Nabari No Ou

2

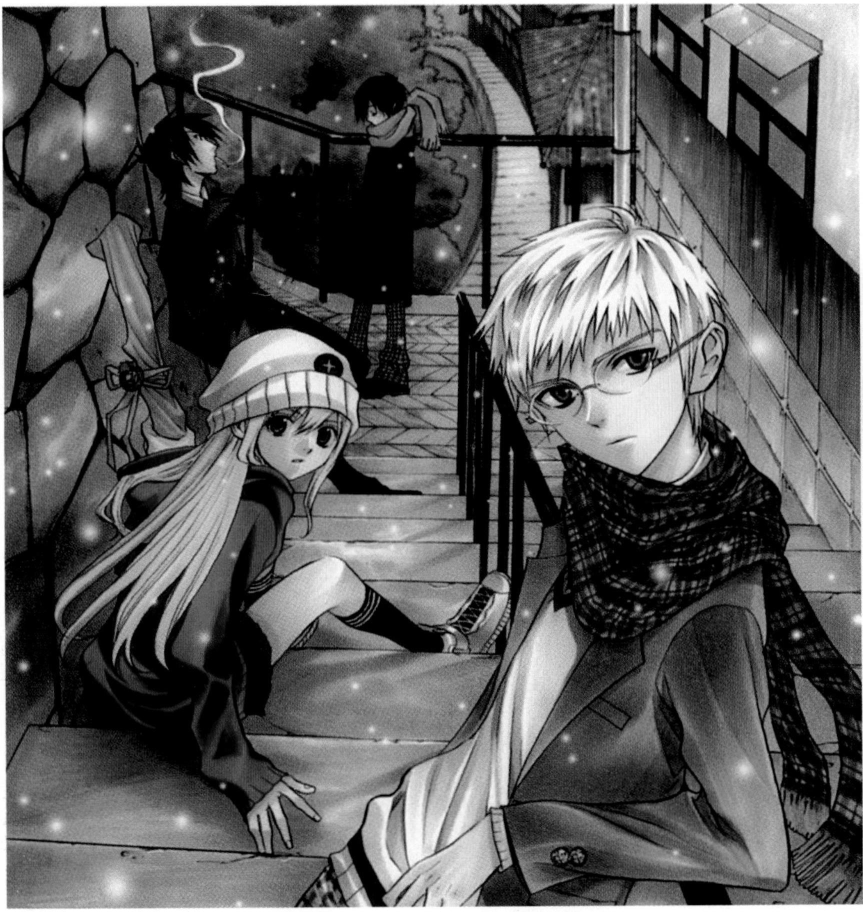

Yuhki Kamatani

Nabari No Ou

2

Yuhki Kamatani

Contents

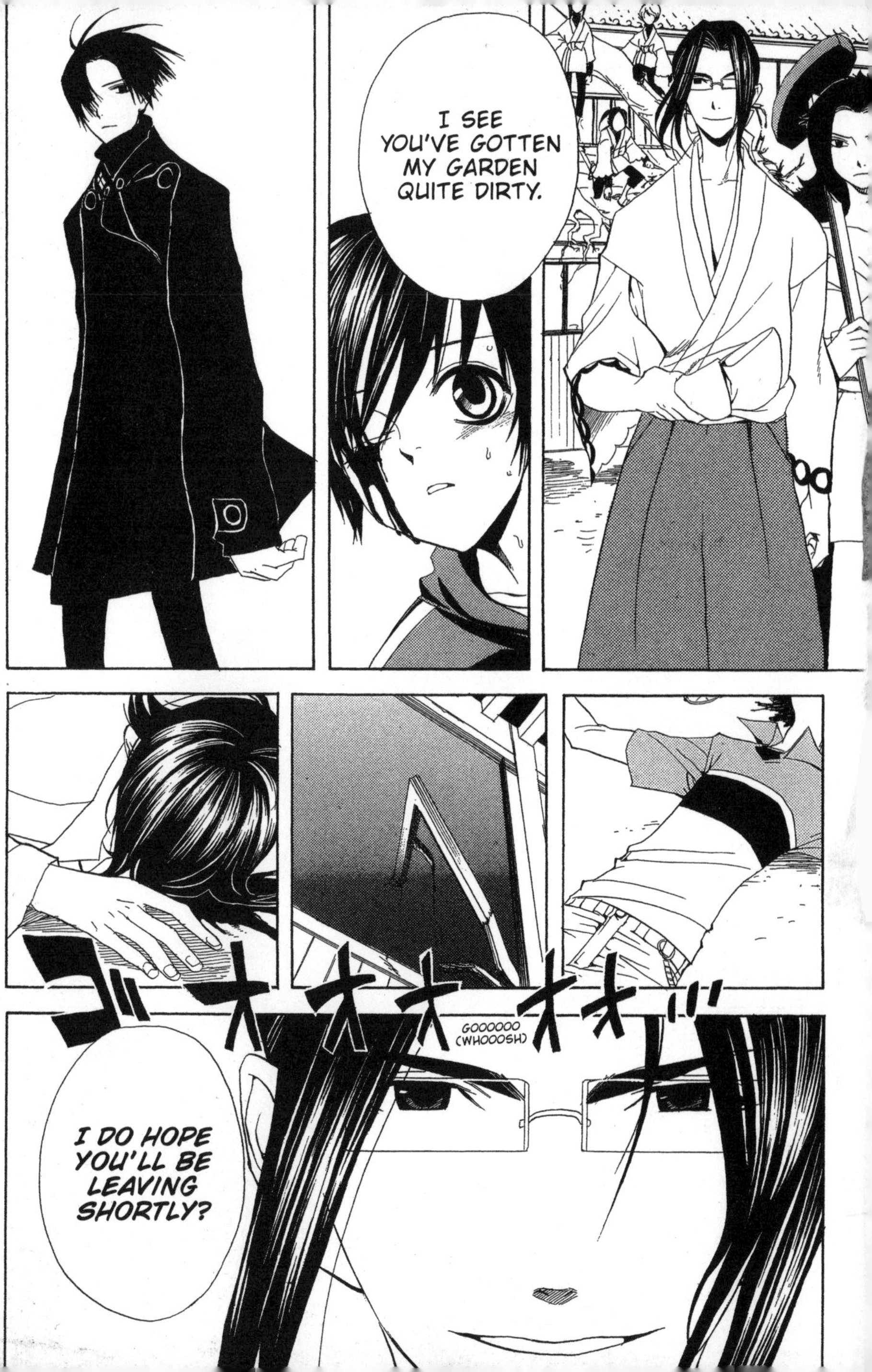
I SEE YOU'VE GOTTEN MY GARDEN QUITE DIRTY.
ゴオオオオオオ
GOOOOOO (WHOOOSH)
I DO HOPE YOU'LL BE LEAVING SHORTLY?

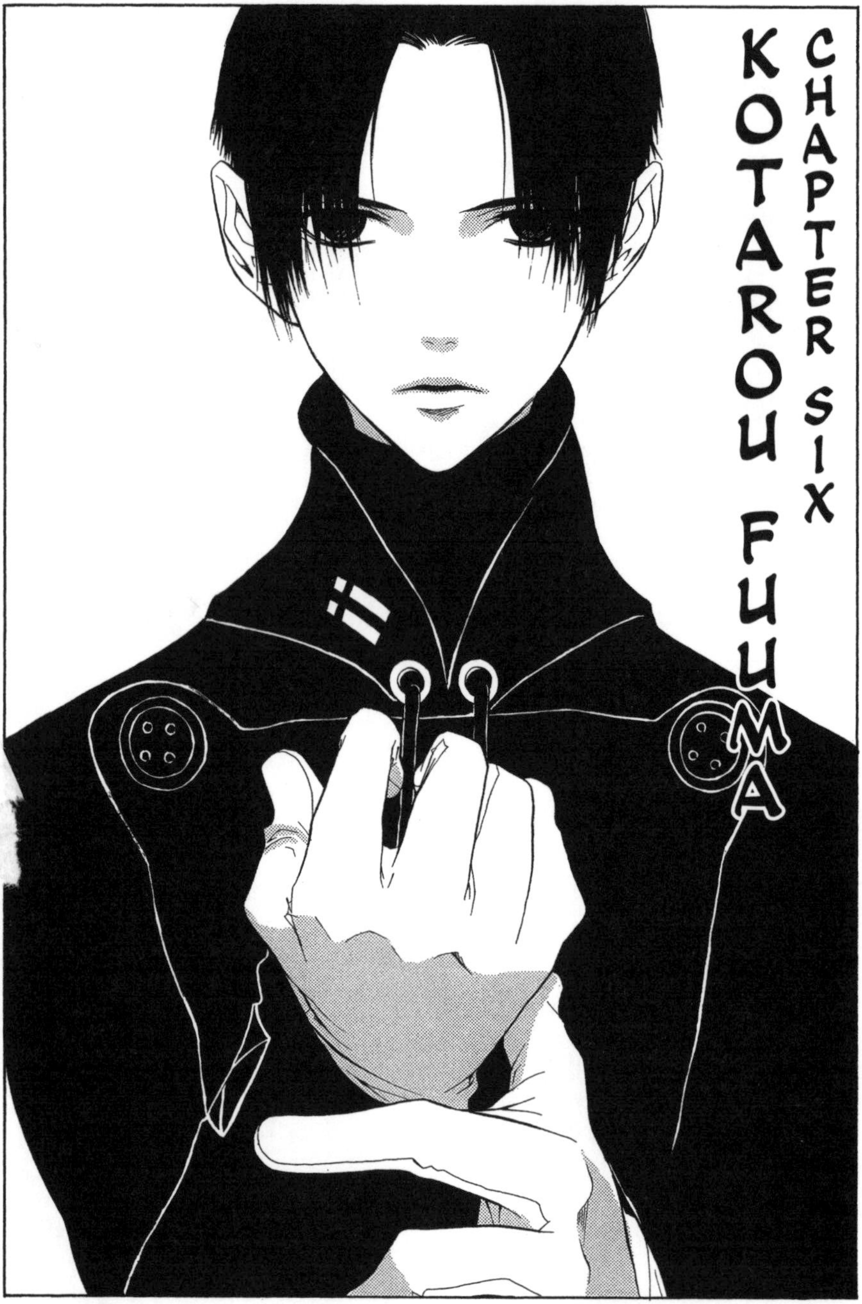
CHAPTER SIX
KOTAROU FUUMA

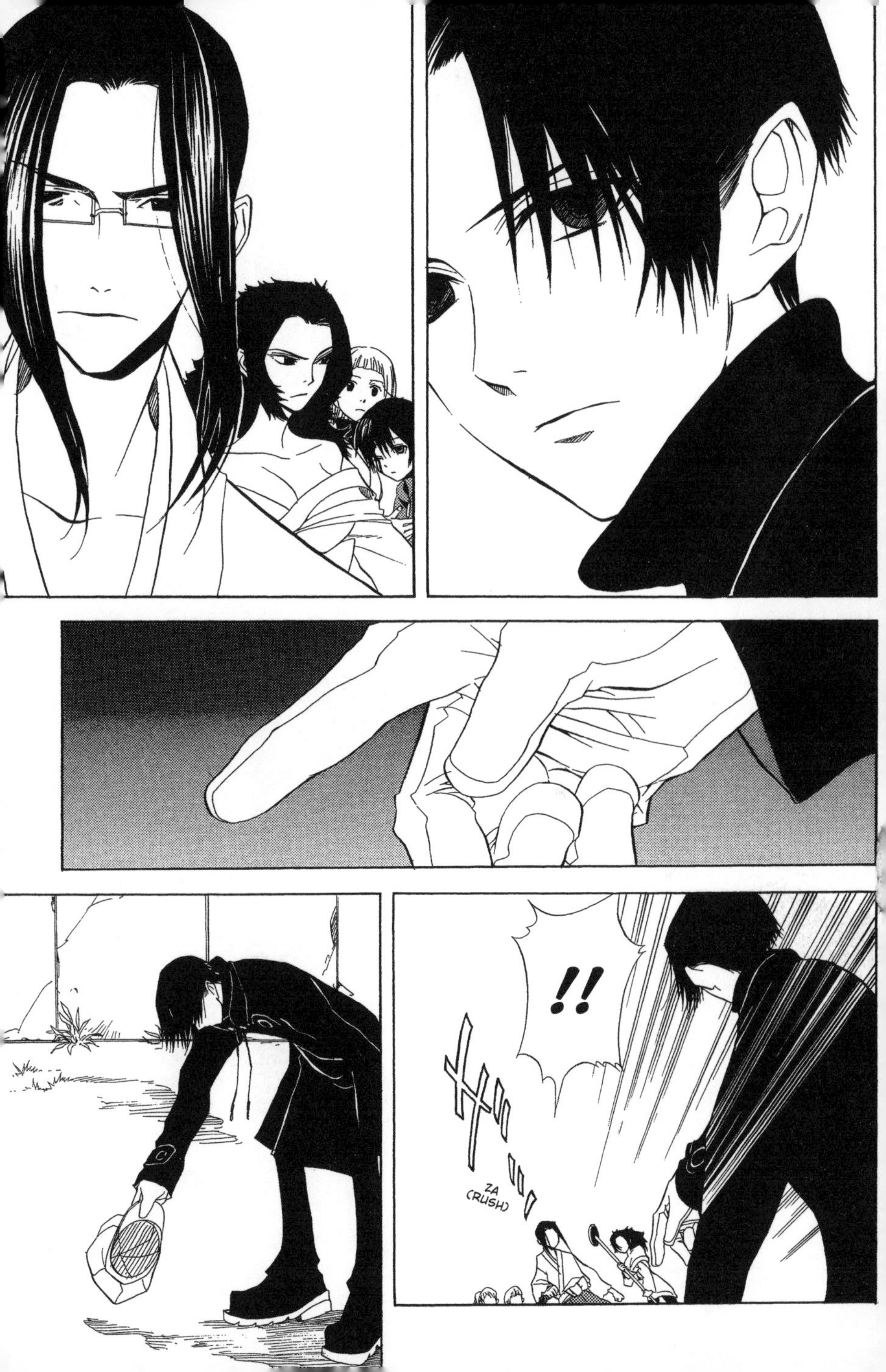
!!
ZA
(RUSH)

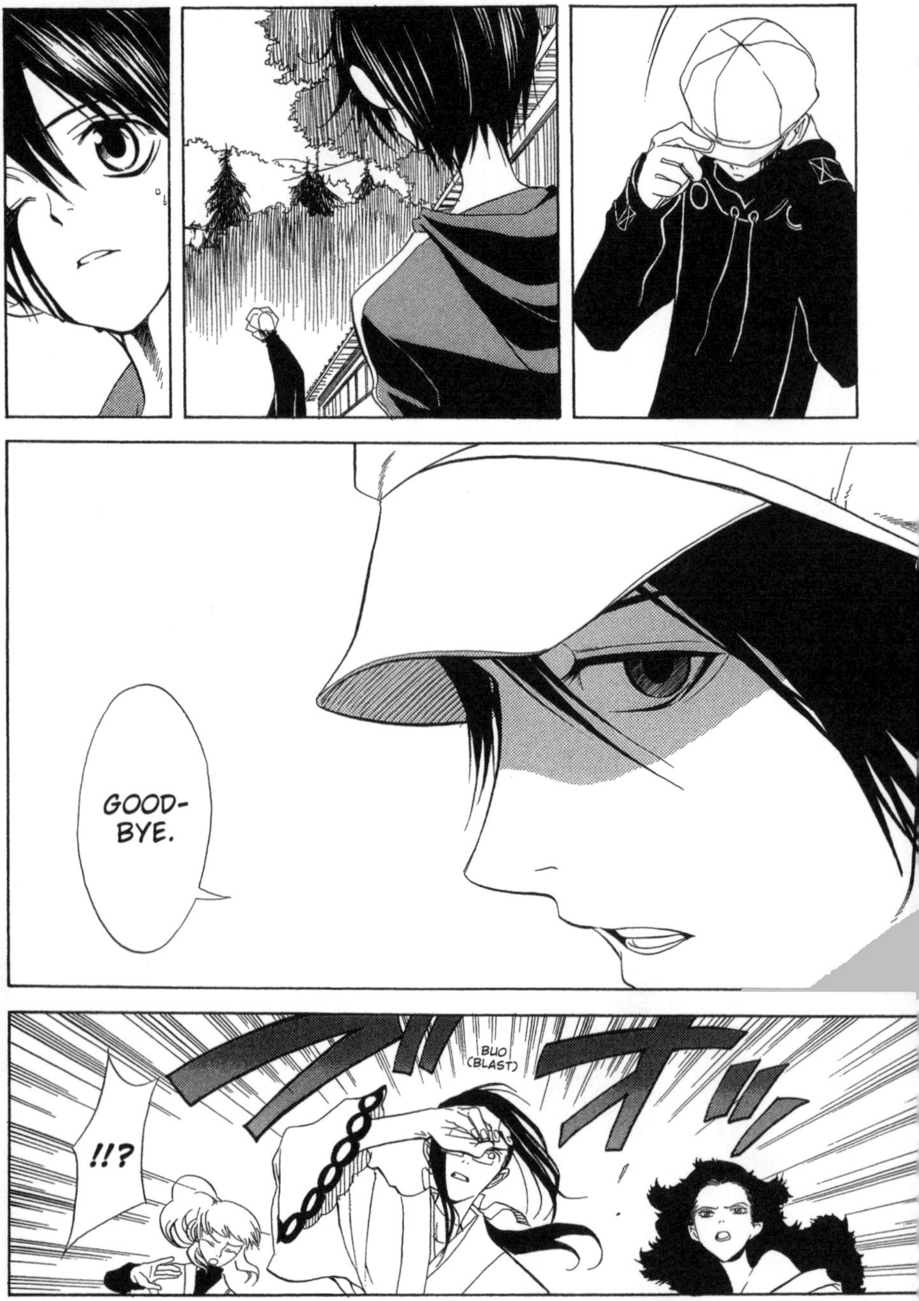
GOOD-BYE.
BUO (BLAST)
!!?

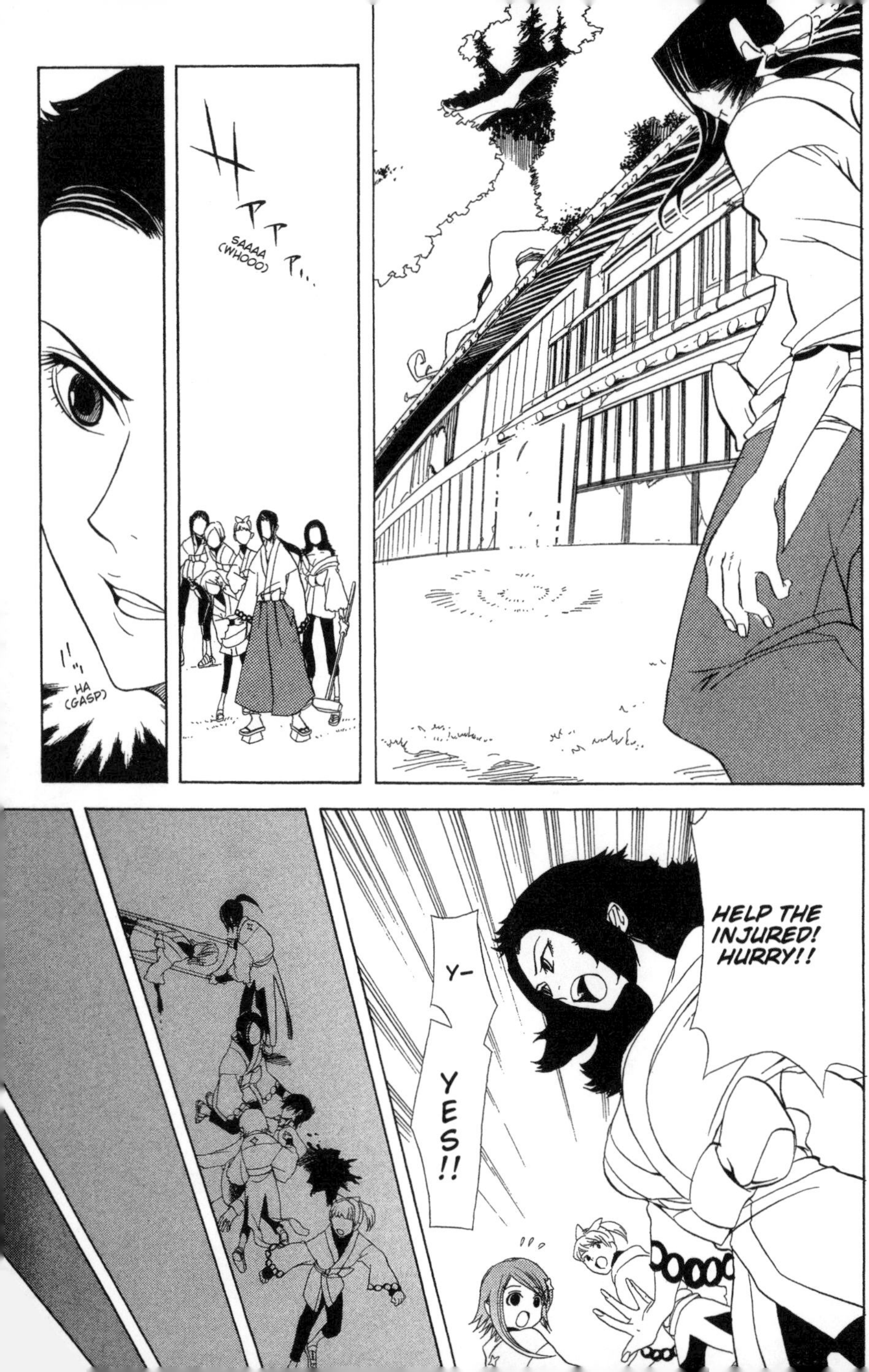
SAAAA (WHOOO)
HA (GASP)
HELP THE INJURED! HURRY!!
Y-
YES!!

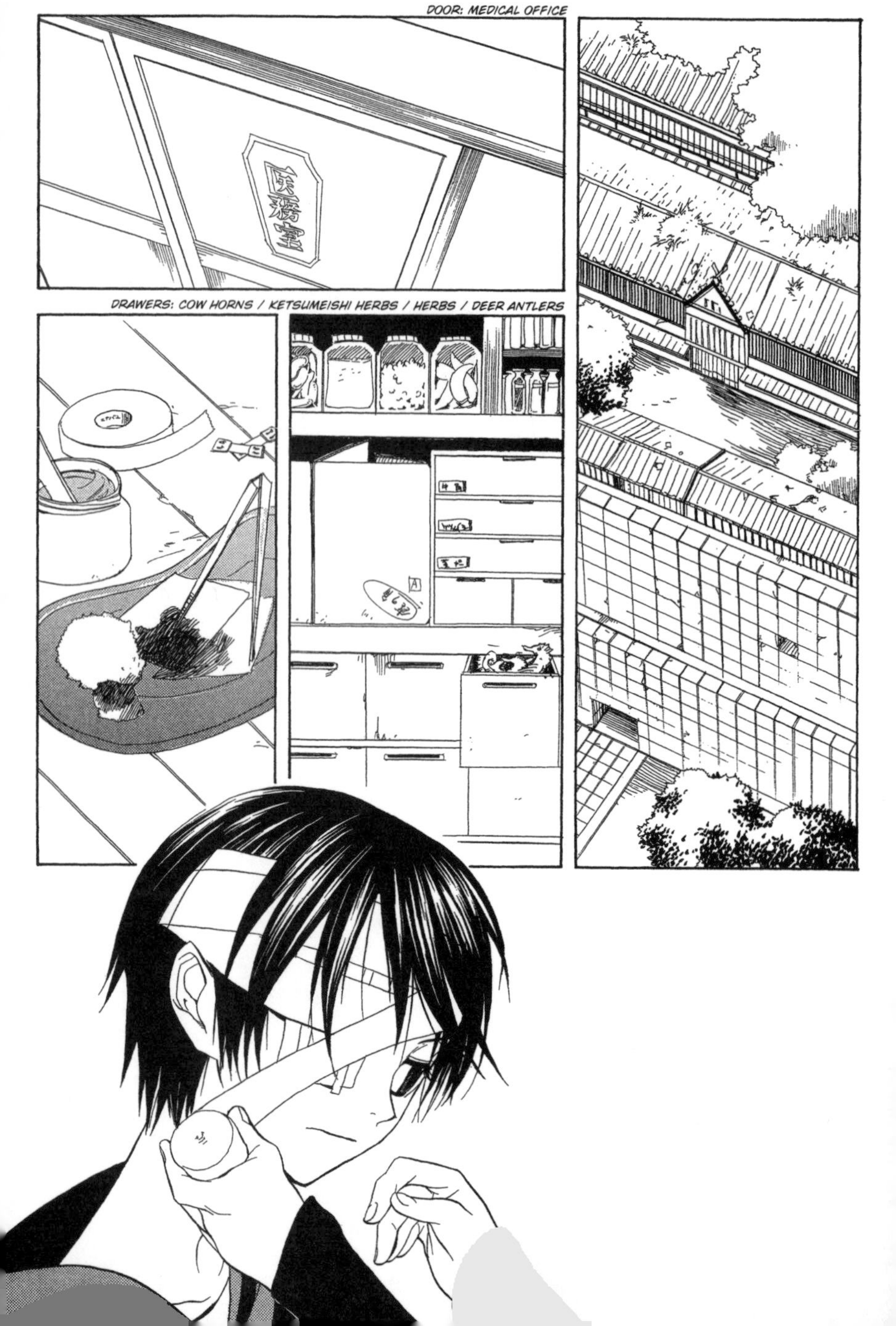
DOOR: MEDICAL OFFICE
医務室
DRAWERS: COW HORNS / KETSUMEISHI HERBS / HERBS / DEER ANTLERS

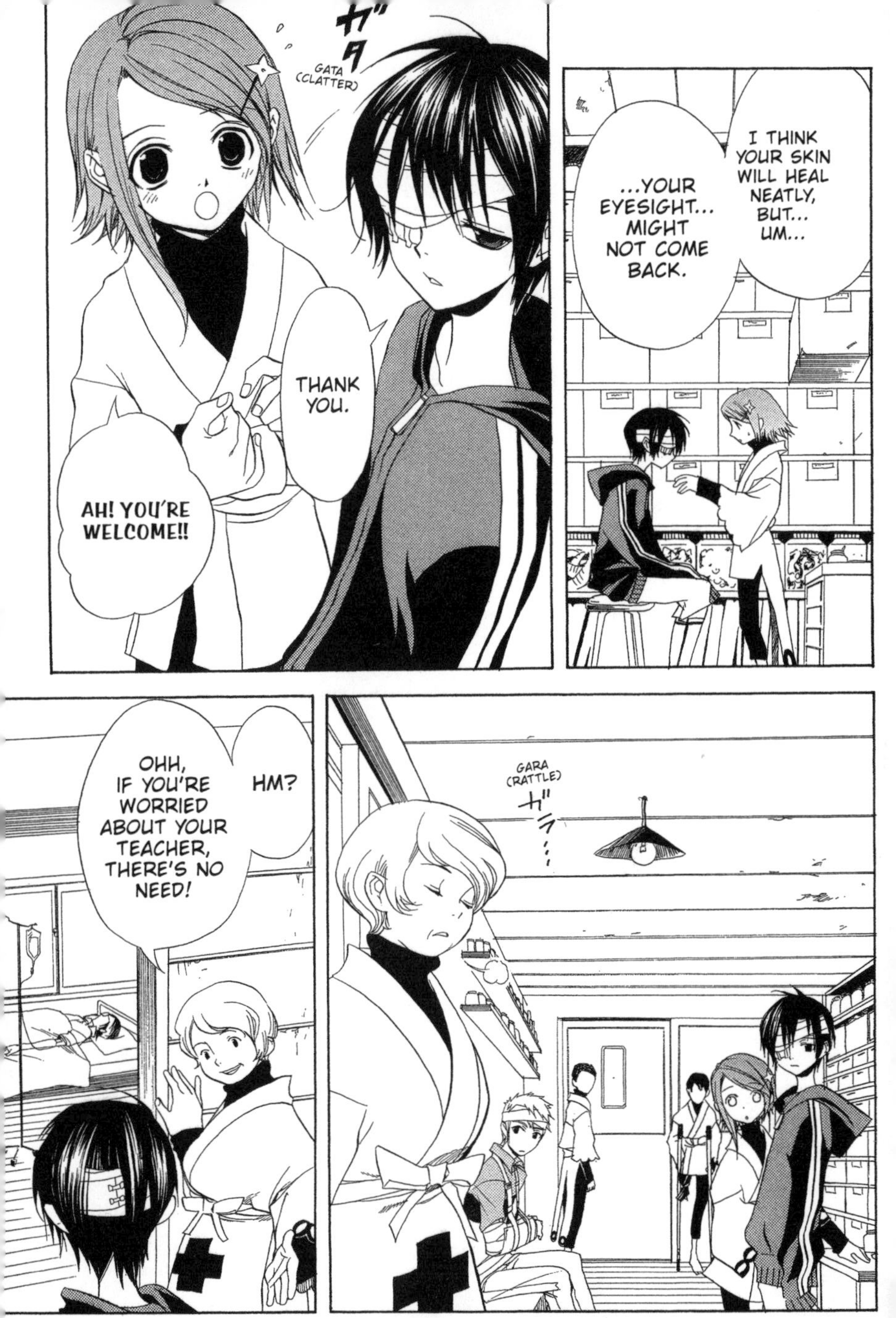
I THINK YOUR SKIN WILL HEAL NEATLY, BUT... UM...
...YOUR EYESIGHT... MIGHT NOT COME BACK.
GATA (CLATTER)
THANK YOU.
AH! YOU'RE WELCOME!!
GARA (RATTLE)
HM?
OHH, IF YOU'RE WORRIED ABOUT YOUR TEACHER, THERE'S NO NEED!

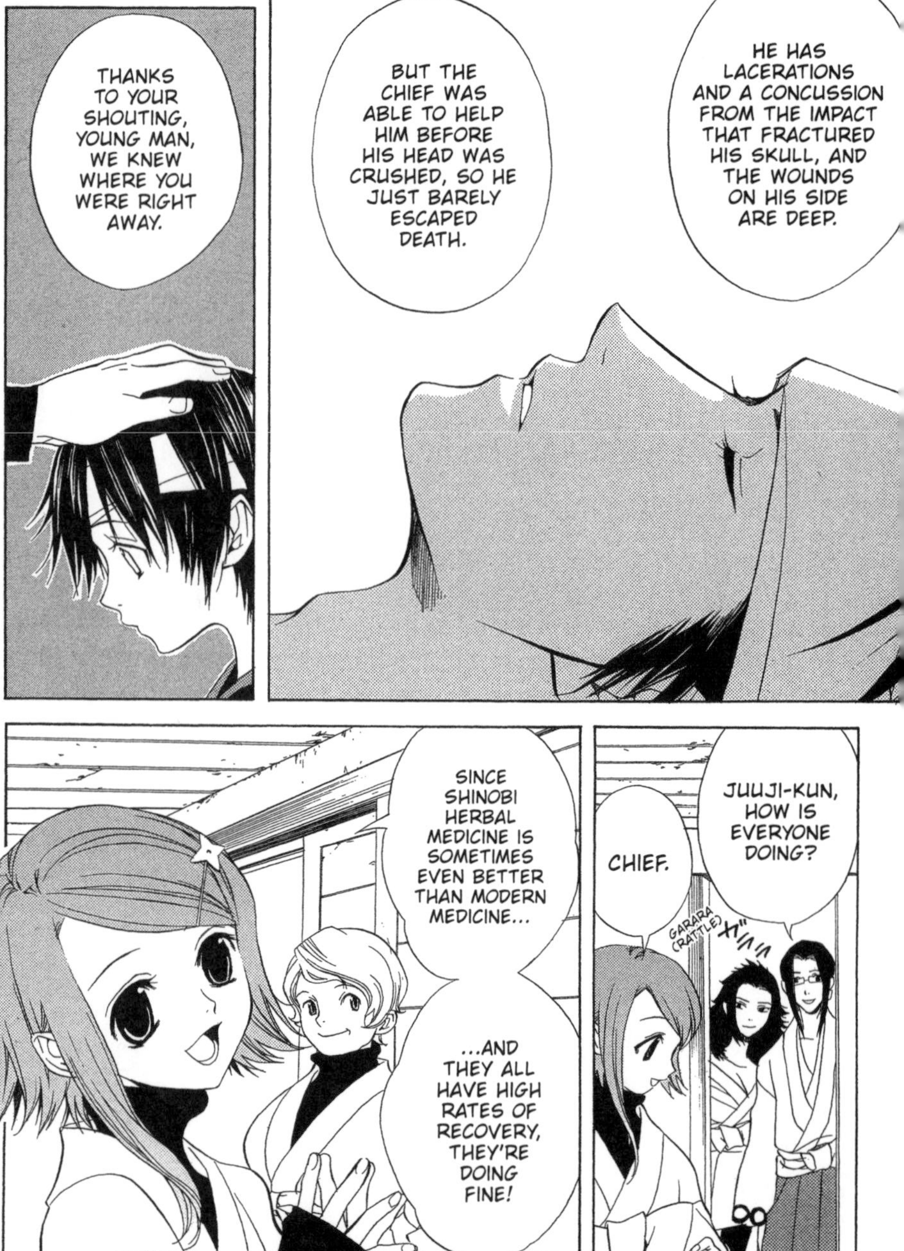
HE HAS LACERATIONS AND A CONCUSSION FROM THE IMPACT THAT FRACTURED HIS SKULL, AND THE WOUNDS ON HIS SIDE ARE DEEP.
BUT THE CHIEF WAS ABLE TO HELP HIM BEFORE HIS HEAD WAS CRUSHED, SO HE JUST BARELY ESCAPED DEATH.
THANKS TO YOUR SHOUTING, YOUNG MAN, WE KNEW WHERE YOU WERE RIGHT AWAY.
JUUJI-KUN, HOW IS EVERYONE DOING?
CHIEF.
GARARA (RATTLE)
SINCE SHINOBI HERBAL MEDICINE IS SOMETIMES EVEN BETTER THAN MODERN MEDICINE...
...AND THEY ALL HAVE HIGH RATES OF RECOVERY, THEY'RE DOING FINE!

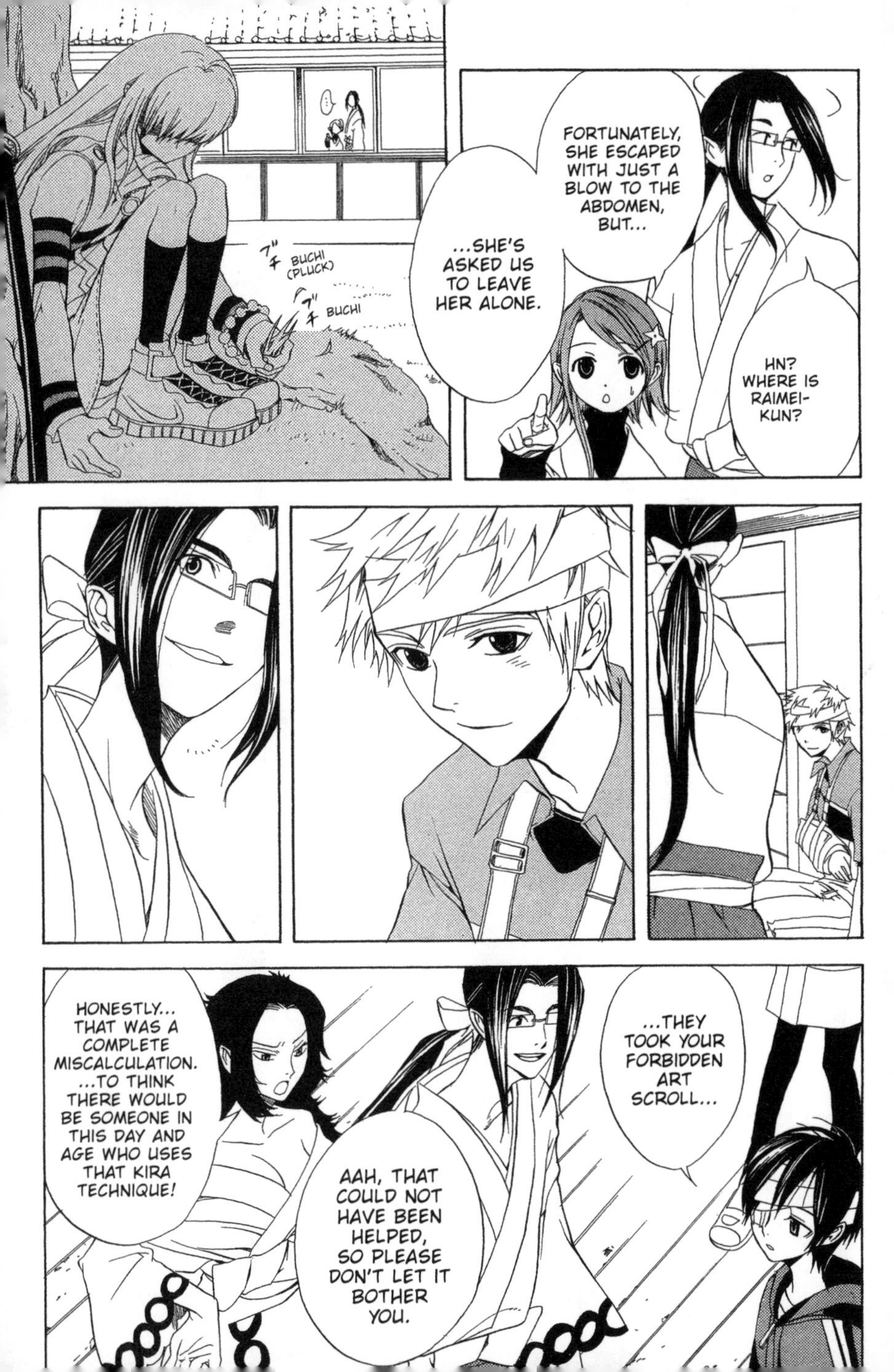
FORTUNATELY, SHE ESCAPED WITH JUST A BLOW TO THE ABDOMEN, BUT...
...SHE'S ASKED US TO LEAVE HER ALONE.
HN? WHERE IS RAIMEI-KUN?
...
ブチ BUCHI (PLUCK)
ブチ BUCHI
...THEY TOOK YOUR FORBIDDEN ART SCROLL...
HONESTLY... THAT WAS A COMPLETE MISCALCULATION. ...TO THINK THERE WOULD BE SOMEONE IN THIS DAY AND AGE WHO USES THAT KIRA TECHNIQUE!
AAH, THAT COULD NOT HAVE BEEN HELPED, SO PLEASE DON'T LET IT BOTHER YOU.

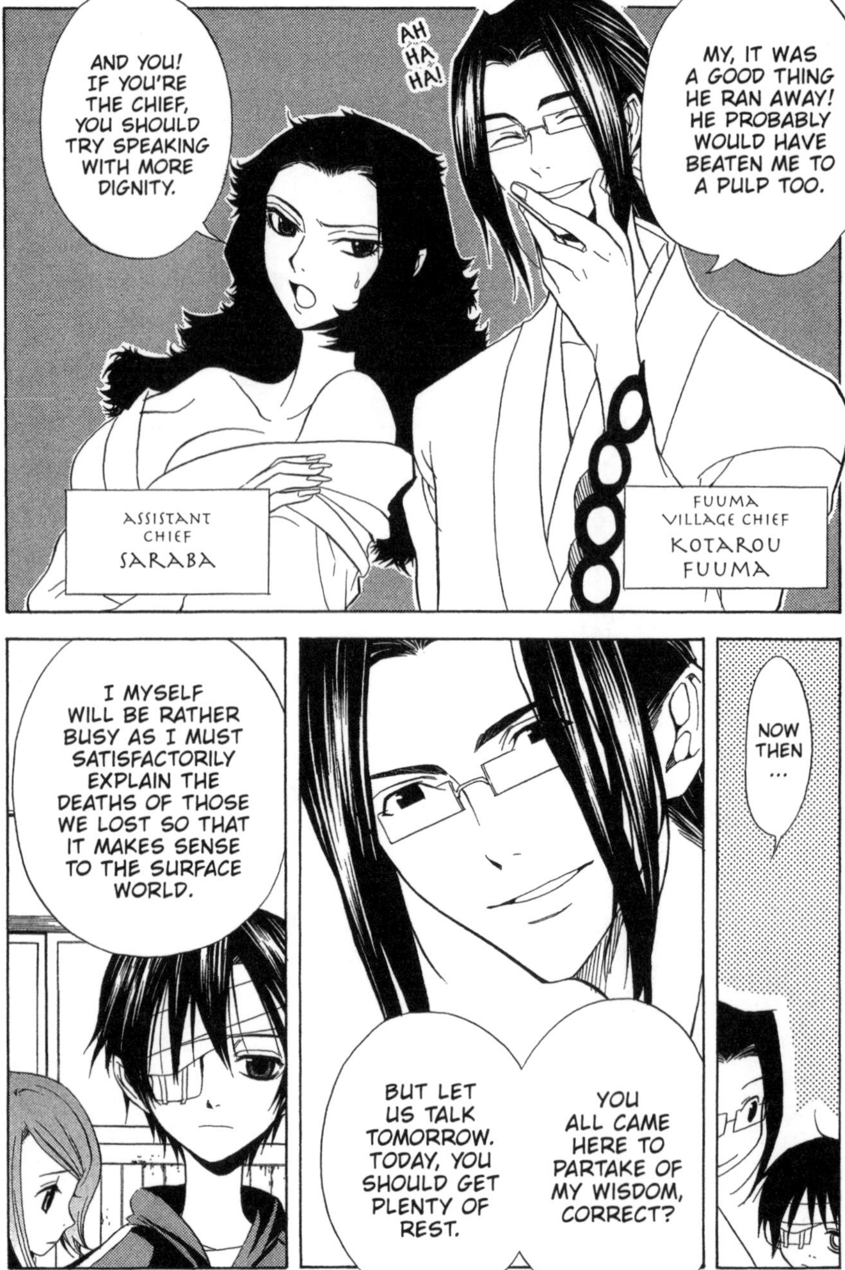
MY, IT WAS A GOOD THING HE RAN AWAY! HE PROBABLY WOULD HAVE BEATEN ME TO A PULP TOO.
AH HA HA!
AND YOU! IF YOU'RE THE CHIEF, YOU SHOULD TRY SPEAKING WITH MORE DIGNITY.
FUUMA VILLAGE CHIEF KOTAROU FUUMA
ASSISTANT CHIEF SARABA
NOW THEN ...
YOU ALL CAME HERE TO PARTAKE OF MY WISDOM, CORRECT?
BUT LET US TALK TOMORROW. TODAY, YOU SHOULD GET PLENTY OF REST.
I MYSELF WILL BE RATHER BUSY AS I MUST SATISFACTORILY EXPLAIN THE DEATHS OF THOSE WE LOST SO THAT IT MAKES SENSE TO THE SURFACE WORLD.

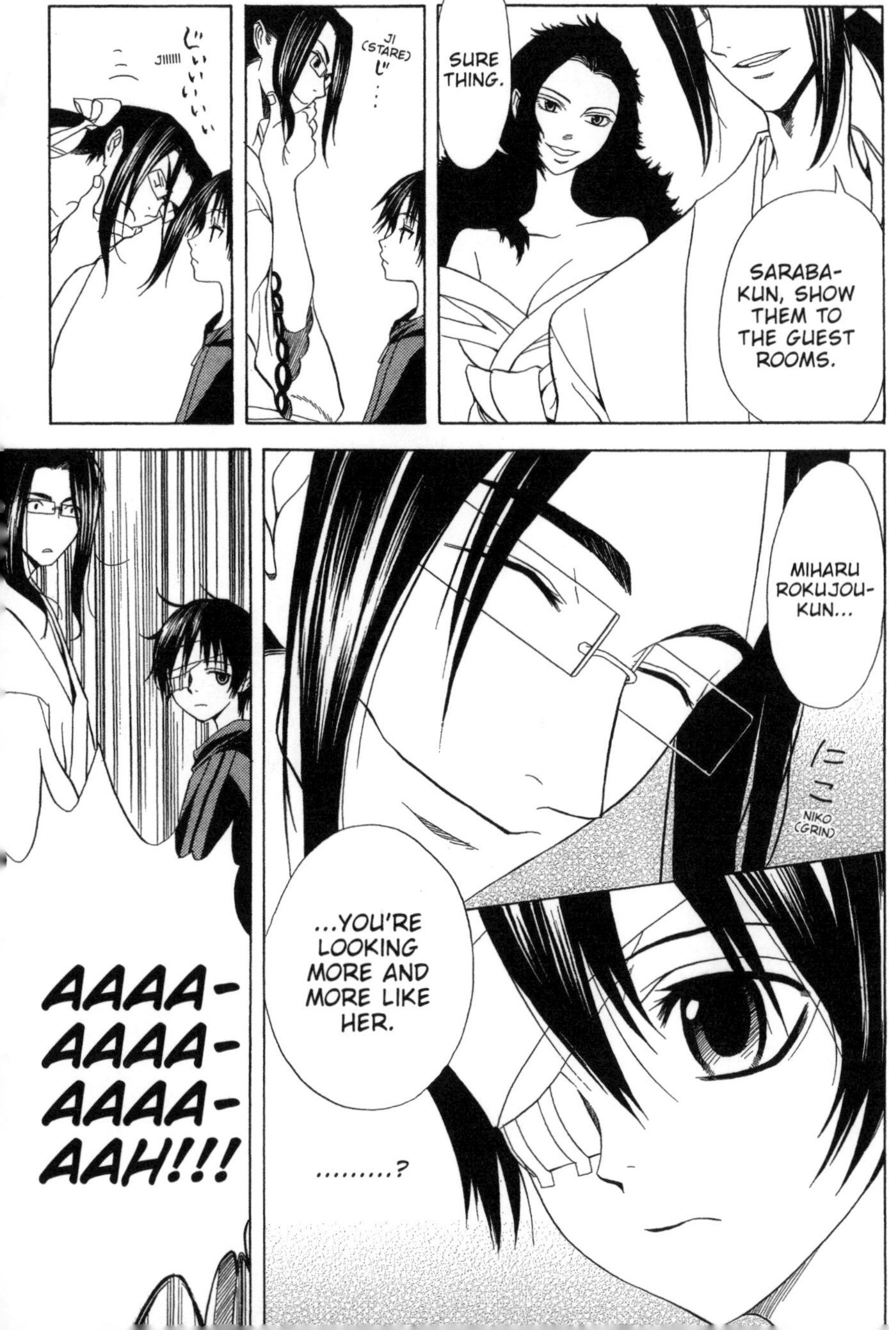
SARABA-KUN, SHOW THEM TO THE GUEST ROOMS.
SURE THING.
JI (STARE)
じ・・・
じいいいいいい
JIIIIII
MIHARU ROKUJOU-KUN...
にこ
NIKO (GRIN)
...YOU'RE LOOKING MORE AND MORE LIKE HER.
.........?
AAAA-AAAA-AAAA-AAH!!!

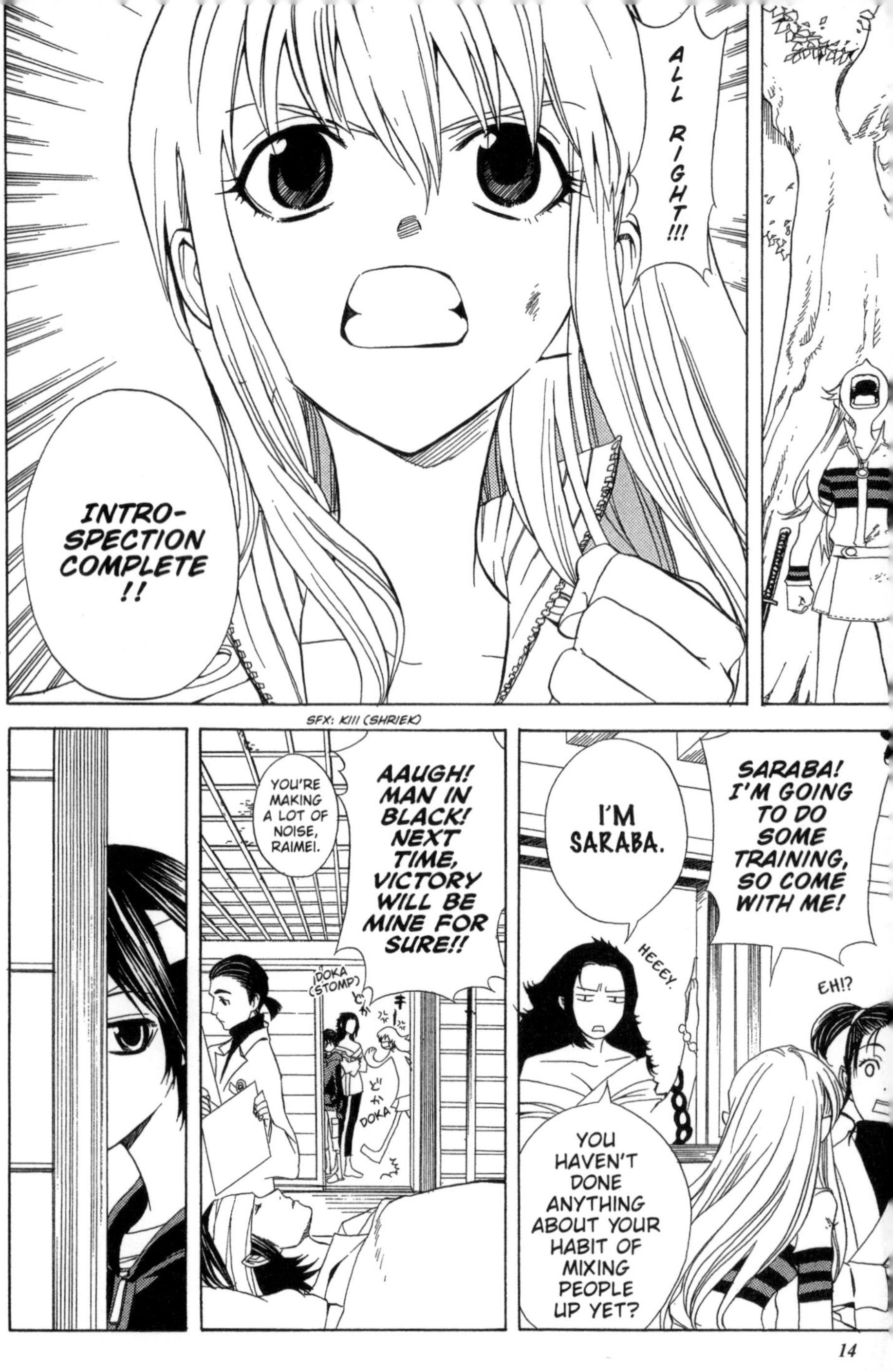
ALL RIGHT!!!
INTRO-SPECTION COMPLETE!!
SFX: KIII (SHRIEK)
SARABA! I'M GOING TO DO SOME TRAINING, SO COME WITH ME!
EH!?
I'M SARABA.
HEEEY.
YOU HAVEN'T DONE ANYTHING ABOUT YOUR HABIT OF MIXING PEOPLE UP YET?
AAUGH! MAN IN BLACK! NEXT TIME, VICTORY WILL BE MINE FOR SURE!!
YOU'RE MAKING A LOT OF NOISE, RAIMEI.
DOKA (STOMP)
DOKA

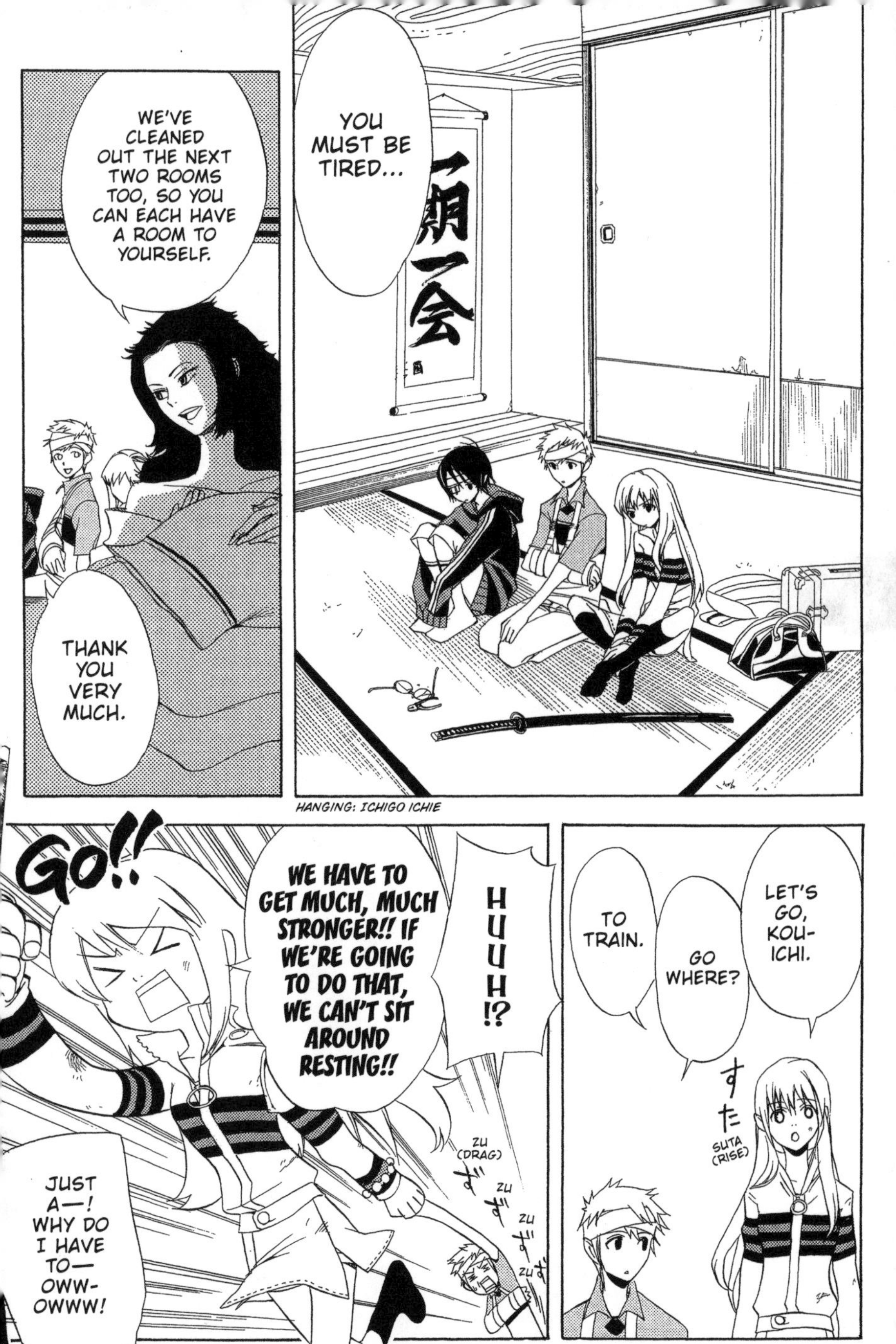
YOU MUST BE TIRED...
HANGING: ICHIGO ICHIE
WE'VE CLEANED OUT THE NEXT TWO ROOMS TOO, SO YOU CAN EACH HAVE A ROOM TO YOURSELF.
THANK YOU VERY MUCH.
LET'S GO, KOU-ICHI.
GO WHERE?
TO TRAIN.
すた
SUTA (RISE)
HUUUH!?
WE HAVE TO GET MUCH, MUCH STRONGER!! IF WE'RE GOING TO DO THAT, WE CAN'T SIT AROUND RESTING!!
GO!!
ZU (DRAG)
ず
ZU
ず
ZU
ず
ZU
ず
JUST A—! WHY DO I HAVE TO— OWW-OWWW!

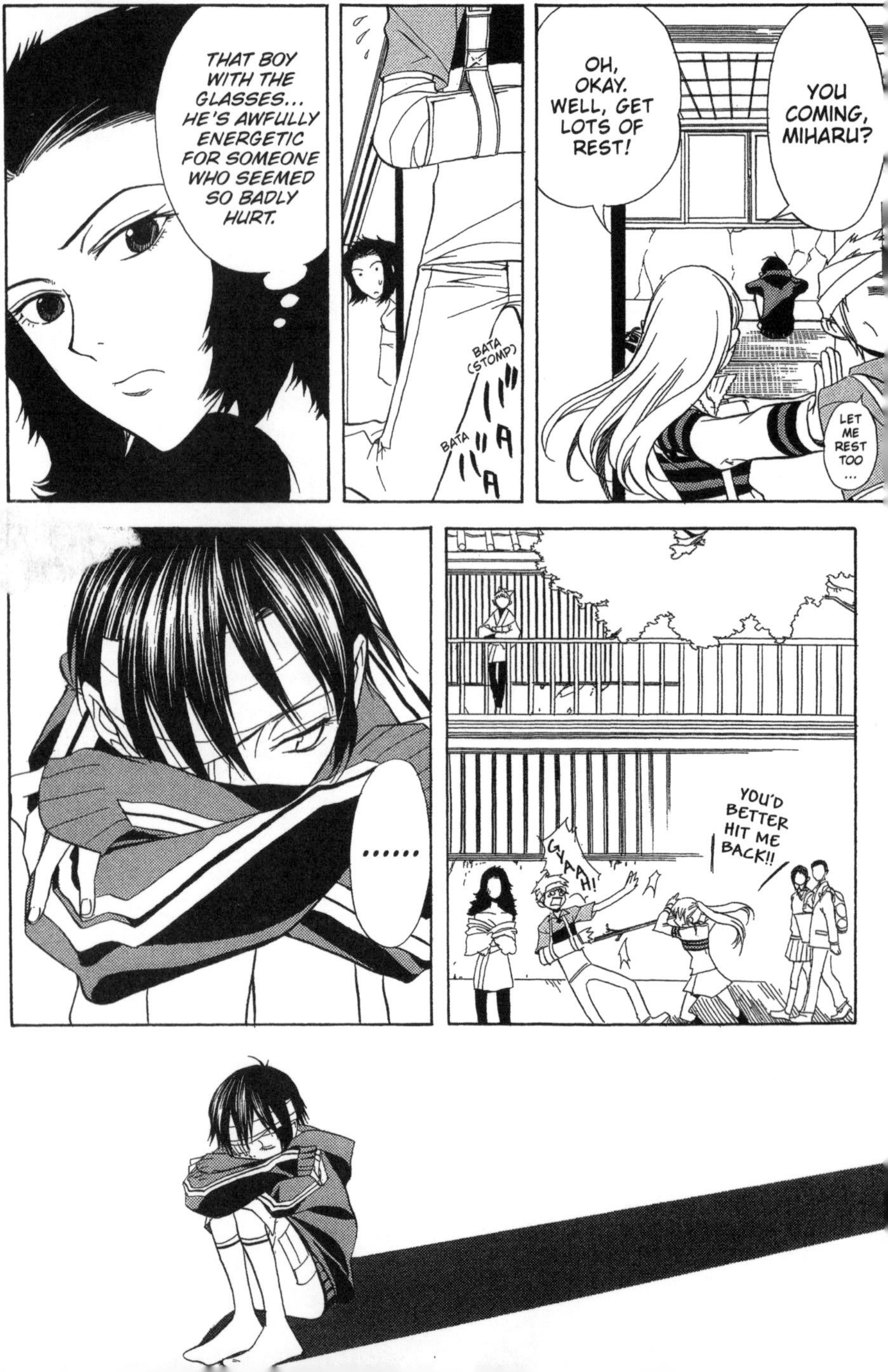
YOU COMING, MIHARU?
OH, OKAY. WELL, GET LOTS OF REST!
LET ME REST TOO ...
BATA (STOMP)
BATA
THAT BOY WITH THE GLASSES... HE'S AWFULLY ENERGETIC FOR SOMEONE WHO SEEMED SO BADLY HURT.
YOU'D BETTER HIT ME BACK!!
GYAAH!
......

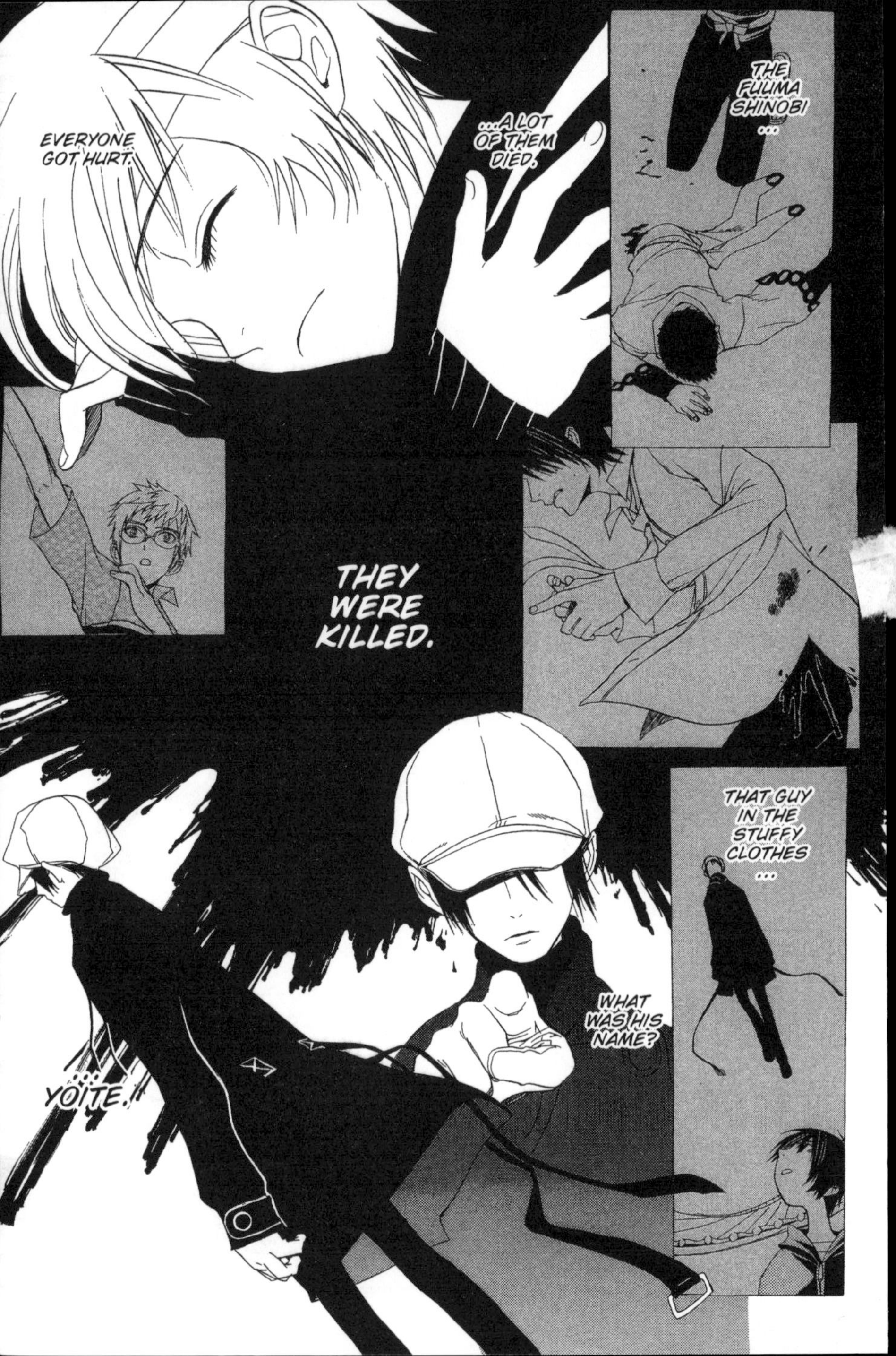
THE FUUMA SHINOBI ...
...A LOT OF THEM DIED.
EVERYONE GOT HURT.
THEY WERE KILLED.
THAT GUY IN THE STUFFY CLOTHES ...
WHAT WAS HIS NAME?
...YOITE.

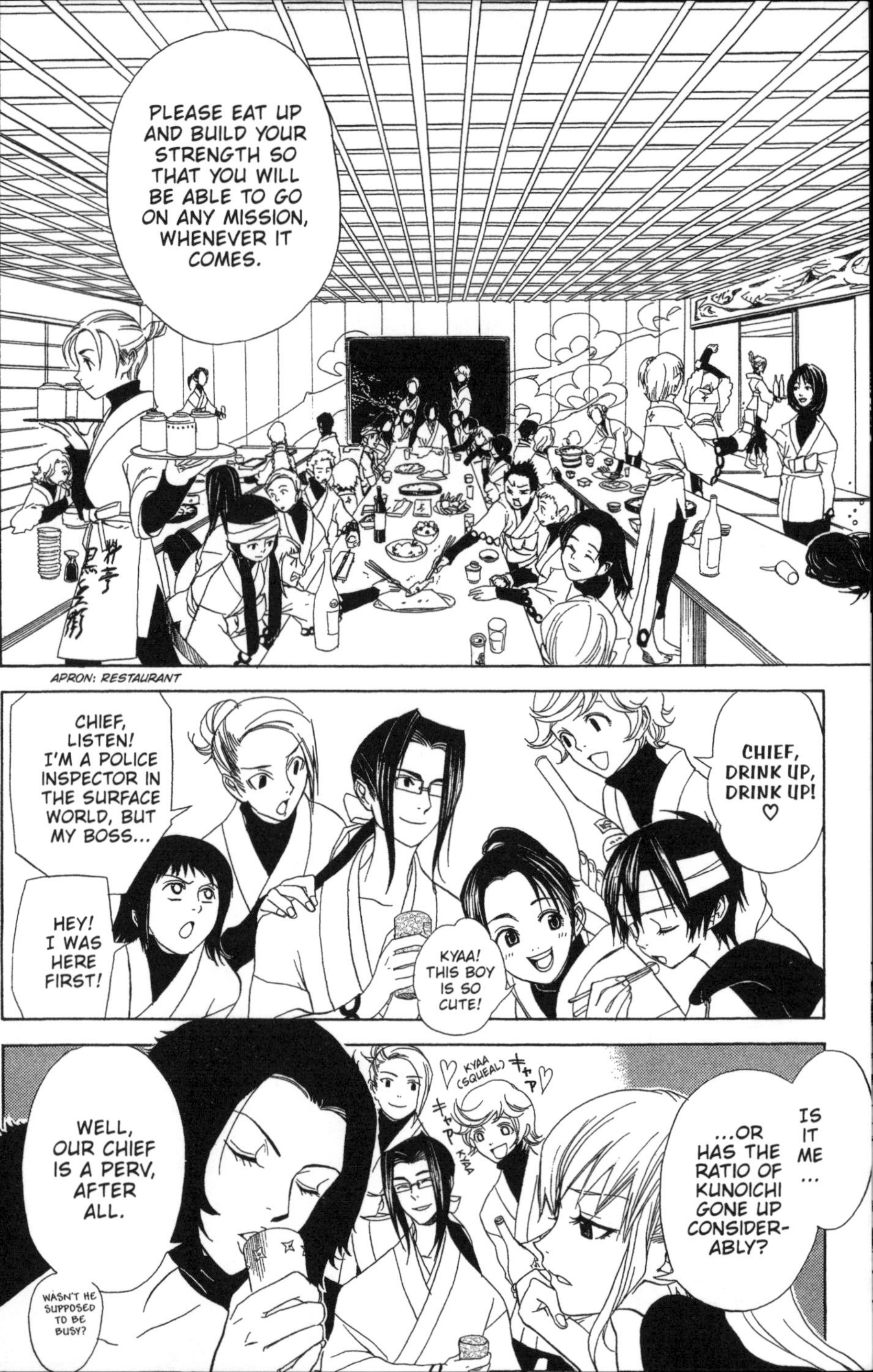
PLEASE EAT UP AND BUILD YOUR STRENGTH SO THAT YOU WILL BE ABLE TO GO ON ANY MISSION, WHENEVER IT COMES.
APRON: RESTAURANT
CHIEF, DRINK UP, DRINK UP! ♡
CHIEF, LISTEN! I'M A POLICE INSPECTOR IN THE SURFACE WORLD, BUT MY BOSS...
KYAA! THIS BOY IS SO CUTE!
HEY! I WAS HERE FIRST!
IS IT ME ...
...OR HAS THE RATIO OF KUNOICHI GONE UP CONSIDERABLY?
KYAA (SQUEAL) キャア
キャア KYAA
WELL, OUR CHIEF IS A PERV, AFTER ALL.
WASN'T HE SUPPOSED TO BE BUSY?

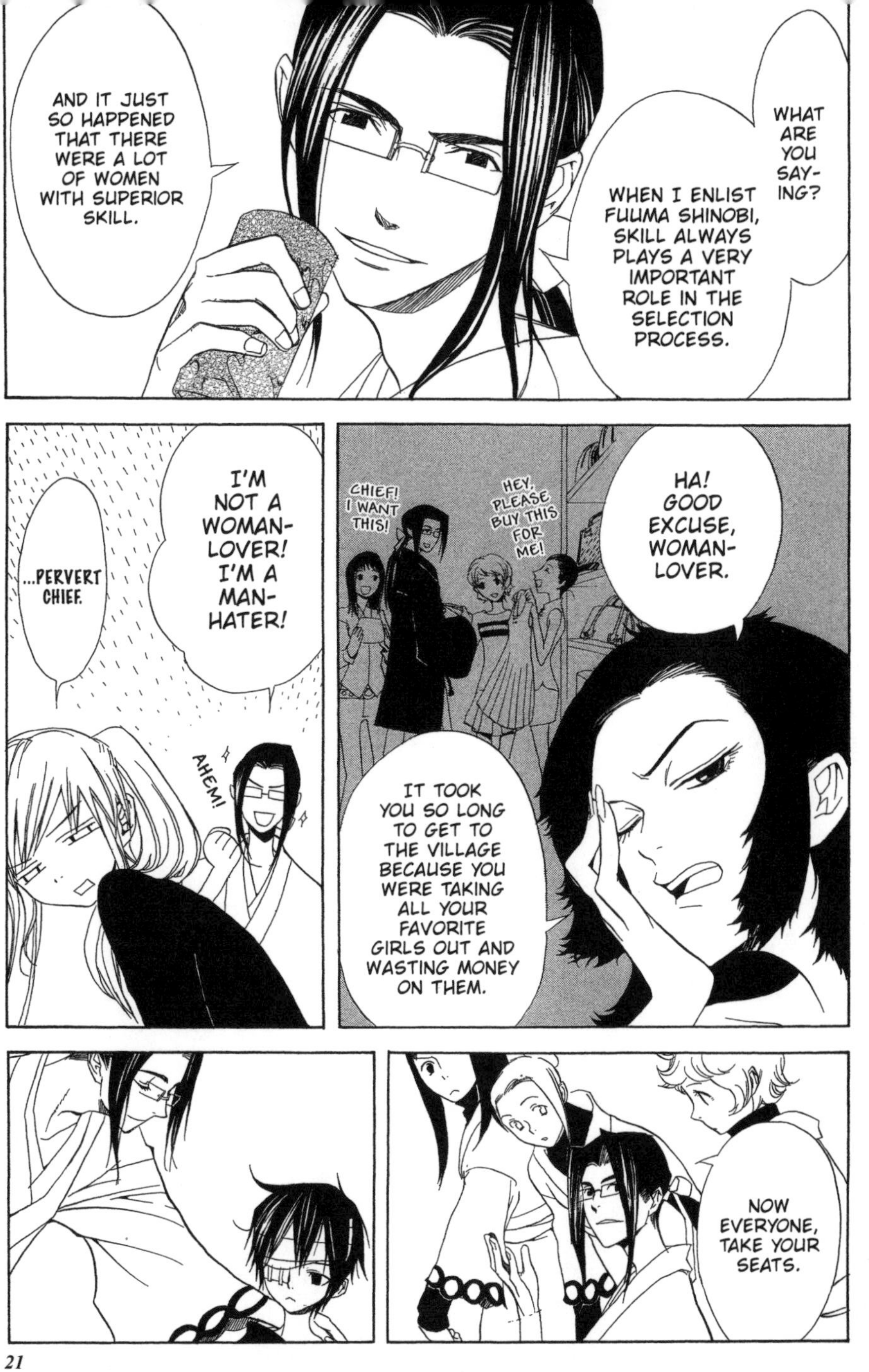
WHAT ARE YOU SAYING?
WHEN I ENLIST FUUMA SHINOBI, SKILL ALWAYS PLAYS A VERY IMPORTANT ROLE IN THE SELECTION PROCESS.
AND IT JUST SO HAPPENED THAT THERE WERE A LOT OF WOMEN WITH SUPERIOR SKILL.
HA! GOOD EXCUSE, WOMAN-LOVER.
HEY, PLEASE BUY THIS FOR ME!
CHIEF! I WANT THIS!
IT TOOK YOU SO LONG TO GET TO THE VILLAGE BECAUSE YOU WERE TAKING ALL YOUR FAVORITE GIRLS OUT AND WASTING MONEY ON THEM.
I'M NOT A WOMAN-LOVER! I'M A MAN-HATER!
...PERVERT CHIEF.
AHEM!
NOW EVERYONE, TAKE YOUR SEATS.

SFX: ZAWA (MURMUR) ZAWA

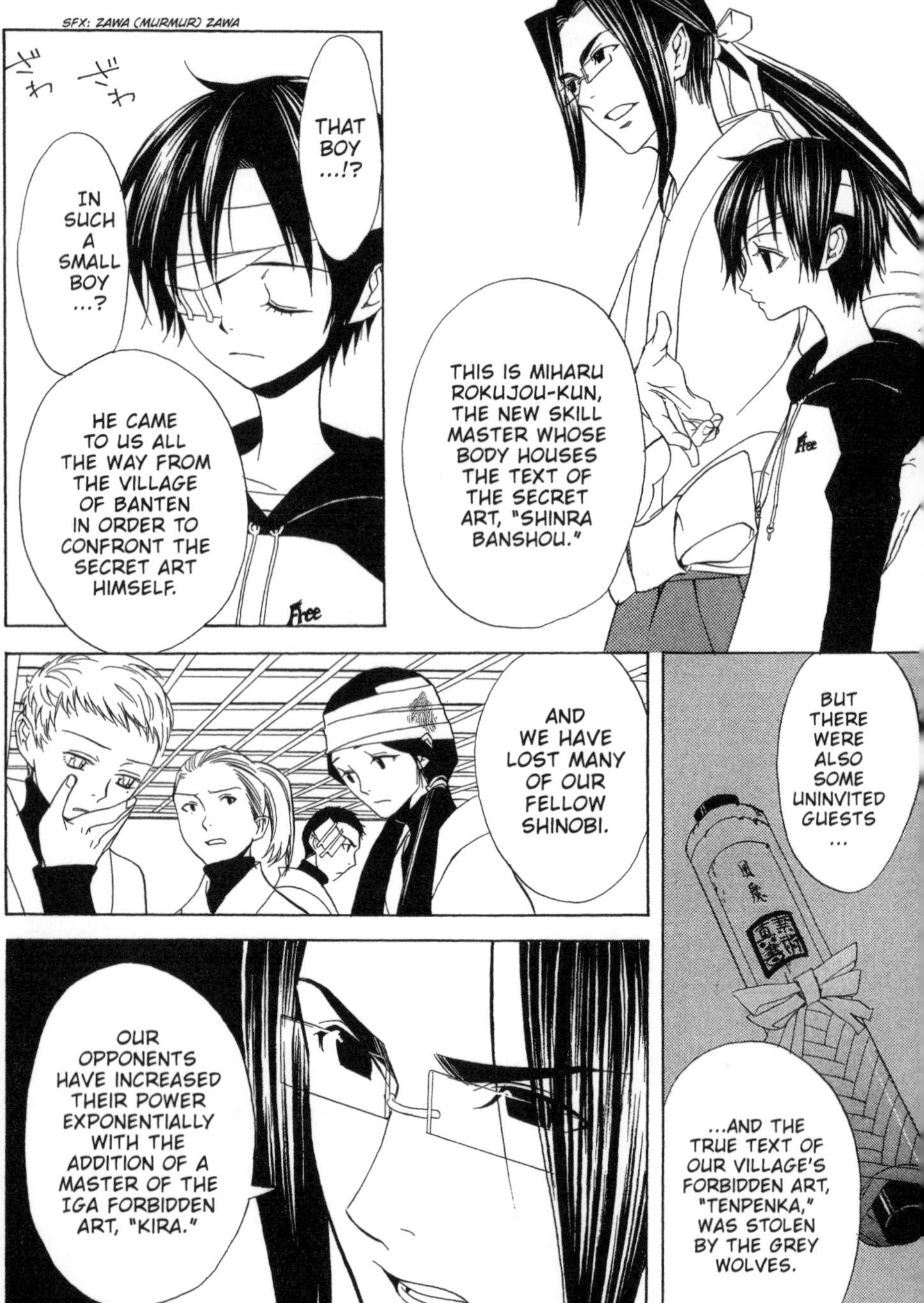

THIS IS MIHARU ROKUJOU-KUN, THE NEW SKILL MASTER WHOSE BODY HOUSES THE TEXT OF THE SECRET ART, "SHINRA BANSHOU."
ざわ ざわ
THAT BOY ...!?
IN SUCH A SMALL BOY ...?
HE CAME TO US ALL THE WAY FROM THE VILLAGE OF BANTEN IN ORDER TO CONFRONT THE SECRET ART HIMSELF.
BUT THERE WERE ALSO SOME UNINVITED GUESTS ...
...AND THE TRUE TEXT OF OUR VILLAGE'S FORBIDDEN ART, "TENPENKA," WAS STOLEN BY THE GREY WOLVES.
AND WE HAVE LOST MANY OF OUR FELLOW SHINOBI.
OUR OPPONENTS HAVE INCREASED THEIR POWER EXPONENTIALLY WITH THE ADDITION OF A MASTER OF THE IGA FORBIDDEN ART, "KIRA."

SCROLL: FORBIDDEN ART TRUE TEXT

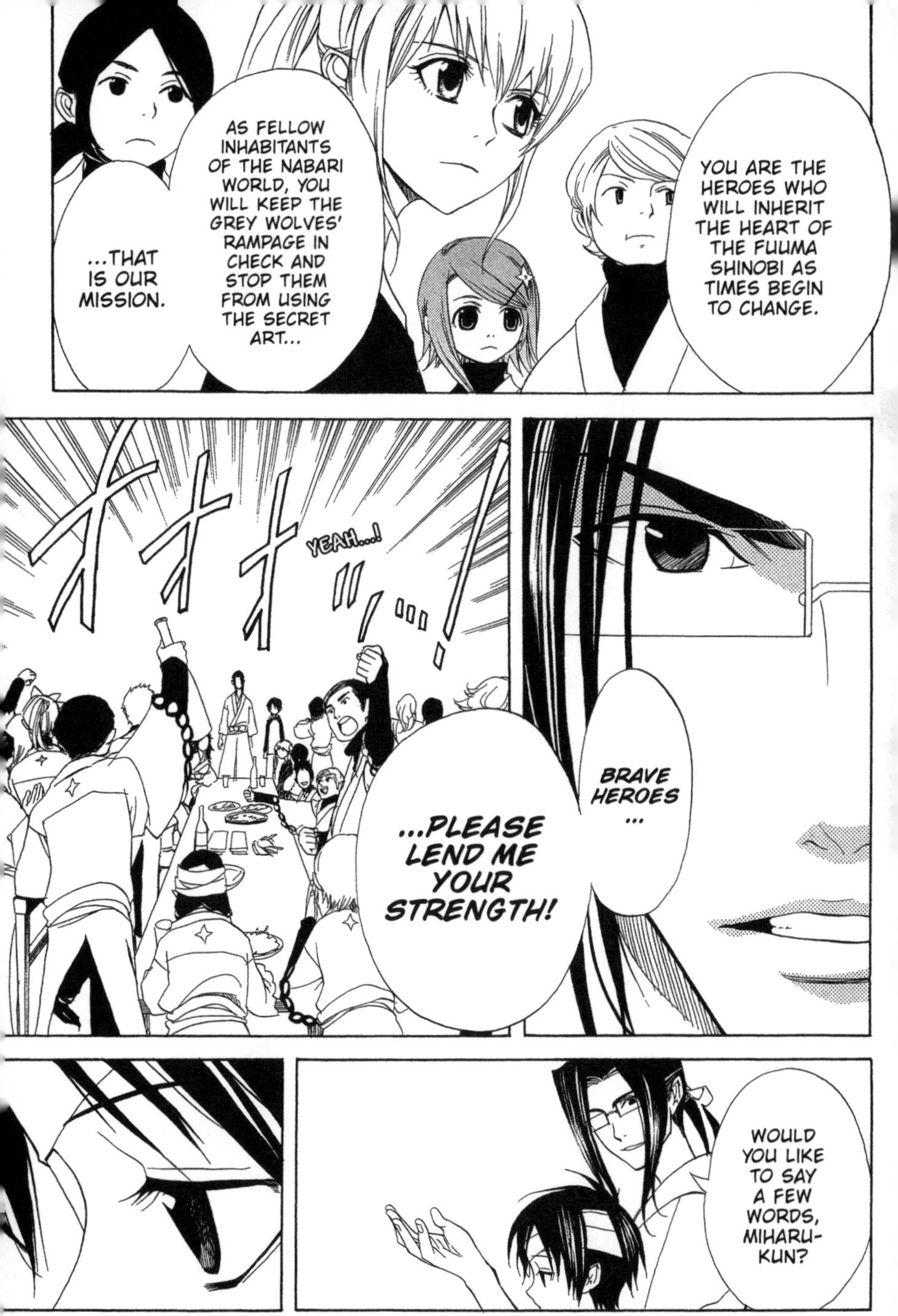
YOU ARE THE HEROES WHO WILL INHERIT THE HEART OF THE FUUMA SHINOBI AS TIMES BEGIN TO CHANGE.
AS FELLOW INHABITANTS OF THE NABARI WORLD, YOU WILL KEEP THE GREY WOLVES' RAMPAGE IN CHECK AND STOP THEM FROM USING THE SECRET ART...
...THAT IS OUR MISSION.
BRAVE HEROES ...
...PLEASE LEND ME YOUR STRENGTH!
YEAH...!
WOULD YOU LIKE TO SAY A FEW WORDS, MIHARU-KUN?

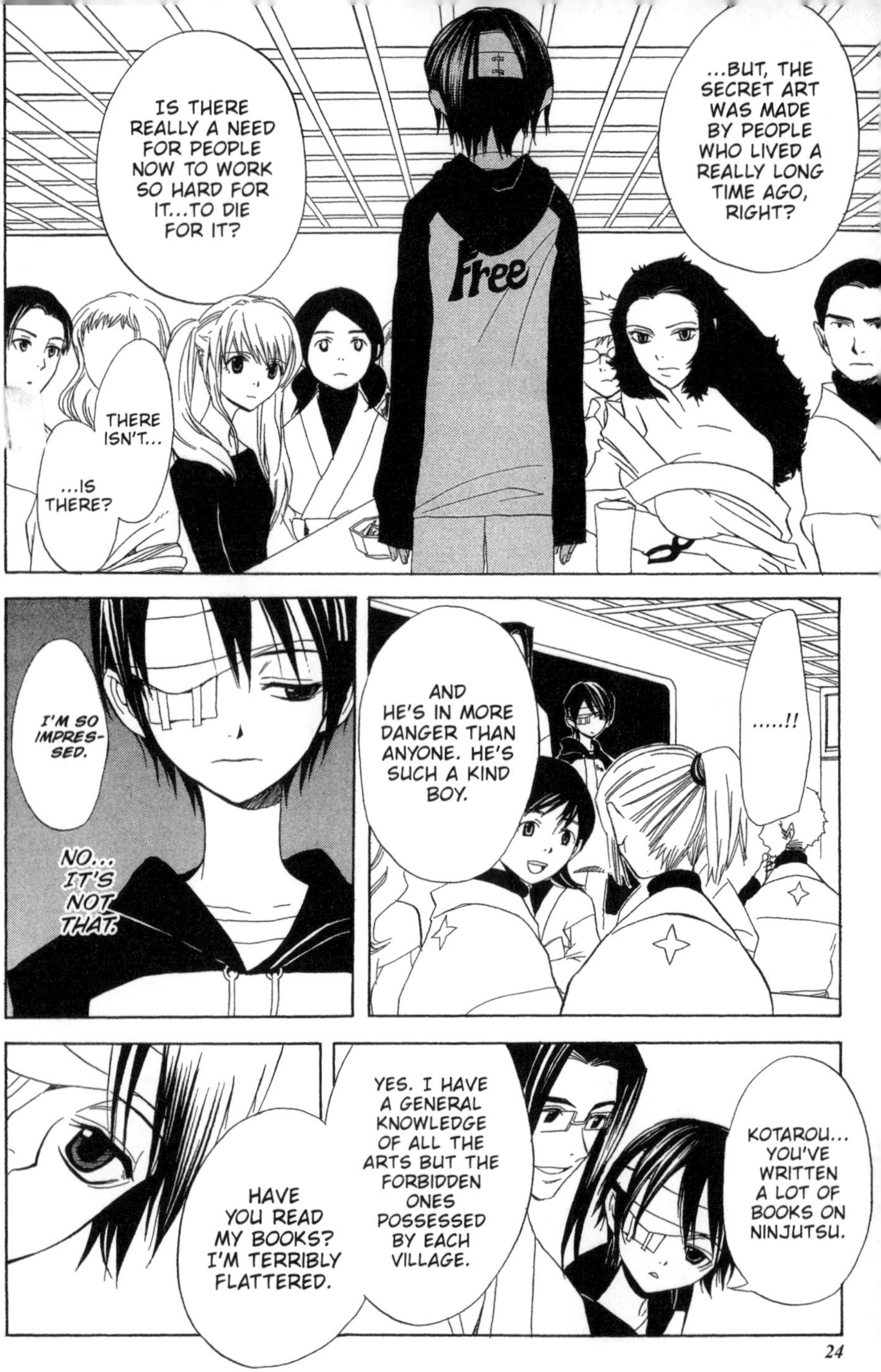

...BUT, THE SECRET ART WAS MADE BY PEOPLE WHO LIVED A REALLY LONG TIME AGO, RIGHT?
IS THERE REALLY A NEED FOR PEOPLE NOW TO WORK SO HARD FOR IT...TO DIE FOR IT?
THERE ISN'T...
...IS THERE?
.....!!
AND HE'S IN MORE DANGER THAN ANYONE. HE'S SUCH A KIND BOY.
I'M SO IMPRESSED.
NO... IT'S NOT THAT.
KOTAROU... YOU'VE WRITTEN A LOT OF BOOKS ON NINJUTSU.
HAVE YOU READ MY BOOKS? I'M TERRIBLY FLATTERED.
YES. I HAVE A GENERAL KNOWLEDGE OF ALL THE ARTS BUT THE FORBIDDEN ONES POSSESSED BY EACH VILLAGE.

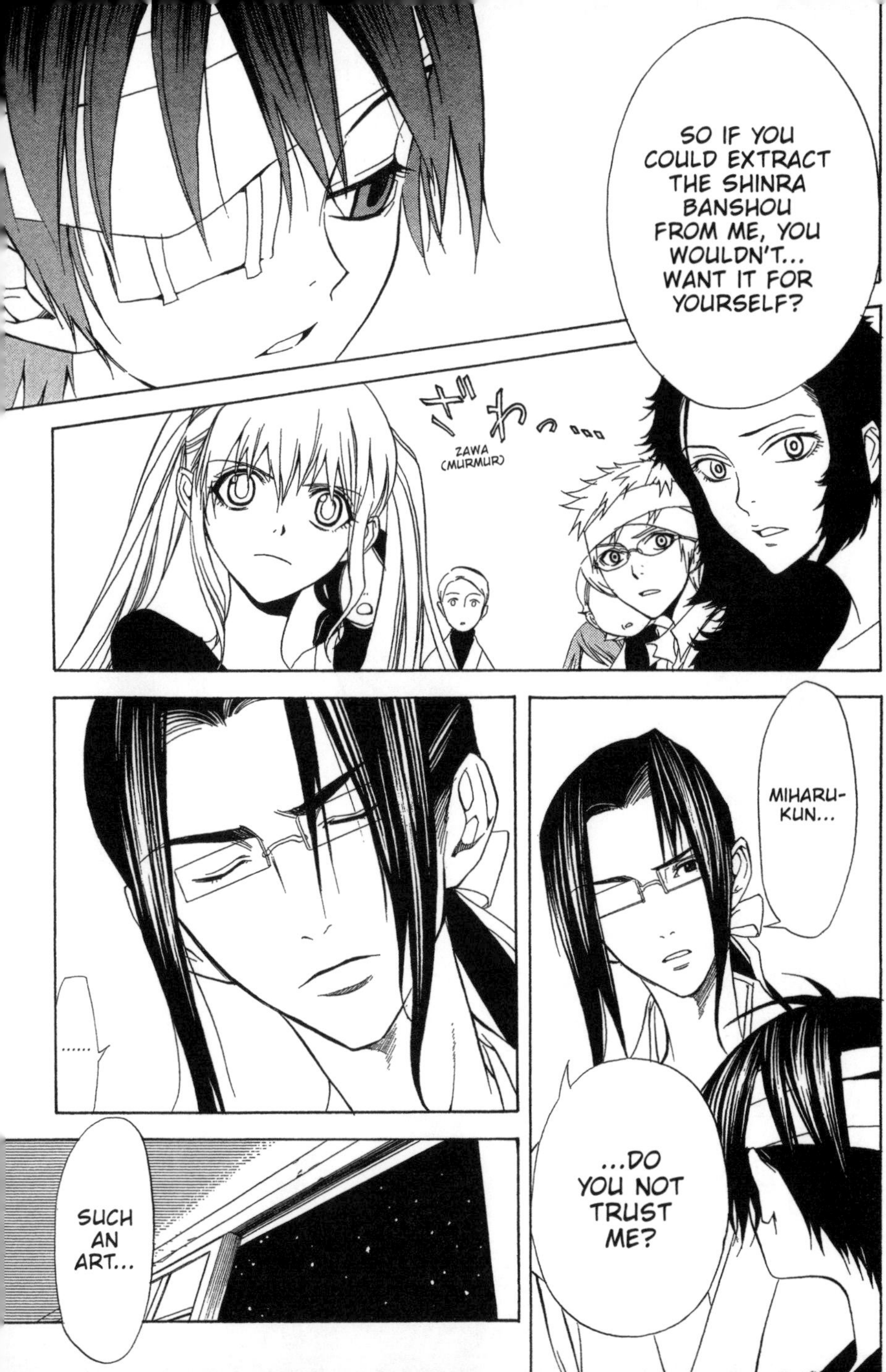
SO IF YOU COULD EXTRACT THE SHINRA BANSHOU FROM ME, YOU WOULDN'T... WANT IT FOR YOURSELF?
ざわっ...
ZAWA (MURMUR)
MIHARU-KUN...
...DO YOU NOT TRUST ME?
......
SUCH AN ART...

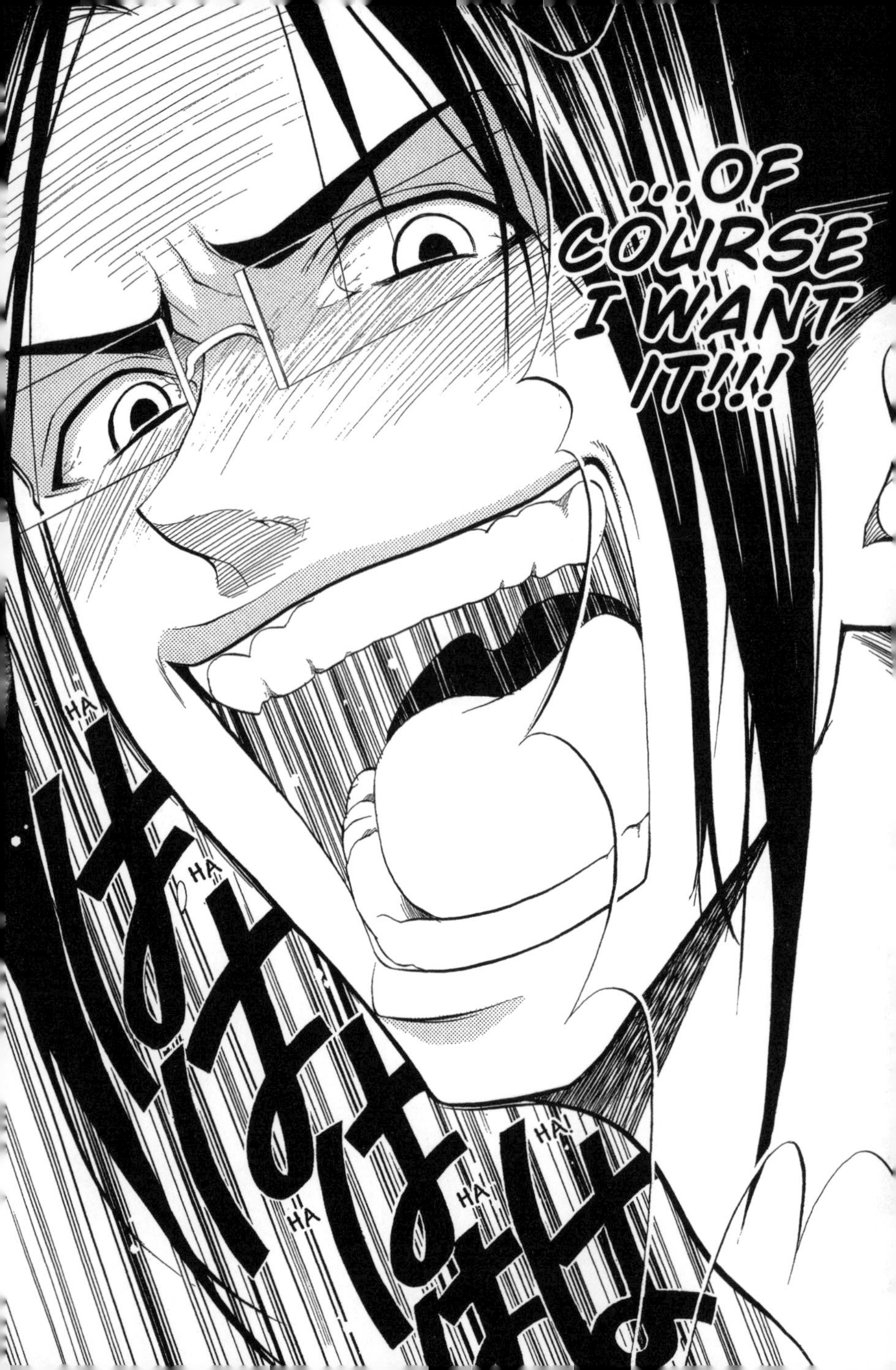
...OF COURSE I WANT IT!!!
HA
HA
HA!
HA
HA

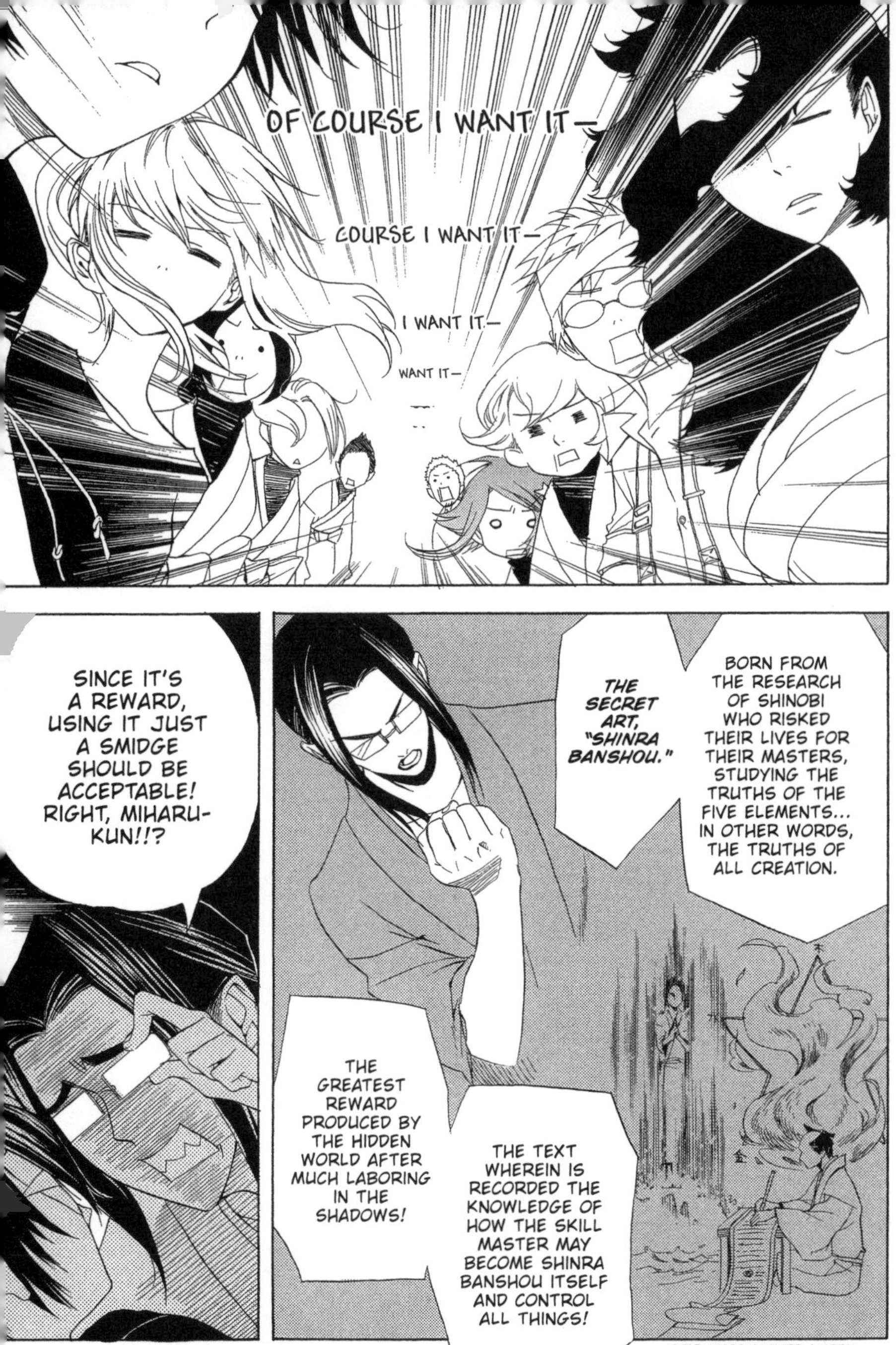
OF COURSE I WANT IT—
COURSE I WANT IT—
I WANT IT—
WANT IT—
BORN FROM THE RESEARCH OF SHINOBI WHO RISKED THEIR LIVES FOR THEIR MASTERS, STUDYING THE TRUTHS OF THE FIVE ELEMENTS... IN OTHER WORDS, THE TRUTHS OF ALL CREATION.
THE SECRET ART, "SHINRA BANSHOU."
THE GREATEST REWARD PRODUCED BY THE HIDDEN WORLD AFTER MUCH LABORING IN THE SHADOWS!
THE TEXT WHEREIN IS RECORDED THE KNOWLEDGE OF HOW THE SKILL MASTER MAY BECOME SHINRA BANSHOU ITSELF AND CONTROL ALL THINGS!
SINCE IT'S A REWARD, USING IT JUST A SMIDGE SHOULD BE ACCEPTABLE! RIGHT, MIHARU-KUN!!?

STAR: WOOD / WATER / METAL

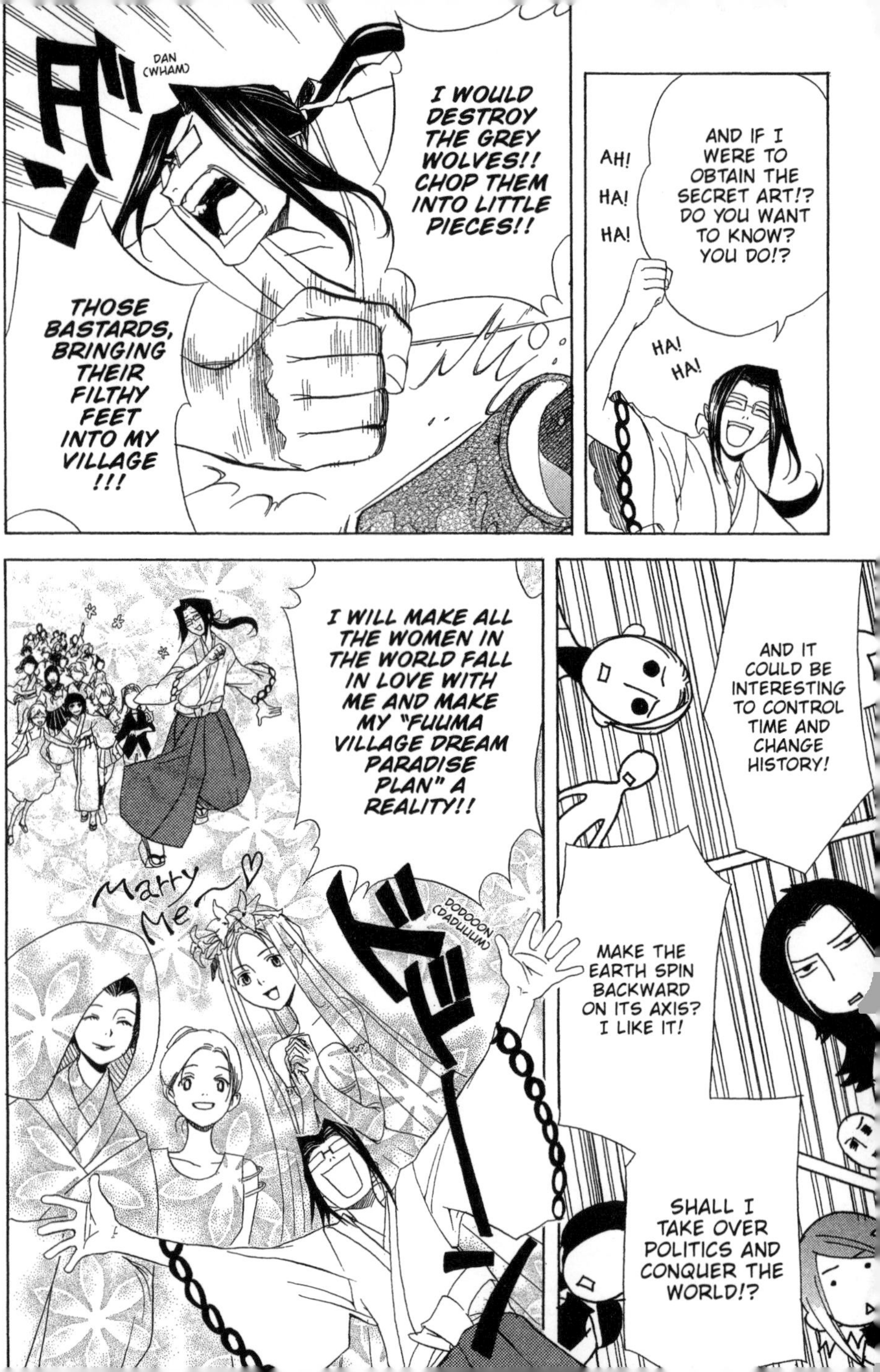
AND IF I WERE TO OBTAIN THE SECRET ART!? DO YOU WANT TO KNOW? YOU DO!?
AH! HA! HA!
HA! HA!
DAN (WHAM)
I WOULD DESTROY THE GREY WOLVES!! CHOP THEM INTO LITTLE PIECES!!
THOSE BASTARDS, BRINGING THEIR FILTHY FEET INTO MY VILLAGE!!!
AND IT COULD BE INTERESTING TO CONTROL TIME AND CHANGE HISTORY!
MAKE THE EARTH SPIN BACKWARD ON ITS AXIS? I LIKE IT!
SHALL I TAKE OVER POLITICS AND CONQUER THE WORLD!?
I WILL MAKE ALL THE WOMEN IN THE WORLD FALL IN LOVE WITH ME AND MAKE MY "FUUMA VILLAGE DREAM PARADISE PLAN" A REALITY!!
Marry Me~♡
DODOOON (DADUUUM)

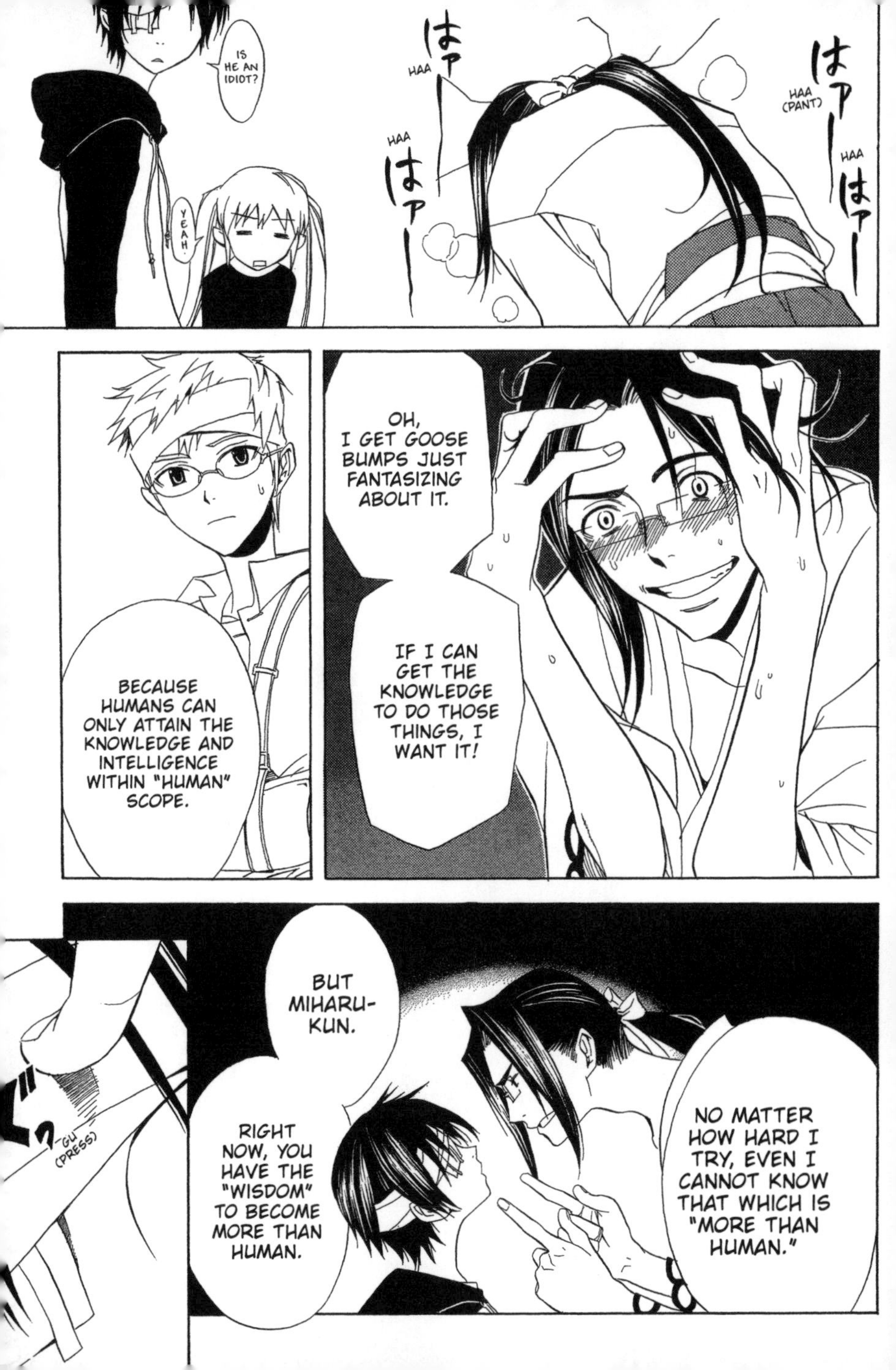

はァー
HAA (PANT)
はァー
HAA
はァー
HAA
はァー
HAA
IS HE AN IDIOT?
YEAH.
OH, I GET GOOSE BUMPS JUST FANTASIZING ABOUT IT.
IF I CAN GET THE KNOWLEDGE TO DO THOSE THINGS, I WANT IT!
BECAUSE HUMANS CAN ONLY ATTAIN THE KNOWLEDGE AND INTELLIGENCE WITHIN "HUMAN" SCOPE.
NO MATTER HOW HARD I TRY, EVEN I CANNOT KNOW THAT WHICH IS "MORE THAN HUMAN."
BUT MIHARU-KUN.
RIGHT NOW, YOU HAVE THE "WISDOM" TO BECOME MORE THAN HUMAN.
ぐっ
GU (PRESS)

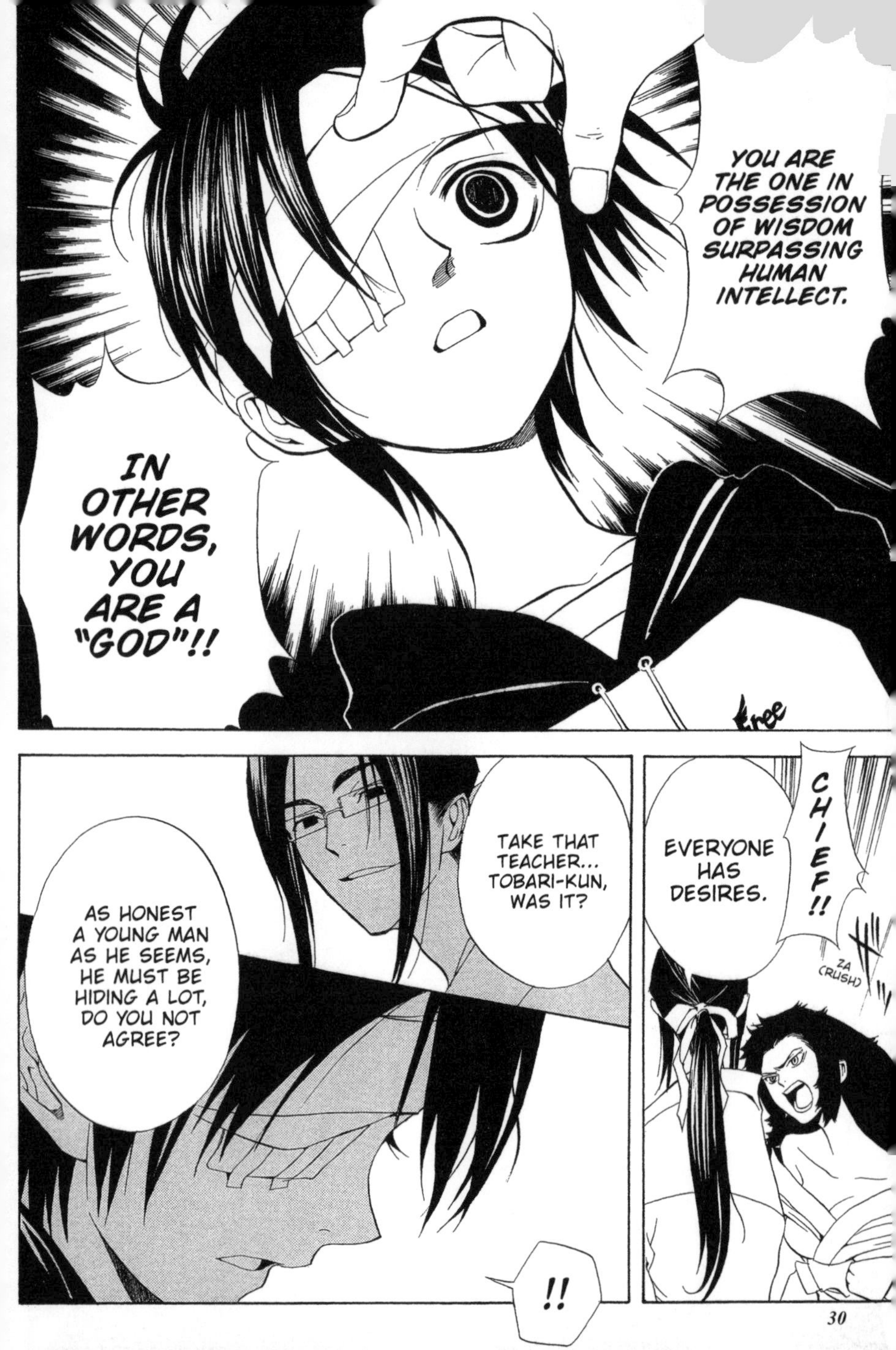
YOU ARE THE ONE IN POSSESSION OF WISDOM SURPASSING HUMAN INTELLECT.
IN OTHER WORDS, YOU ARE A "GOD"!!
CHIEF!!
EVERYONE HAS DESIRES.
ZA (RUSH)
TAKE THAT TEACHER... TOBARI-KUN, WAS IT?
AS HONEST A YOUNG MAN AS HE SEEMS, HE MUST BE HIDING A LOT, DO YOU NOT AGREE?
!!

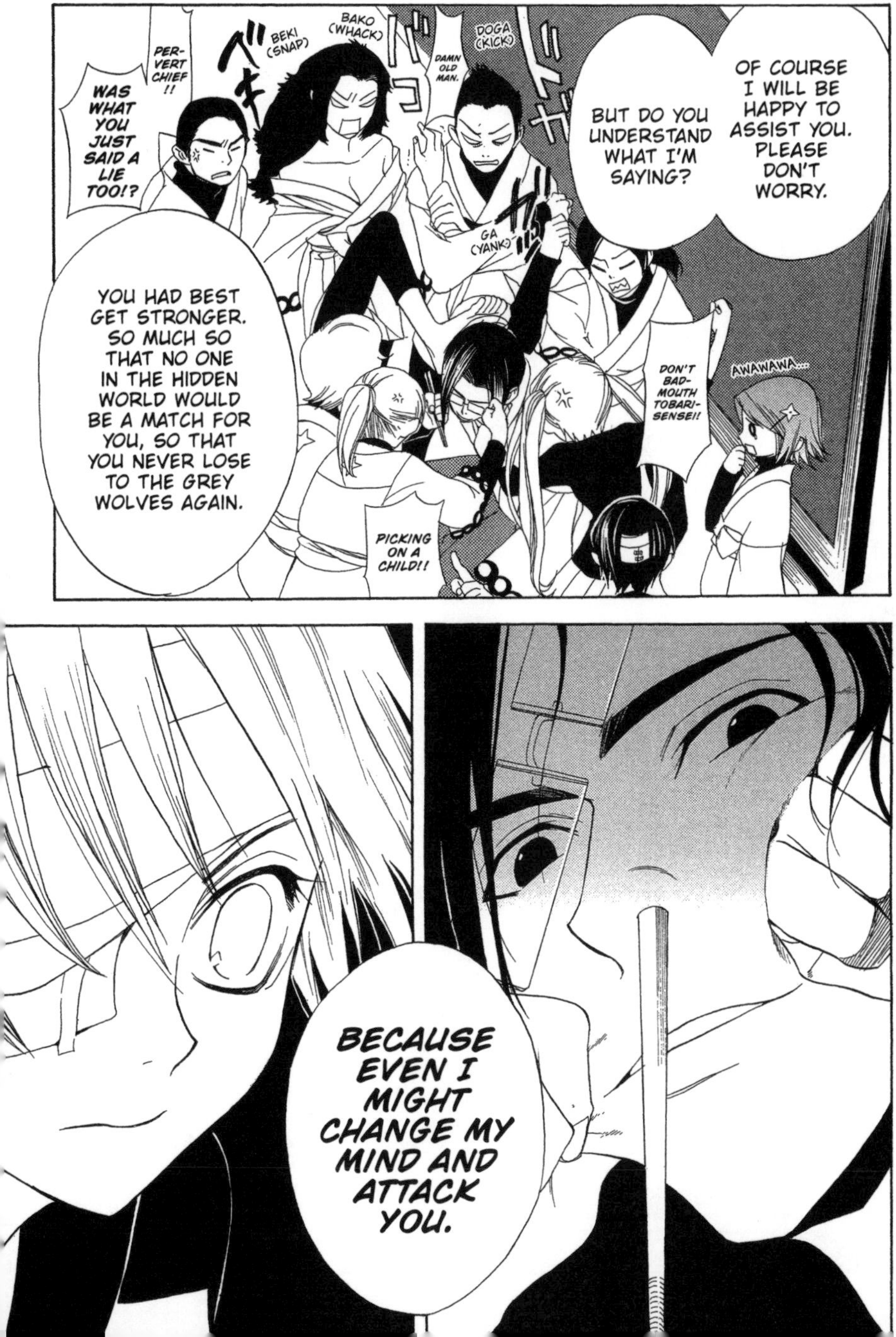
OF COURSE I WILL BE HAPPY TO ASSIST YOU. PLEASE DON'T WORRY.
BUT DO YOU UNDERSTAND WHAT I'M SAYING?
DOGA (KICK)
DAMN OLD MAN.
BAKO (WHACK)
BEKI (SNAP)
PER-VERT CHIEF!!
WAS WHAT YOU JUST SAID A LIE TOO!?
GA (YANK)
AWAWAWA...
DON'T BAD-MOUTH TOBARI-SENSEI!!
YOU HAD BEST GET STRONGER. SO MUCH SO THAT NO ONE IN THE HIDDEN WORLD WOULD BE A MATCH FOR YOU, SO THAT YOU NEVER LOSE TO THE GREY WOLVES AGAIN.
PICKING ON A CHILD!!
BECAUSE EVEN I MIGHT CHANGE MY MIND AND ATTACK YOU.

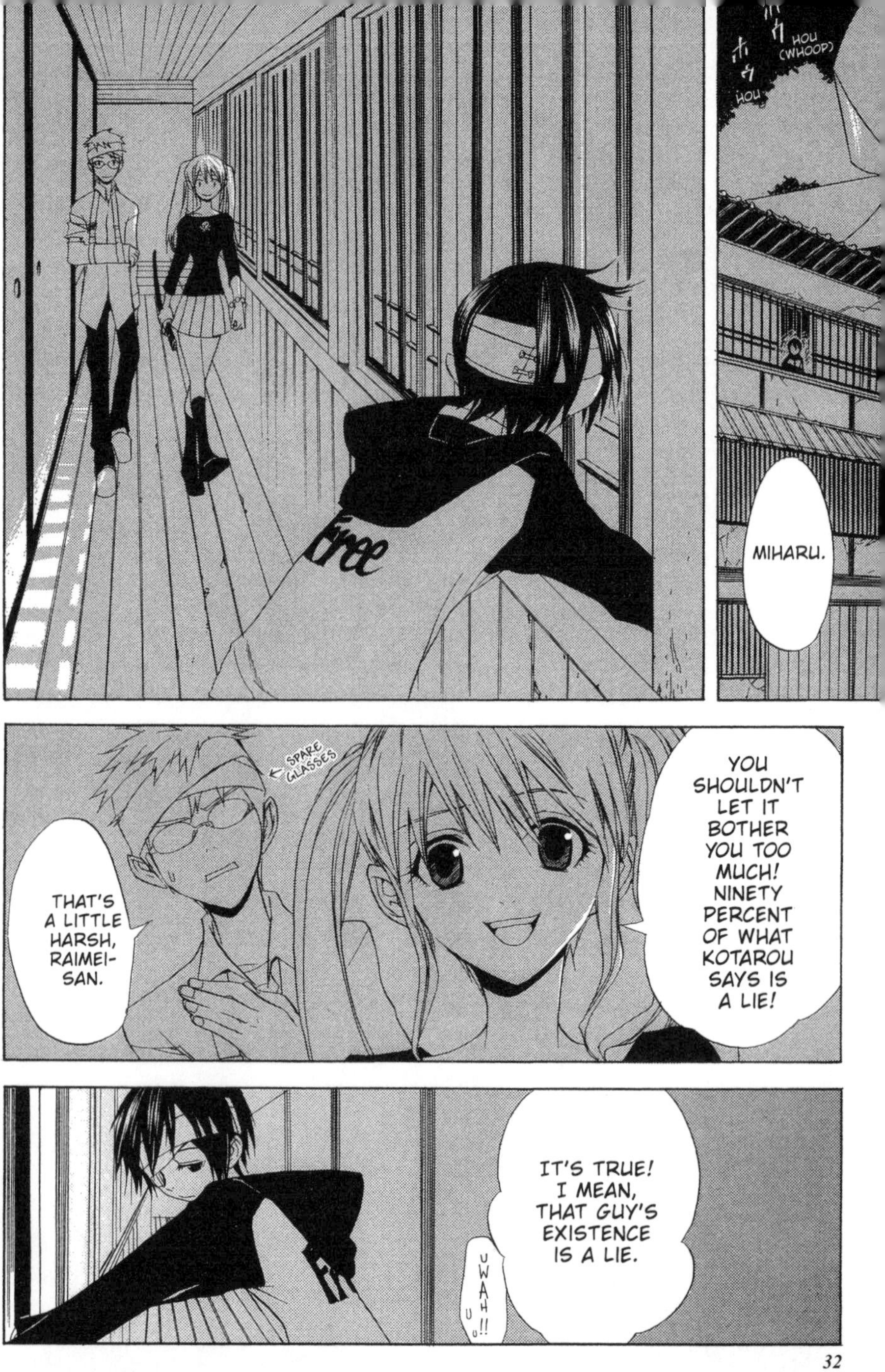
HOU (WHOOP)
HOU
MIHARU.
YOU SHOULDN'T LET IT BOTHER YOU TOO MUCH! NINETY PERCENT OF WHAT KOTAROU SAYS IS A LIE!
SPARE GLASSES
THAT'S A LITTLE HARSH, RAIMEI-SAN.
IT'S TRUE! I MEAN, THAT GUY'S EXISTENCE IS A LIE.
UWAH!!

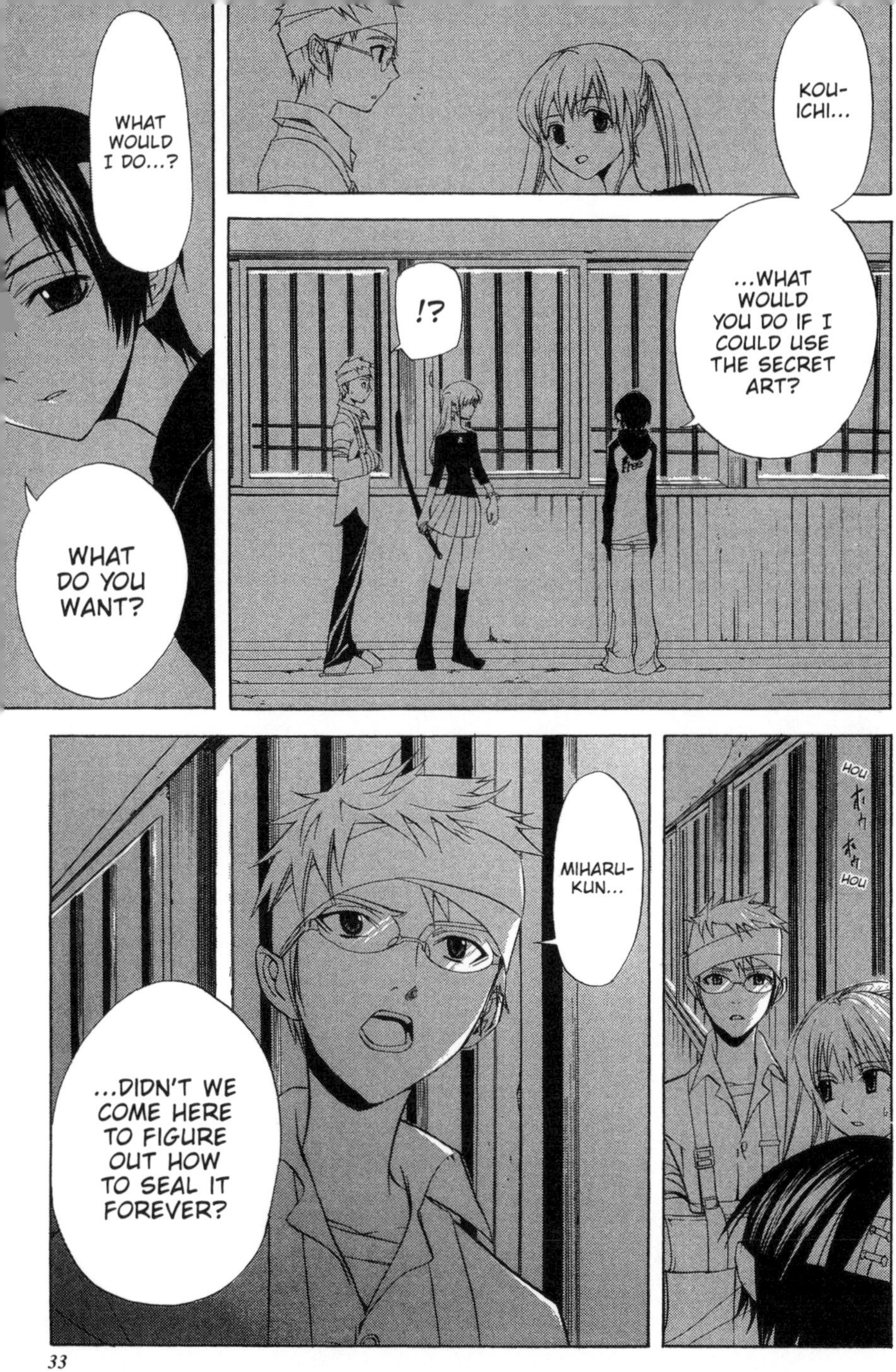
KOU-ICHI...
...WHAT WOULD YOU DO IF I COULD USE THE SECRET ART?
!?
WHAT WOULD I DO...?
WHAT DO YOU WANT?
HOU HOU
MIHARU-KUN...
...DIDN'T WE COME HERE TO FIGURE OUT HOW TO SEAL IT FOREVER?

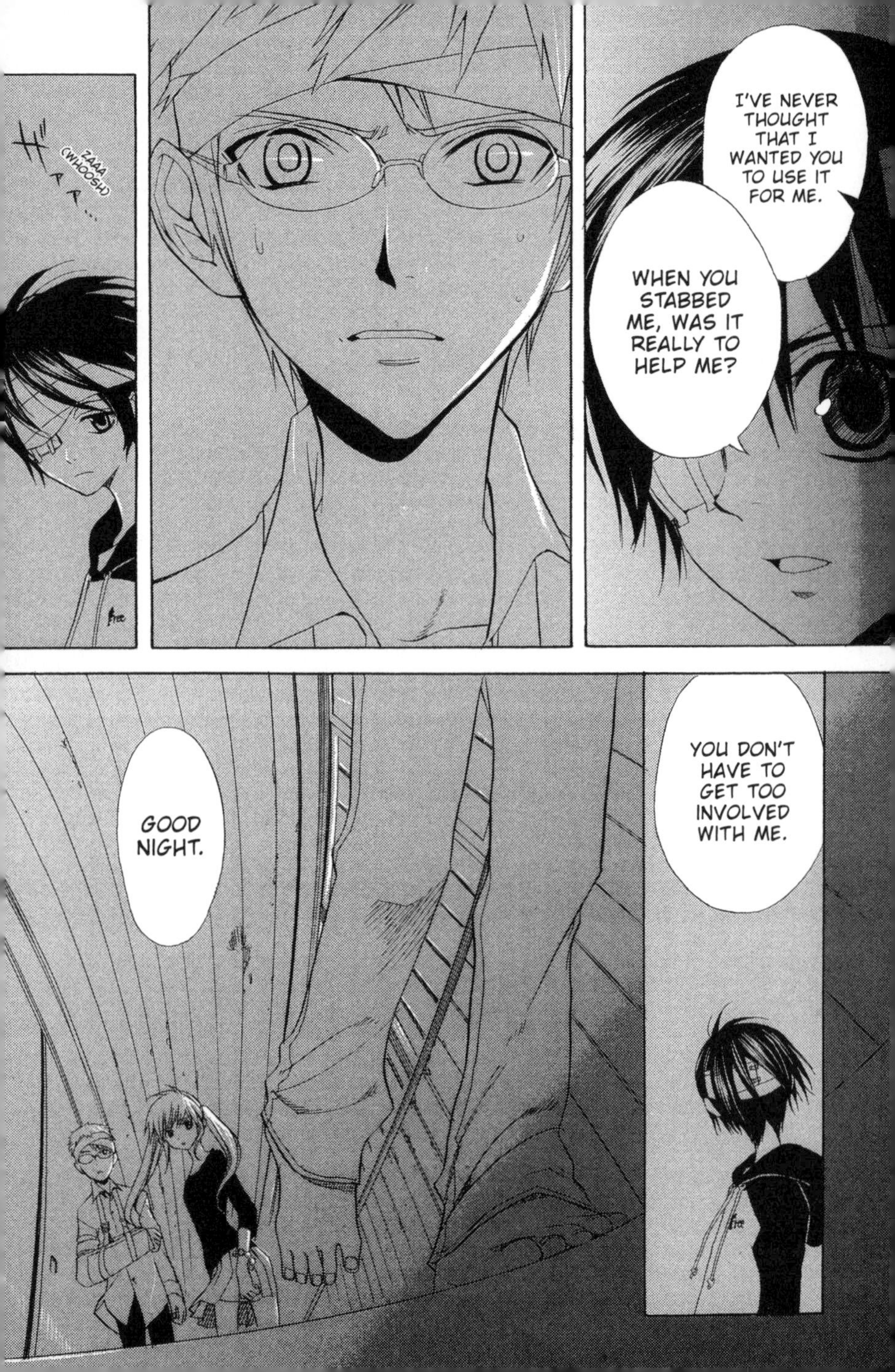

I'VE NEVER THOUGHT THAT I WANTED YOU TO USE IT FOR ME.
WHEN YOU STABBED ME, WAS IT REALLY TO HELP ME?
ザァァ…
ZAAA (WHOOSH)
YOU DON'T HAVE TO GET TOO INVOLVED WITH ME.
GOOD NIGHT.

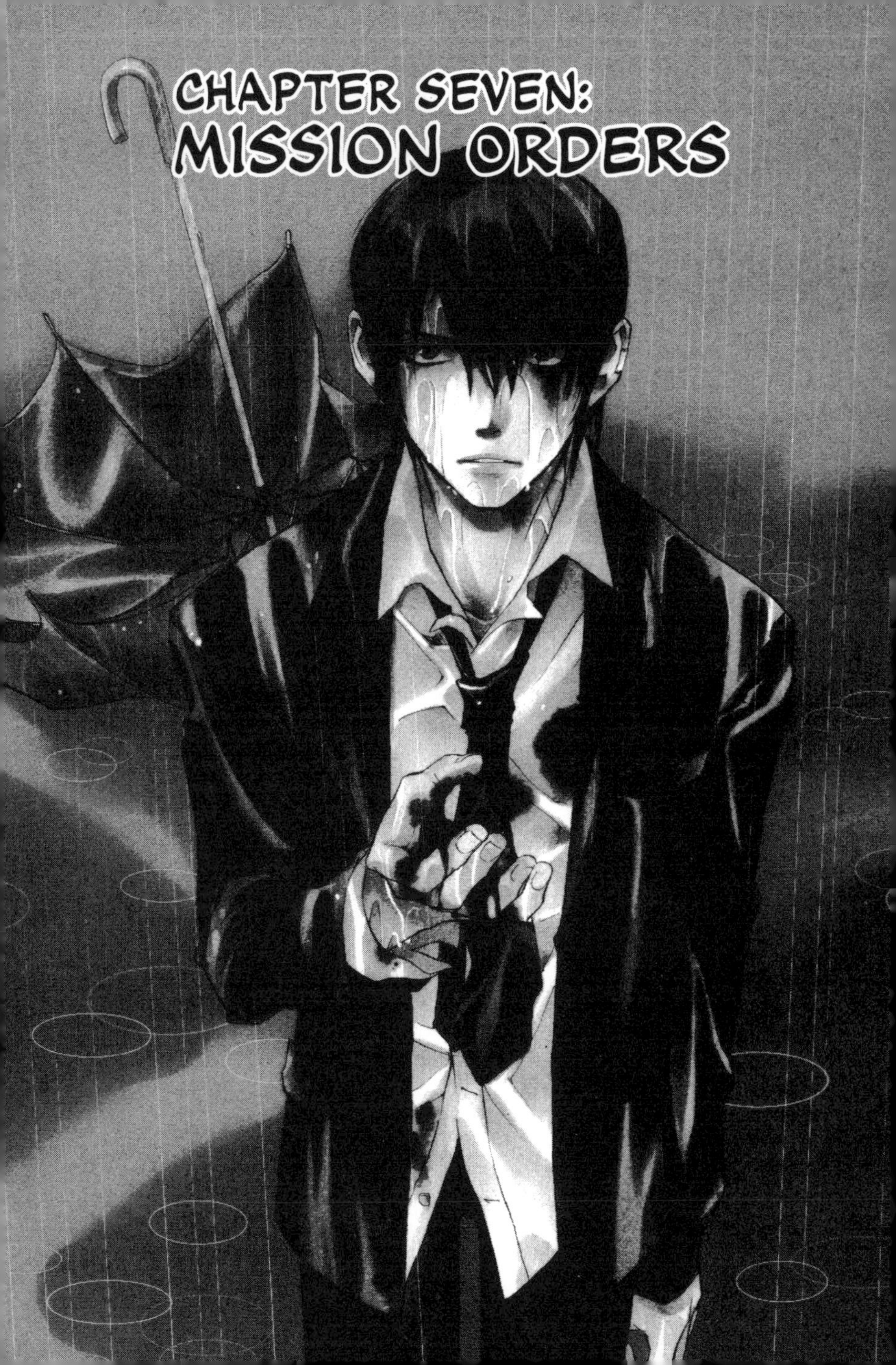
CHAPTER SEVEN:
MISSION ORDERS

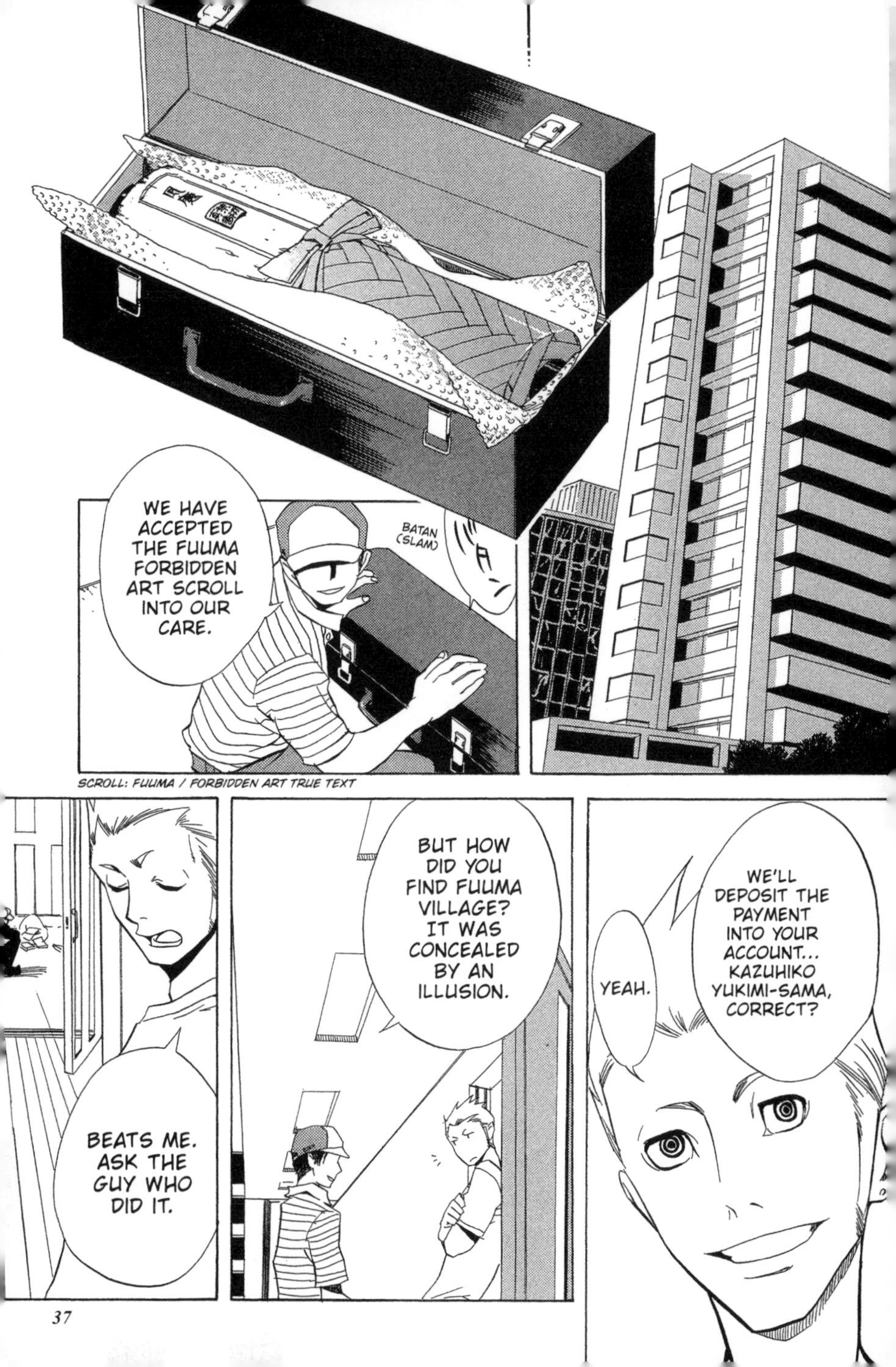
WE HAVE ACCEPTED THE FUUMA FORBIDDEN ART SCROLL INTO OUR CARE.
BATAN (SLAM)
SCROLL: FUUMA / FORBIDDEN ART TRUE TEXT
WE'LL DEPOSIT THE PAYMENT INTO YOUR ACCOUNT... KAZUHIKO YUKIMI-SAMA, CORRECT?
YEAH.
BUT HOW DID YOU FIND FUUMA VILLAGE? IT WAS CONCEALED BY AN ILLUSION.
BEATS ME. ASK THE GUY WHO DID IT.

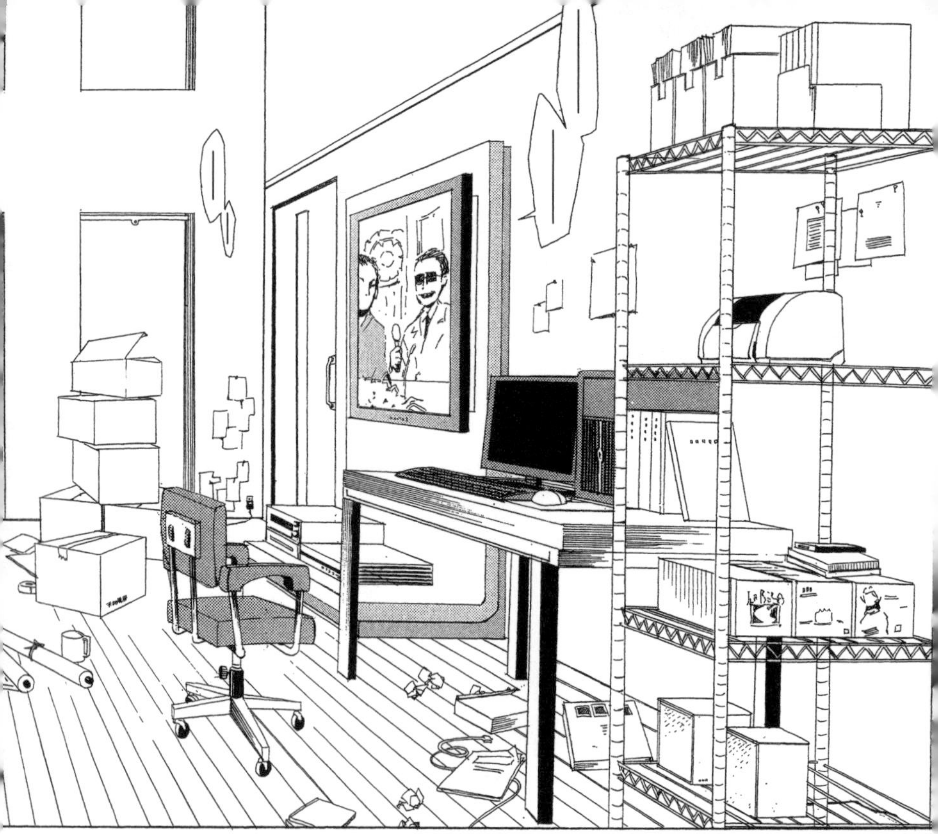

HAT: DELIVERY

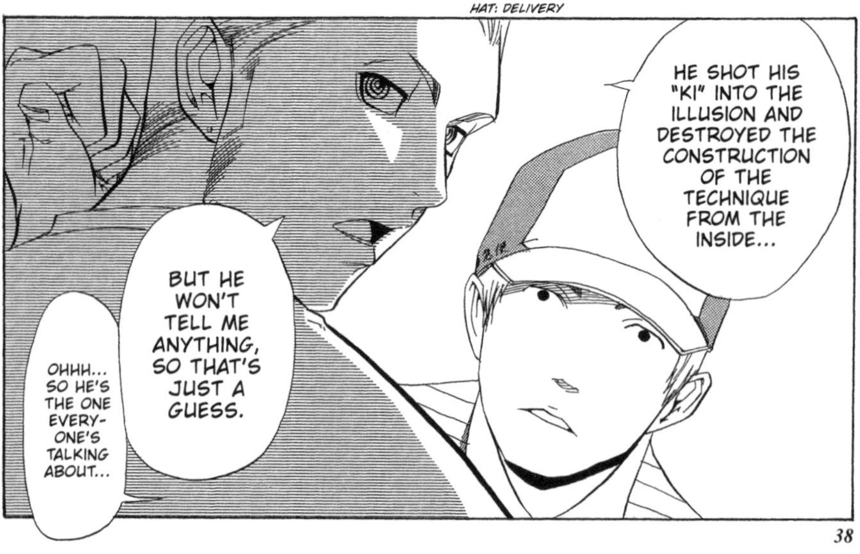
HE SHOT HIS "KI" INTO THE ILLUSION AND DESTROYED THE CONSTRUCTION OF THE TECHNIQUE FROM THE INSIDE...
BUT HE WON'T TELL ME ANYTHING, SO THAT'S JUST A GUESS.
OHHH... SO HE'S THE ONE EVERY-ONE'S TALKING ABOUT...

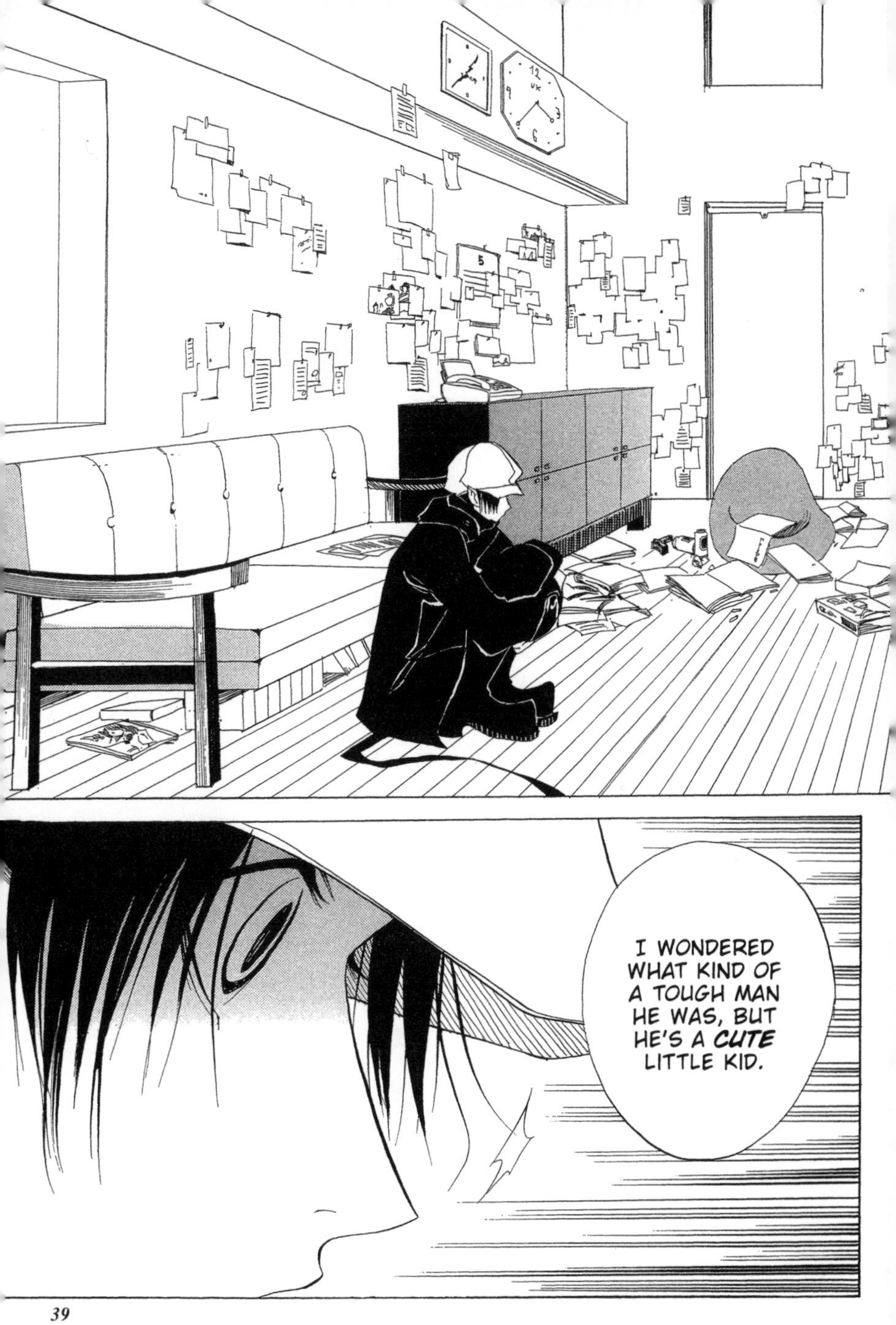
I WONDERED WHAT KIND OF A TOUGH MAN HE WAS, BUT HE'S A CUTE LITTLE KID.

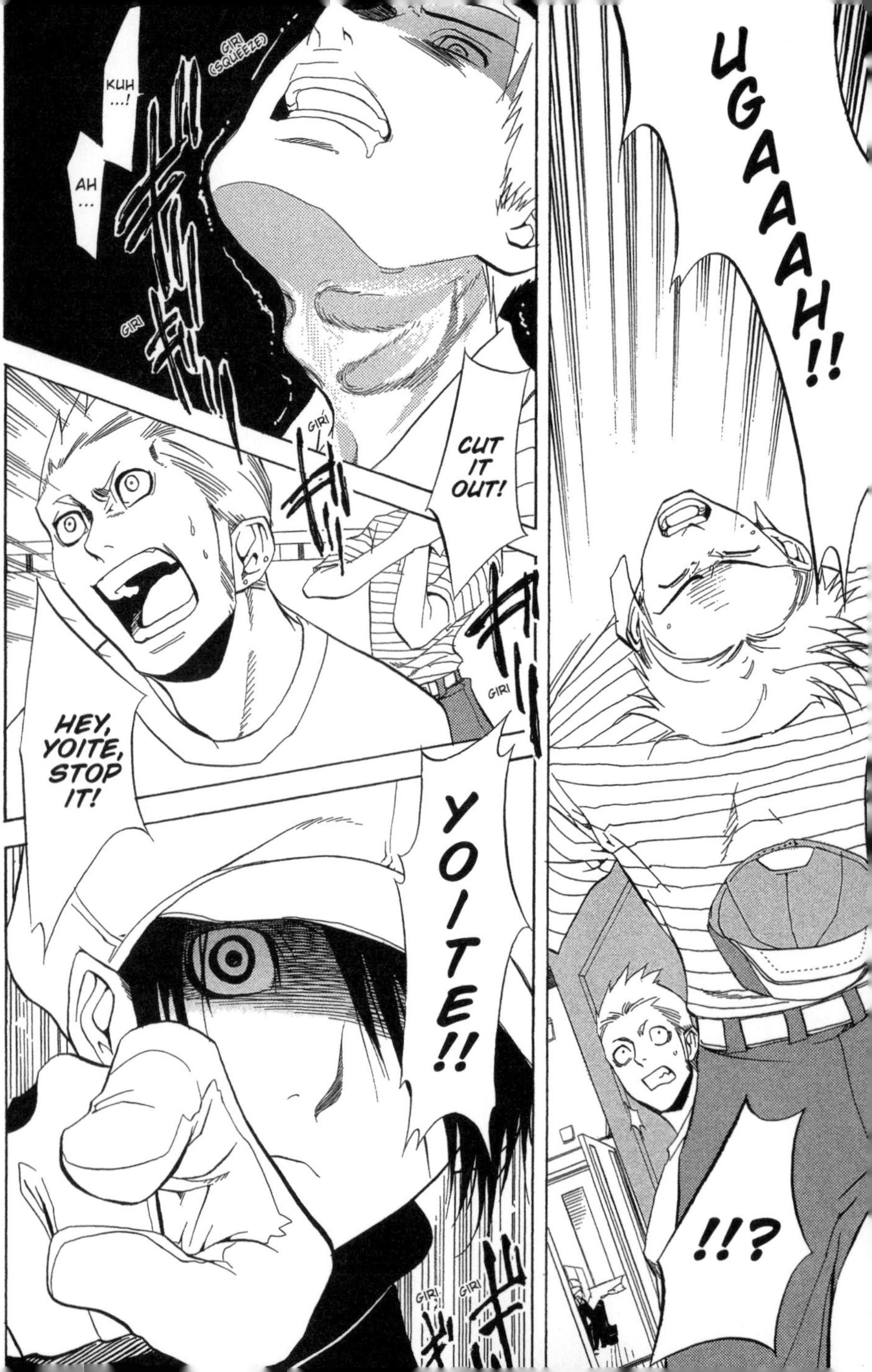
UGAAAH!!
!!?
GIRI (SQUEEZE)
KUH ...!
AH ...
GIRI
GIRI
CUT IT OUT!
GIRI
HEY, YOITE, STOP IT!
YOITE!!
GIRI
GIRI

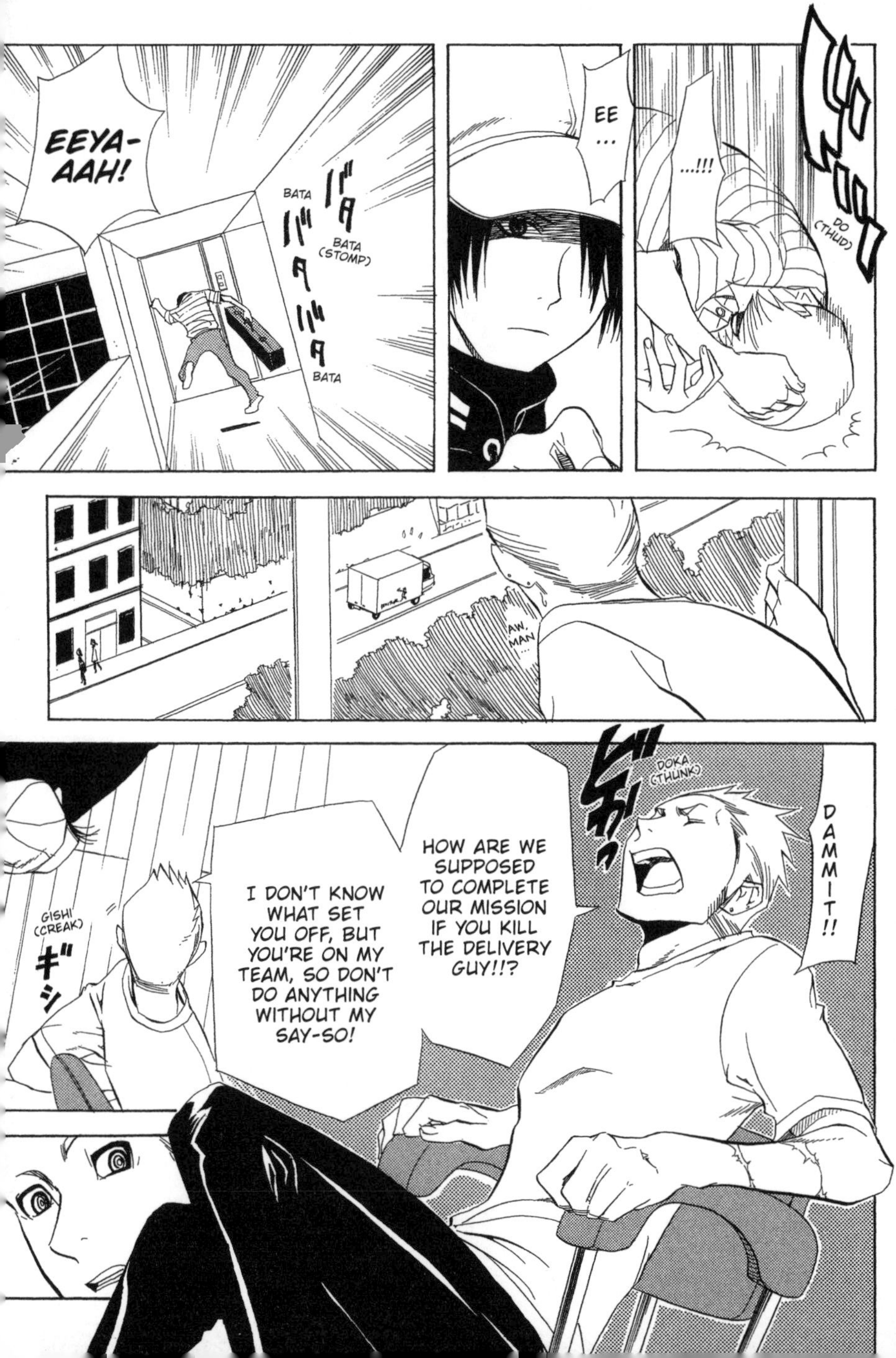
...!!!
DO (THUD)
EE ...
EEYA-AAH!
バタ
BATA
BATA (STOMP)
バタバタ
BATA
AW, MAN ...
DAMMIT!!
DOKA (THUNK)
HOW ARE WE SUPPOSED TO COMPLETE OUR MISSION IF YOU KILL THE DELIVERY GUY!!?
I DON'T KNOW WHAT SET YOU OFF, BUT YOU'RE ON MY TEAM, SO DON'T DO ANYTHING WITHOUT MY SAY-SO!
GISHI (CREAK)
ギシ

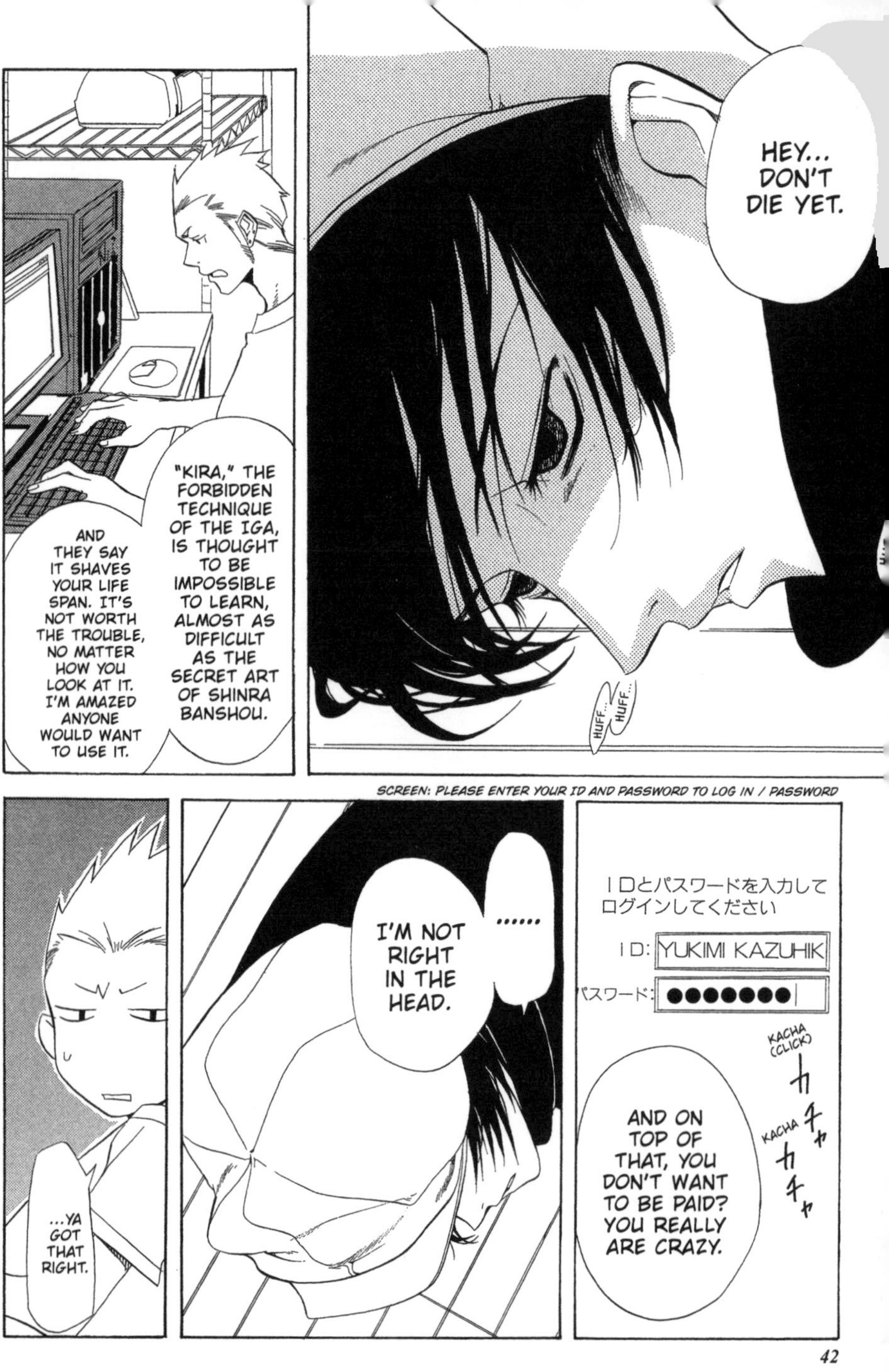
HEY... DON'T DIE YET.
HUFF... HUFF...
"KIRA," THE FORBIDDEN TECHNIQUE OF THE IGA, IS THOUGHT TO BE IMPOSSIBLE TO LEARN, ALMOST AS DIFFICULT AS THE SECRET ART OF SHINRA BANSHOU.
AND THEY SAY IT SHAVES YOUR LIFE SPAN. IT'S NOT WORTH THE TROUBLE, NO MATTER HOW YOU LOOK AT IT. I'M AMAZED ANYONE WOULD WANT TO USE IT.
SCREEN: PLEASE ENTER YOUR ID AND PASSWORD TO LOG IN / PASSWORD
ＩＤとパスワードを入力して
ログインしてください
ＩＤ: YUKIMI KAZUHIK
パスワード: ●●●●●●●●
KACHA (CLICK) カチャ
KACHA カチャ
AND ON TOP OF THAT, YOU DON'T WANT TO BE PAID? YOU REALLY ARE CRAZY.
......
I'M NOT RIGHT IN THE HEAD.
...YA GOT THAT RIGHT.

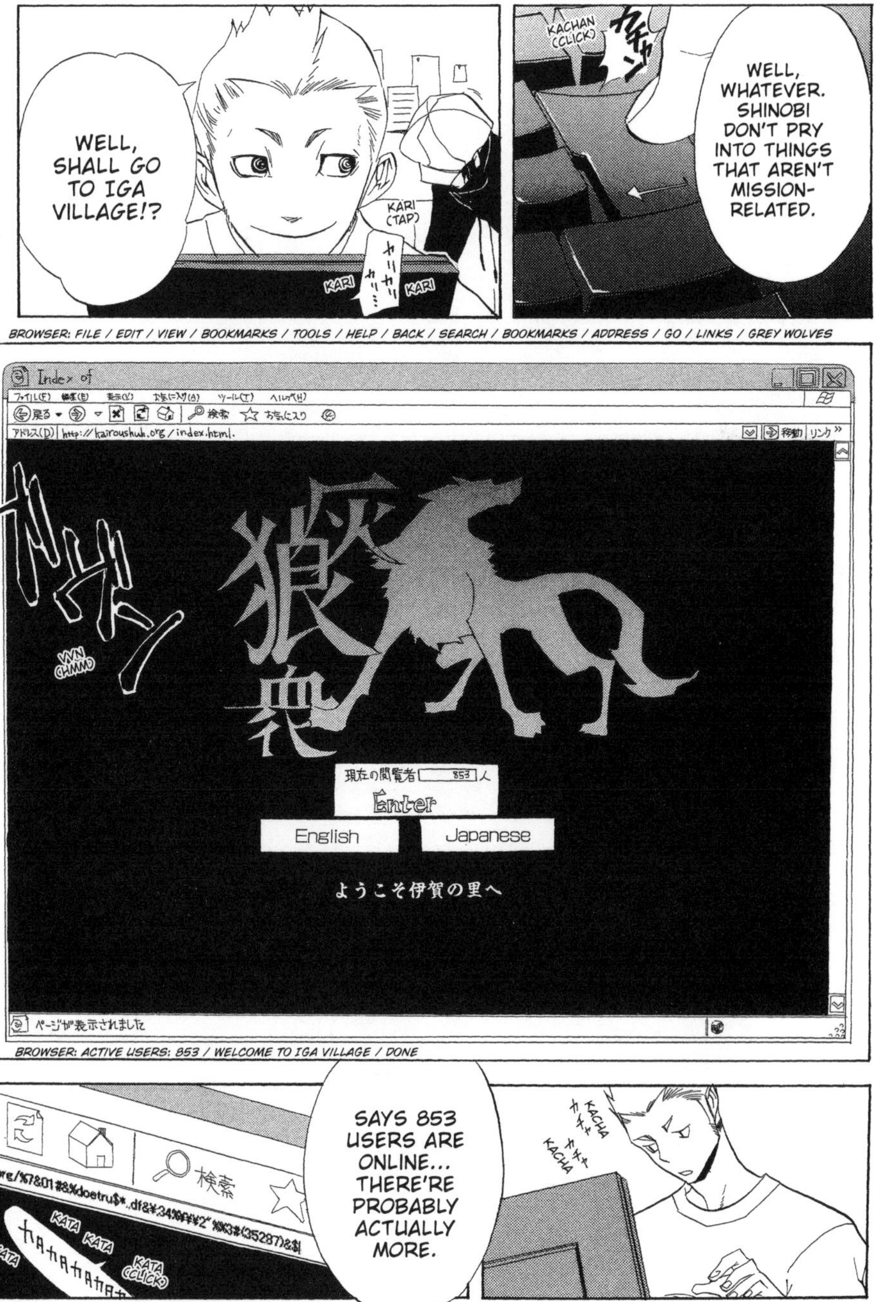
KACHAN (CLICK)
カチャン
WELL, WHATEVER. SHINOBI DON'T PRY INTO THINGS THAT AREN'T MISSION-RELATED.
WELL, SHALL GO TO IGA VILLAGE!?
KARI (TAP)
カリカリカリッ
KARI
KARI
BROWSER: FILE / EDIT / VIEW / BOOKMARKS / TOOLS / HELP / BACK / SEARCH / BOOKMARKS / ADDRESS / GO / LINKS / GREY WOLVES
Index of
http://kairoushuh.org/index.html
現在の閲覧者 853 人
Enter
English
Japanese
ようこそ伊賀の里へ
ページが表示されました
VVN (HMM)
BROWSER: ACTIVE USERS: 853 / WELCOME TO IGA VILLAGE / DONE
KACHA
カチャ
カチャ
KACHA
SAYS 853 USERS ARE ONLINE... THERE'RE PROBABLY ACTUALLY MORE.
検索
KATA
KATA
KATA
KATA (CLICK)
カタカタカタカタカ

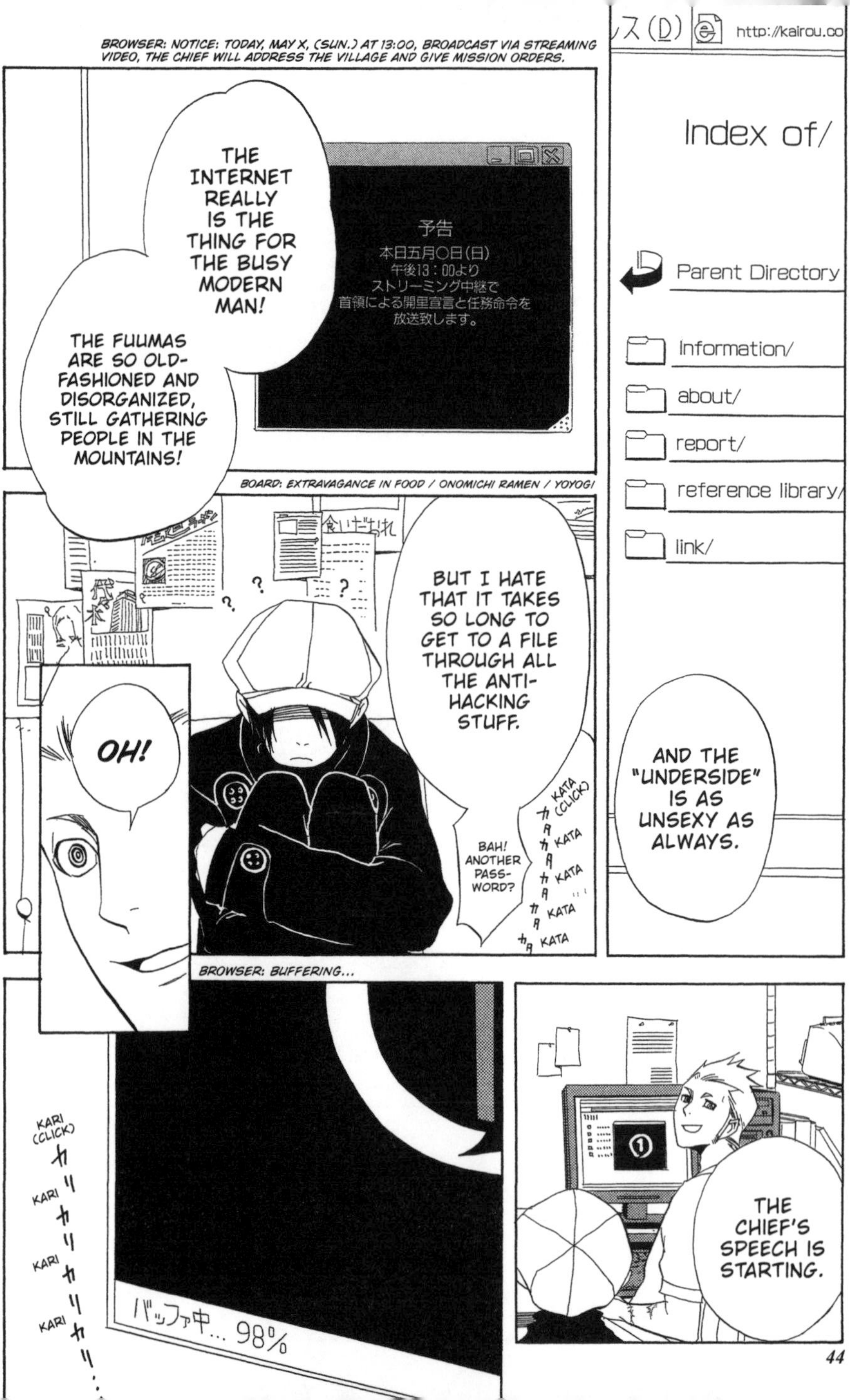

ス(D) http://kairou.co
Index of/
Parent Directory
Information/
about/
report/
reference library/
link/
AND THE "UNDERSIDE" IS AS UNSEXY AS ALWAYS.
BROWSER: NOTICE: TODAY, MAY X, (SUN.) AT 13:00, BROADCAST VIA STREAMING VIDEO, THE CHIEF WILL ADDRESS THE VILLAGE AND GIVE MISSION ORDERS.
予告
本日五月〇日(日)
午後13：00より
ストリーミング中継で
首領による開里宣言と任務命令を
放送致します。
THE INTERNET REALLY IS THE THING FOR THE BUSY MODERN MAN!
THE FUUMAS ARE SO OLD-FASHIONED AND DISORGANIZED, STILL GATHERING PEOPLE IN THE MOUNTAINS!
BOARD: EXTRAVAGANCE IN FOOD / ONOMICHI RAMEN / YOYOGI
食いだおれ
BUT I HATE THAT IT TAKES SO LONG TO GET TO A FILE THROUGH ALL THE ANTI-HACKING STUFF.
KATA (CLICK) KATA KATA KATA KATA
BAH! ANOTHER PASS-WORD?
OH!
BROWSER: BUFFERING...
THE CHIEF'S SPEECH IS STARTING.
KARI (CLICK) KARI KARI KARI
バッファ中… 98%

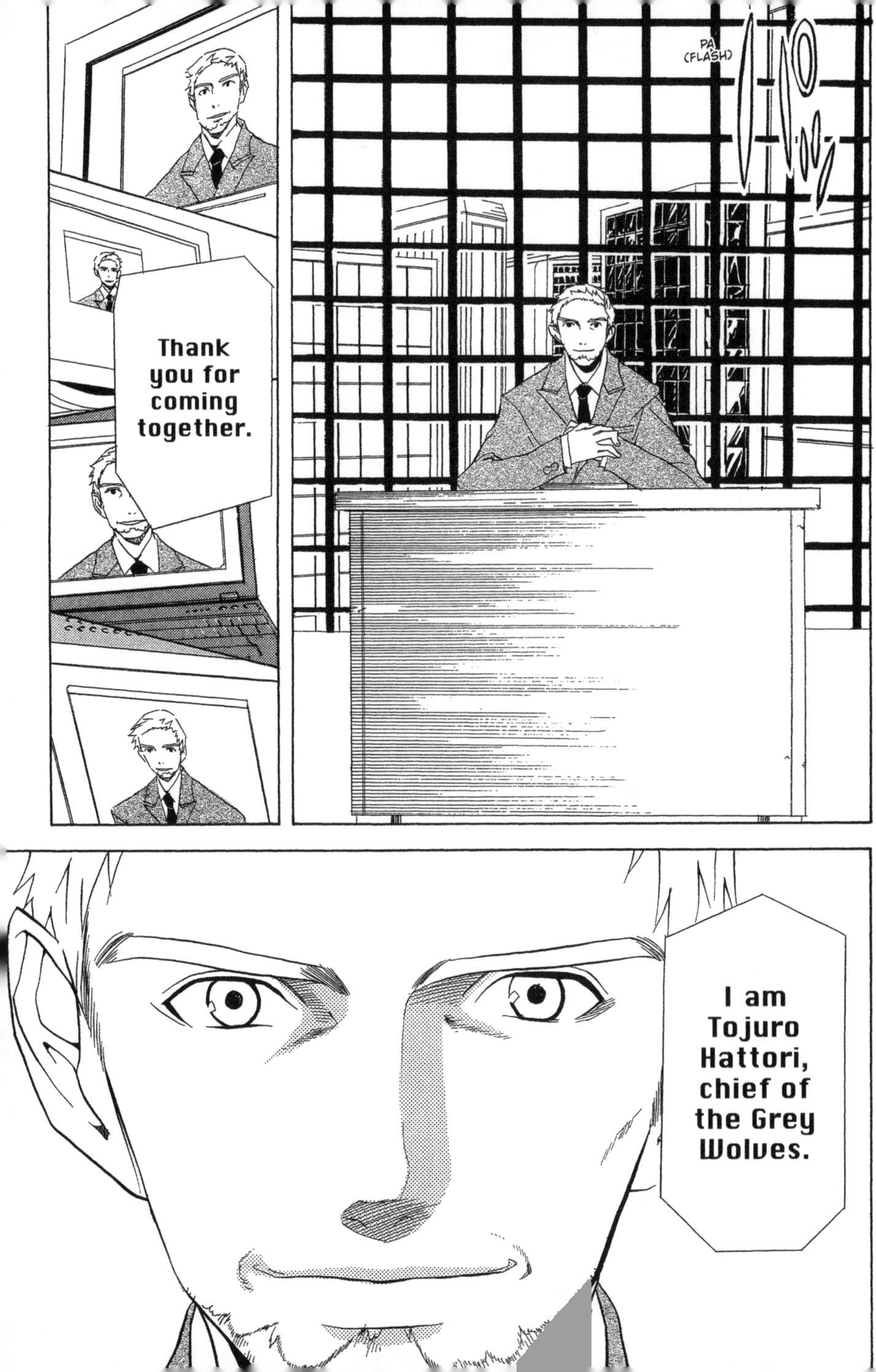
PA (FLASH)
Thank you for coming together.
I am Tojuro Hattori, chief of the Grey Wolves.

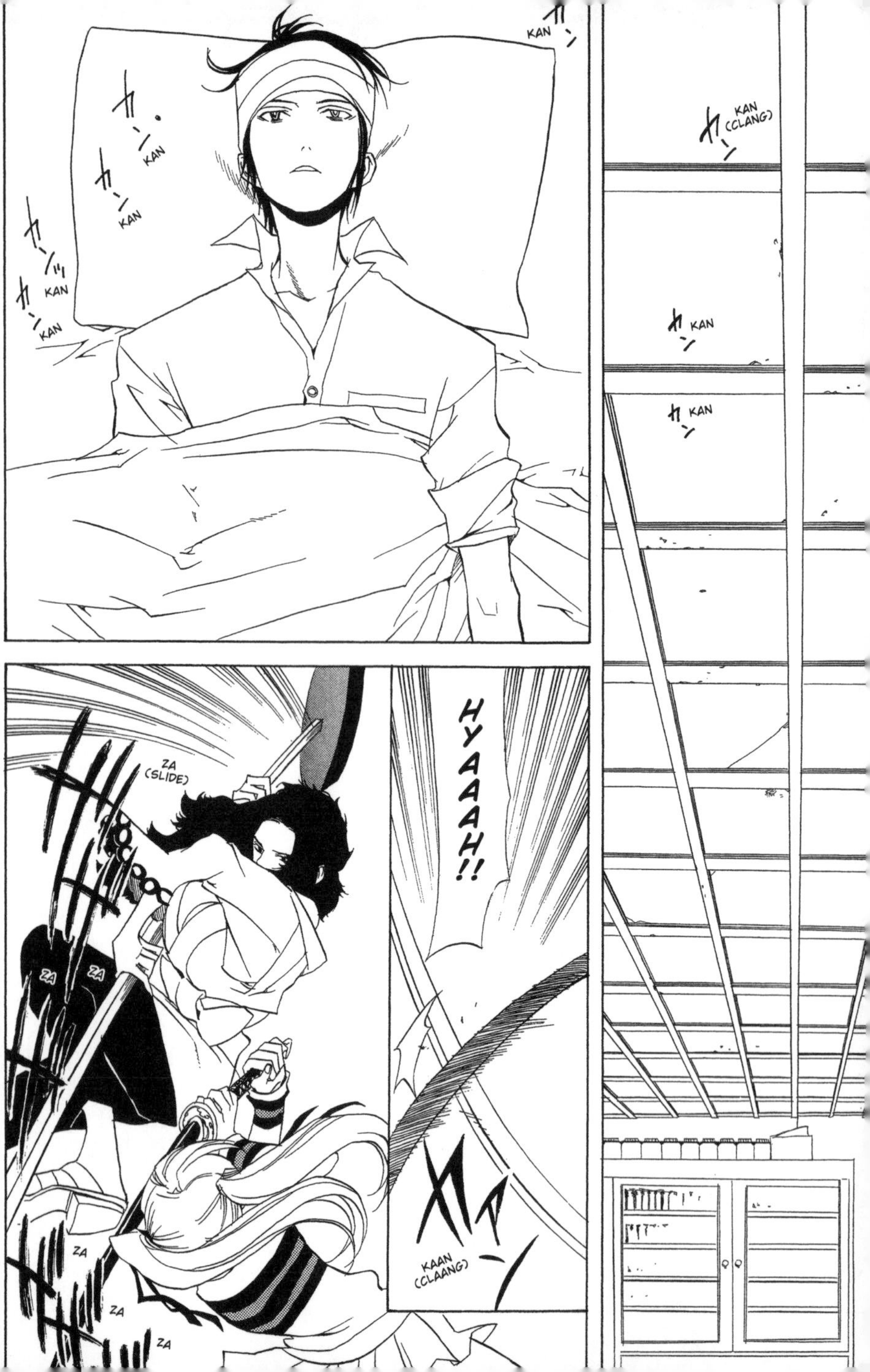
KAN (CLANG)
KAN
KAN
KAN
KAN
KAN
KAN
KAN
HYAAAAH!!
KAAN (CLAANG)
ZA (SLIDE)
ZA
ZA
ZA
ZA
ZA

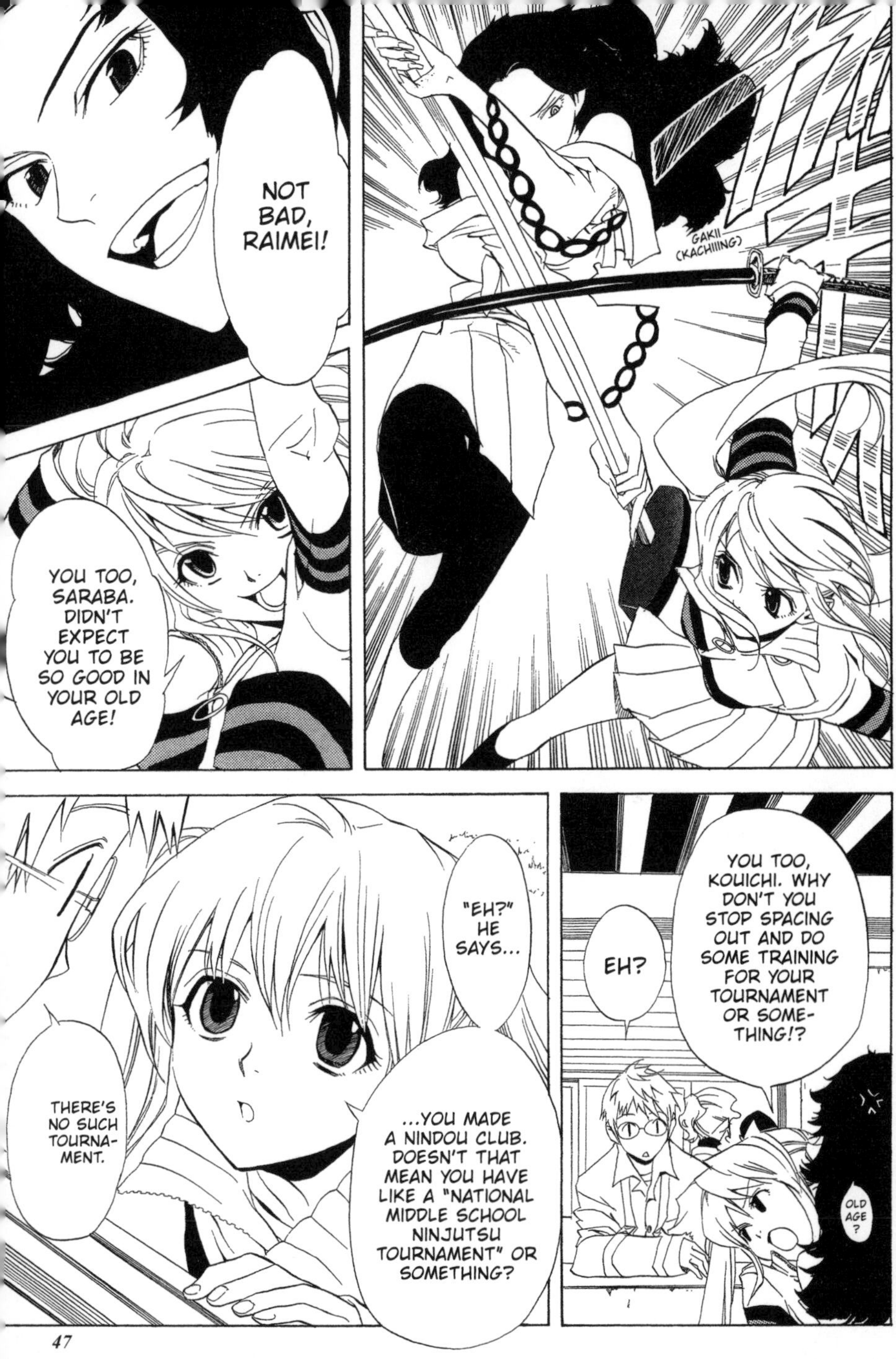
GAKII (KACHIIING)
NOT BAD, RAIMEI!
YOU TOO, SARABA. DIDN'T EXPECT YOU TO BE SO GOOD IN YOUR OLD AGE!
YOU TOO, KOUICHI. WHY DON'T YOU STOP SPACING OUT AND DO SOME TRAINING FOR YOUR TOURNAMENT OR SOME-THING!?
EH?
OLD AGE?
"EH?" HE SAYS...
...YOU MADE A NINDOU CLUB. DOESN'T THAT MEAN YOU HAVE LIKE A "NATIONAL MIDDLE SCHOOL NINJUTSU TOURNAMENT" OR SOMETHING?
THERE'S NO SUCH TOURNA-MENT.

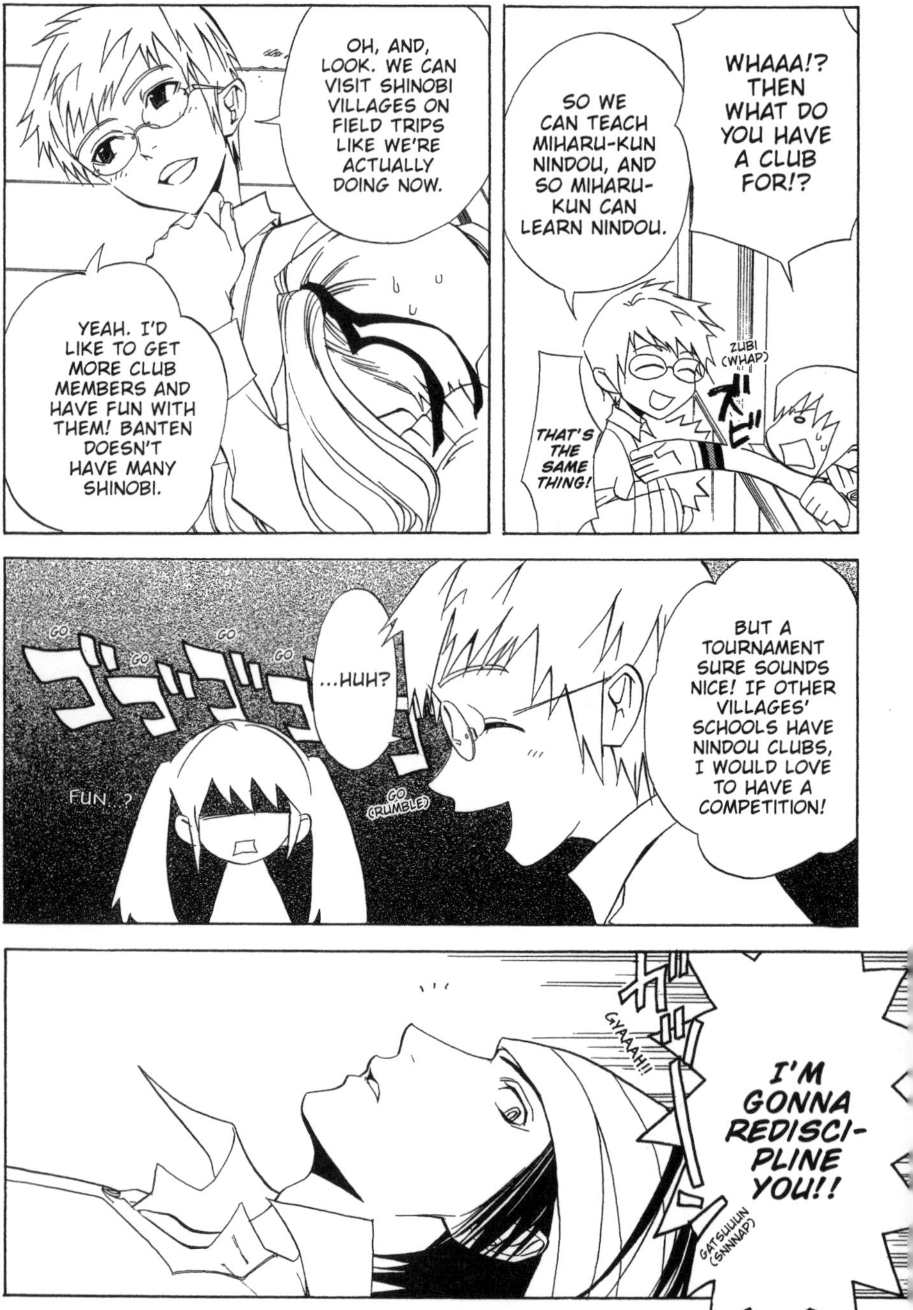
WHAAA!? THEN WHAT DO YOU HAVE A CLUB FOR!?
SO WE CAN TEACH MIHARU-KUN NINDOU, AND SO MIHARU-KUN CAN LEARN NINDOU.
ZUBI (WHAP)
THAT'S THE SAME THING!
OH, AND, LOOK. WE CAN VISIT SHINOBI VILLAGES ON FIELD TRIPS LIKE WE'RE ACTUALLY DOING NOW.
YEAH. I'D LIKE TO GET MORE CLUB MEMBERS AND HAVE FUN WITH THEM! BANTEN DOESN'T HAVE MANY SHINOBI.
BUT A TOURNAMENT SURE SOUNDS NICE! IF OTHER VILLAGES' SCHOOLS HAVE NINDOU CLUBS, I WOULD LOVE TO HAVE A COMPETITION!
...HUH?
GO GO GO GO
GO (RUMBLE)
FUN...?
I'M GONNA REDISCI-PLINE YOU!!
GYAAAH!!
GATSUUUN (SNNNAP)

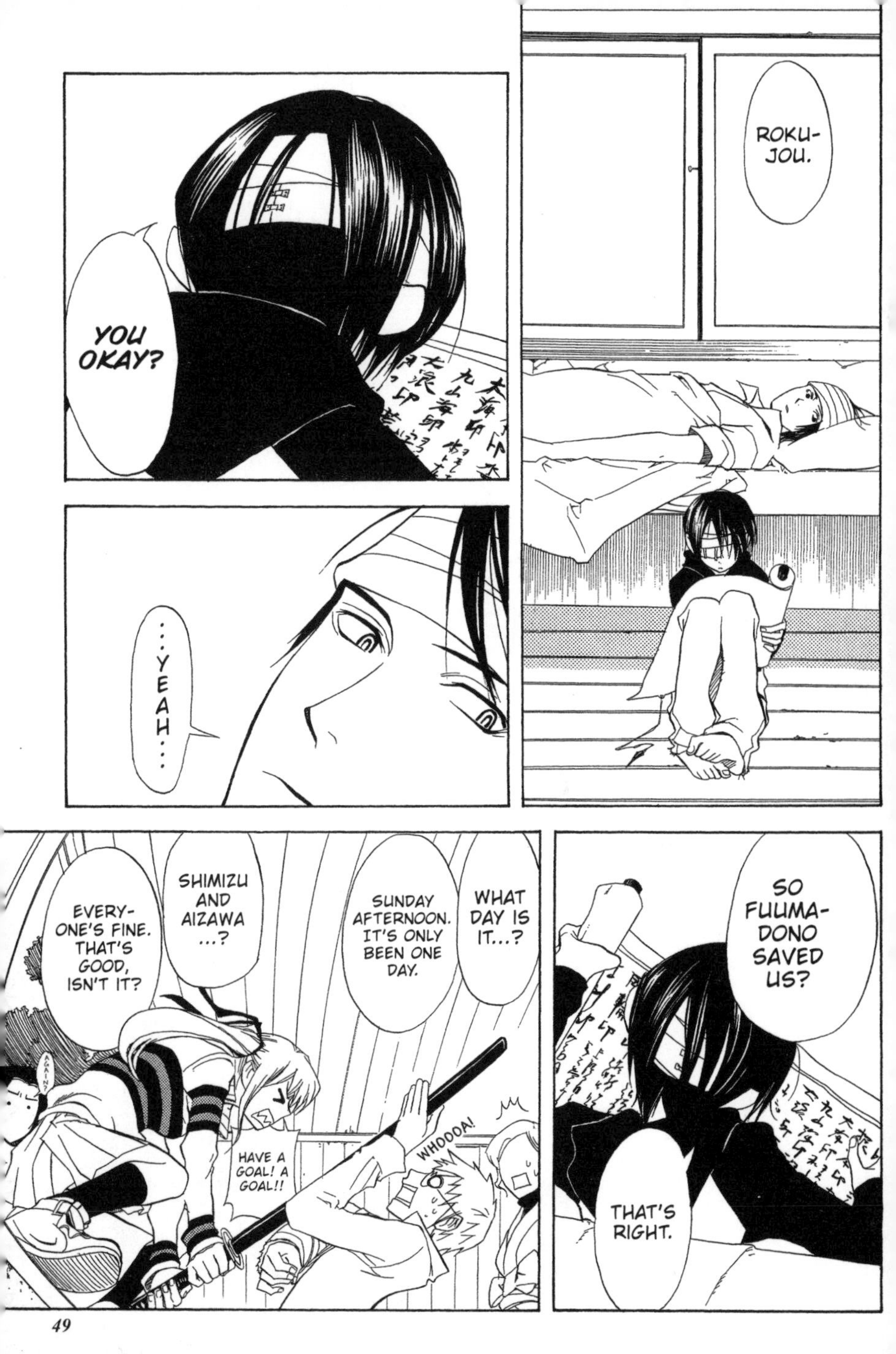
ROKU-JOU.
YOU OKAY?
...YEAH...
SO FUUMA-DONO SAVED US?
THAT'S RIGHT.
WHAT DAY IS IT...?
SUNDAY AFTERNOON. IT'S ONLY BEEN ONE DAY.
SHIMIZU AND AIZAWA ...?
EVERY-ONE'S FINE. THAT'S GOOD, ISN'T IT?
WHOOOA!
HAVE A GOAL! A GOAL!!
AGAIN?

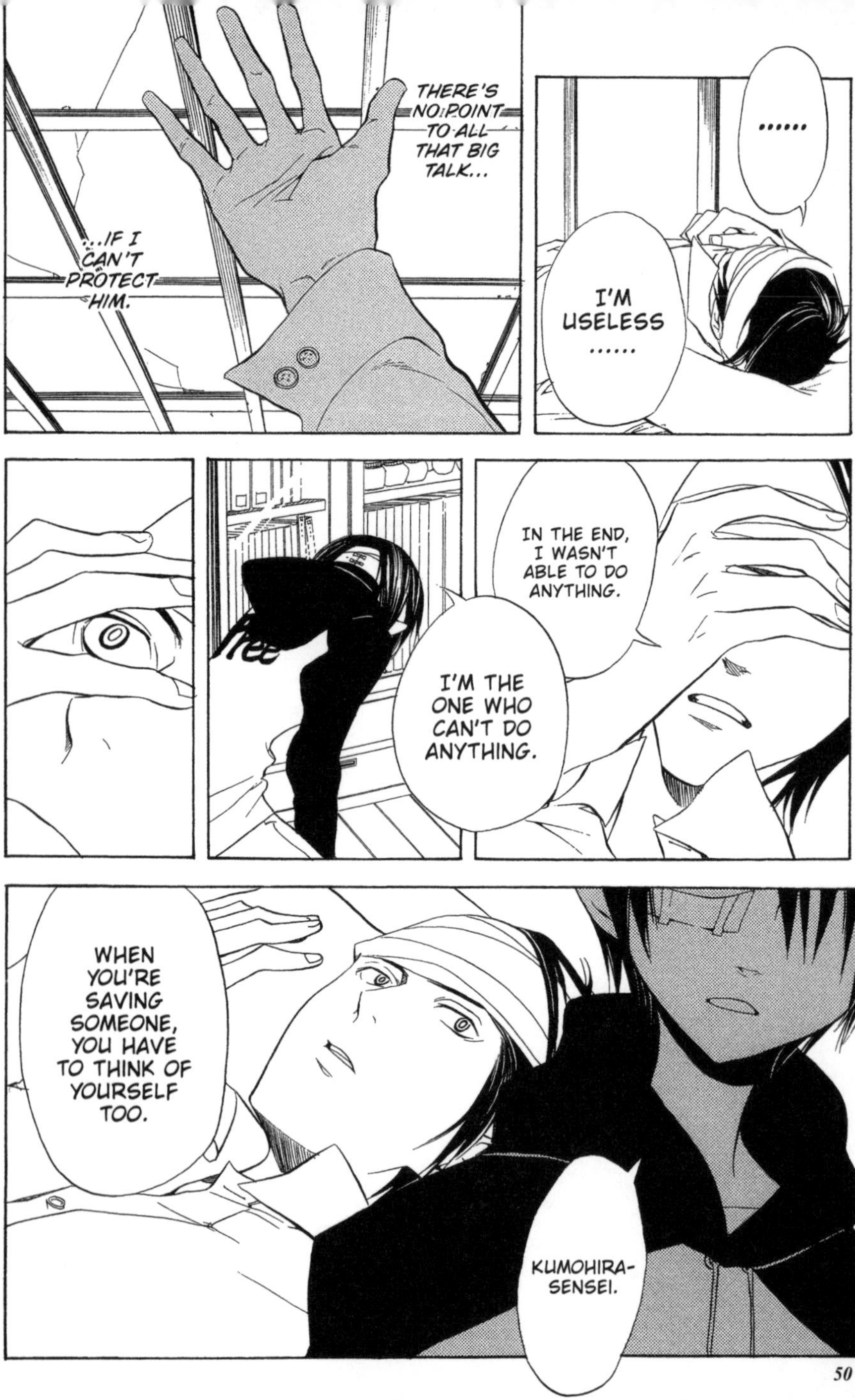
......
I'M USELESS ......
THERE'S NO POINT TO ALL THAT BIG TALK...
...IF I CAN'T PROTECT HIM.
IN THE END, I WASN'T ABLE TO DO ANYTHING.
I'M THE ONE WHO CAN'T DO ANYTHING.
WHEN YOU'RE SAVING SOMEONE, YOU HAVE TO THINK OF YOURSELF TOO.
KUMOHIRA-SENSEI.

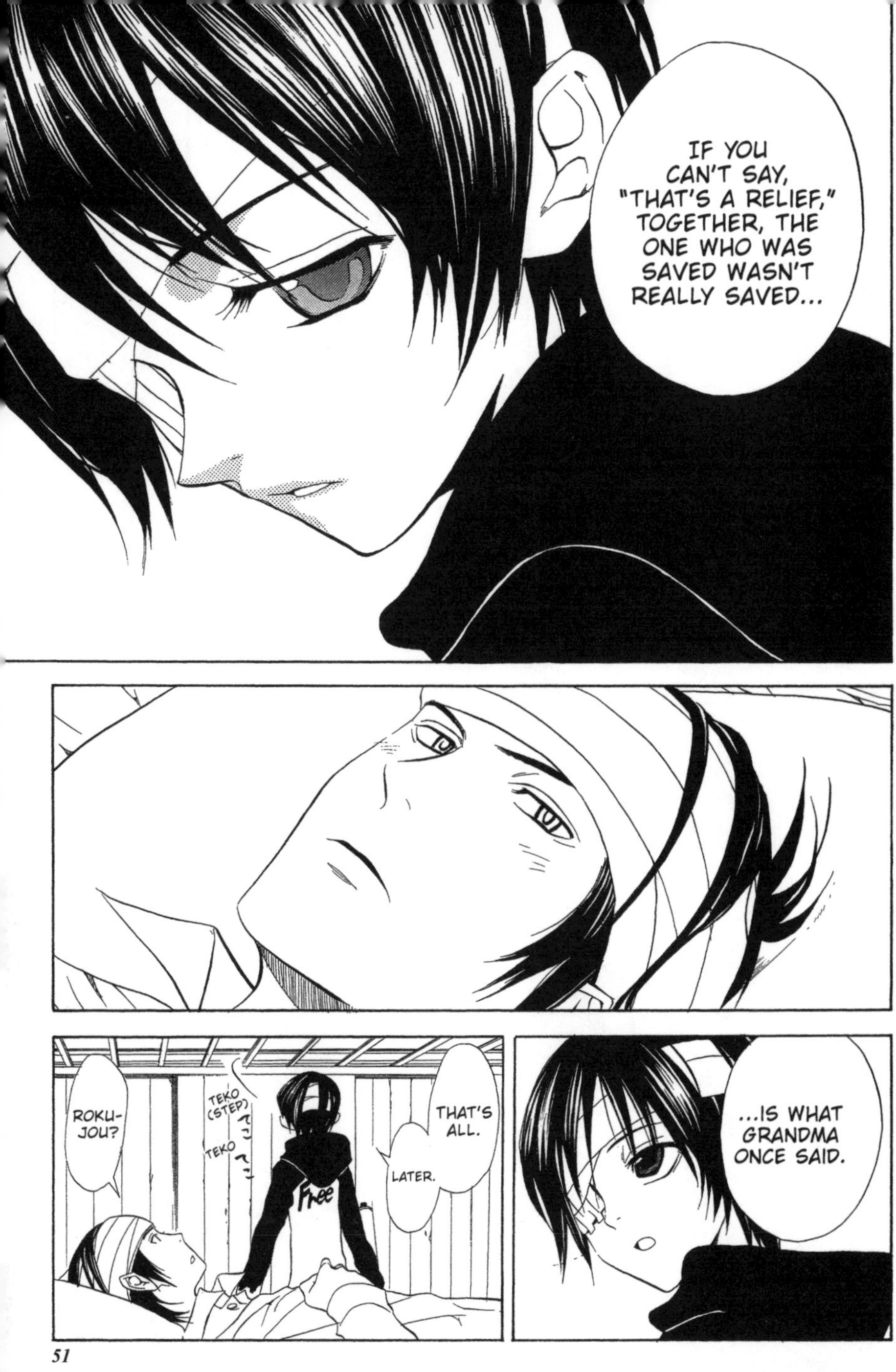
IF YOU CAN'T SAY, "THAT'S A RELIEF," TOGETHER, THE ONE WHO WAS SAVED WASN'T REALLY SAVED...
...IS WHAT GRANDMA ONCE SAID.
THAT'S ALL.
LATER.
TEKO (STEP)
TEKO
ROKU-JOU?
Free

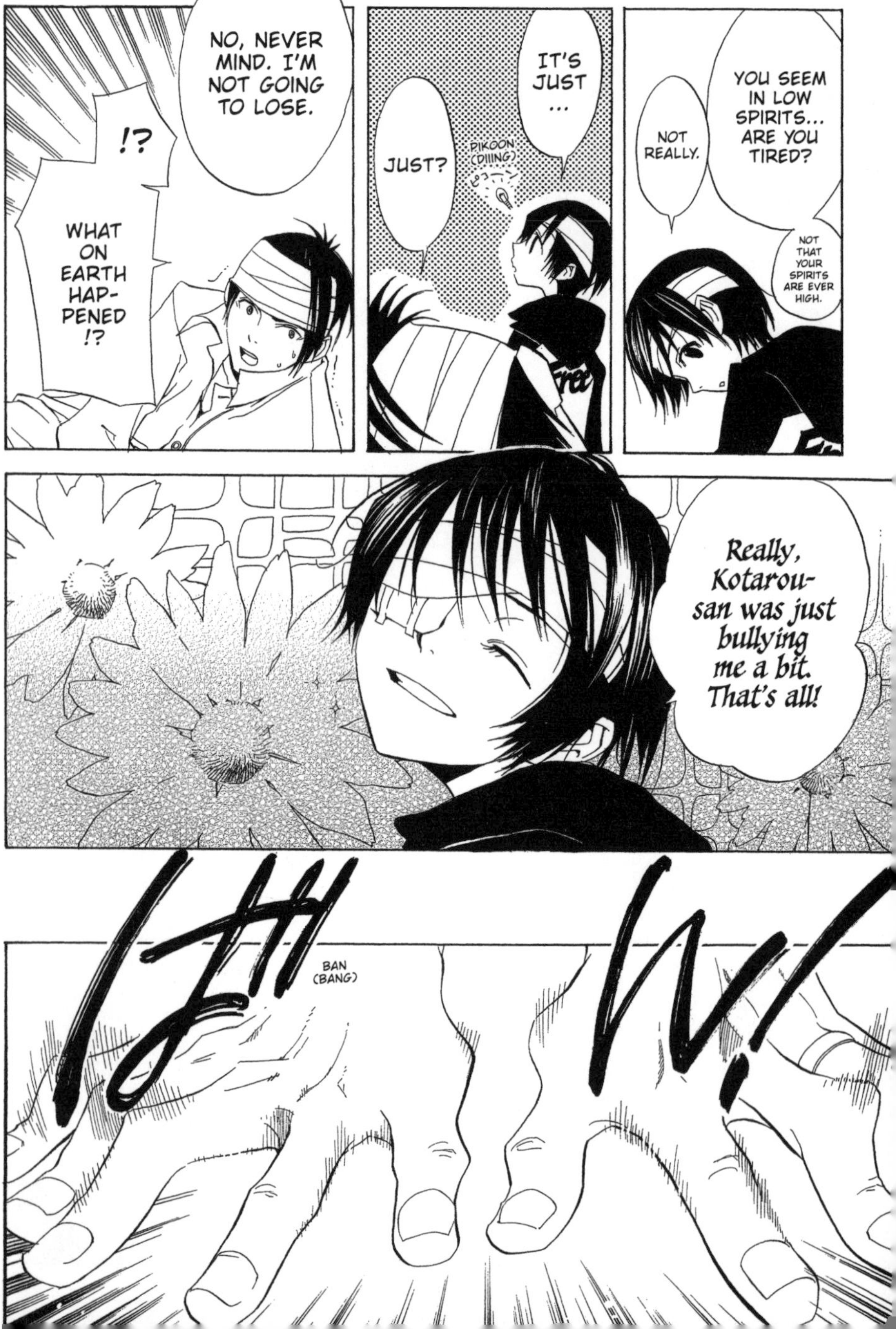
YOU SEEM IN LOW SPIRITS... ARE YOU TIRED?
NOT REALLY.
NOT THAT YOUR SPIRITS ARE EVER HIGH.
IT'S JUST ...
PIKOON (DIIING)
JUST?
NO, NEVER MIND. I'M NOT GOING TO LOSE.
!?
WHAT ON EARTH HAP-PENED !?
Really, Kotarou-san was just bullying me a bit. That's all!
BAN (BANG)

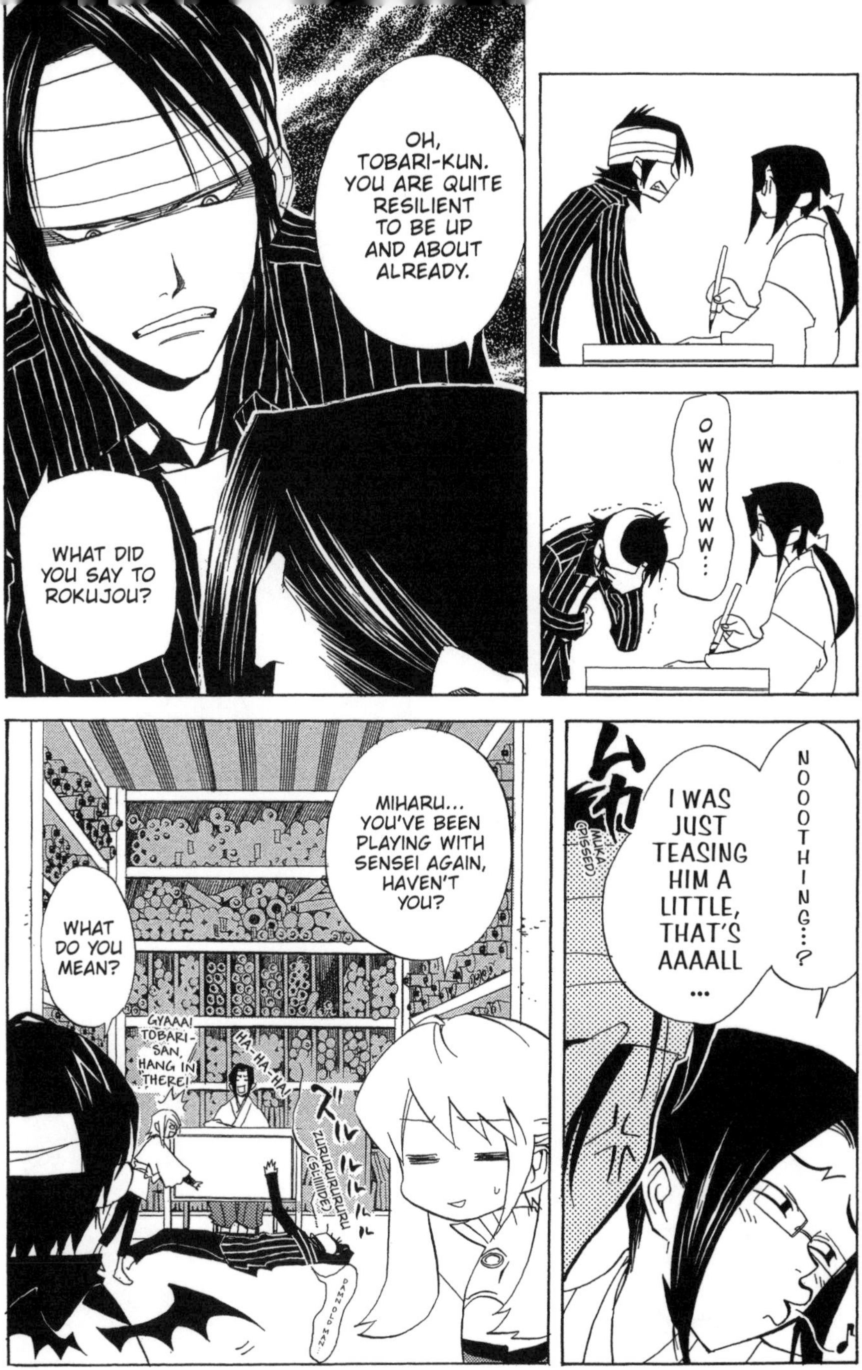
OWWWWWWW...
OH, TOBARI-KUN. YOU ARE QUITE RESILIENT TO BE UP AND ABOUT ALREADY.
WHAT DID YOU SAY TO ROKUJOU?
NOOOTHING...?
I WAS JUST TEASING HIM A LITTLE, THAT'S AAAALL ...
MUKA (PISSED)
MIHARU... YOU'VE BEEN PLAYING WITH SENSEI AGAIN, HAVEN'T YOU?
WHAT DO YOU MEAN?
GYAAA! TOBARI-SAN, HANG IN THERE!
HA-HA-HA!
ZURURURURURU (SLIIIIIDE)
DAMN OLD MAN...

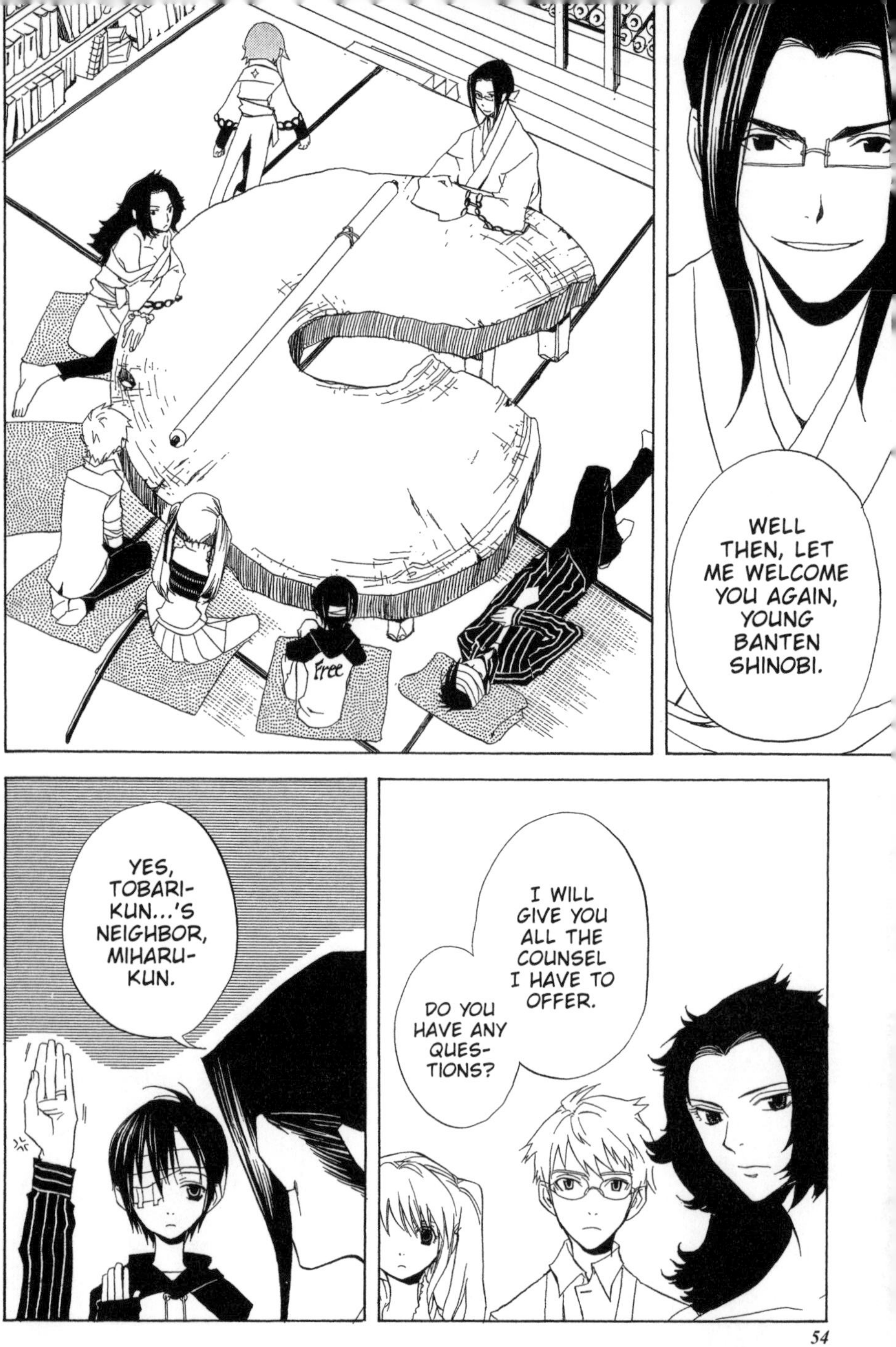
WELL THEN, LET ME WELCOME YOU AGAIN, YOUNG BANTEN SHINOBI.
I WILL GIVE YOU ALL THE COUNSEL I HAVE TO OFFER.
DO YOU HAVE ANY QUES-TIONS?
YES, TOBARI-KUN...'S NEIGHBOR, MIHARU-KUN.

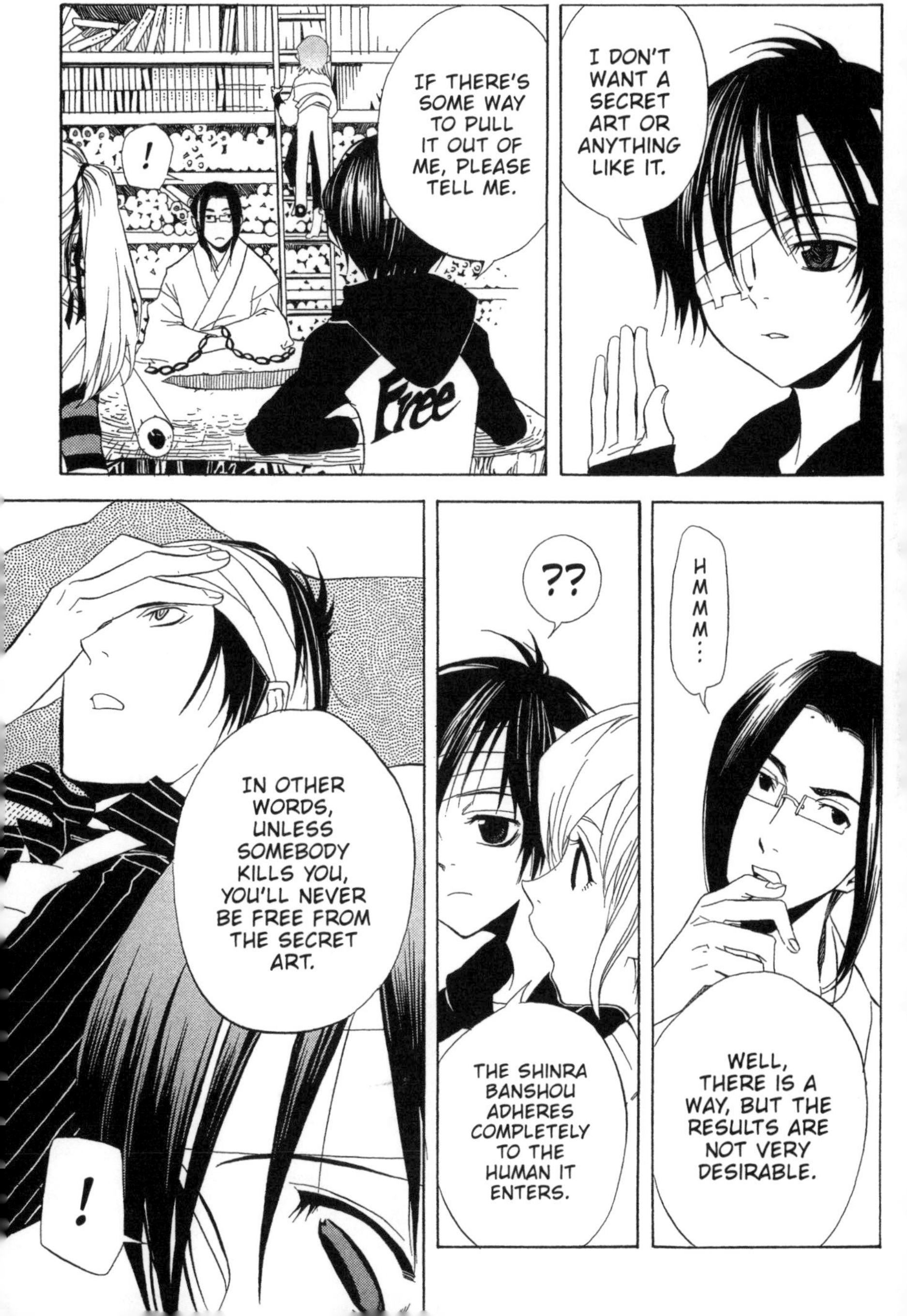
I DON'T WANT A SECRET ART OR ANYTHING LIKE IT.
IF THERE'S SOME WAY TO PULL IT OUT OF ME, PLEASE TELL ME.
!
Free
HMMM...
WELL, THERE IS A WAY, BUT THE RESULTS ARE NOT VERY DESIRABLE.
??
THE SHINRA BANSHOU ADHERES COMPLETELY TO THE HUMAN IT ENTERS.
IN OTHER WORDS, UNLESS SOMEBODY KILLS YOU, YOU'LL NEVER BE FREE FROM THE SECRET ART.
!

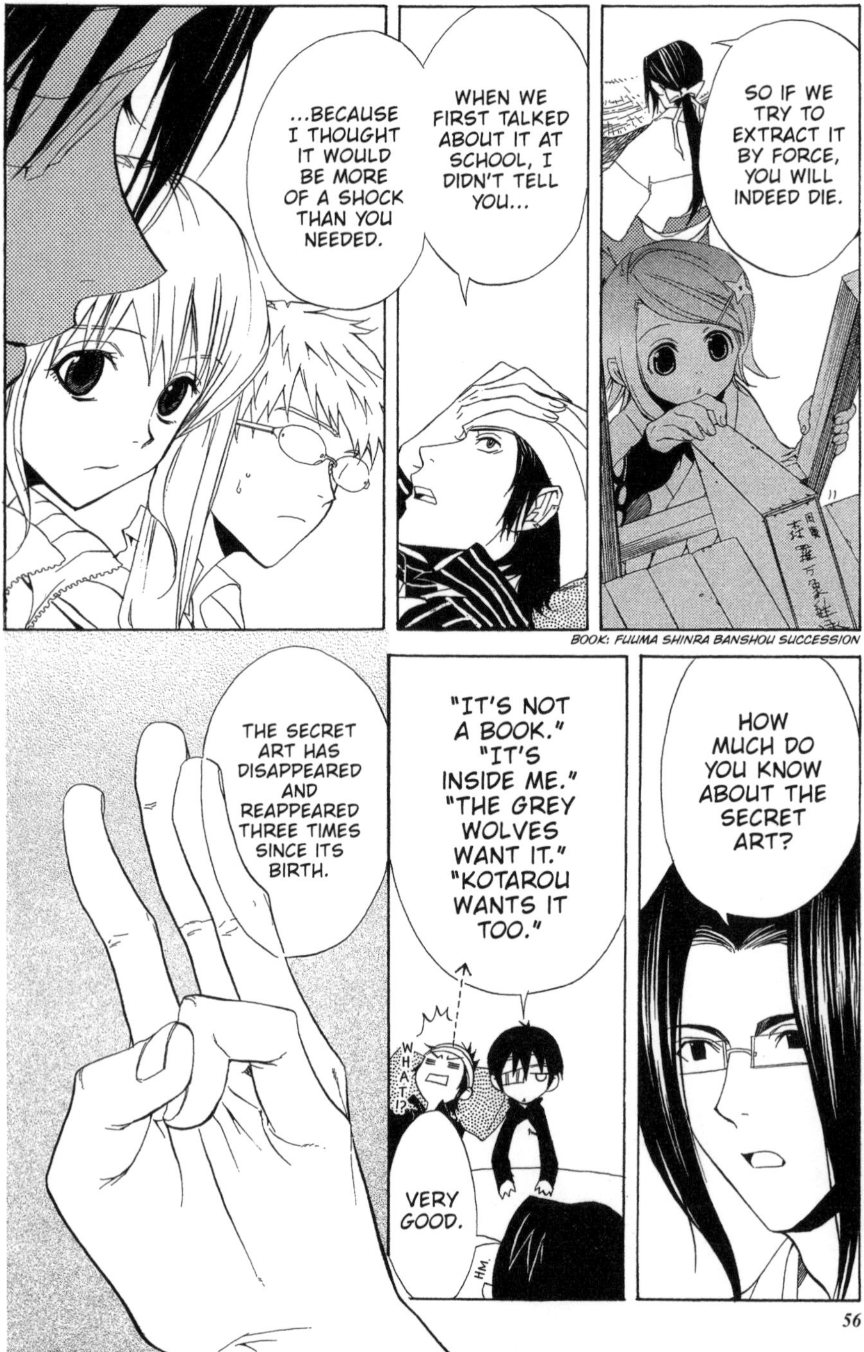
SO IF WE TRY TO EXTRACT IT BY FORCE, YOU WILL INDEED DIE.
BOOK: FUUMA SHINRA BANSHOU SUCCESSION
WHEN WE FIRST TALKED ABOUT IT AT SCHOOL, I DIDN'T TELL YOU...
...BECAUSE I THOUGHT IT WOULD BE MORE OF A SHOCK THAN YOU NEEDED.
HOW MUCH DO YOU KNOW ABOUT THE SECRET ART?
"IT'S NOT A BOOK." "IT'S INSIDE ME." "THE GREY WOLVES WANT IT." "KOTAROU WANTS IT TOO."
WHAT!?
VERY GOOD.
HM.
THE SECRET ART HAS DISAPPEARED AND REAPPEARED THREE TIMES SINCE ITS BIRTH.

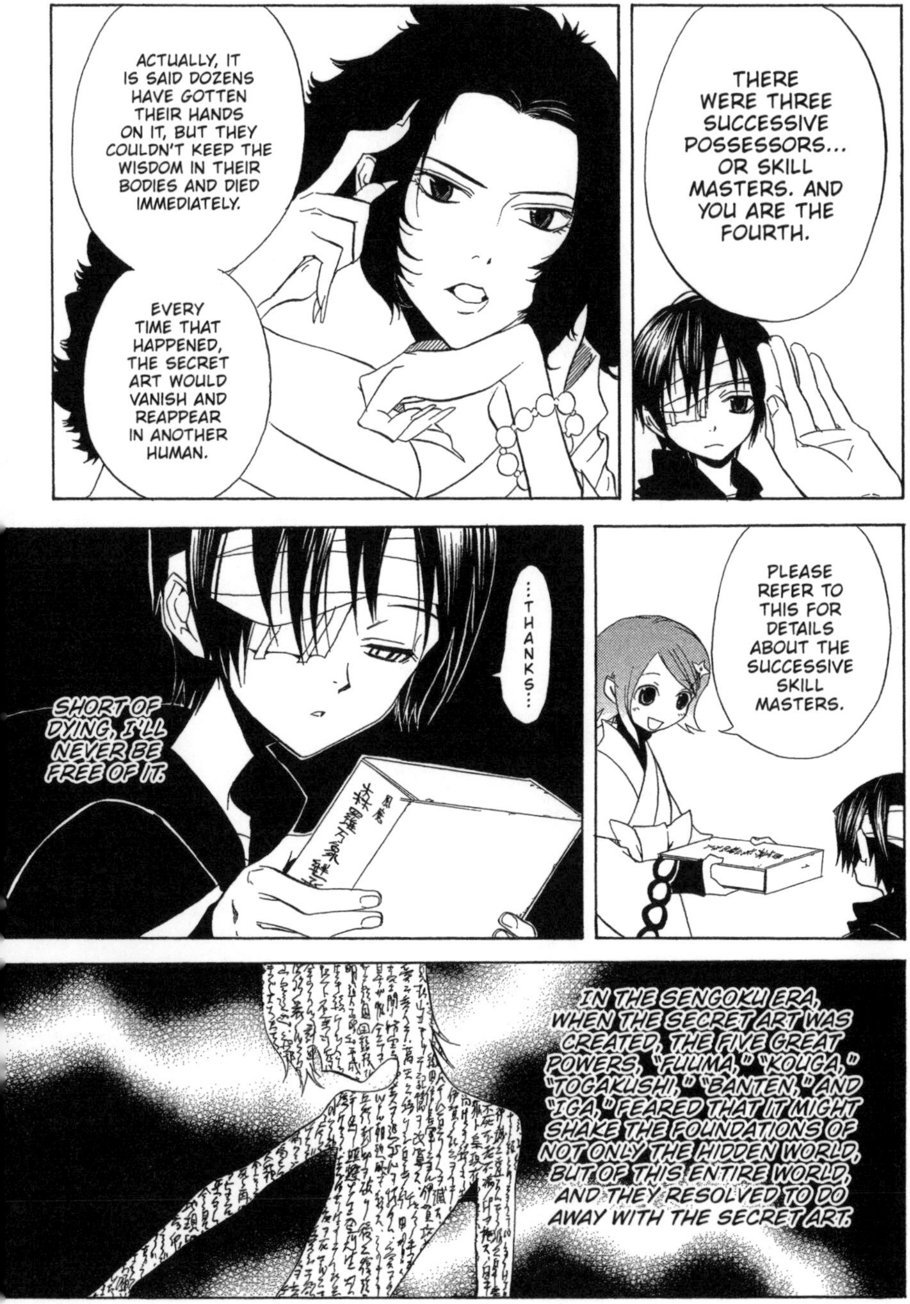
THERE WERE THREE SUCCESSIVE POSSESSORS... OR SKILL MASTERS. AND YOU ARE THE FOURTH.
ACTUALLY, IT IS SAID DOZENS HAVE GOTTEN THEIR HANDS ON IT, BUT THEY COULDN'T KEEP THE WISDOM IN THEIR BODIES AND DIED IMMEDIATELY.
EVERY TIME THAT HAPPENED, THE SECRET ART WOULD VANISH AND REAPPEAR IN ANOTHER HUMAN.
PLEASE REFER TO THIS FOR DETAILS ABOUT THE SUCCESSIVE SKILL MASTERS.
...THANKS...
SHORT OF DYING, I'LL NEVER BE FREE OF IT.
IN THE SENGOKU ERA, WHEN THE SECRET ART WAS CREATED, THE FIVE GREAT POWERS, "FUUMA," "KOUGA," "TOGAKUSHI," "BANTEN," AND "IGA," FEARED THAT IT MIGHT SHAKE THE FOUNDATIONS OF NOT ONLY THE HIDDEN WORLD, BUT OF THIS ENTIRE WORLD, AND THEY RESOLVED TO DO AWAY WITH THE SECRET ART.

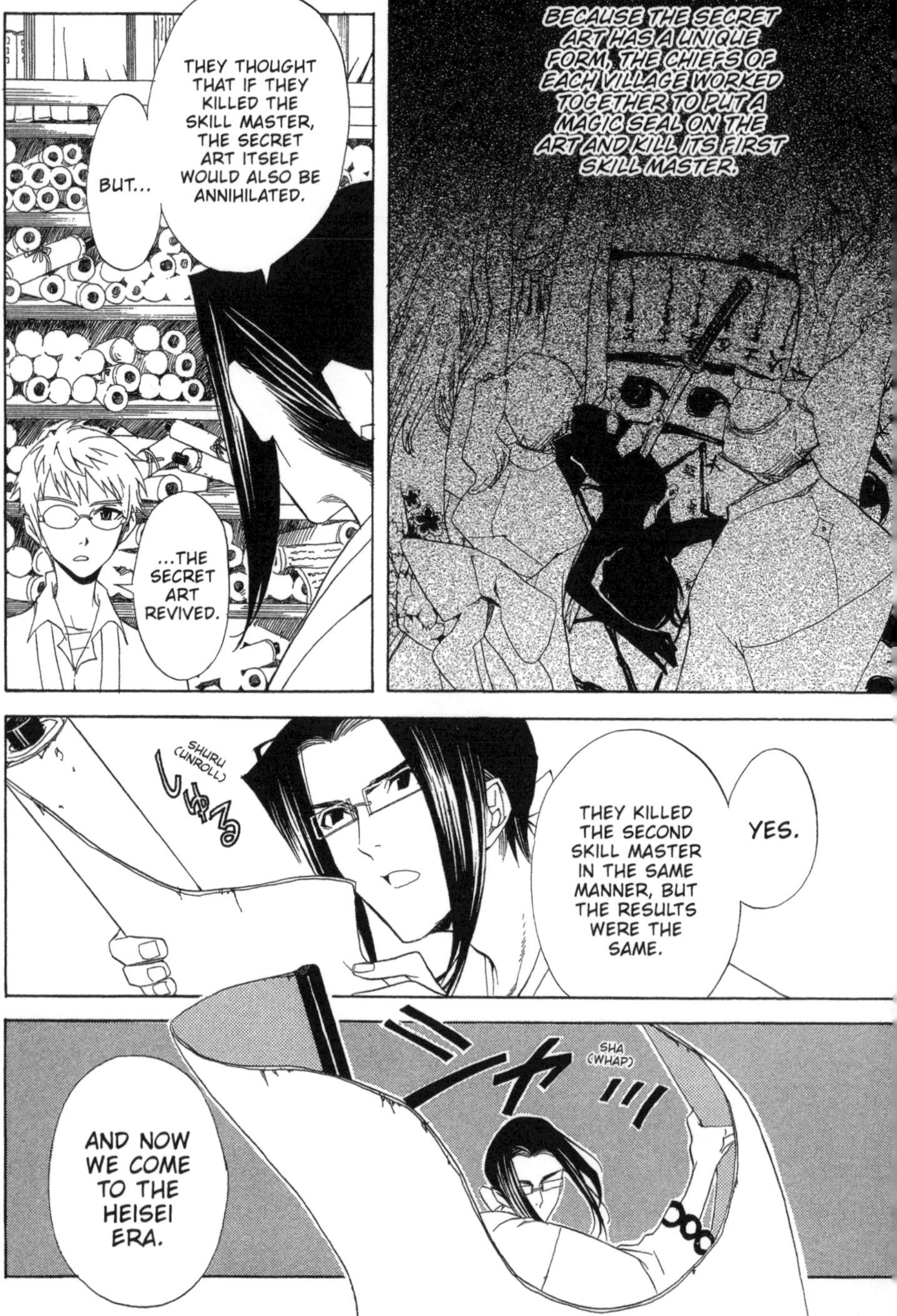
BECAUSE THE SECRET ART HAS A UNIQUE FORM, THE CHIEFS OF EACH VILLAGE WORKED TOGETHER TO PUT A MAGIC SEAL ON THE ART AND KILL ITS FIRST SKILL MASTER.
THEY THOUGHT THAT IF THEY KILLED THE SKILL MASTER, THE SECRET ART ITSELF WOULD ALSO BE ANNIHILATED.
BUT...
...THE SECRET ART REVIVED.
YES.
THEY KILLED THE SECOND SKILL MASTER IN THE SAME MANNER, BUT THE RESULTS WERE THE SAME.
SHURU (UNROLL)
SHA (WHAP)
AND NOW WE COME TO THE HEISEI ERA.

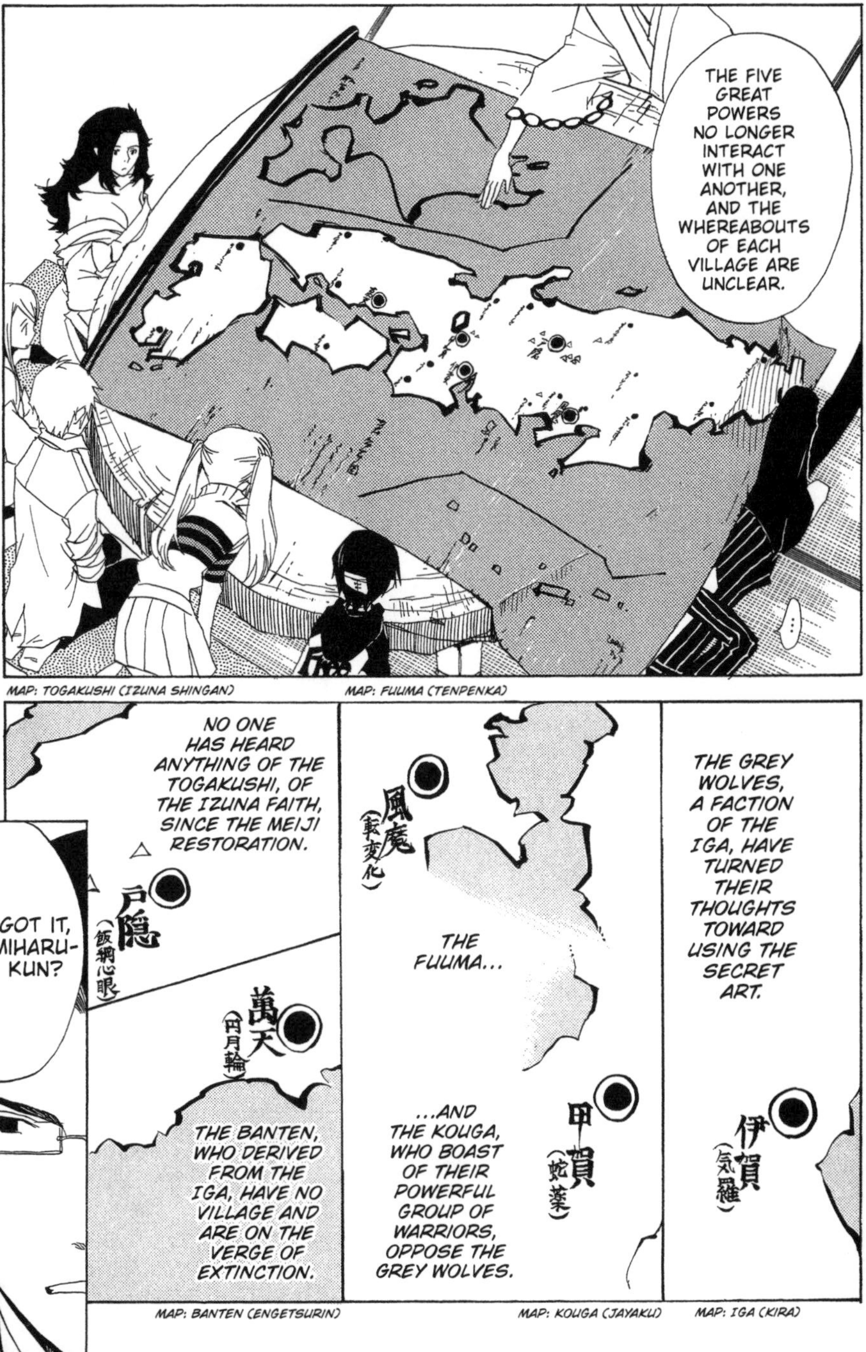
THE FIVE GREAT POWERS NO LONGER INTERACT WITH ONE ANOTHER, AND THE WHEREABOUTS OF EACH VILLAGE ARE UNCLEAR.
...
THE GREY WOLVES, A FACTION OF THE IGA, HAVE TURNED THEIR THOUGHTS TOWARD USING THE SECRET ART.
伊賀（気羅）
風魔（転変化）
THE FUUMA...
...AND THE KOUGA, WHO BOAST OF THEIR POWERFUL GROUP OF WARRIORS, OPPOSE THE GREY WOLVES.
甲賀（蛇薬）
NO ONE HAS HEARD ANYTHING OF THE TOGAKUSHI, OF THE IZUNA FAITH, SINCE THE MEIJI RESTORATION.
戸隠（飯綱心眼）
萬天（円月輪）
THE BANTEN, WHO DERIVED FROM THE IGA, HAVE NO VILLAGE AND ARE ON THE VERGE OF EXTINCTION.
GOT IT, MIHARU-KUN?
MAP: TOGAKUSHI (IZUNA SHINGAN)
MAP: FUUMA (TENPENKA)
MAP: BANTEN (ENGETSURIN)
MAP: KOUGA (JAYAKU)
MAP: IGA (KIRA)

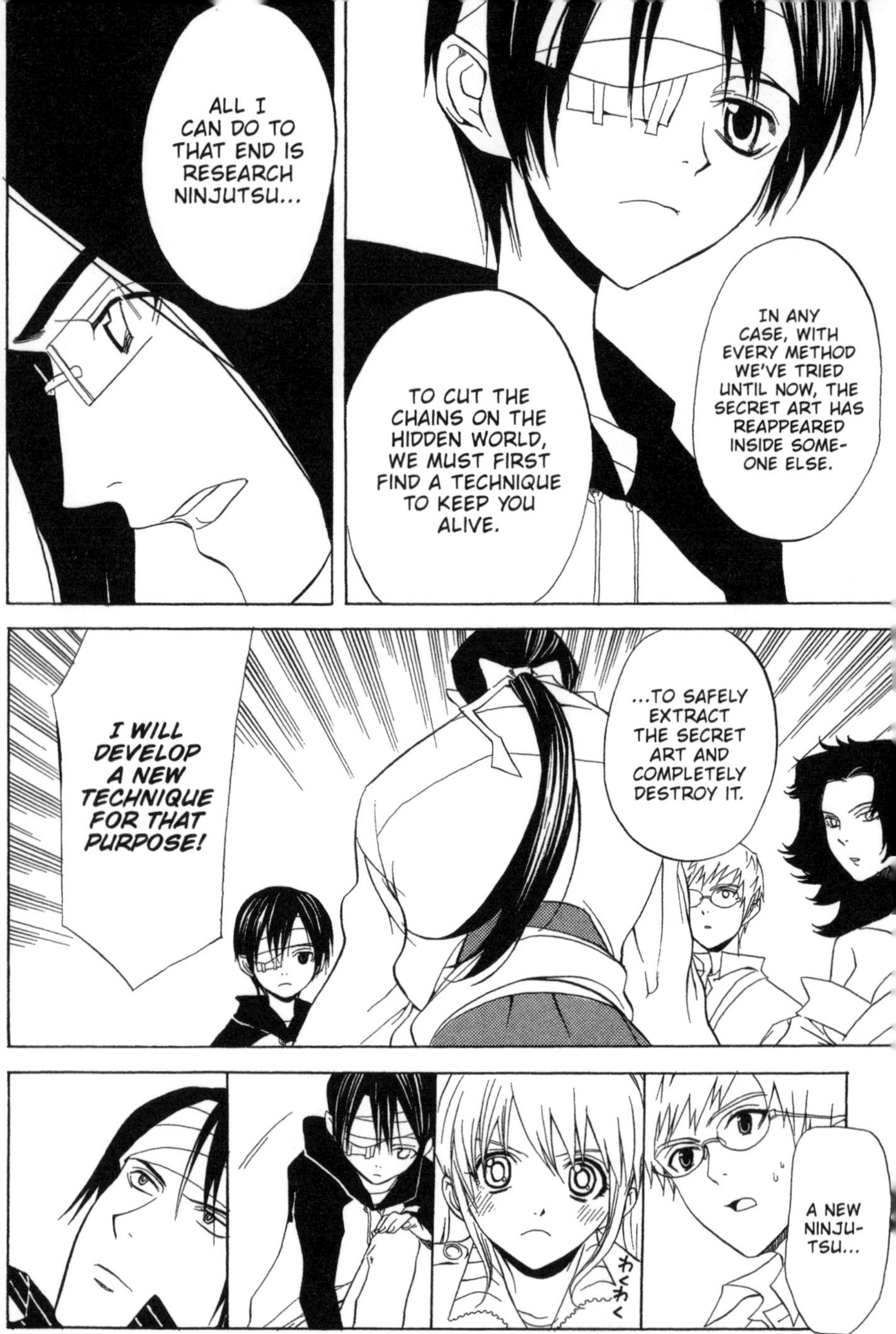
IN ANY CASE, WITH EVERY METHOD WE'VE TRIED UNTIL NOW, THE SECRET ART HAS REAPPEARED INSIDE SOME-ONE ELSE.
TO CUT THE CHAINS ON THE HIDDEN WORLD, WE MUST FIRST FIND A TECHNIQUE TO KEEP YOU ALIVE.
ALL I CAN DO TO THAT END IS RESEARCH NINJUTSU...
...TO SAFELY EXTRACT THE SECRET ART AND COMPLETELY DESTROY IT.
I WILL DEVELOP A NEW TECHNIQUE FOR THAT PURPOSE!
A NEW NINJU-TSU...
わくわく
SFX: WAKU (EXCITED) WAKU

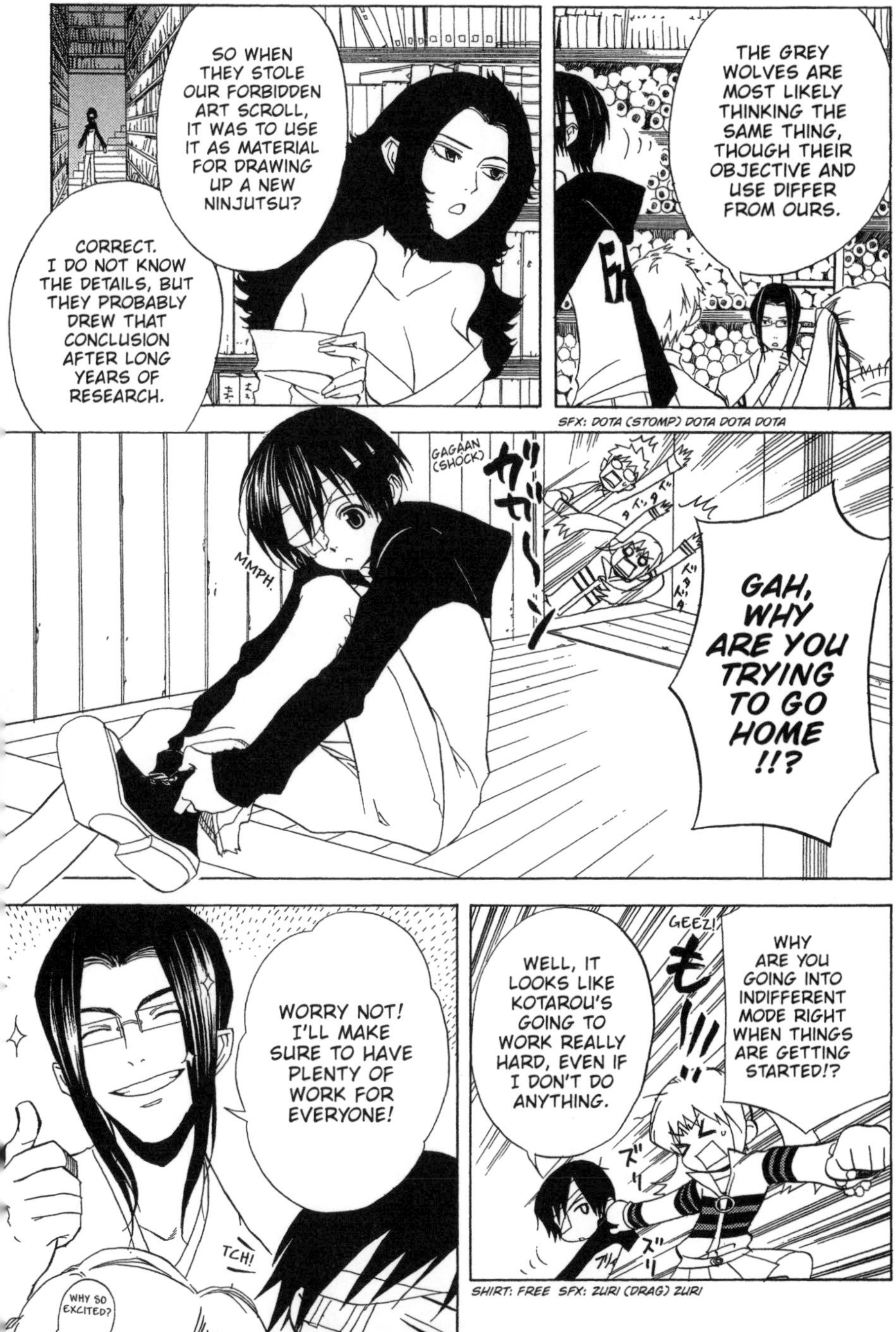
THE GREY WOLVES ARE MOST LIKELY THINKING THE SAME THING, THOUGH THEIR OBJECTIVE AND USE DIFFER FROM OURS.
SFX: DOTA (STOMP) DOTA DOTA DOTA
SO WHEN THEY STOLE OUR FORBIDDEN ART SCROLL, IT WAS TO USE IT AS MATERIAL FOR DRAWING UP A NEW NINJUTSU?
CORRECT. I DO NOT KNOW THE DETAILS, BUT THEY PROBABLY DREW THAT CONCLUSION AFTER LONG YEARS OF RESEARCH.
GAH, WHY ARE YOU TRYING TO GO HOME!!?
GAGAAN (SHOCK)
MMPH.
WHY ARE YOU GOING INTO INDIFFERENT MODE RIGHT WHEN THINGS ARE GETTING STARTED!?
GEEZ!
WELL, IT LOOKS LIKE KOTAROU'S GOING TO WORK REALLY HARD, EVEN IF I DON'T DO ANYTHING.
SHIRT: FREE SFX: ZURI (DRAG) ZURI
WORRY NOT! I'LL MAKE SURE TO HAVE PLENTY OF WORK FOR EVERYONE!
TCH!
WHY SO EXCITED?

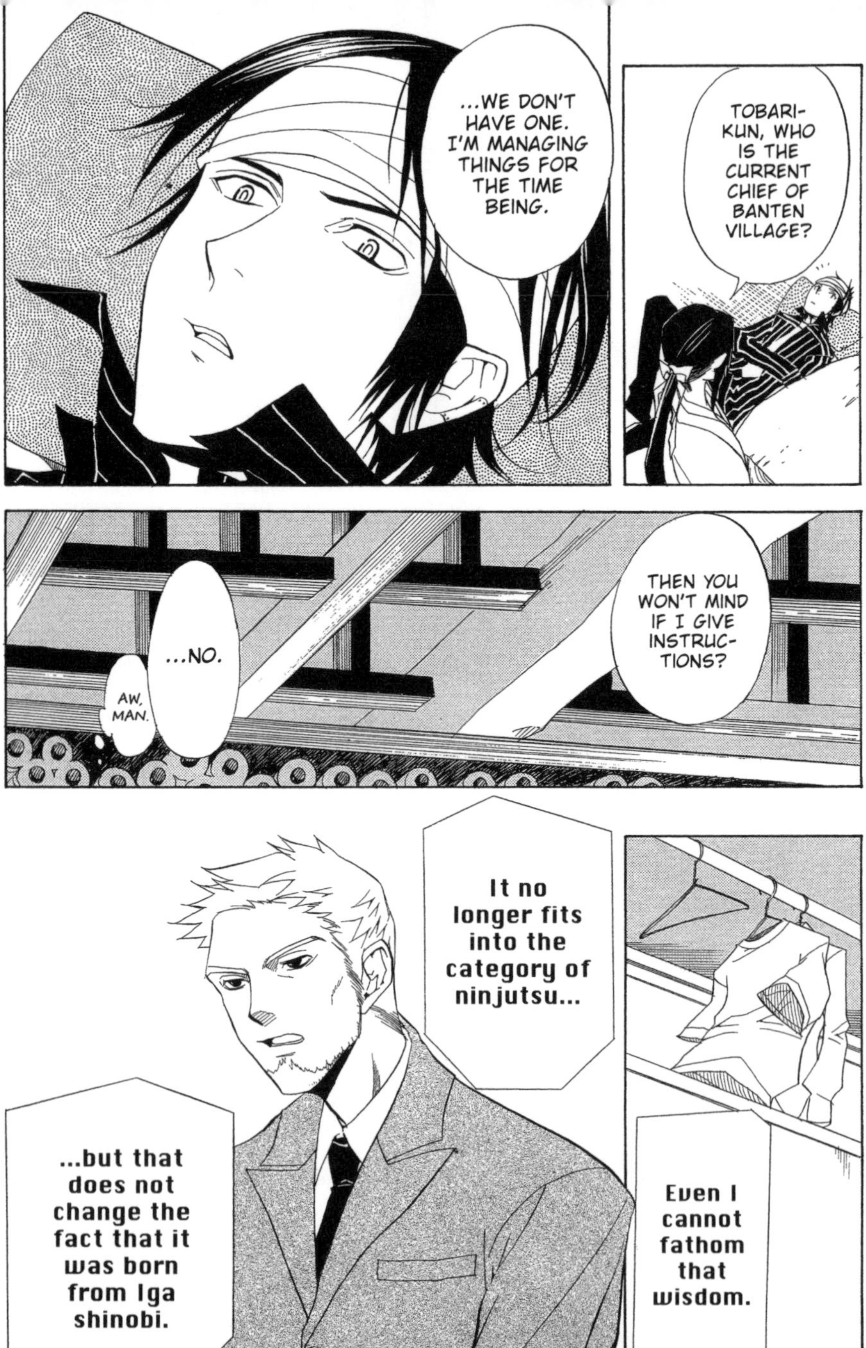
TOBARI-KUN, WHO IS THE CURRENT CHIEF OF BANTEN VILLAGE?
...WE DON'T HAVE ONE. I'M MANAGING THINGS FOR THE TIME BEING.
THEN YOU WON'T MIND IF I GIVE INSTRUCTIONS?
...NO.
AW, MAN.
It no longer fits into the category of ninjutsu...
...but that does not change the fact that it was born from Iga shinobi.
Even I cannot fathom that wisdom.

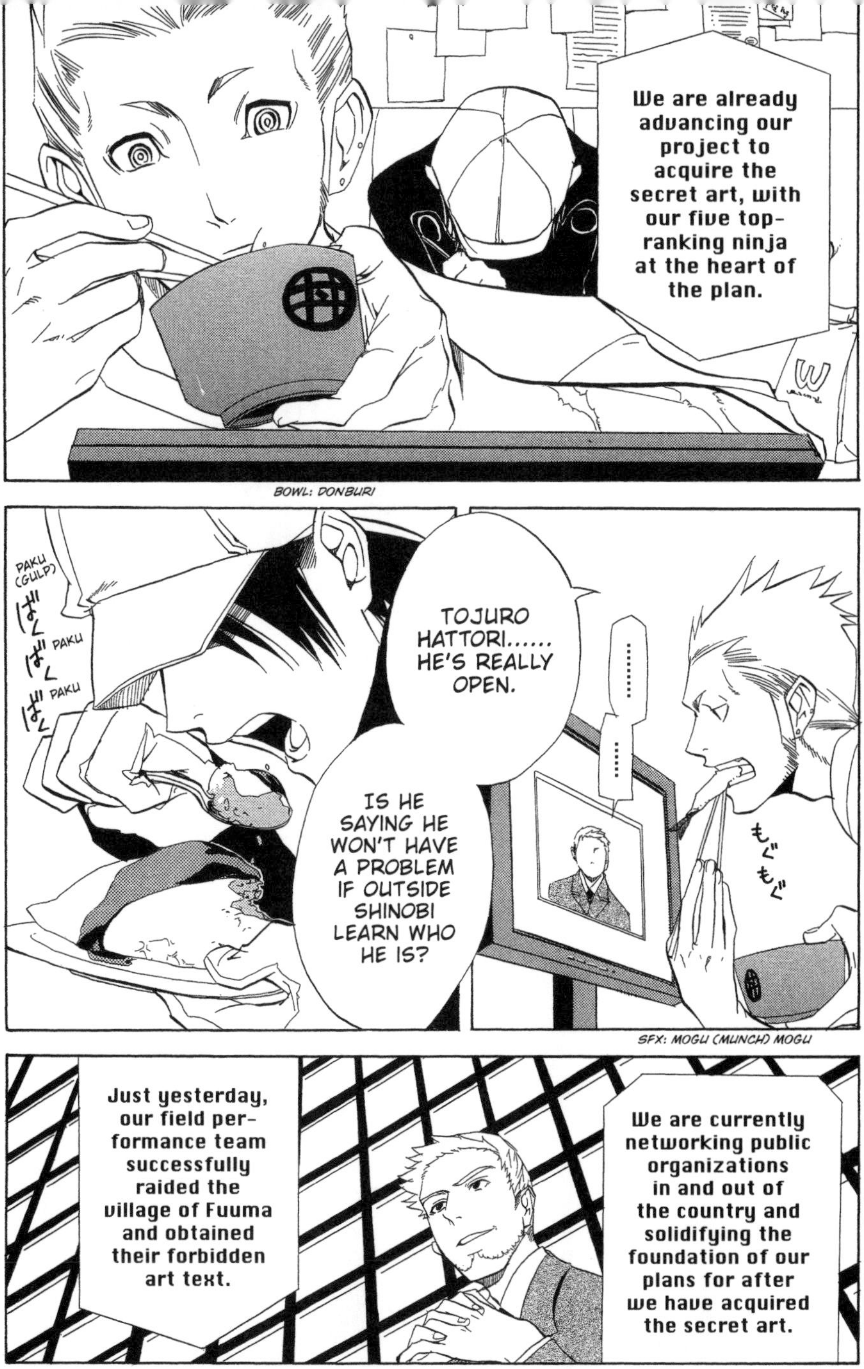

We are already advancing our project to acquire the secret art, with our five top-ranking ninja at the heart of the plan.
BOWL: DONBURI
TOJURO HATTORI...... HE'S REALLY OPEN.
......
......
もぐもぐ
SFX: MOGU (MUNCH) MOGU
PAKU (GULP) ぱく PAKU ぱく PAKU ぱく
IS HE SAYING HE WON'T HAVE A PROBLEM IF OUTSIDE SHINOBI LEARN WHO HE IS?
We are currently networking public organizations in and out of the country and solidifying the foundation of our plans for after we have acquired the secret art.
Just yesterday, our field performance team successfully raided the village of Fuuma and obtained their forbidden art text.

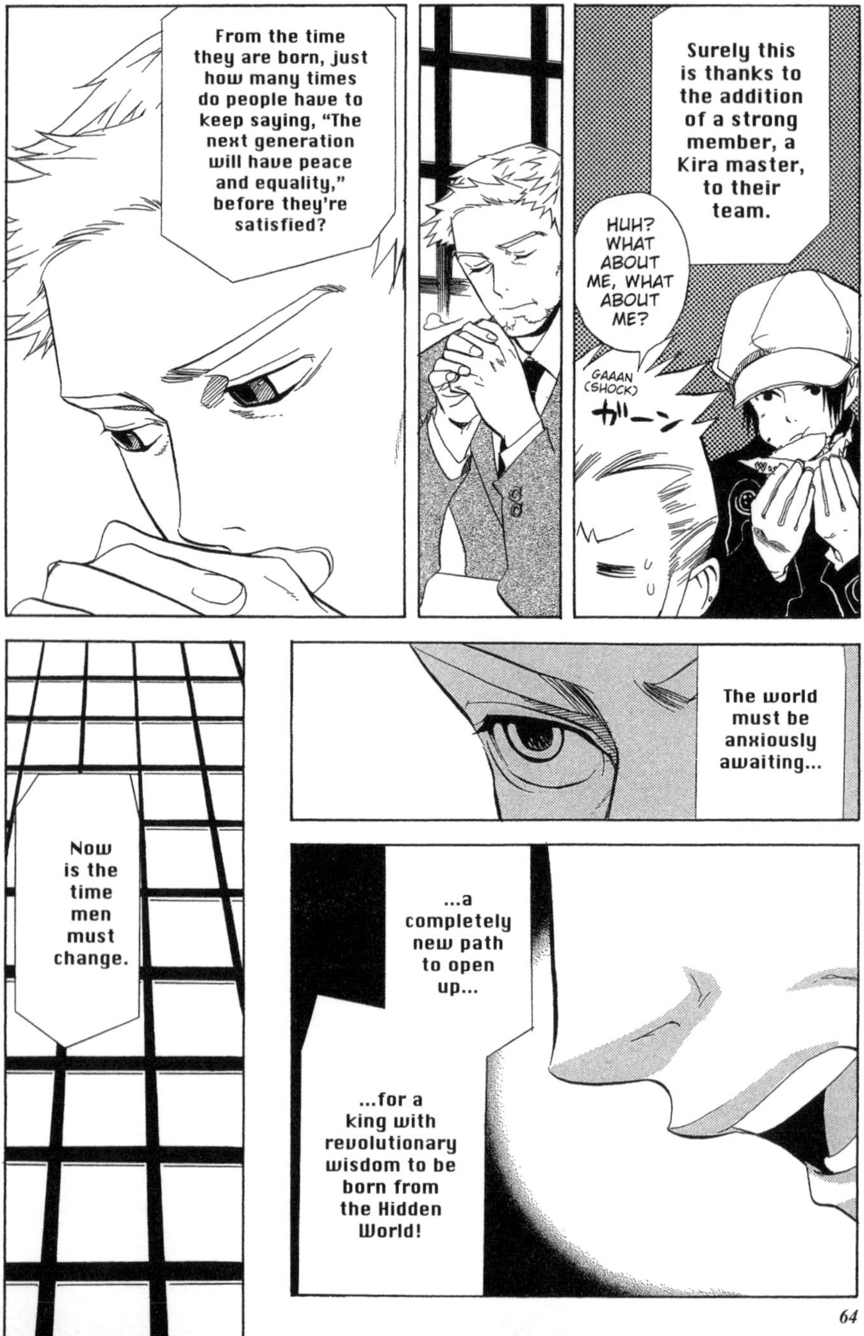
Surely this is thanks to the addition of a strong member, a Kira master, to their team.
HUH? WHAT ABOUT ME, WHAT ABOUT ME?
GAAAN (SHOCK)
ガーン
From the time they are born, just how many times do people have to keep saying, "The next generation will have peace and equality," before they're satisfied?
The world must be anxiously awaiting...
...a completely new path to open up...
...for a king with revolutionary wisdom to be born from the Hidden World!
Now is the time men must change.

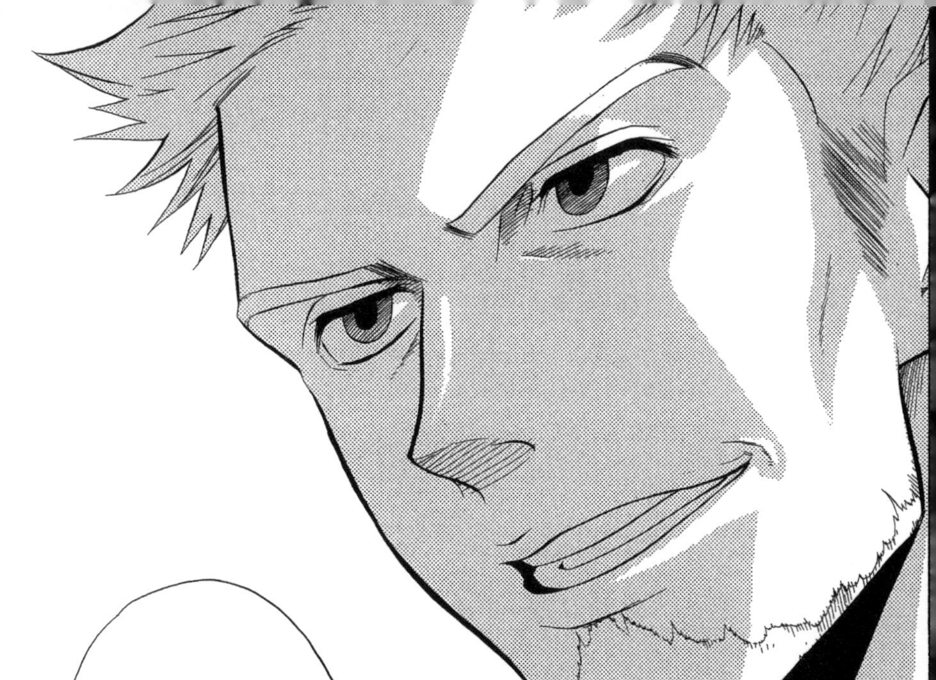
WE WILL BRING ABOUT THE EVOLUTION OF MANKIND.

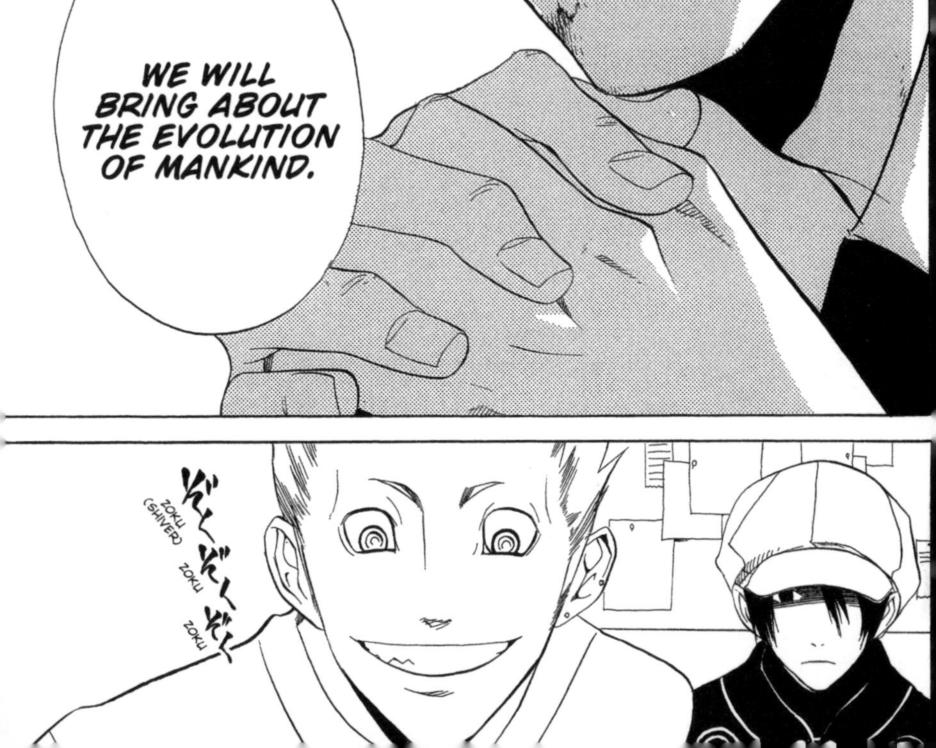
ZOKU (SHIVER)
ZOKU
ZOKU

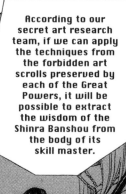

According to our secret art research team, if we can apply the techniques from the forbidden art scrolls preserved by each of the Great Powers, it will be possible to extract the wisdom of the Shinra Banshou from the body of its skill master.

And so... I would like all of you to collect and report information regarding the remaining three villages, be it on the Surface World or the Hidden World.

EACH VILLAGE PRESERVES ONE FORBIDDEN ART SCROLL AS A MAJOR ASSET MAINTAINED BY EACH GREAT POWER. EVEN NOW, THEY ARE PASSED DOWN FROM CHIEF TO CHIEF...

I WOULD LIKE YOU ALL TO GO TO EACH VILLAGE AND BRING THEM TO ME.

AT ANY RATE, THE ENEMY SHOULD BE AFTER ALL THE VILLAGES' FORBIDDEN ART SCROLLS SO THAT THEY CAN ACQUIRE THE SECRET ART WITHOUT FAIL.

LET'S FOLLOW THEIR PLAN FOR NOW AND USE THEM FOR MY RESEARCH.

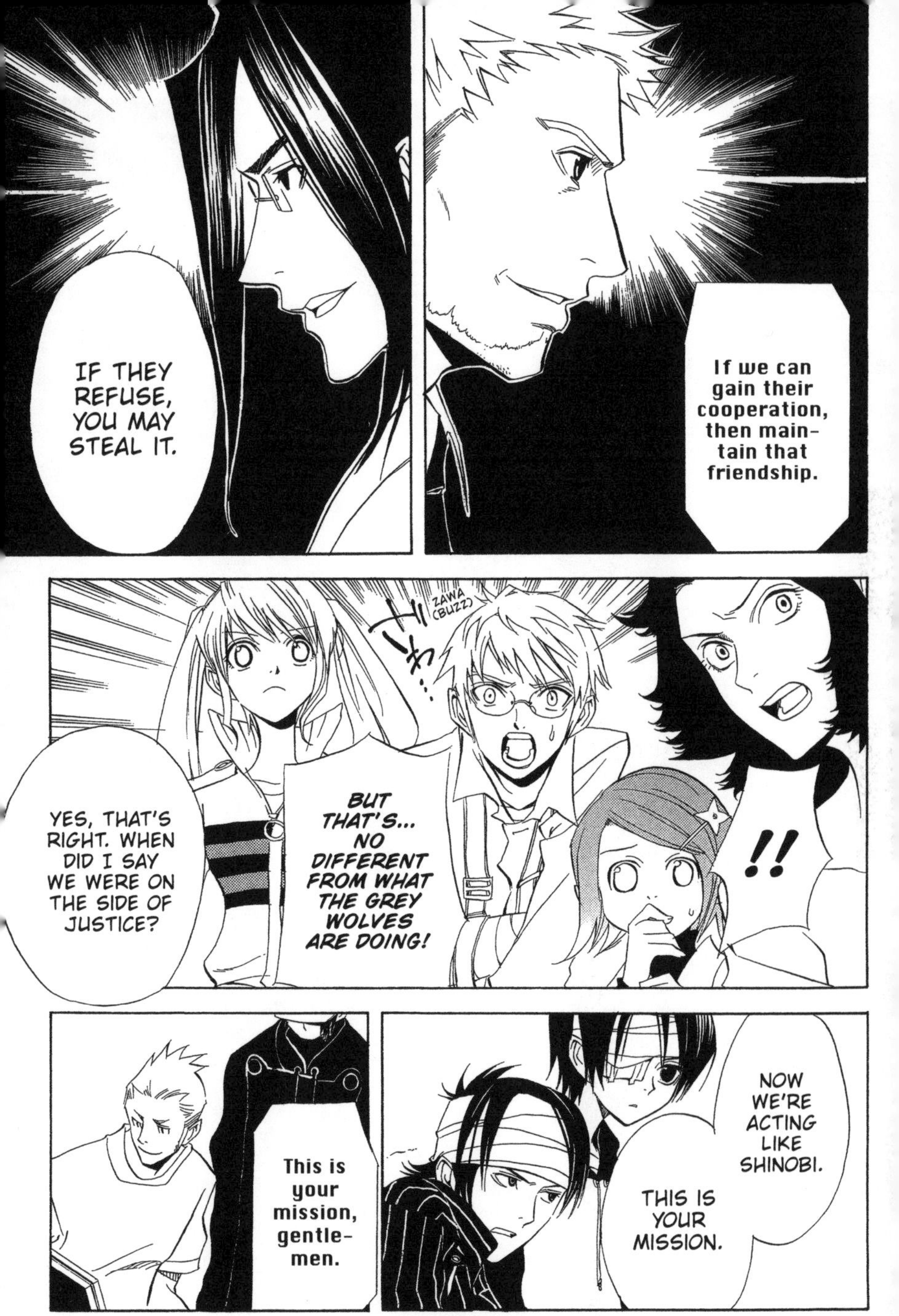
If we can gain their cooperation, then main- tain that friendship.
IF THEY REFUSE, YOU MAY STEAL IT.
!!
ZAWA (BUZZ)
BUT THAT'S... NO DIFFERENT FROM WHAT THE GREY WOLVES ARE DOING!
YES, THAT'S RIGHT. WHEN DID I SAY WE WERE ON THE SIDE OF JUSTICE?
NOW WE'RE ACTING LIKE SHINOBI.
THIS IS YOUR MISSION.
This is your mission, gentle- men.

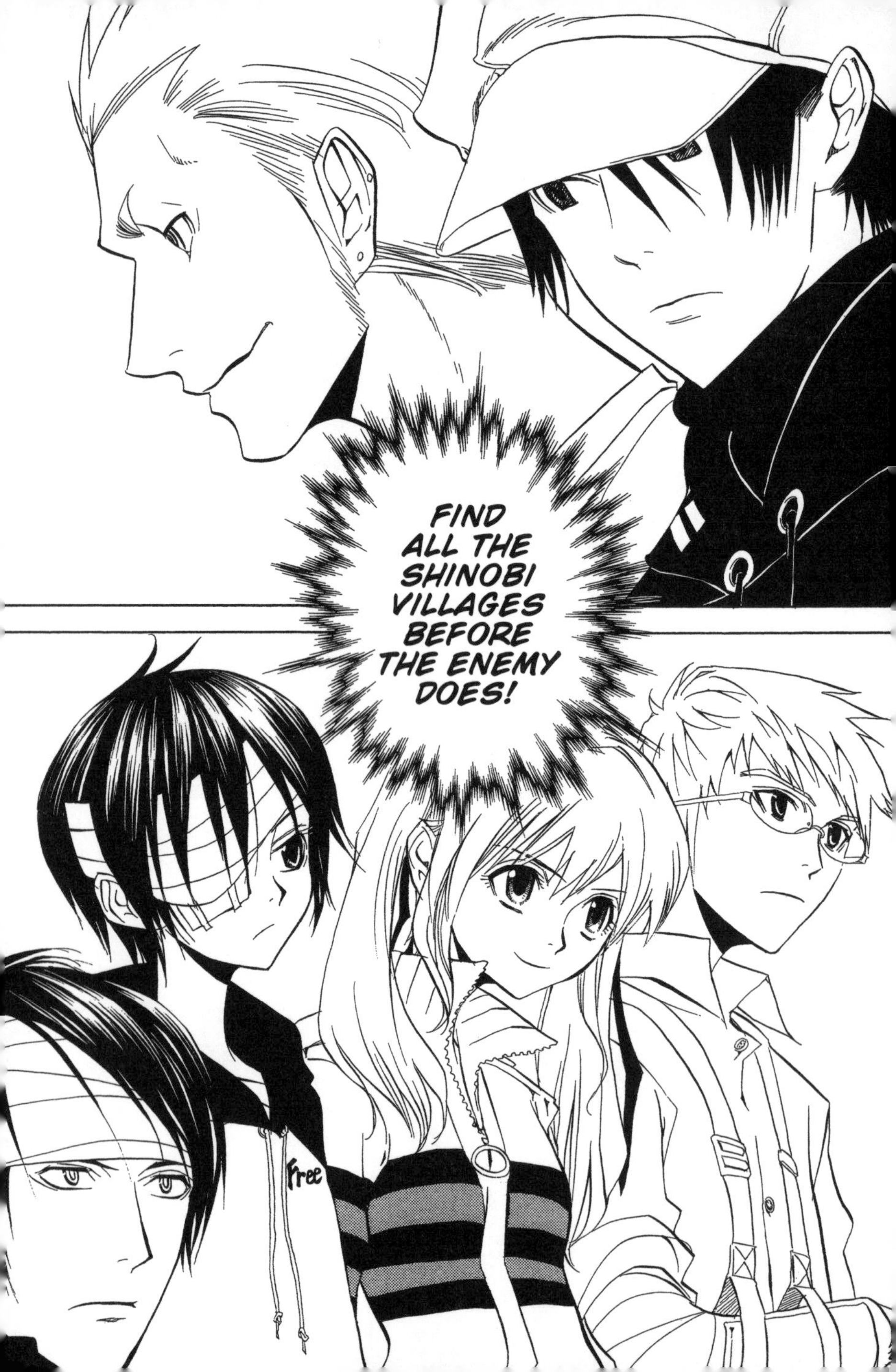
FIND ALL THE SHINOBI VILLAGES BEFORE THE ENEMY DOES!
Free

CHAPTER EIGHT: DESIRE

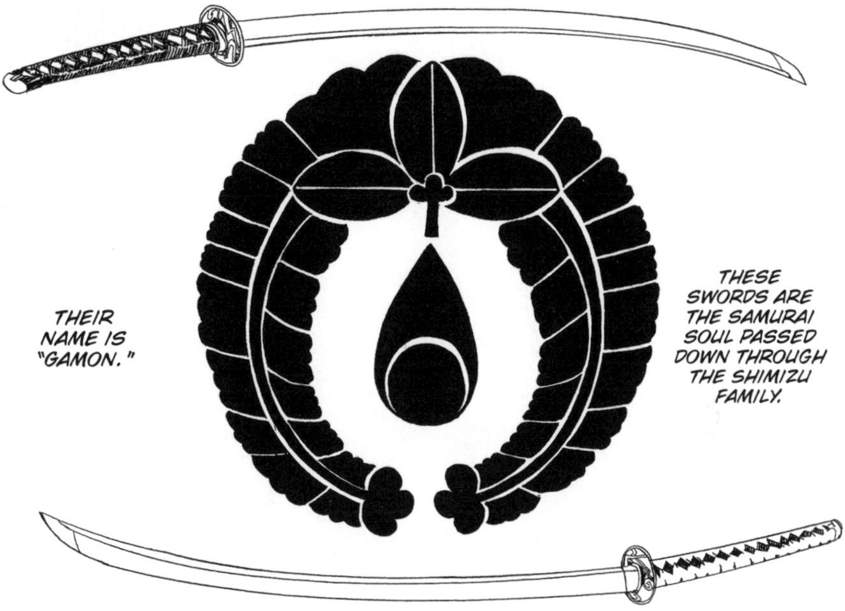
THESE SWORDS ARE THE SAMURAI SOUL PASSED DOWN THROUGH THE SHIMIZU FAMILY.
THEIR NAME IS "GAMON."

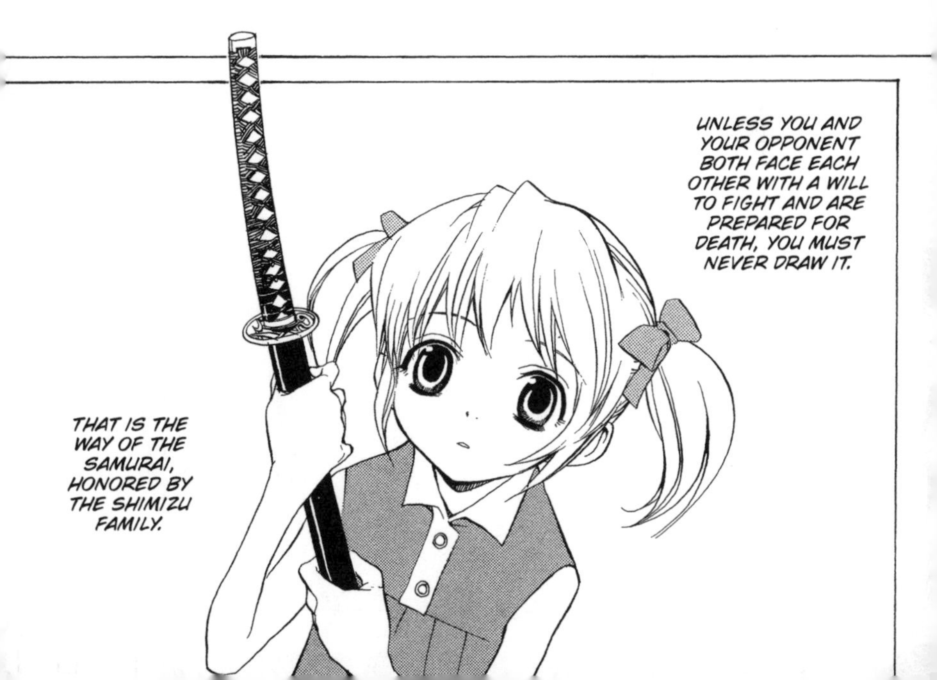
UNLESS YOU AND YOUR OPPONENT BOTH FACE EACH OTHER WITH A WILL TO FIGHT AND ARE PREPARED FOR DEATH, YOU MUST NEVER DRAW IT.
THAT IS THE WAY OF THE SAMURAI, HONORED BY THE SHIMIZU FAMILY.

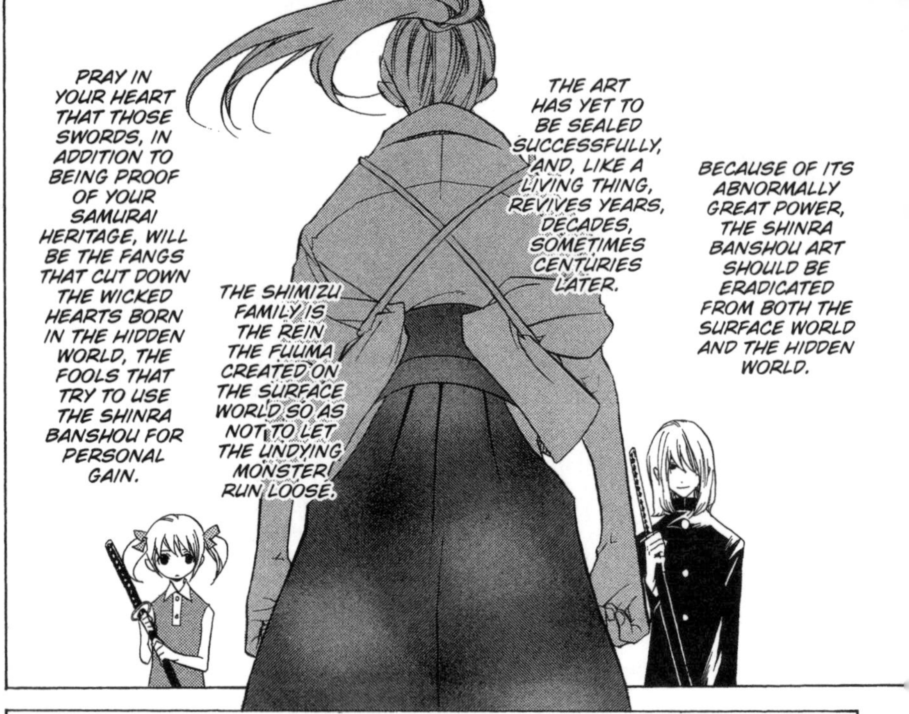
BECAUSE OF ITS ABNORMALLY GREAT POWER, THE SHINRA BANSHOU ART SHOULD BE ERADICATED FROM BOTH THE SURFACE WORLD AND THE HIDDEN WORLD.
THE ART HAS YET TO BE SEALED SUCCESSFULLY, AND, LIKE A LIVING THING, REVIVES YEARS, DECADES, SOMETIMES CENTURIES LATER.
THE SHIMIZU FAMILY IS THE REIN THE FUUMA CREATED ON THE SURFACE WORLD SO AS NOT TO LET THE UNDYING MONSTER RUN LOOSE.
PRAY IN YOUR HEART THAT THOSE SWORDS, IN ADDITION TO BEING PROOF OF YOUR SAMURAI HERITAGE, WILL BE THE FANGS THAT CUT DOWN THE WICKED HEARTS BORN IN THE HIDDEN WORLD, THE FOOLS THAT TRY TO USE THE SHINRA BANSHOU FOR PERSONAL GAIN.

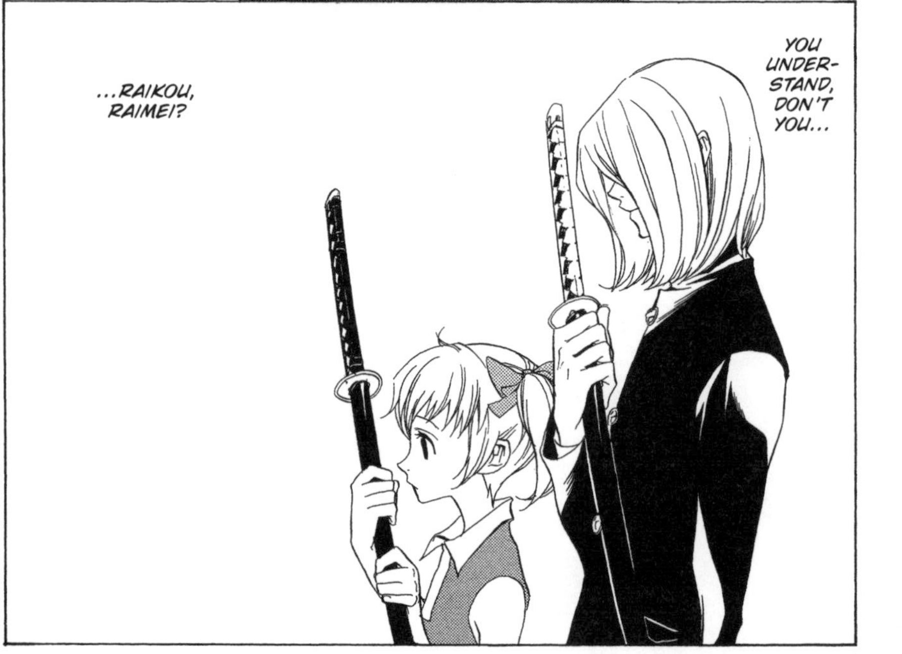
YOU UNDER-STAND, DON'T YOU...
...RAIKOU, RAIMEI?

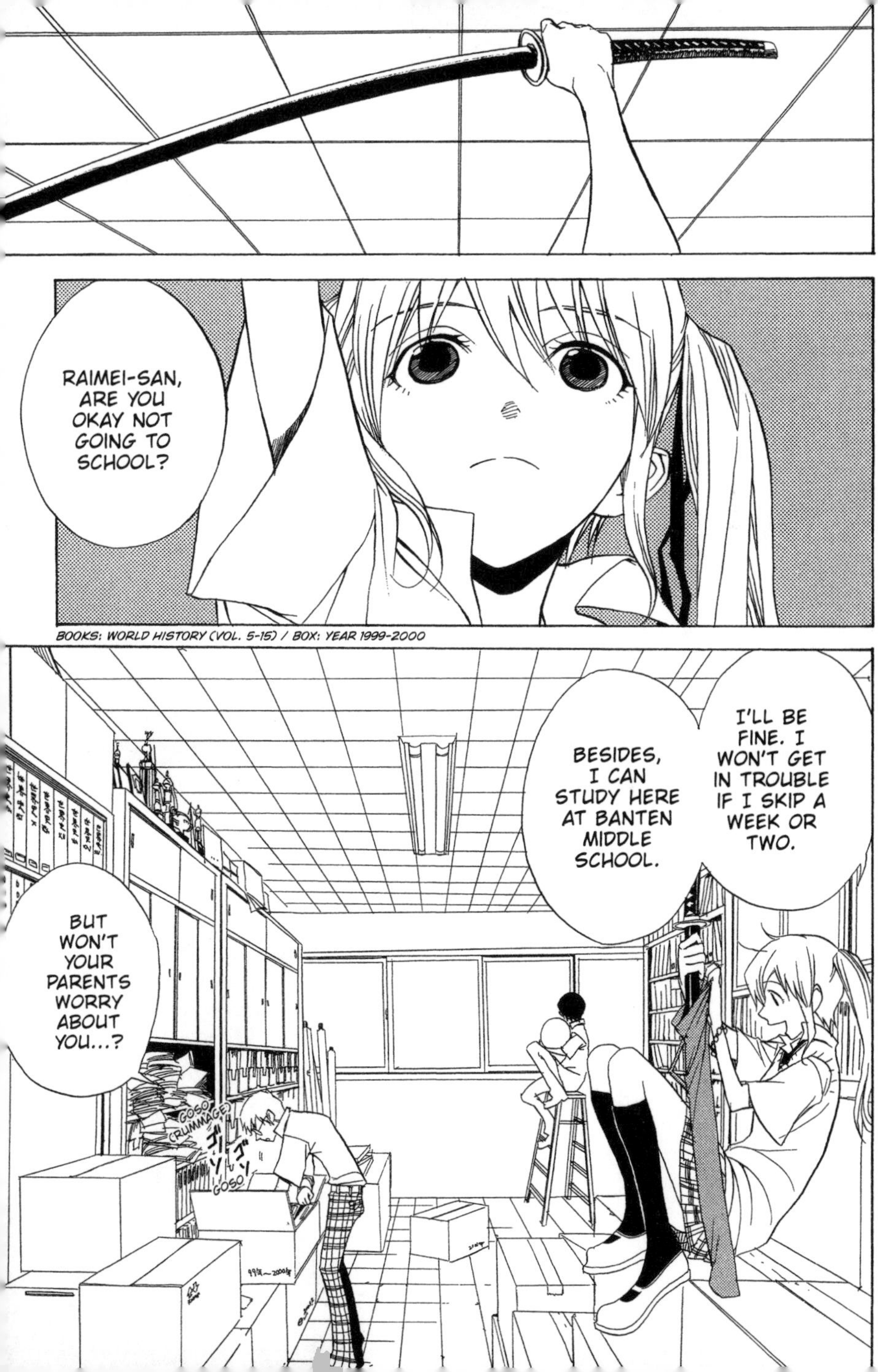
RAIMEI-SAN, ARE YOU OKAY NOT GOING TO SCHOOL?
BOOKS: WORLD HISTORY (VOL. 5-15) / BOX: YEAR 1999-2000
I'LL BE FINE. I WON'T GET IN TROUBLE IF I SKIP A WEEK OR TWO.
BESIDES, I CAN STUDY HERE AT BANTEN MIDDLE SCHOOL.
BUT WON'T YOUR PARENTS WORRY ABOUT YOU...?
GOSO (RUMMAGE)
GOSO

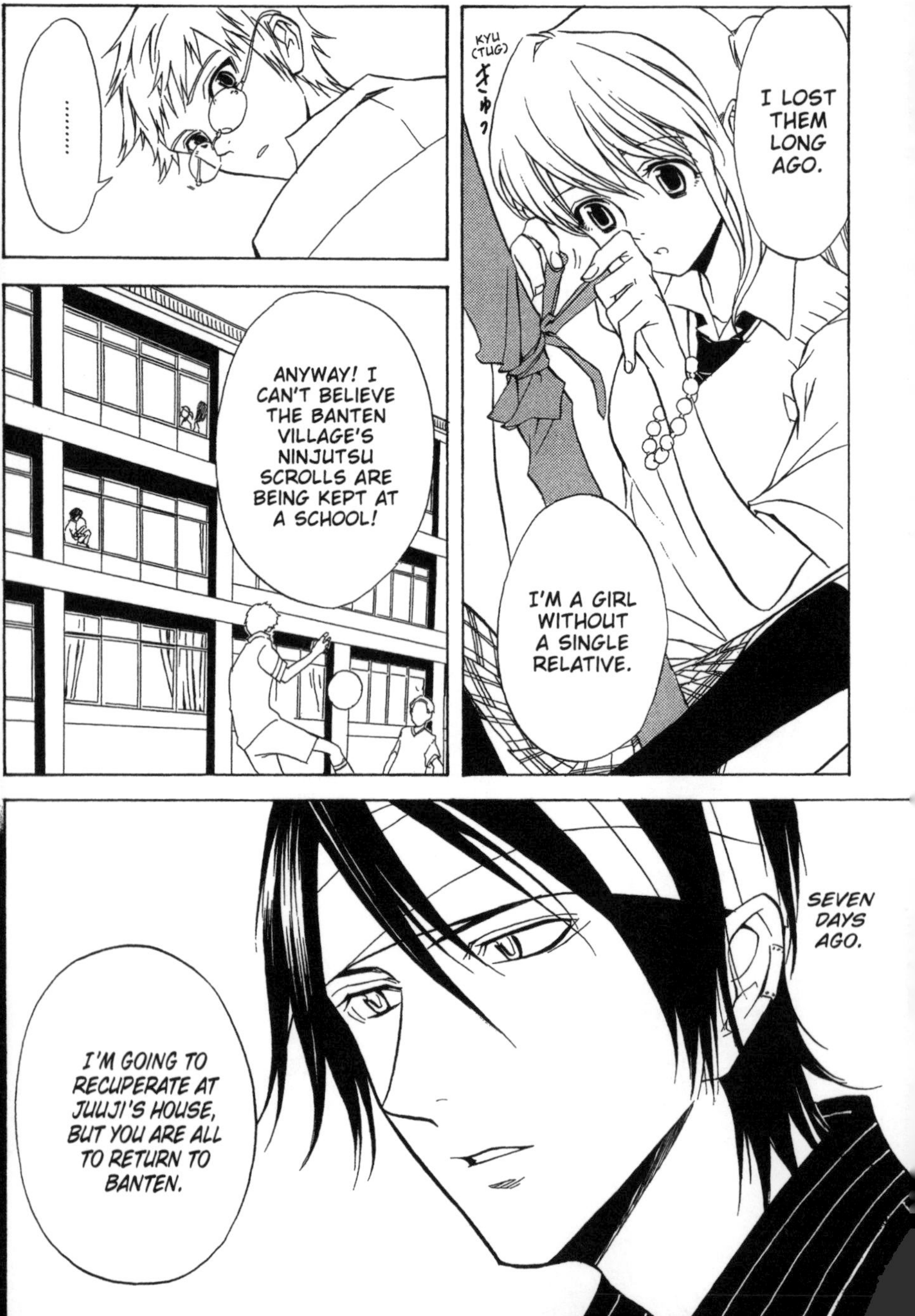
KYU (TUG)
きゅっ
I LOST THEM LONG AGO.
I'M A GIRL WITHOUT A SINGLE RELATIVE.
......
ANYWAY! I CAN'T BELIEVE THE BANTEN VILLAGE'S NINJUTSU SCROLLS ARE BEING KEPT AT A SCHOOL!
SEVEN DAYS AGO.
I'M GOING TO RECUPERATE AT JUUJI'S HOUSE, BUT YOU ARE ALL TO RETURN TO BANTEN.

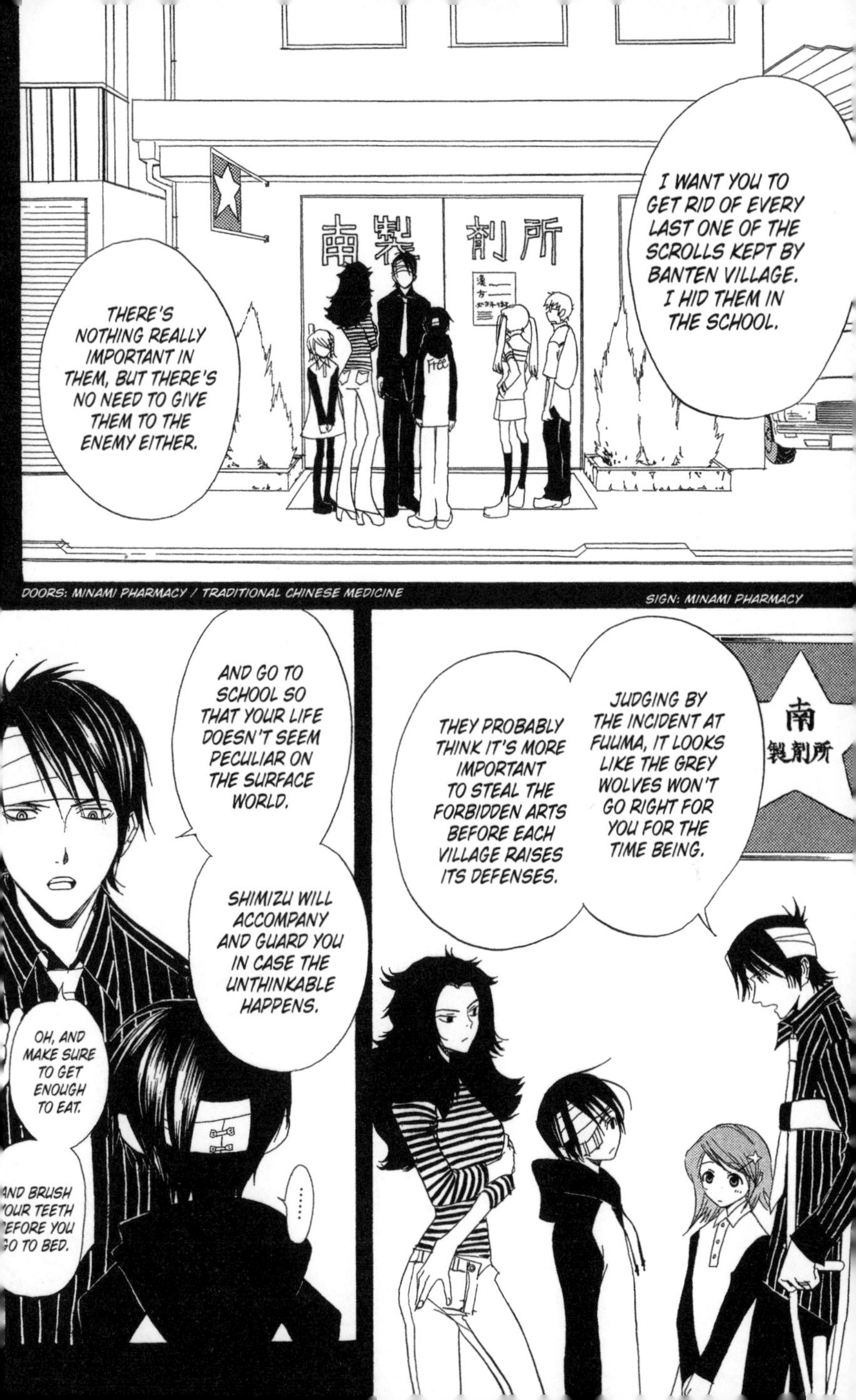
I WANT YOU TO GET RID OF EVERY LAST ONE OF THE SCROLLS KEPT BY BANTEN VILLAGE. I HID THEM IN THE SCHOOL.
THERE'S NOTHING REALLY IMPORTANT IN THEM, BUT THERE'S NO NEED TO GIVE THEM TO THE ENEMY EITHER.
南製剤所
DOORS: MINAMI PHARMACY / TRADITIONAL CHINESE MEDICINE
SIGN: MINAMI PHARMACY
南 製剤所
JUDGING BY THE INCIDENT AT FUUMA, IT LOOKS LIKE THE GREY WOLVES WON'T GO RIGHT FOR YOU FOR THE TIME BEING.
THEY PROBABLY THINK IT'S MORE IMPORTANT TO STEAL THE FORBIDDEN ARTS BEFORE EACH VILLAGE RAISES ITS DEFENSES.
AND GO TO SCHOOL SO THAT YOUR LIFE DOESN'T SEEM PECULIAR ON THE SURFACE WORLD.
SHIMIZU WILL ACCOMPANY AND GUARD YOU IN CASE THE UNTHINKABLE HAPPENS.
OH, AND MAKE SURE TO GET ENOUGH TO EAT.
AND BRUSH OUR TEETH EFORE YOU O TO BED.
......

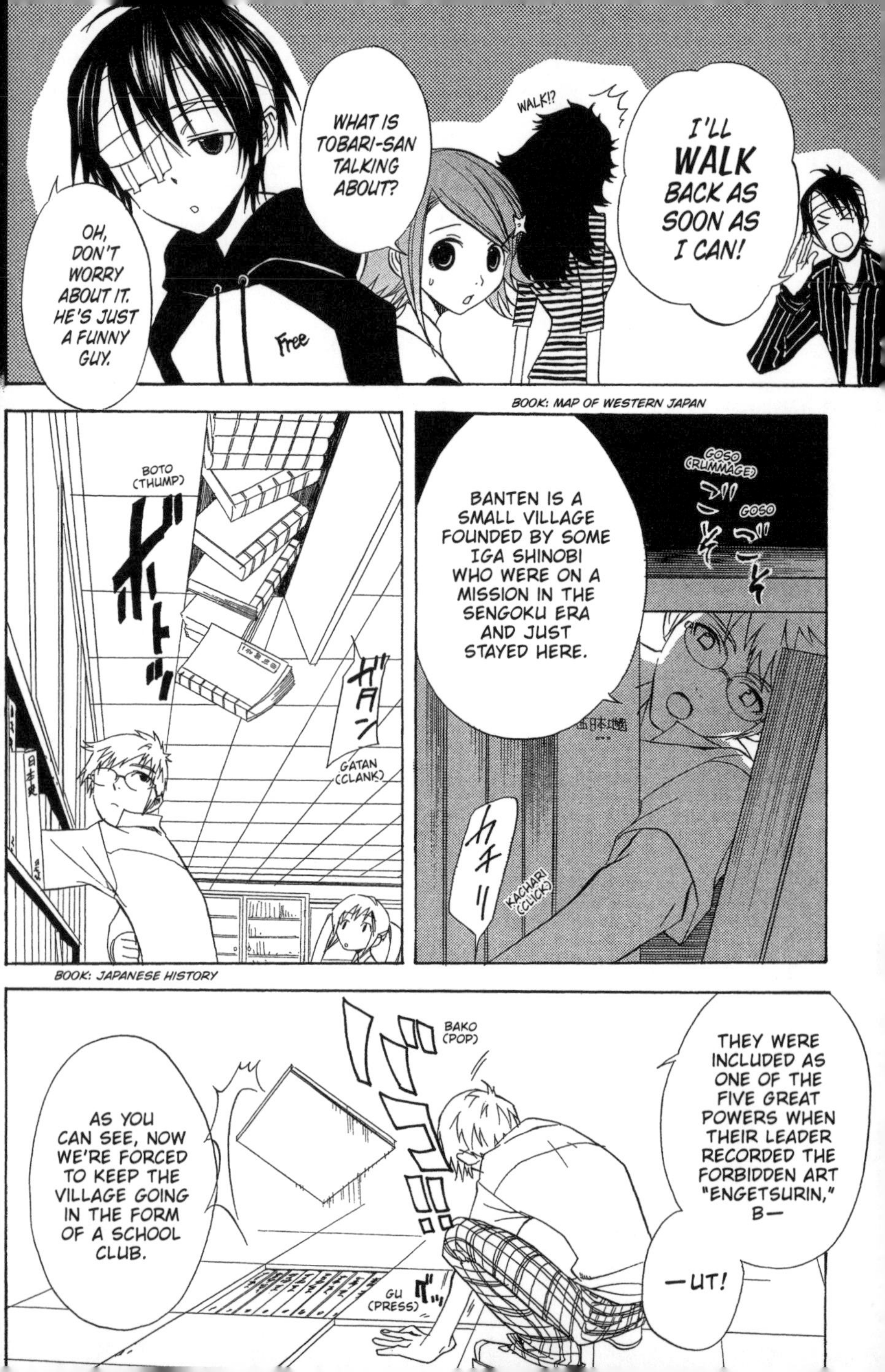
I'LL WALK BACK AS SOON AS I CAN!
WALK!?
WHAT IS TOBARI-SAN TALKING ABOUT?
OH, DON'T WORRY ABOUT IT. HE'S JUST A FUNNY GUY.
Free
BOOK: MAP OF WESTERN JAPAN
GOSO (RUMMAGE)
GOSO
BANTEN IS A SMALL VILLAGE FOUNDED BY SOME IGA SHINOBI WHO WERE ON A MISSION IN THE SENGOKU ERA AND JUST STAYED HERE.
KACHARI (CLICK)
BOTO (THUMP)
GATAN (CLANK)
BOOK: JAPANESE HISTORY
THEY WERE INCLUDED AS ONE OF THE FIVE GREAT POWERS WHEN THEIR LEADER RECORDED THE FORBIDDEN ART "ENGETSURIN," B—
—UT!
GU (PRESS)
BAKO (POP)
AS YOU CAN SEE, NOW WE'RE FORCED TO KEEP THE VILLAGE GOING IN THE FORM OF A SCHOOL CLUB.

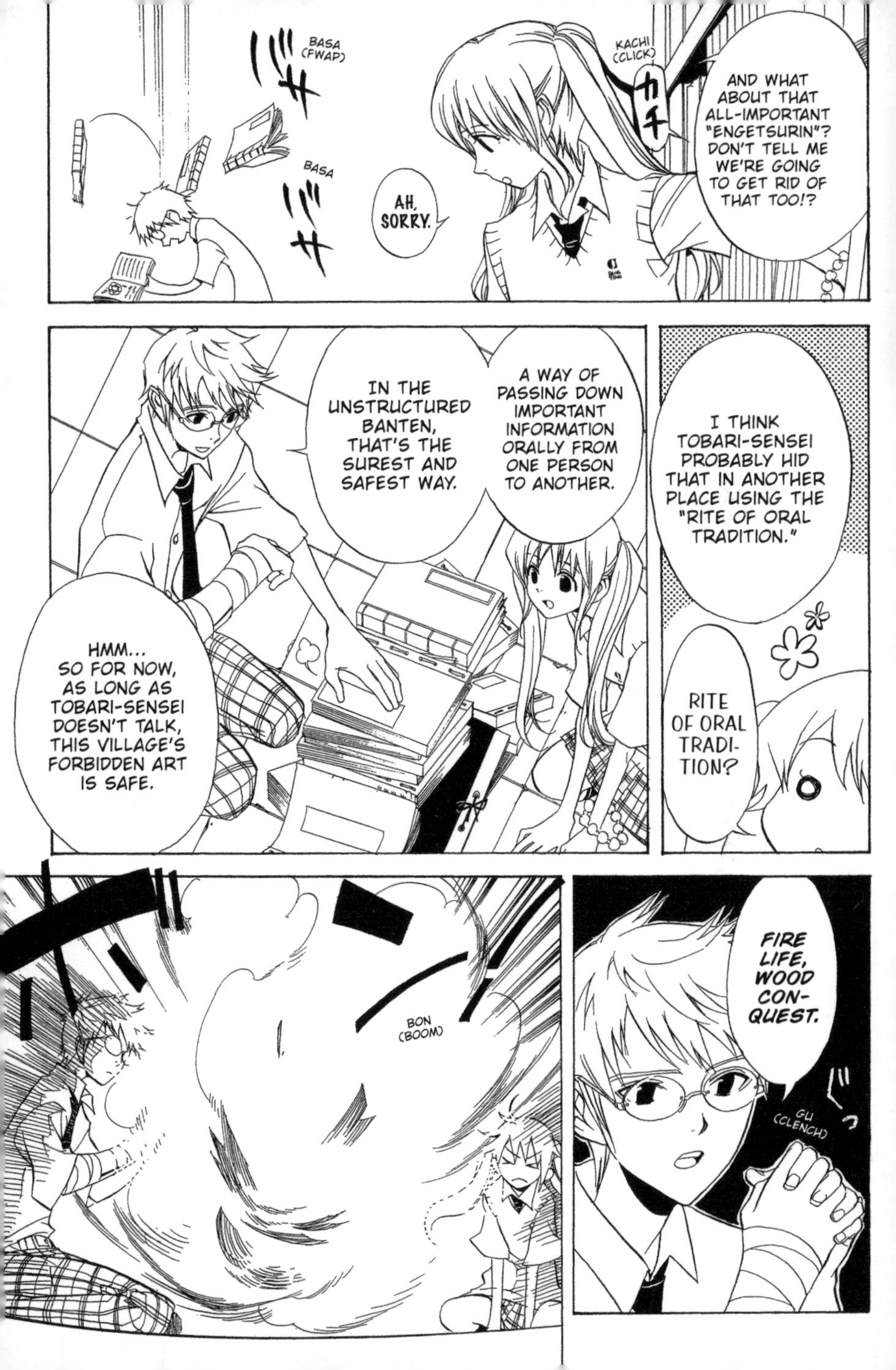
KACHI (CLICK)
AND WHAT ABOUT THAT ALL-IMPORTANT "ENGETSURIN"? DON'T TELL ME WE'RE GOING TO GET RID OF THAT TOO!?
AH, SORRY.
BASA (FWAP)
BASA
I THINK TOBARI-SENSEI PROBABLY HID THAT IN ANOTHER PLACE USING THE "RITE OF ORAL TRADITION."
RITE OF ORAL TRADI-TION?
A WAY OF PASSING DOWN IMPORTANT INFORMATION ORALLY FROM ONE PERSON TO ANOTHER.
IN THE UNSTRUCTURED BANTEN, THAT'S THE SUREST AND SAFEST WAY.
HMM... SO FOR NOW, AS LONG AS TOBARI-SENSEI DOESN'T TALK, THIS VILLAGE'S FORBIDDEN ART IS SAFE.
FIRE LIFE, WOOD CON-QUEST.
GU (CLENCH)
BON (BOOM)

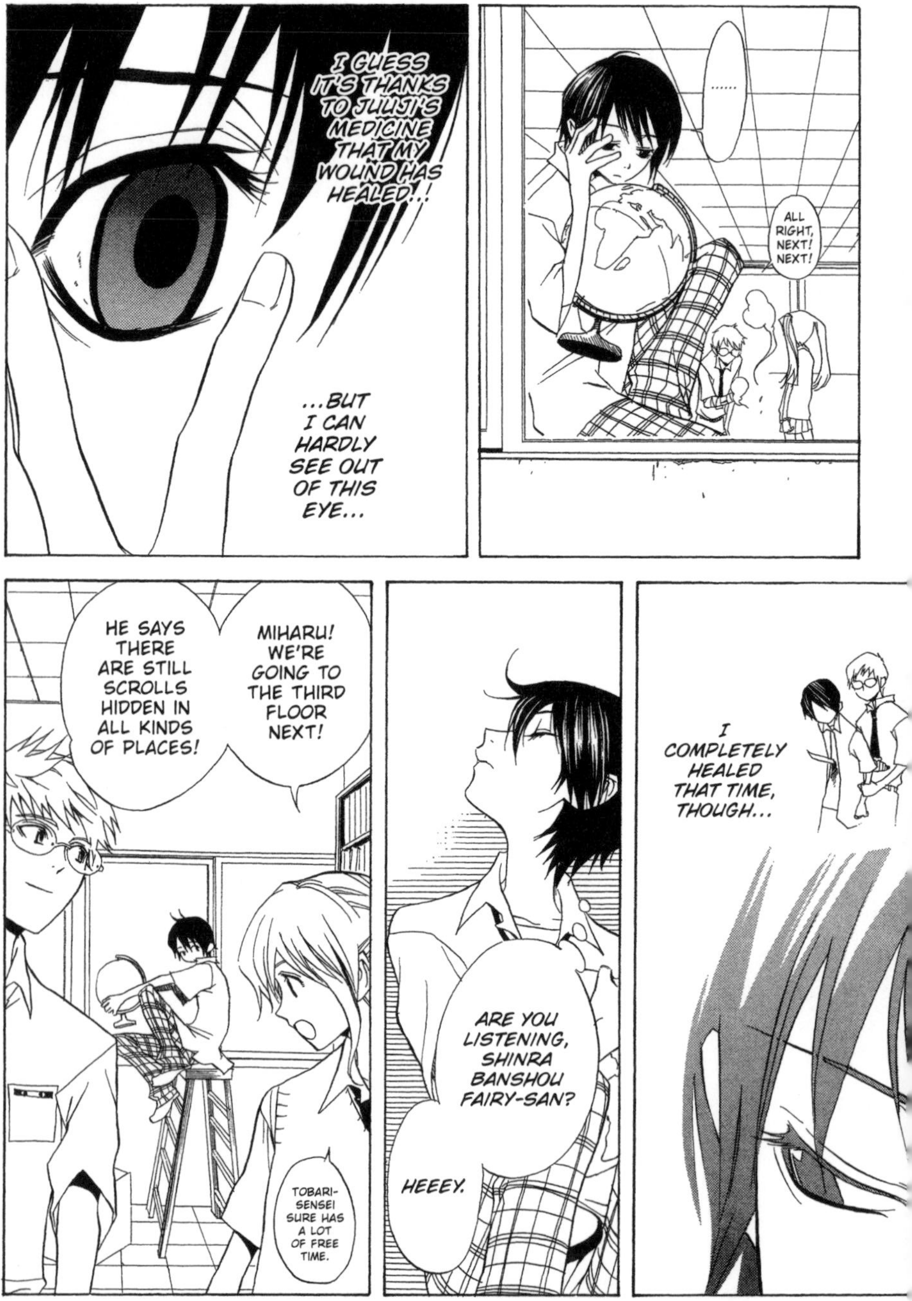
......
ALL RIGHT, NEXT! NEXT!
I GUESS IT'S THANKS TO JUUJI'S MEDICINE THAT MY WOUND HAS HEALED...
...BUT I CAN HARDLY SEE OUT OF THIS EYE...
I COMPLETELY HEALED THAT TIME, THOUGH...
ARE YOU LISTENING, SHINRA BANSHOU FAIRY-SAN?
HEEEY.
MIHARU! WE'RE GOING TO THE THIRD FLOOR NEXT!
HE SAYS THERE ARE STILL SCROLLS HIDDEN IN ALL KINDS OF PLACES!
TOBARI-SENSEI SURE HAS A LOT OF FREE TIME.

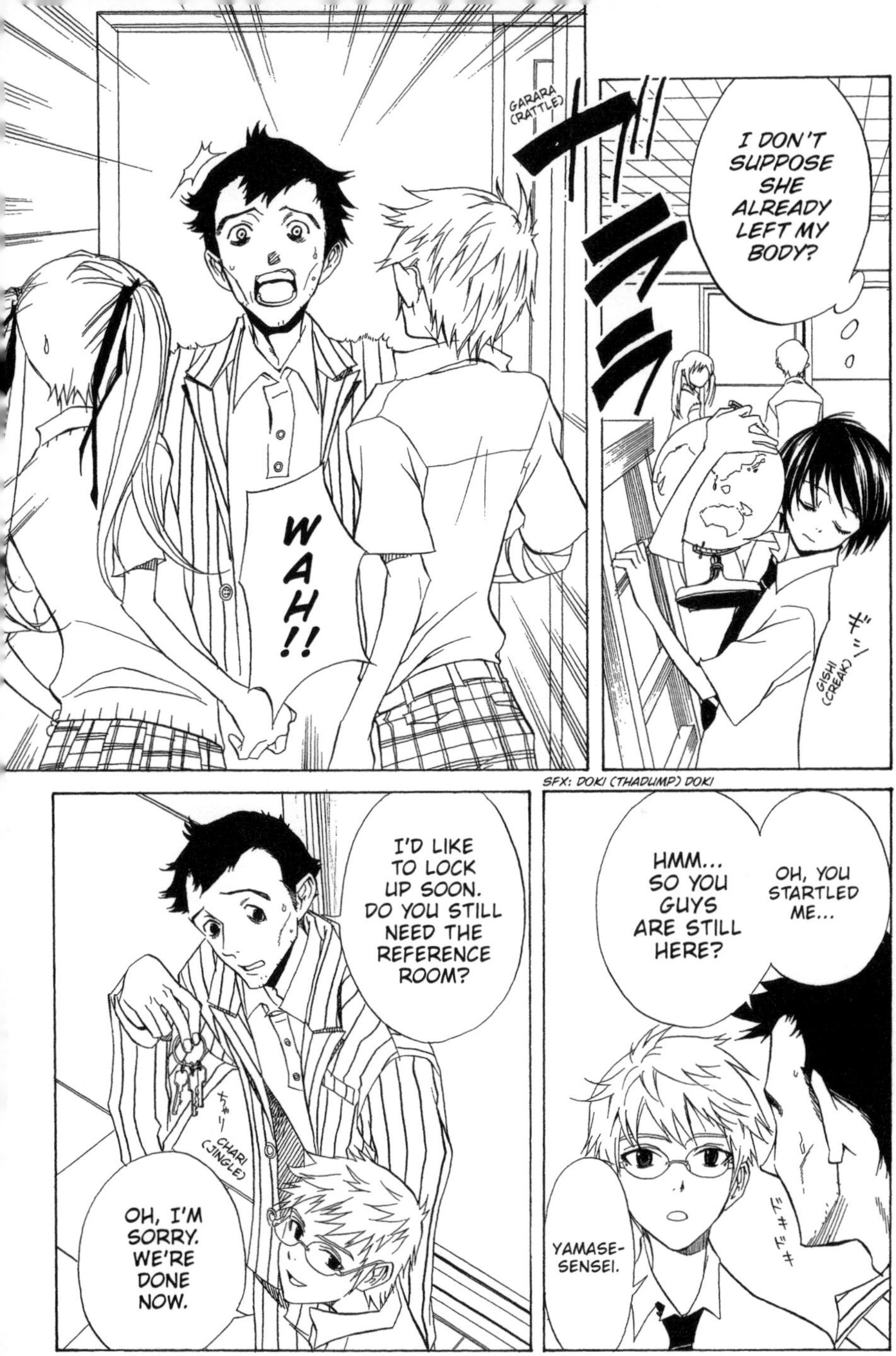
I DON'T SUPPOSE SHE ALREADY LEFT MY BODY?
GISHI (CREAK)
GARARA (RATTLE)
WAH!!
SFX: DOKI (THADUMP) DOKI
OH, YOU STARTLED ME...
HMM... SO YOU GUYS ARE STILL HERE?
YAMASE-SENSEI.
I'D LIKE TO LOCK UP SOON. DO YOU STILL NEED THE REFERENCE ROOM?
CHARI (JINGLE)
OH, I'M SORRY. WE'RE DONE NOW.

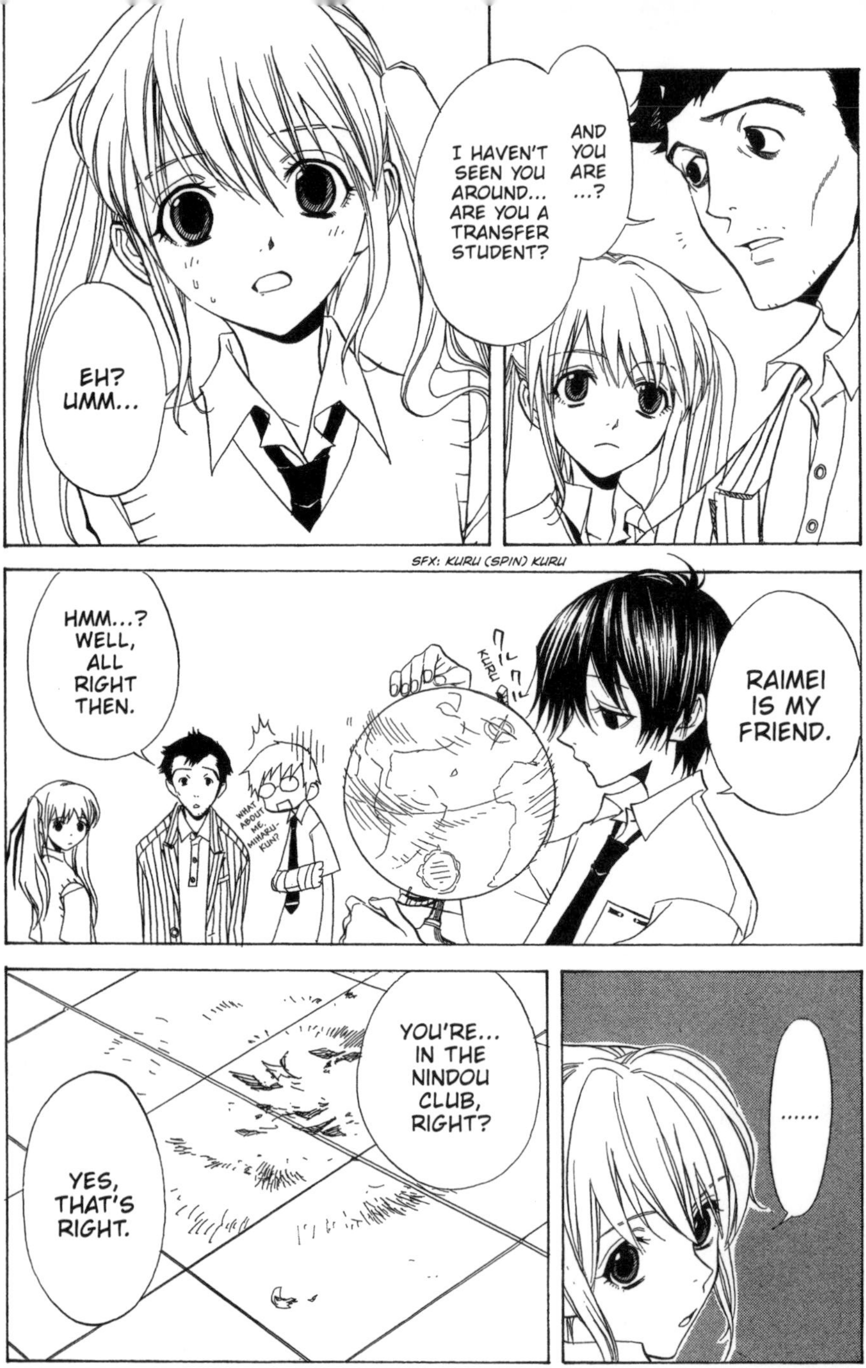
AND YOU ARE ...?
I HAVEN'T SEEN YOU AROUND... ARE YOU A TRANSFER STUDENT?
EH? UMM...
SFX: KURU (SPIN) KURU
RAIMEI IS MY FRIEND.
KURU
WHAT ABOUT ME, MIHARU-KUN?
HMM...? WELL, ALL RIGHT THEN.
......
YOU'RE... IN THE NINDOU CLUB, RIGHT?
YES, THAT'S RIGHT.

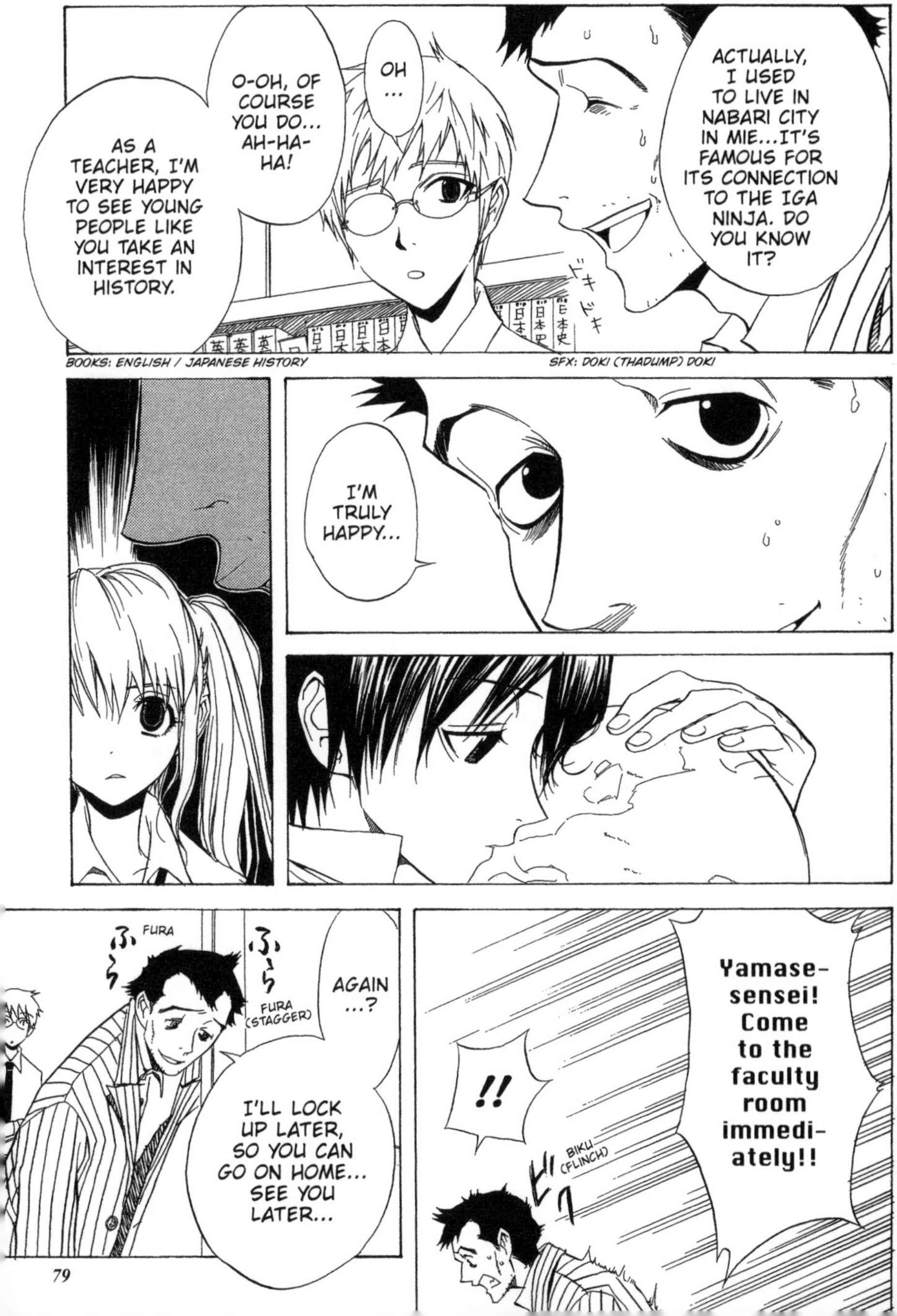
ACTUALLY, I USED TO LIVE IN NABARI CITY IN MIE...IT'S FAMOUS FOR ITS CONNECTION TO THE IGA NINJA. DO YOU KNOW IT?
ドキドキ
SFX: DOKI (THADUMP) DOKI
OH ...
O-OH, OF COURSE YOU DO... AH-HA-HA!
AS A TEACHER, I'M VERY HAPPY TO SEE YOUNG PEOPLE LIKE YOU TAKE AN INTEREST IN HISTORY.
BOOKS: ENGLISH / JAPANESE HISTORY
I'M TRULY HAPPY...
Yamase-sensei! Come to the faculty room immedi-ately!!
!!
ビク
BIKU (FLINCH)
AGAIN ...?
ふら
FURA (STAGGER)
ふら
FURA
I'LL LOCK UP LATER, SO YOU CAN GO ON HOME... SEE YOU LATER...

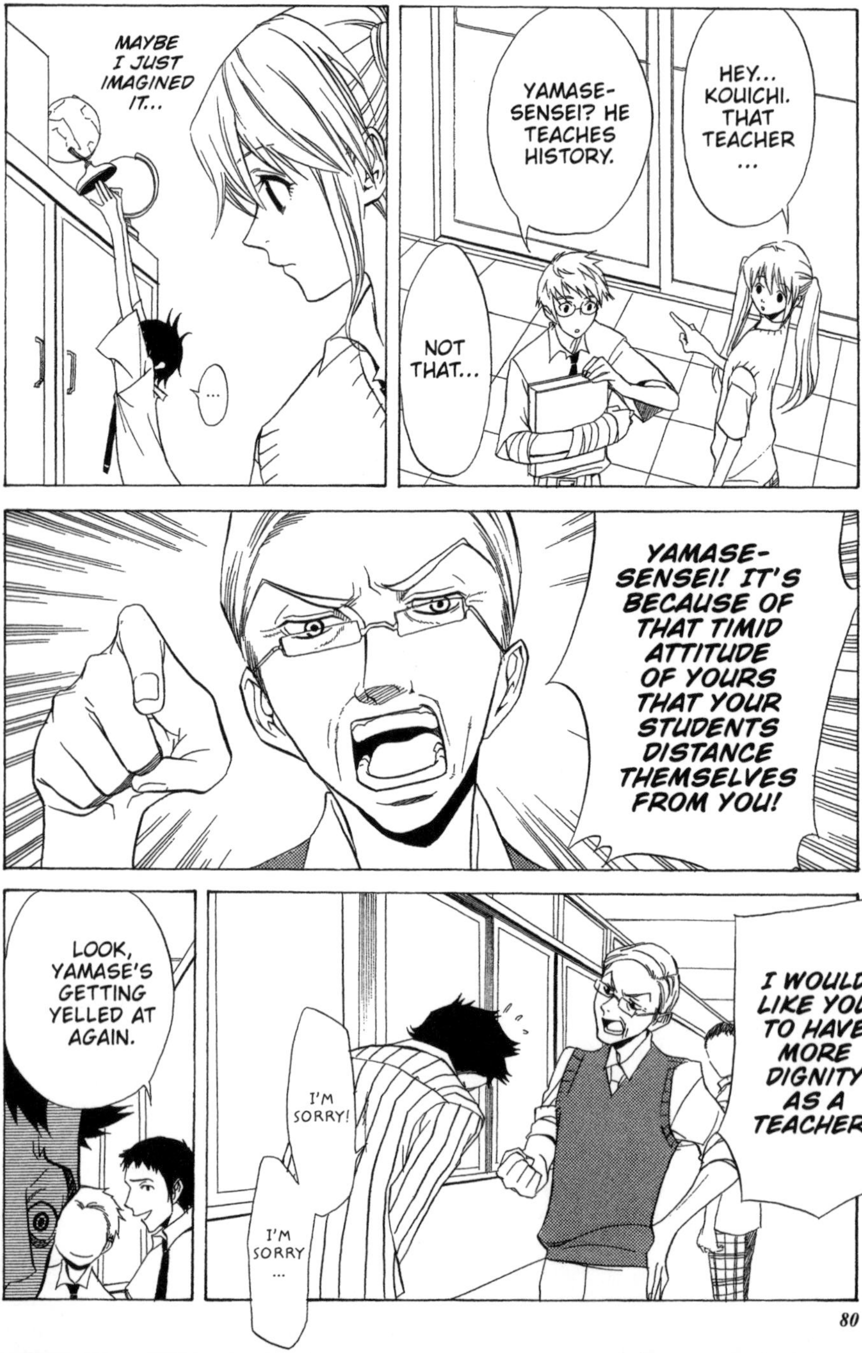
HEY... KOUICHI. THAT TEACHER ...
YAMASE-SENSEI? HE TEACHES HISTORY.
NOT THAT...
MAYBE I JUST IMAGINED IT...
...
YAMASE-SENSEI! IT'S BECAUSE OF THAT TIMID ATTITUDE OF YOURS THAT YOUR STUDENTS DISTANCE THEMSELVES FROM YOU!
I WOULD LIKE YOU TO HAVE MORE DIGNITY AS A TEACHER!
I'M SORRY!
I'M SORRY ...
LOOK, YAMASE'S GETTING YELLED AT AGAIN.

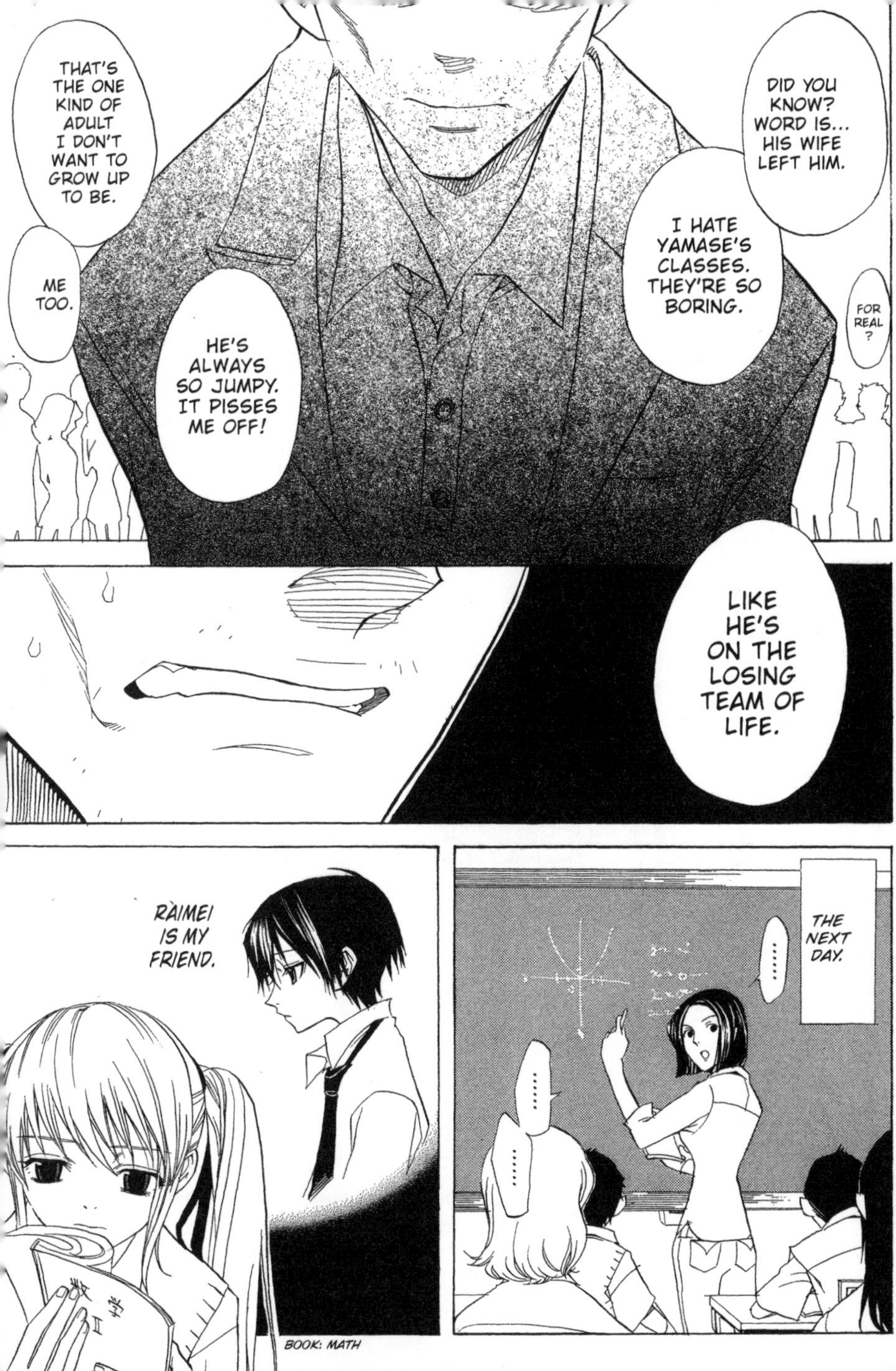
DID YOU KNOW? WORD IS... HIS WIFE LEFT HIM.
FOR REAL?
I HATE YAMASE'S CLASSES. THEY'RE SO BORING.
HE'S ALWAYS SO JUMPY. IT PISSES ME OFF!
THAT'S THE ONE KIND OF ADULT I DON'T WANT TO GROW UP TO BE.
ME TOO.
LIKE HE'S ON THE LOSING TEAM OF LIFE.
THE NEXT DAY.
......
......
RAIMEI IS MY FRIEND.
数学 II
BOOK: MATH

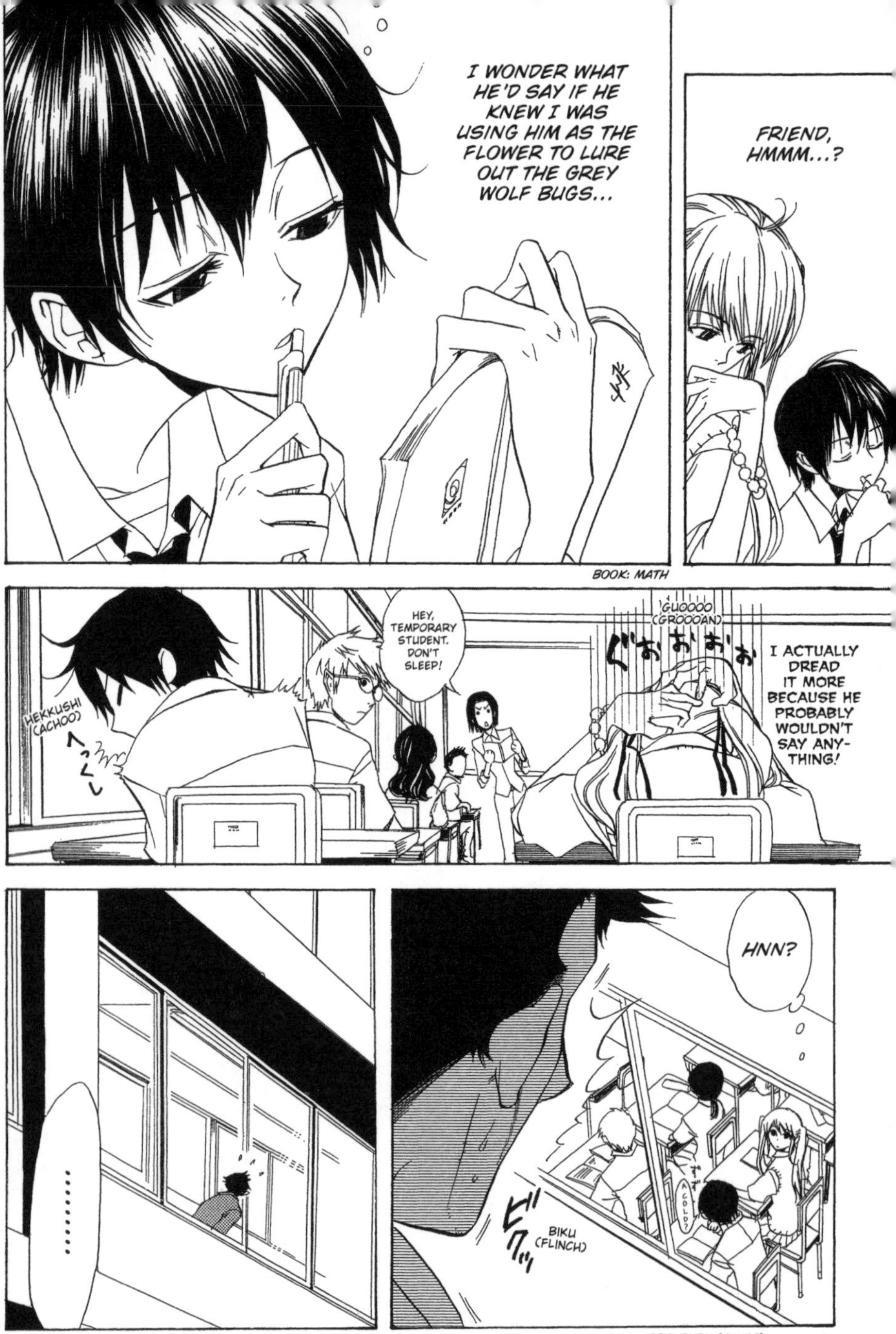
FRIEND, HMMM...?
I WONDER WHAT HE'D SAY IF HE KNEW I WAS USING HIM AS THE FLOWER TO LURE OUT THE GREY WOLF BUGS...
BOOK: MATH
I ACTUALLY DREAD IT MORE BECAUSE HE PROBABLY WOULDN'T SAY ANY-THING!
GUOOOO (GROOOAN)
ぐおおおお
HEY, TEMPORARY STUDENT. DON'T SLEEP!
HEKKUSHI (ACHOO)
へっくし
HNN?
ずず
A COLD?
ビクッ
BIKU (FLINCH)
......

SFX: ZUZU (SNIFF)

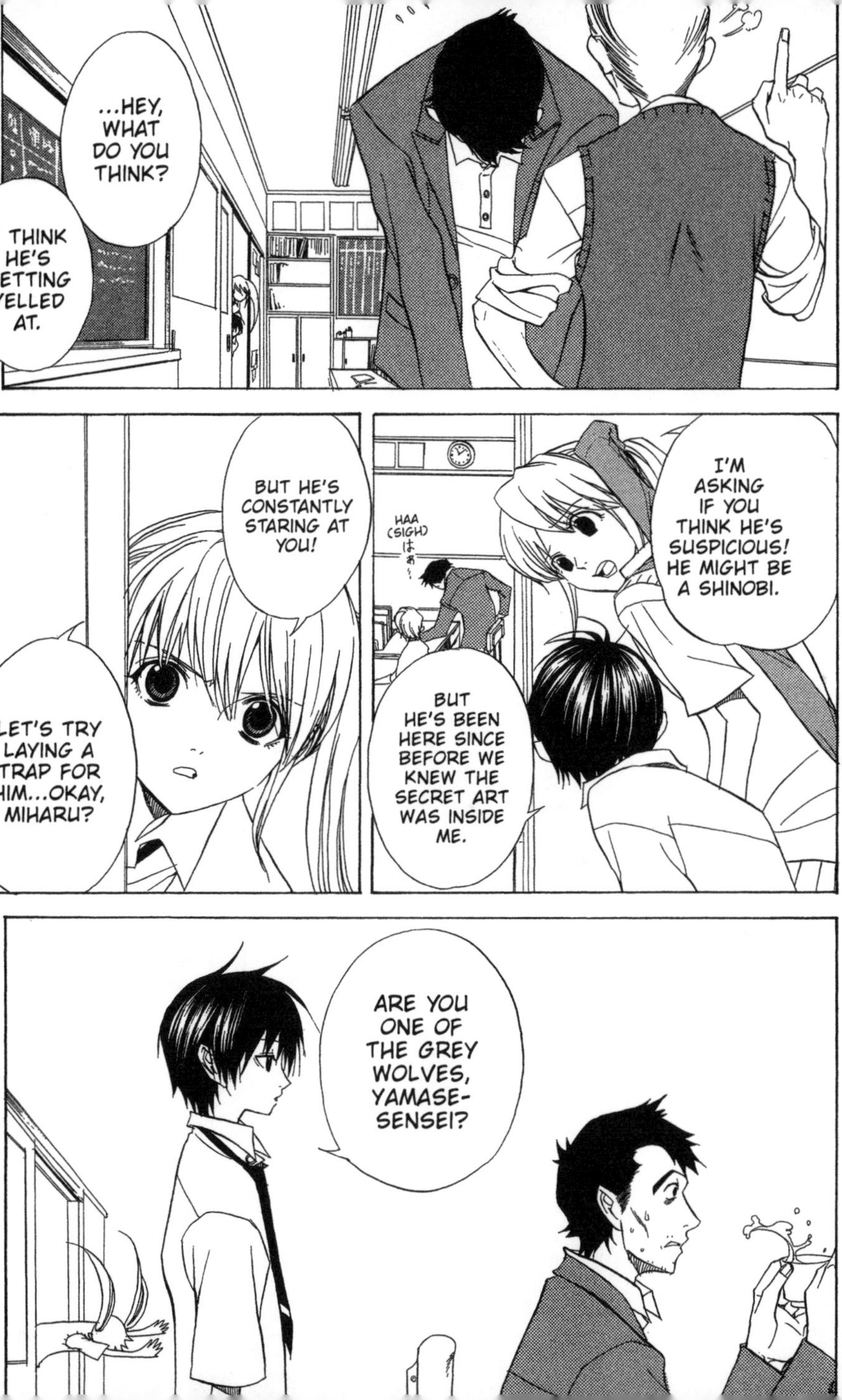
...HEY, WHAT DO YOU THINK?
I THINK HE'S GETTING YELLED AT.
I'M ASKING IF YOU THINK HE'S SUSPICIOUS! HE MIGHT BE A SHINOBI.
HAA (SIGH) はぁ…
BUT HE'S BEEN HERE SINCE BEFORE WE KNEW THE SECRET ART WAS INSIDE ME.
BUT HE'S CONSTANTLY STARING AT YOU!
LET'S TRY LAYING A TRAP FOR HIM...OKAY, MIHARU?
ARE YOU ONE OF THE GREY WOLVES, YAMASE-SENSEI?

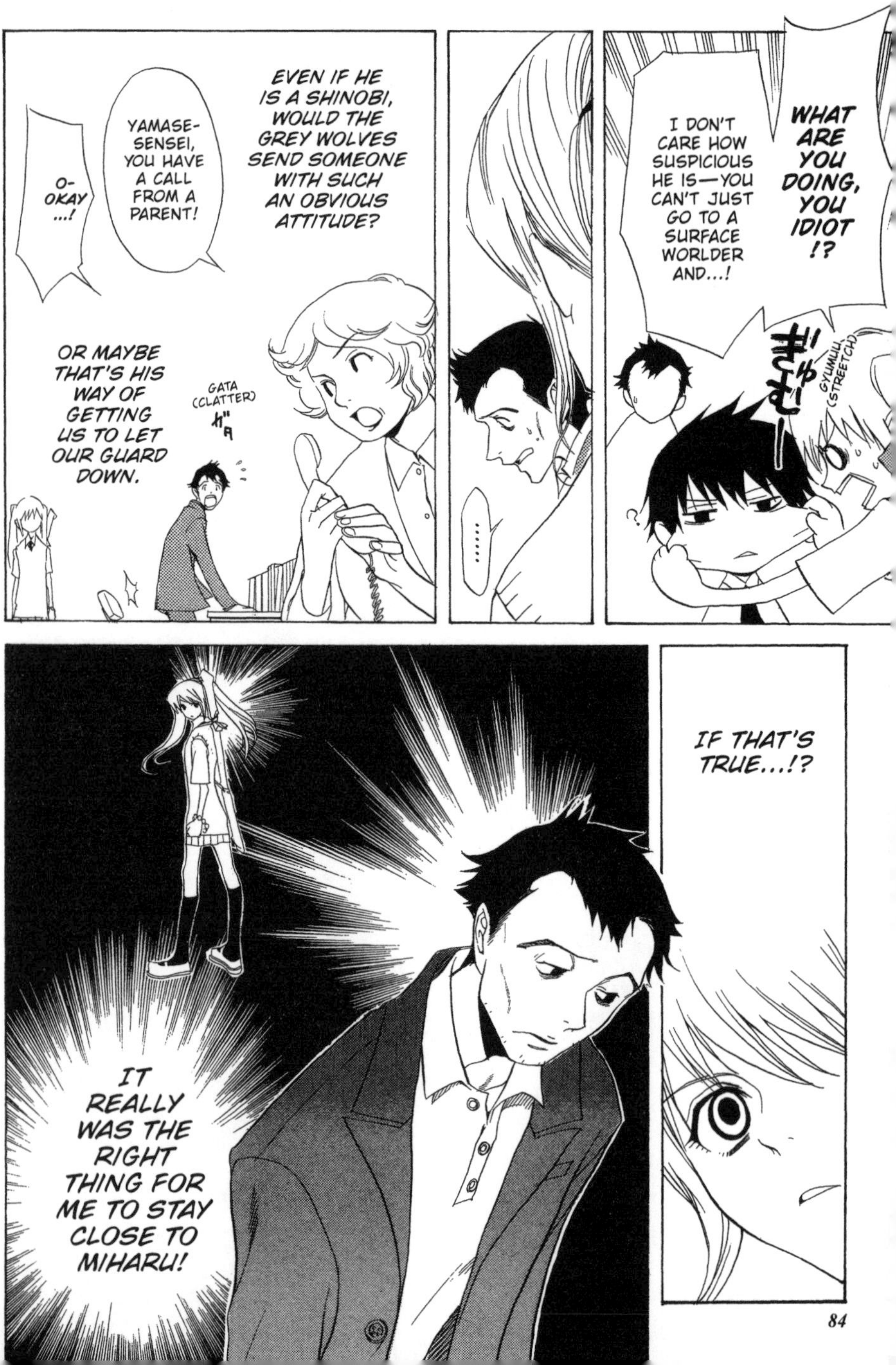
WHAT ARE YOU DOING, YOU IDIOT!?
I DON'T CARE HOW SUSPICIOUS HE IS—YOU CAN'T JUST GO TO A SURFACE WORLDER AND...!
ぎゅむー
GYUMUU (STRETCH)
......
EVEN IF HE IS A SHINOBI, WOULD THE GREY WOLVES SEND SOMEONE WITH SUCH AN OBVIOUS ATTITUDE?
YAMASE-SENSEI, YOU HAVE A CALL FROM A PARENT!
O-OKAY...!
OR MAYBE THAT'S HIS WAY OF GETTING US TO LET OUR GUARD DOWN.
GATA (CLATTER)
ガタ
IF THAT'S TRUE...!?
IT REALLY WAS THE RIGHT THING FOR ME TO STAY CLOSE TO MIHARU!

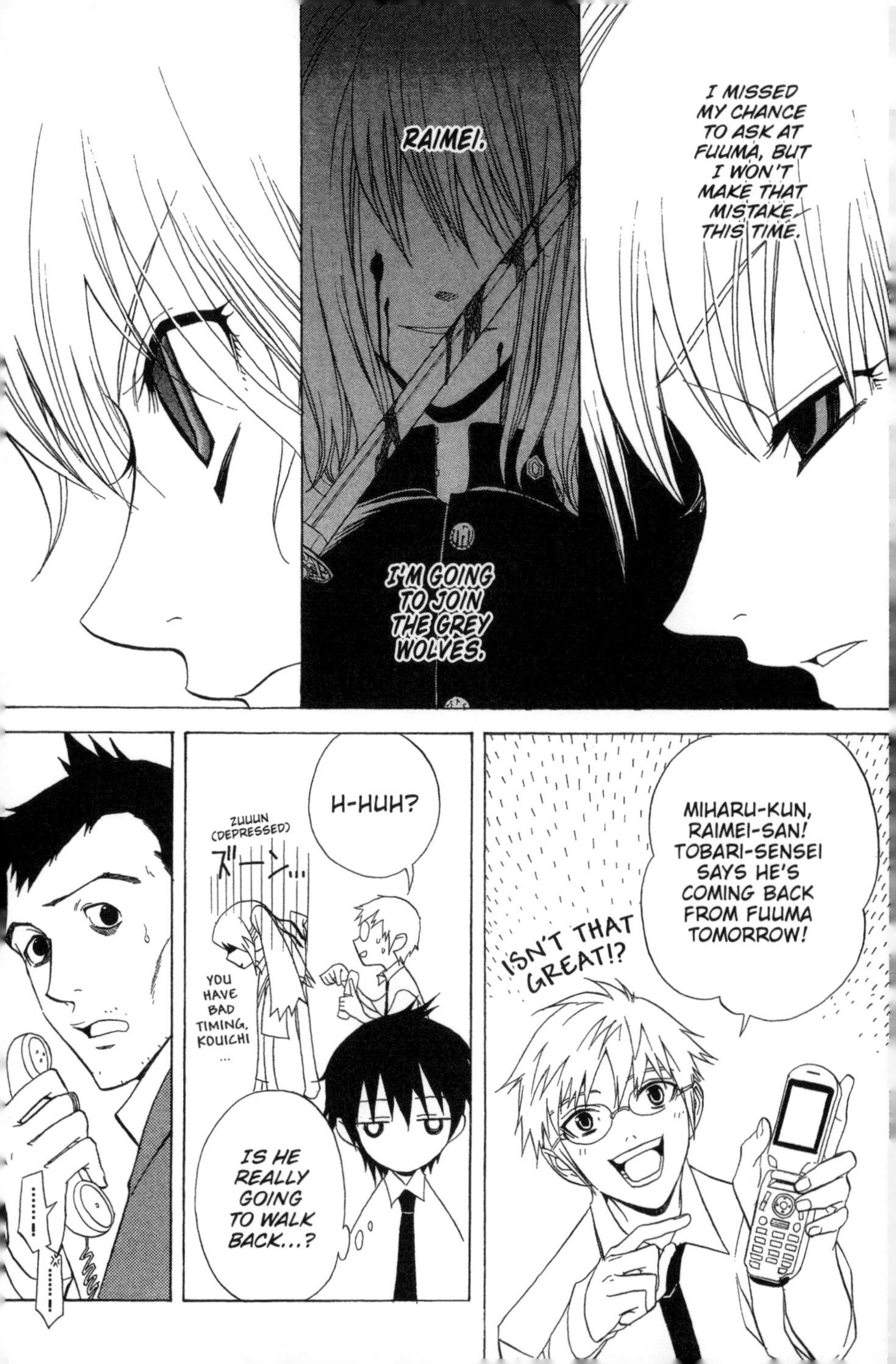

I MISSED MY CHANCE TO ASK AT FUUMA, BUT I WON'T MAKE THAT MISTAKE THIS TIME.
RAIMEI.
I'M GOING TO JOIN THE GREY WOLVES.
MIHARU-KUN, RAIMEI-SAN! TOBARI-SENSEI SAYS HE'S COMING BACK FROM FUUMA TOMORROW!
ISN'T THAT GREAT!?
H-HUH?
ZUUUN (DEPRESSED)
ズーン…
YOU HAVE BAD TIMING, KOUICHI...
IS HE REALLY GOING TO WALK BACK...?
......!
......!

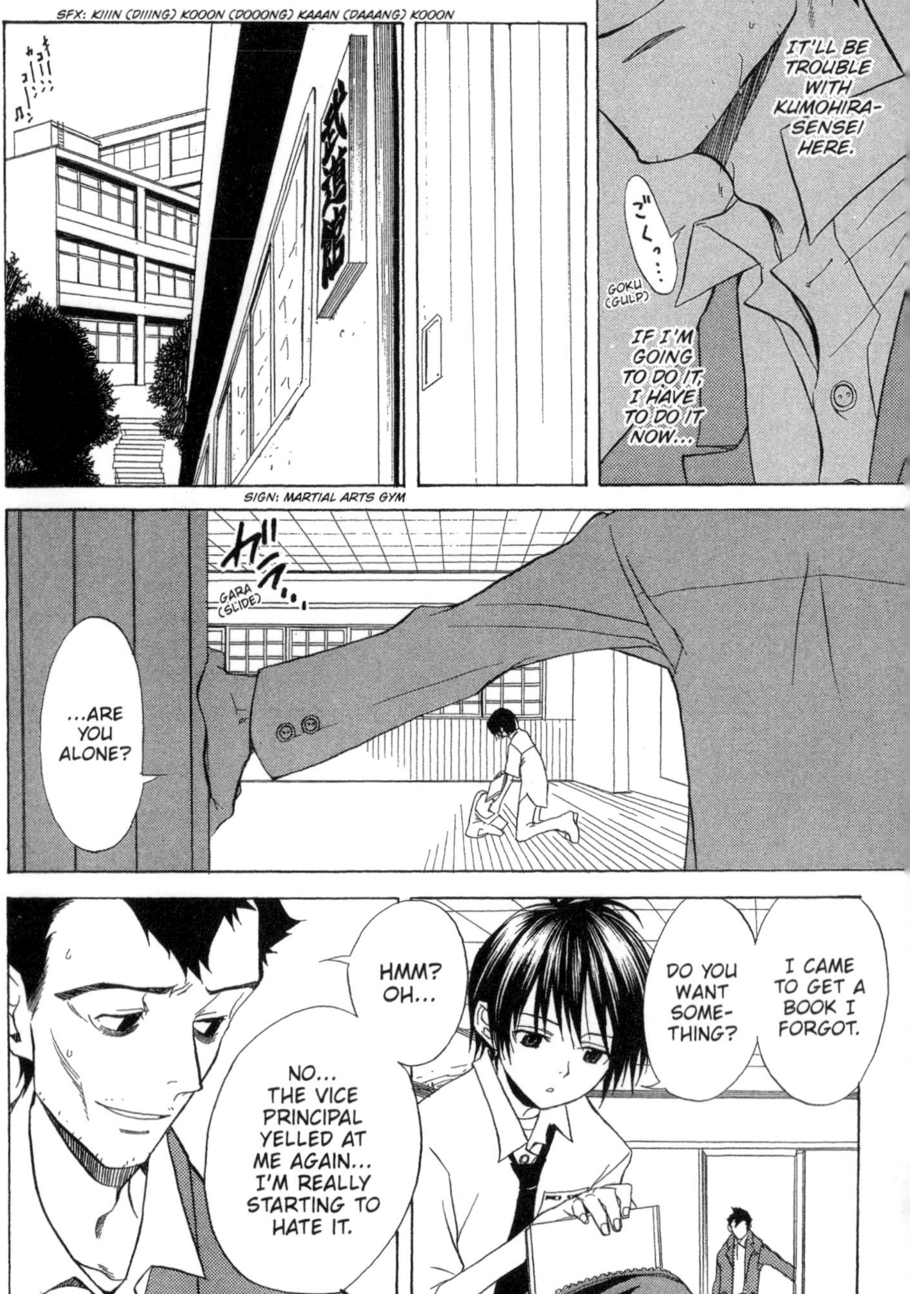
IT'LL BE TROUBLE WITH KUMOHIRA-SENSEI HERE.
ごくっ…
GOKU (GULP)
IF I'M GOING TO DO IT, I HAVE TO DO IT NOW...
武道館
SIGN: MARTIAL ARTS GYM
キーンコーンカーンコーン♪
SFX: KIIIN (DIIING) KOOON (DOOONG) KAAAN (DAAANG) KOOON
ガラ…
GARA (SLIDE)
...ARE YOU ALONE?
I CAME TO GET A BOOK I FORGOT.
DO YOU WANT SOME-THING?
HMM? OH...
NO... THE VICE PRINCIPAL YELLED AT ME AGAIN... I'M REALLY STARTING TO HATE IT.

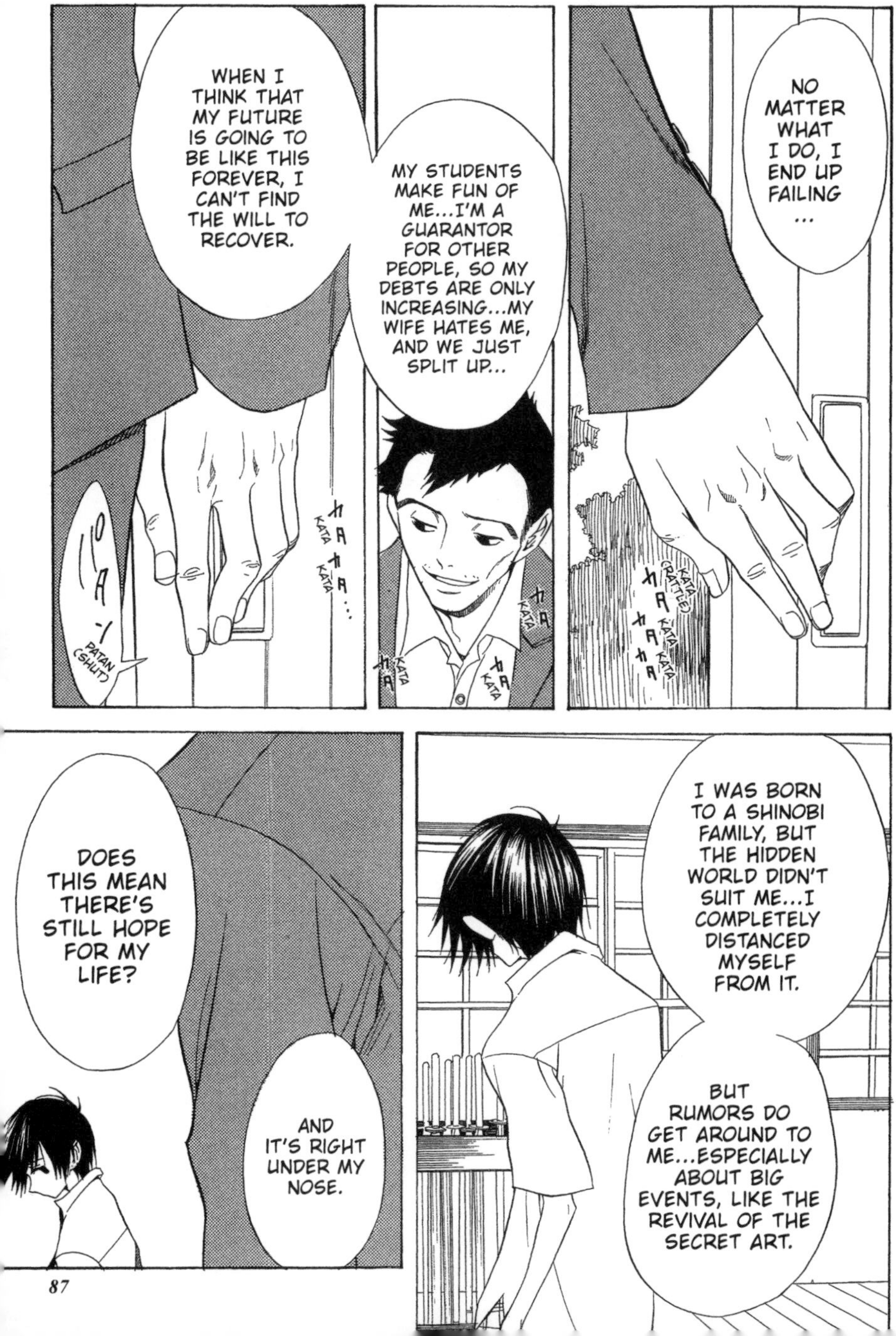
NO MATTER WHAT I DO, I END UP FAILING...
KATA (RATTLE)
KATA
KATA
MY STUDENTS MAKE FUN OF ME...I'M A GUARANTOR FOR OTHER PEOPLE, SO MY DEBTS ARE ONLY INCREASING...MY WIFE HATES ME, AND WE JUST SPLIT UP...
KATA
KATA
KATA
WHEN I THINK THAT MY FUTURE IS GOING TO BE LIKE THIS FOREVER, I CAN'T FIND THE WILL TO RECOVER.
KATA
KATA
PATAN (SHUT)
I WAS BORN TO A SHINOBI FAMILY, BUT THE HIDDEN WORLD DIDN'T SUIT ME...I COMPLETELY DISTANCED MYSELF FROM IT.
BUT RUMORS DO GET AROUND TO ME...ESPECIALLY ABOUT BIG EVENTS, LIKE THE REVIVAL OF THE SECRET ART.
DOES THIS MEAN THERE'S STILL HOPE FOR MY LIFE?
AND IT'S RIGHT UNDER MY NOSE.

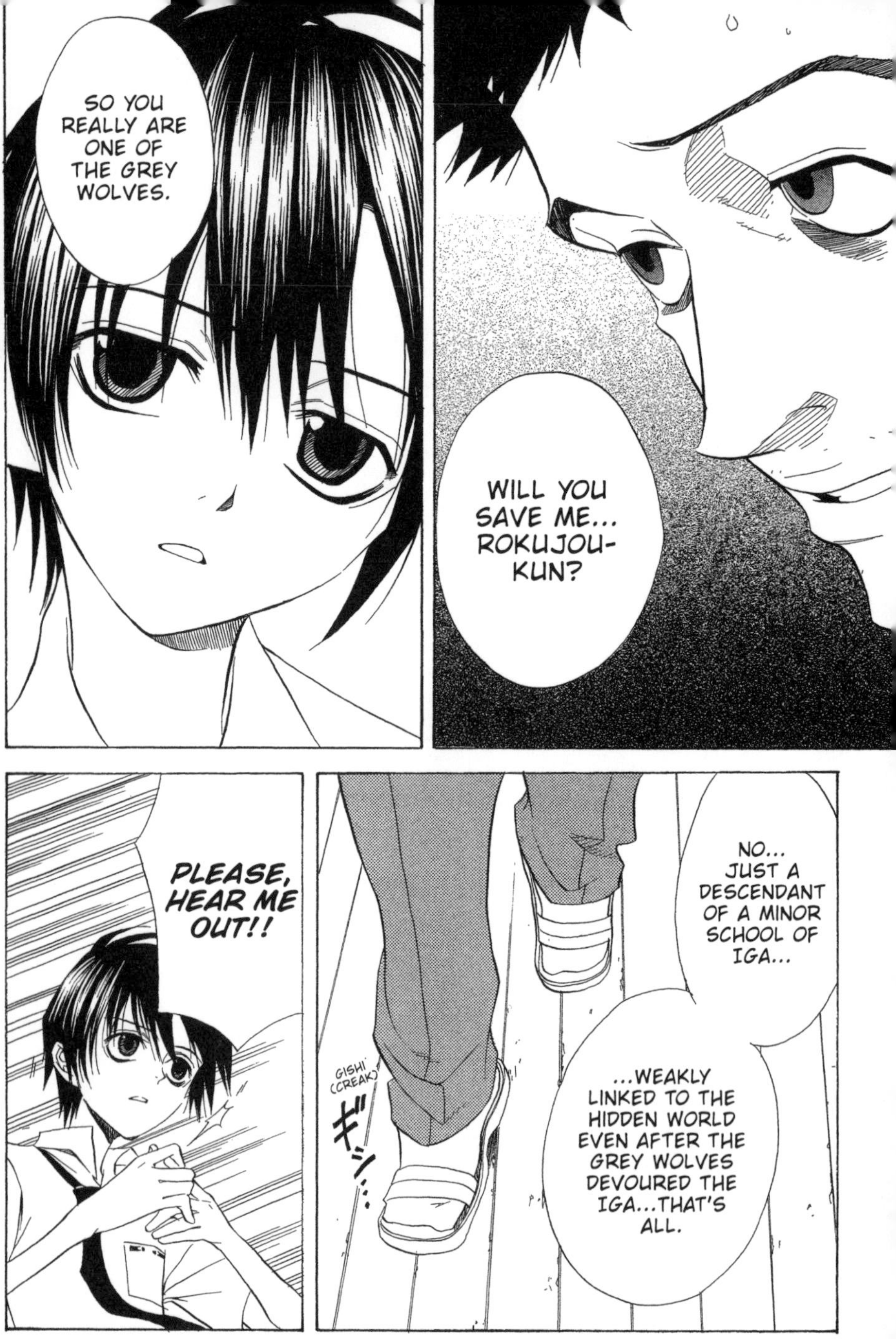
WILL YOU SAVE ME... ROKUJOU-KUN?
SO YOU REALLY ARE ONE OF THE GREY WOLVES.
NO... JUST A DESCENDANT OF A MINOR SCHOOL OF IGA...
...WEAKLY LINKED TO THE HIDDEN WORLD EVEN AFTER THE GREY WOLVES DEVOURED THE IGA...THAT'S ALL.
GISHI (CREAK)
ギッ…
PLEASE, HEAR ME OUT!!

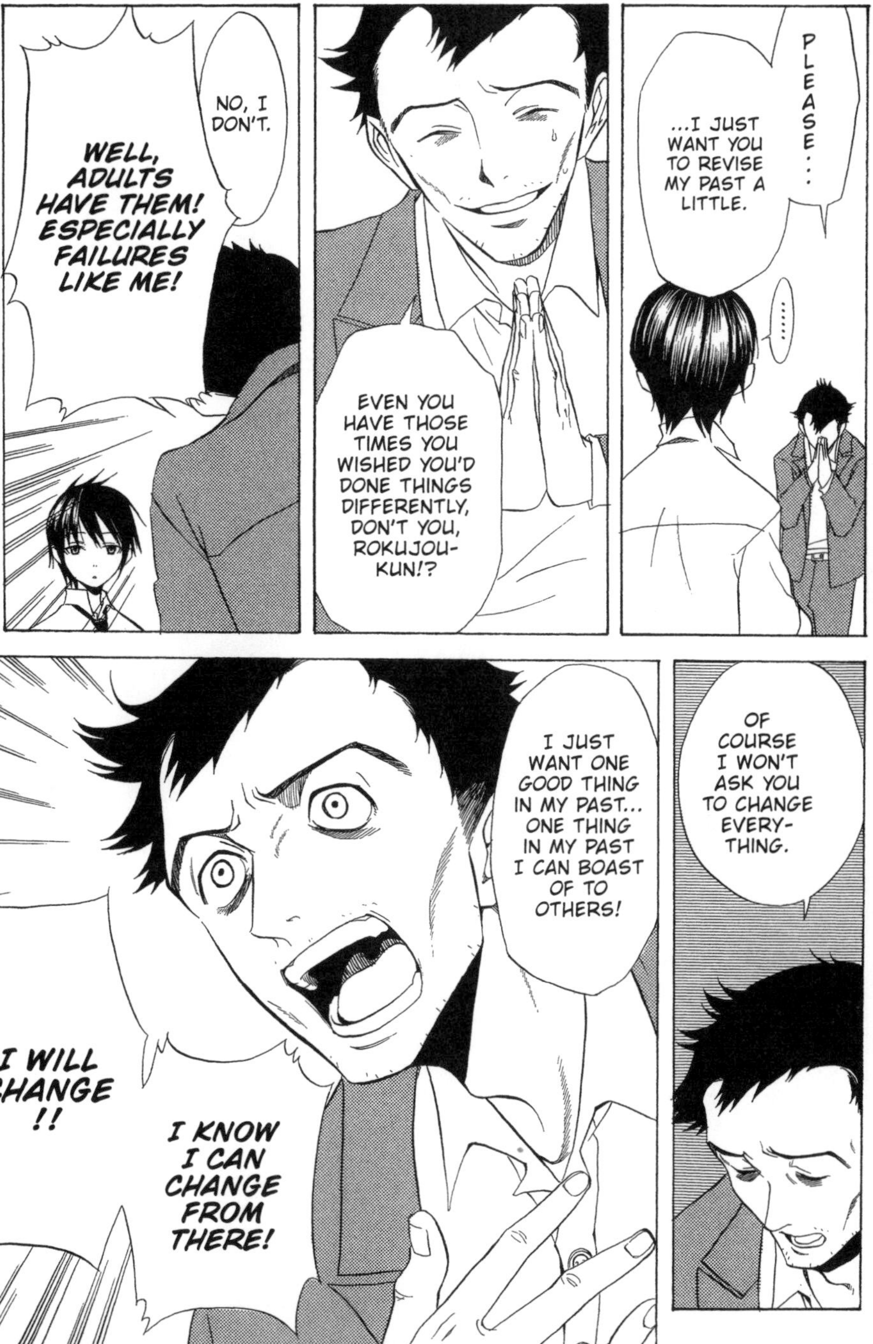
PLEASE...
...I JUST WANT YOU TO REVISE MY PAST A LITTLE.
......
EVEN YOU HAVE THOSE TIMES YOU WISHED YOU'D DONE THINGS DIFFERENTLY, DON'T YOU, ROKUJOU-KUN!?
NO, I DON'T.
WELL, ADULTS HAVE THEM! ESPECIALLY FAILURES LIKE ME!
OF COURSE I WON'T ASK YOU TO CHANGE EVERY-THING.
I JUST WANT ONE GOOD THING IN MY PAST... ONE THING IN MY PAST I CAN BOAST OF TO OTHERS!
I KNOW I CAN CHANGE FROM THERE!
I WILL CHANGE !!

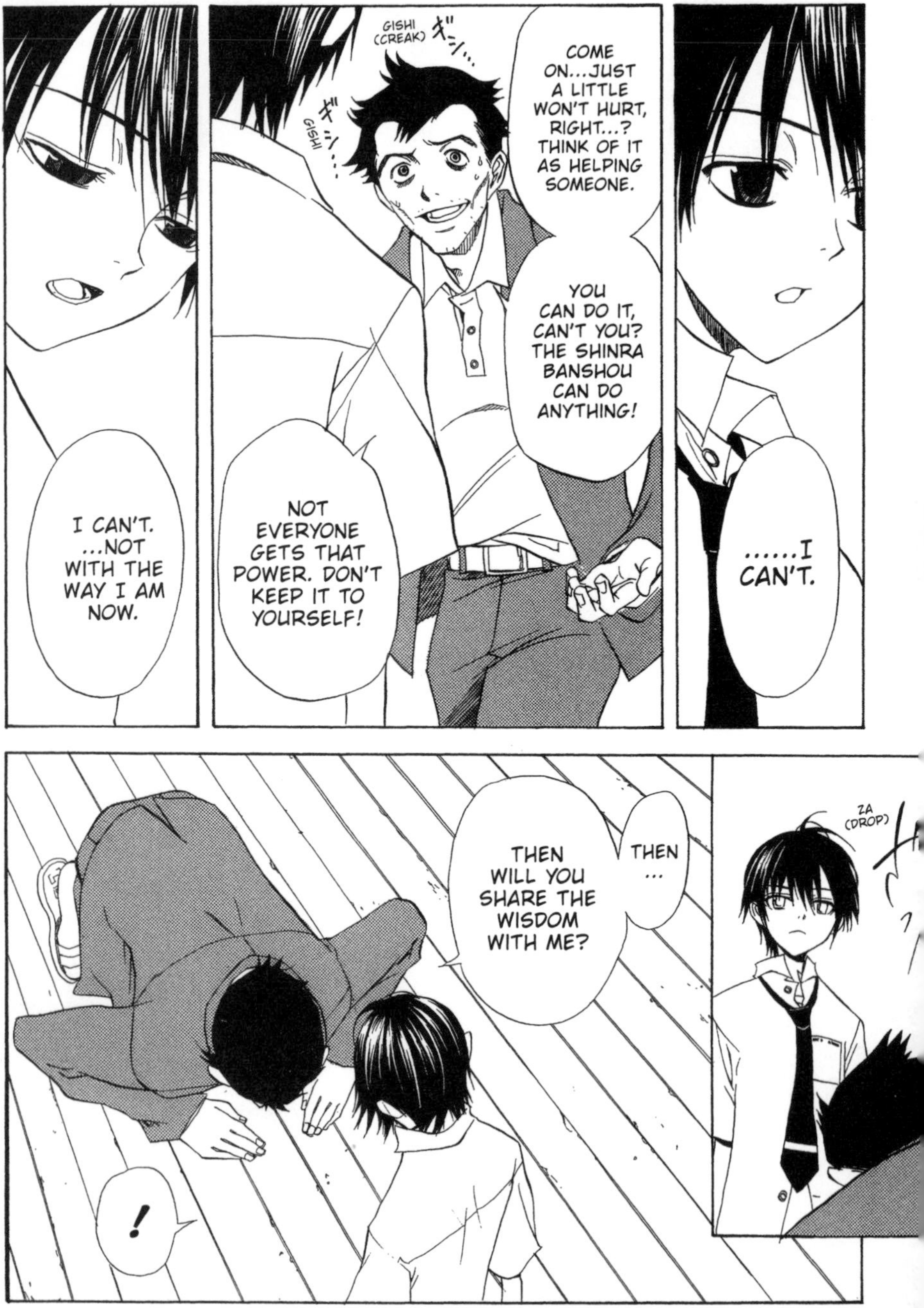
......I CAN'T.
GISHI (CREAK)
GISHI
COME ON...JUST A LITTLE WON'T HURT, RIGHT...? THINK OF IT AS HELPING SOMEONE.
YOU CAN DO IT, CAN'T YOU? THE SHINRA BANSHOU CAN DO ANYTHING!
NOT EVERYONE GETS THAT POWER. DON'T KEEP IT TO YOURSELF!
I CAN'T. ...NOT WITH THE WAY I AM NOW.
ZA (DROP)
THEN ...
THEN WILL YOU SHARE THE WISDOM WITH ME?
!

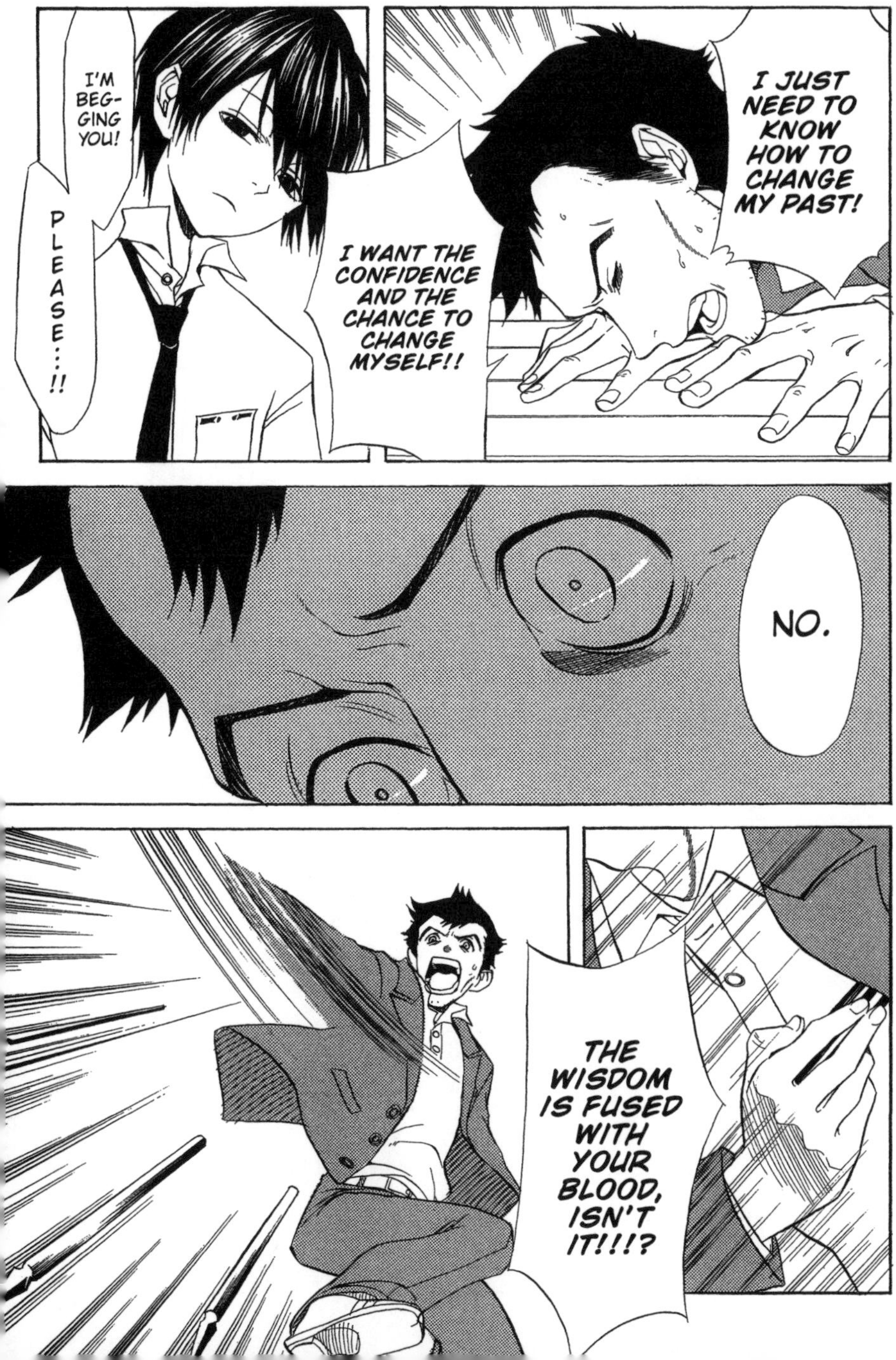
I JUST NEED TO KNOW HOW TO CHANGE MY PAST!
I WANT THE CONFIDENCE AND THE CHANCE TO CHANGE MYSELF!!
I'M BEG-GING YOU!
PLEASE...!!
NO.
THE WISDOM IS FUSED WITH YOUR BLOOD, ISN'T IT!!!?

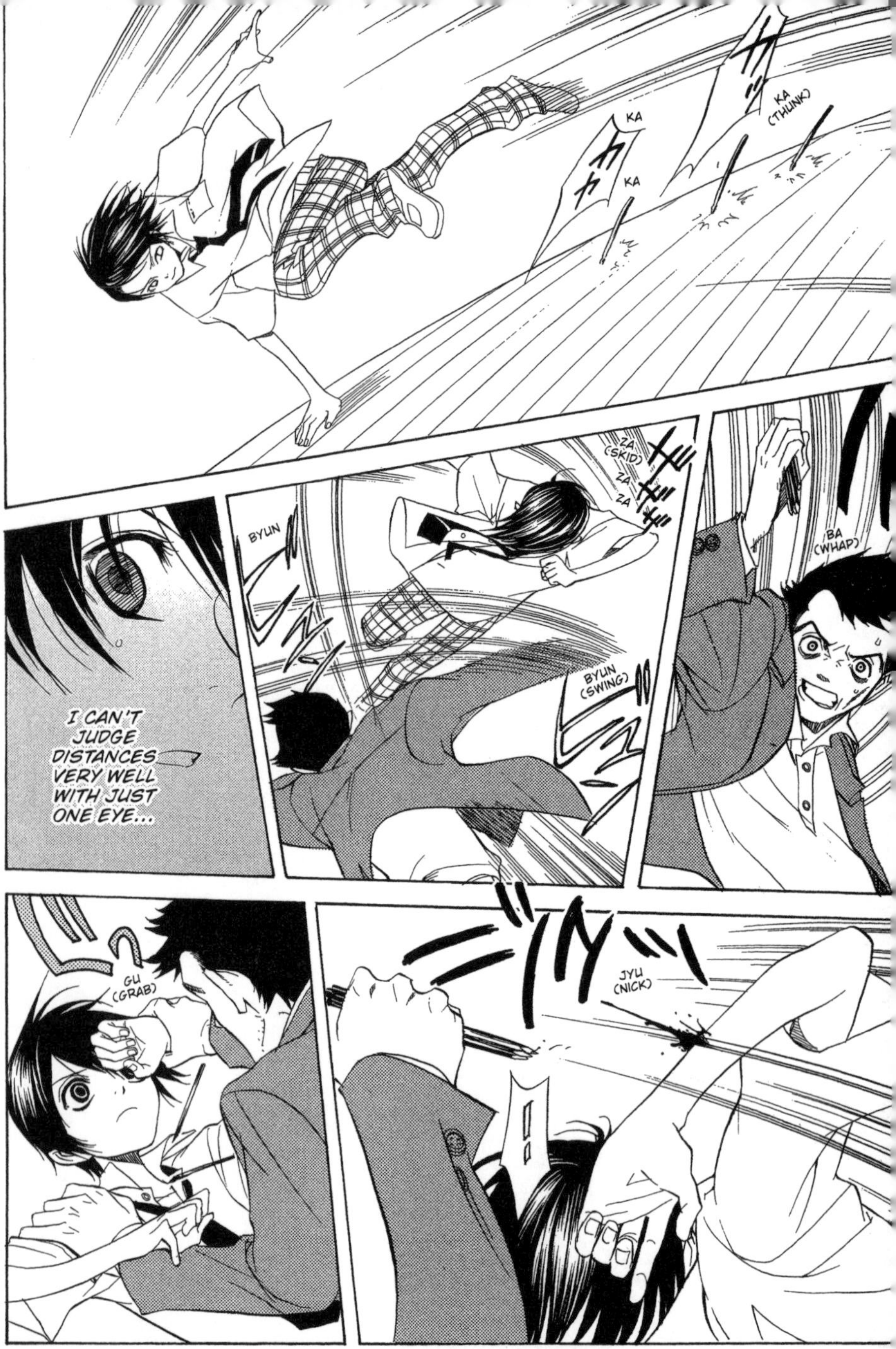
KA (THUNK)
KA
KA
BA (WHAP)
ZA (SKID)
ZA
ZA
BYUN
BYUN (SWING)
I CAN'T JUDGE DISTANCES VERY WELL WITH JUST ONE EYE...
JYU (NICK)
!!
GU (GRAB)

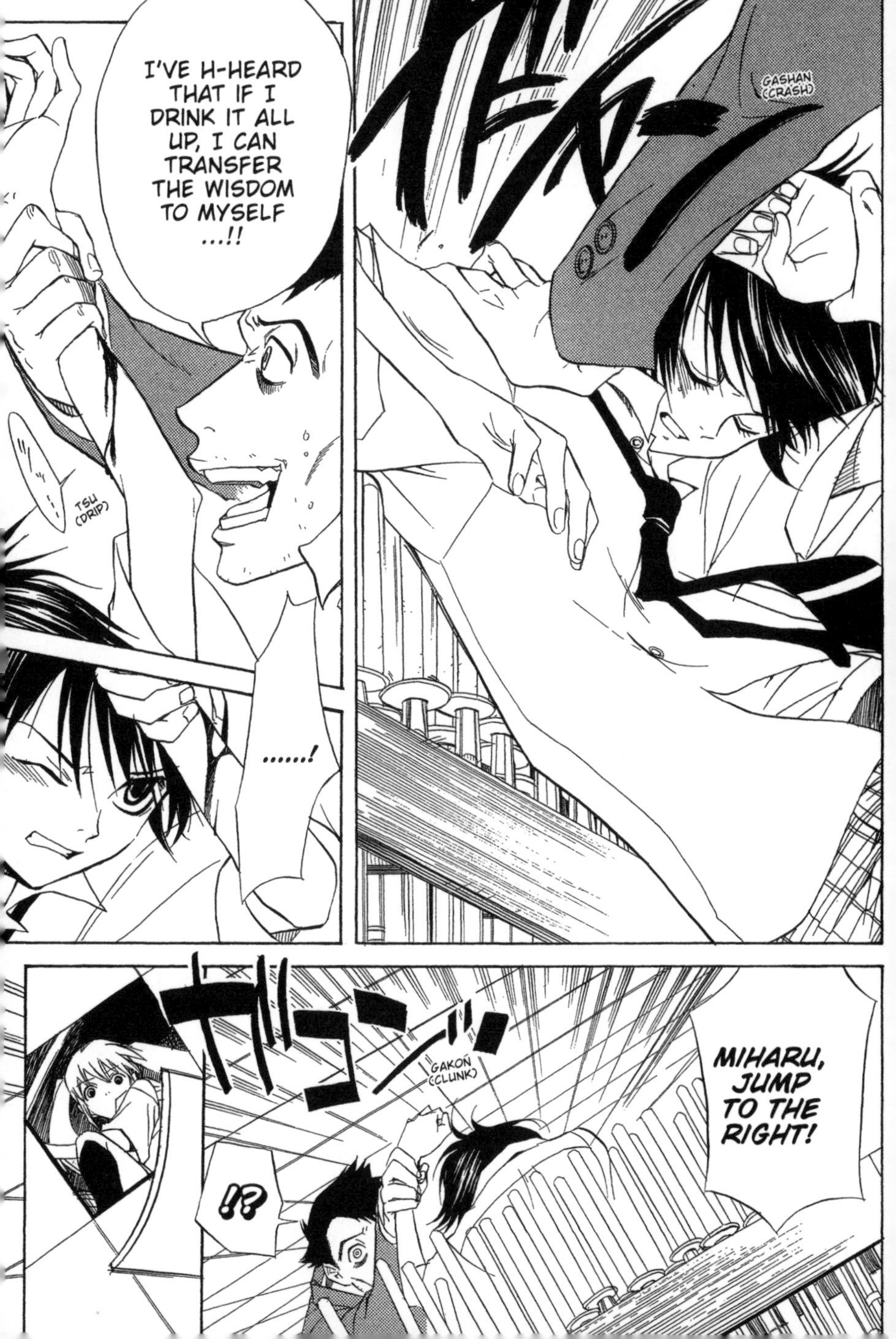
GASHAN (CRASH)
I'VE H-HEARD THAT IF I DRINK IT ALL UP, I CAN TRANSFER THE WISDOM TO MYSELF ...!!
TSU (DRIP)
......!
MIHARU, JUMP TO THE RIGHT!
GAKON (CLUNK)
!?

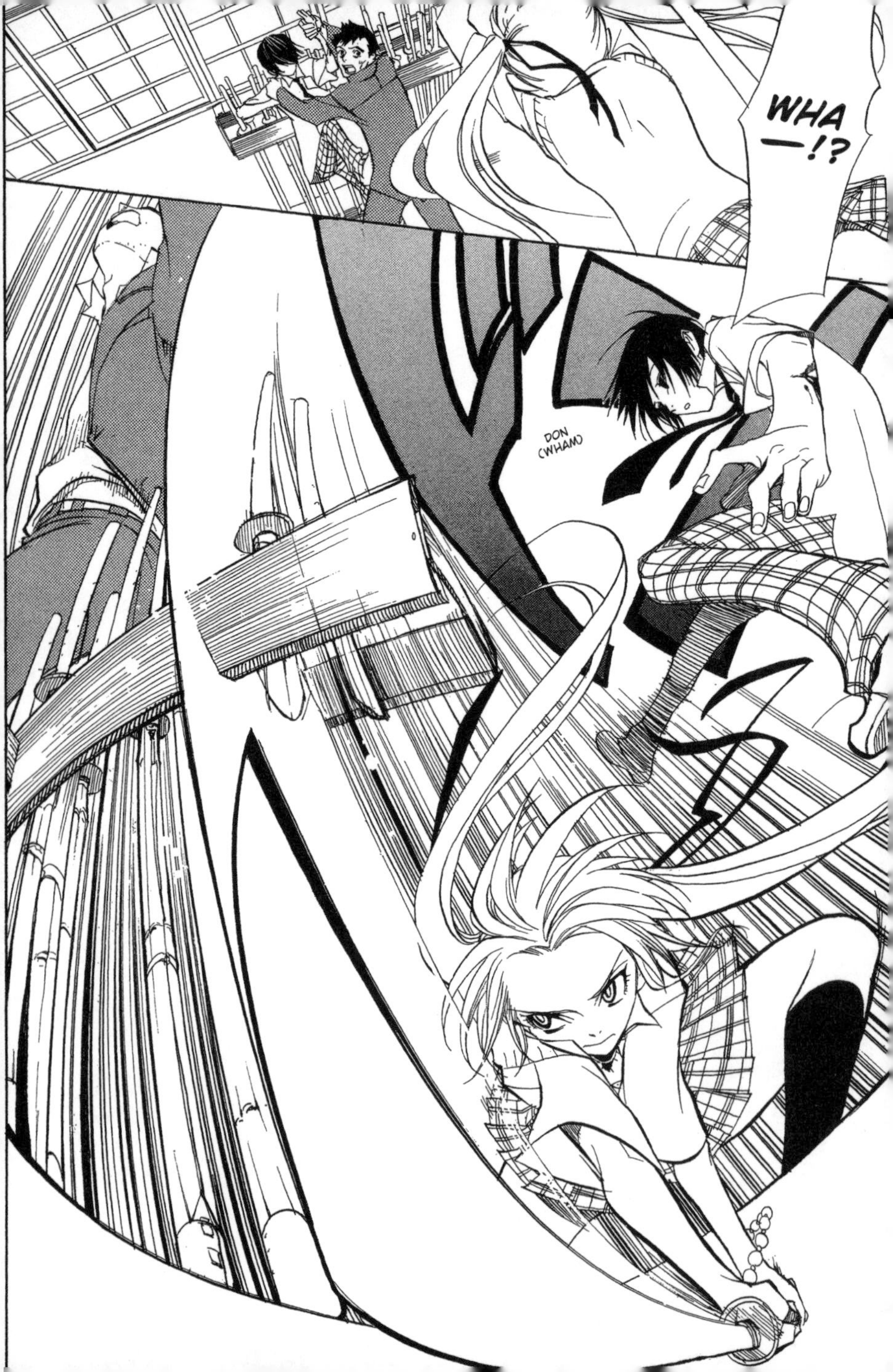
WHA—!?
DON
(WHAM)

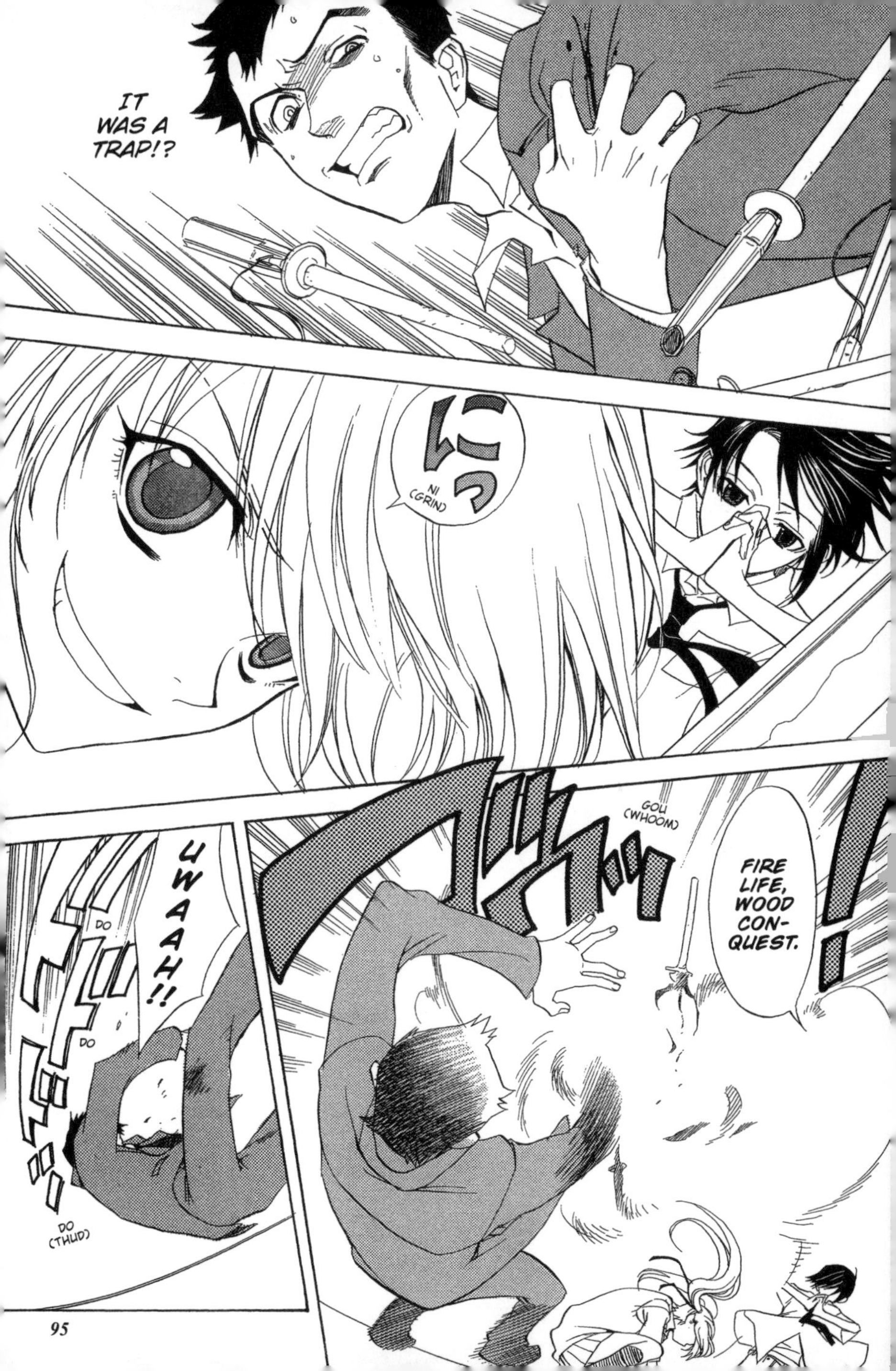
IT WAS A TRAP!?
にっ
NI (GRIN)
GOU (WHOOM)
FIRE LIFE, WOOD CON-QUEST.
UWAAAH!!
DO
DO
DO (THUD)

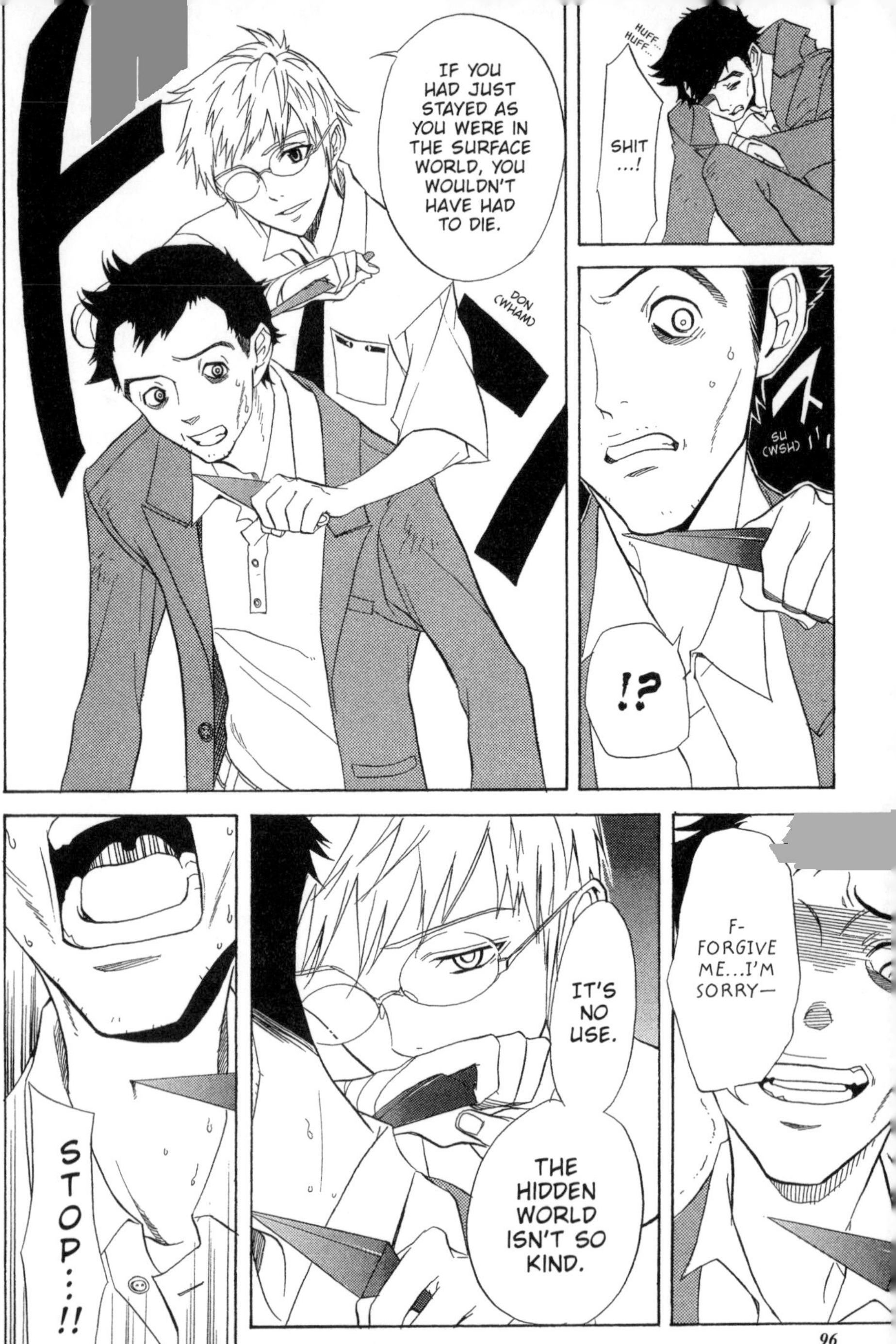
HUFF HUFF...
SHIT ...!
SU (WSH)
!?
IF YOU HAD JUST STAYED AS YOU WERE IN THE SURFACE WORLD, YOU WOULDN'T HAVE HAD TO DIE.
DON (WHAM)
F-FORGIVE ME...I'M SORRY—
IT'S NO USE.
THE HIDDEN WORLD ISN'T SO KIND.
STOP...!!

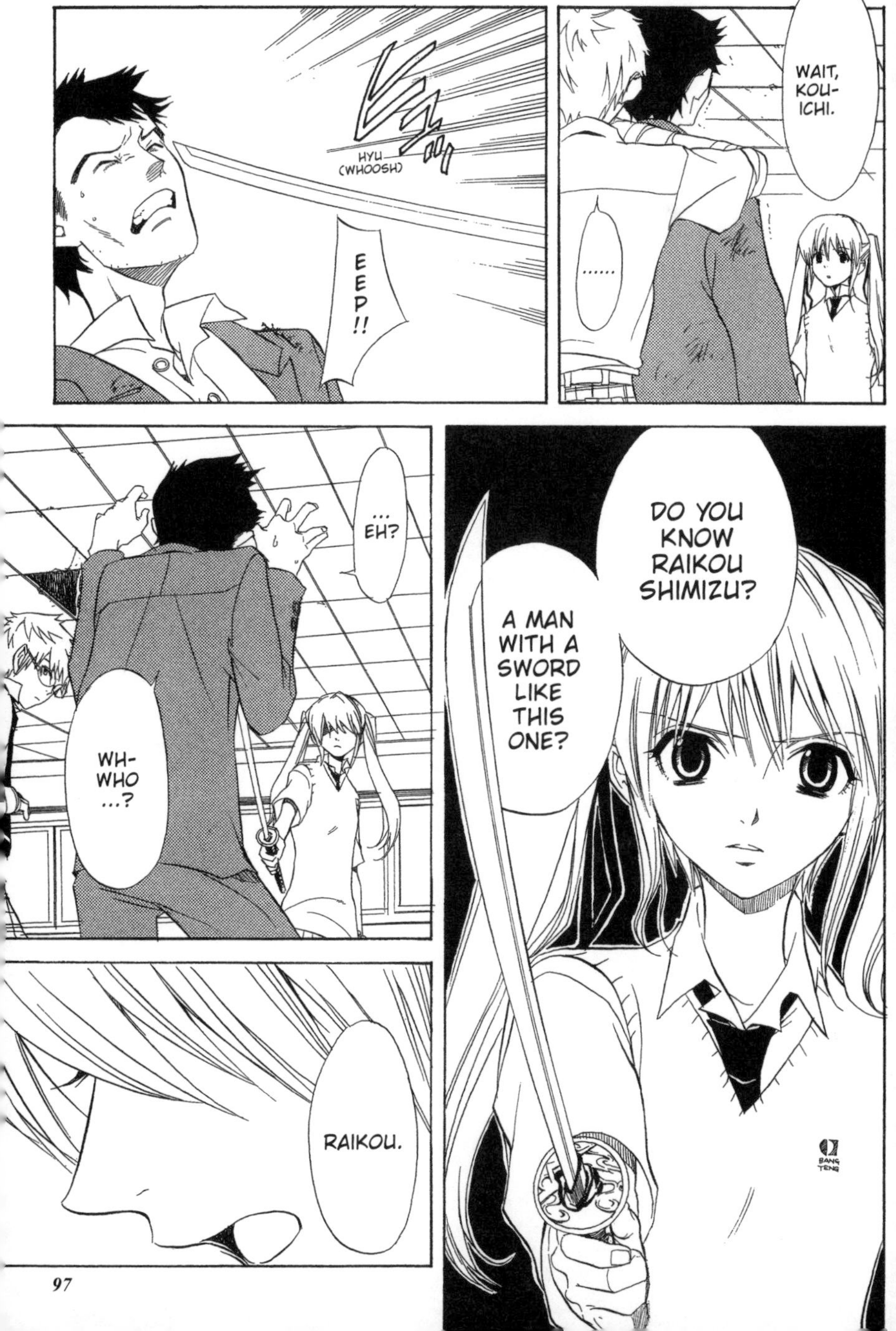
WAIT, KOU-ICHI.
......
HYU (WHOOSH)
EEP!!
DO YOU KNOW RAIKOU SHIMIZU?
A MAN WITH A SWORD LIKE THIS ONE?
BANG TENG
... EH?
WH-WHO ...?
RAIKOU.

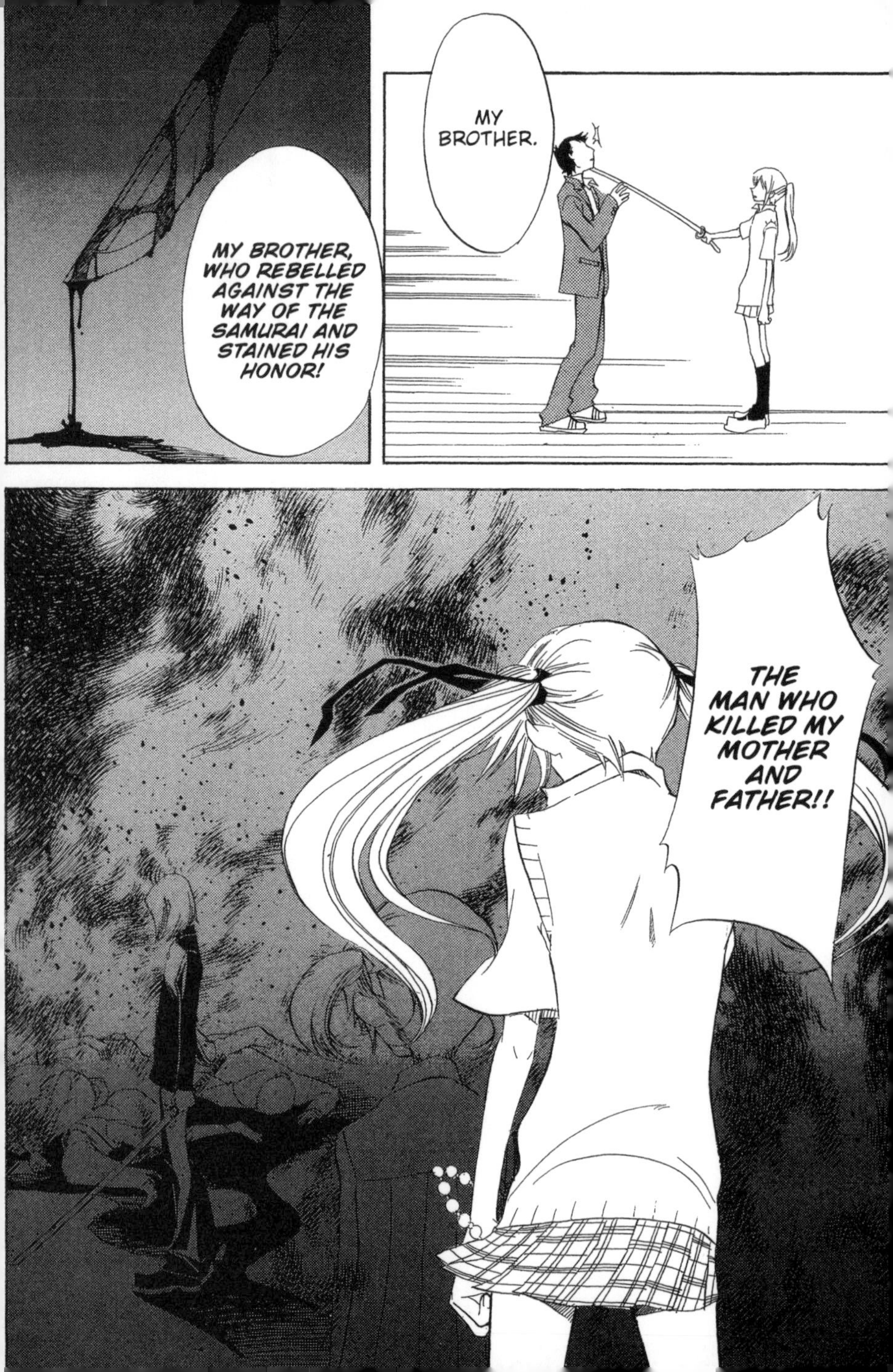
MY BROTHER.
MY BROTHER, WHO REBELLED AGAINST THE WAY OF THE SAMURAI AND STAINED HIS HONOR!
THE MAN WHO KILLED MY MOTHER AND FATHER!!

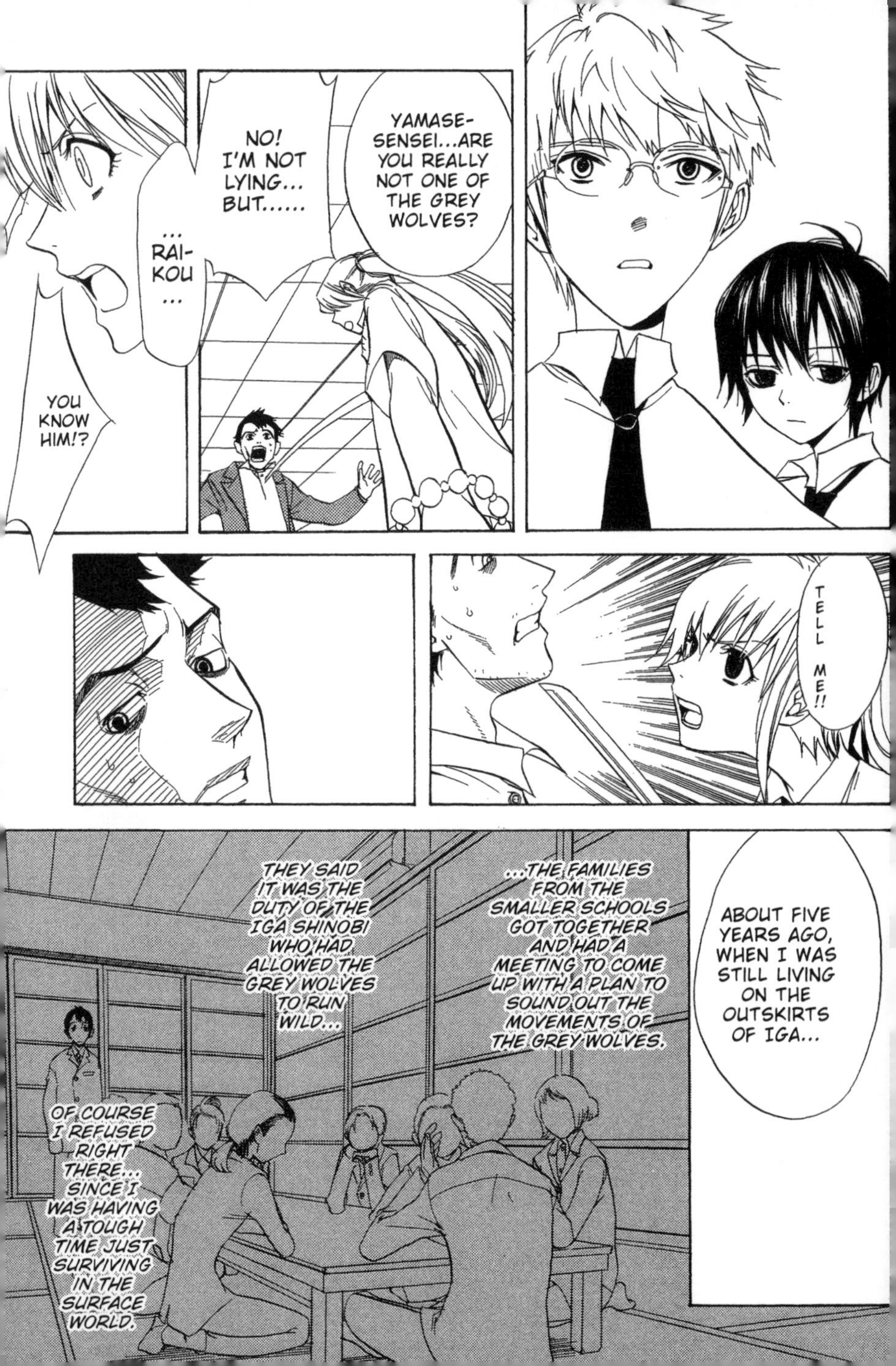
YAMASE-SENSEI...ARE YOU REALLY NOT ONE OF THE GREY WOLVES?
NO! I'M NOT LYING... BUT......
... RAI-KOU ...
YOU KNOW HIM!?
TELL ME!!
ABOUT FIVE YEARS AGO, WHEN I WAS STILL LIVING ON THE OUTSKIRTS OF IGA...
...THE FAMILIES FROM THE SMALLER SCHOOLS GOT TOGETHER AND HAD A MEETING TO COME UP WITH A PLAN TO SOUND OUT THE MOVEMENTS OF THE GREY WOLVES.
THEY SAID IT WAS THE DUTY OF THE IGA SHINOBI WHO HAD ALLOWED THE GREY WOLVES TO RUN WILD...
OF COURSE I REFUSED RIGHT THERE... SINCE I WAS HAVING A TOUGH TIME JUST SURVIVING IN THE SURFACE WORLD.

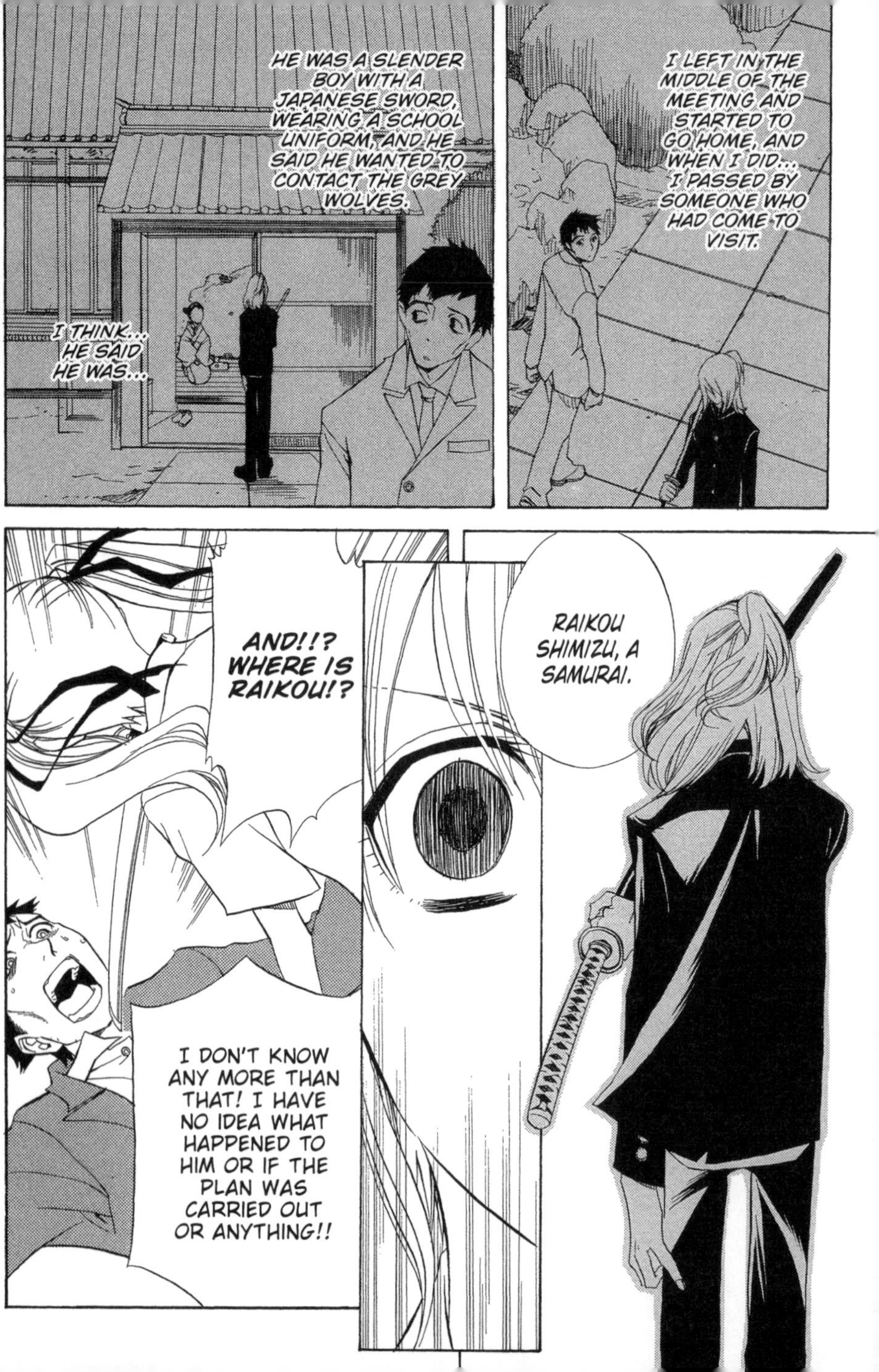
I LEFT IN THE MIDDLE OF THE MEETING AND STARTED TO GO HOME, AND WHEN I DID... I PASSED BY SOMEONE WHO HAD COME TO VISIT.
HE WAS A SLENDER BOY WITH A JAPANESE SWORD, WEARING A SCHOOL UNIFORM, AND HE SAID HE WANTED TO CONTACT THE GREY WOLVES.
I THINK... HE SAID HE WAS...
RAIKOU SHIMIZU, A SAMURAI.
AND!!? WHERE IS RAIKOU!?
I DON'T KNOW ANY MORE THAN THAT! I HAVE NO IDEA WHAT HAPPENED TO HIM OR IF THE PLAN WAS CARRIED OUT OR ANYTHING!!

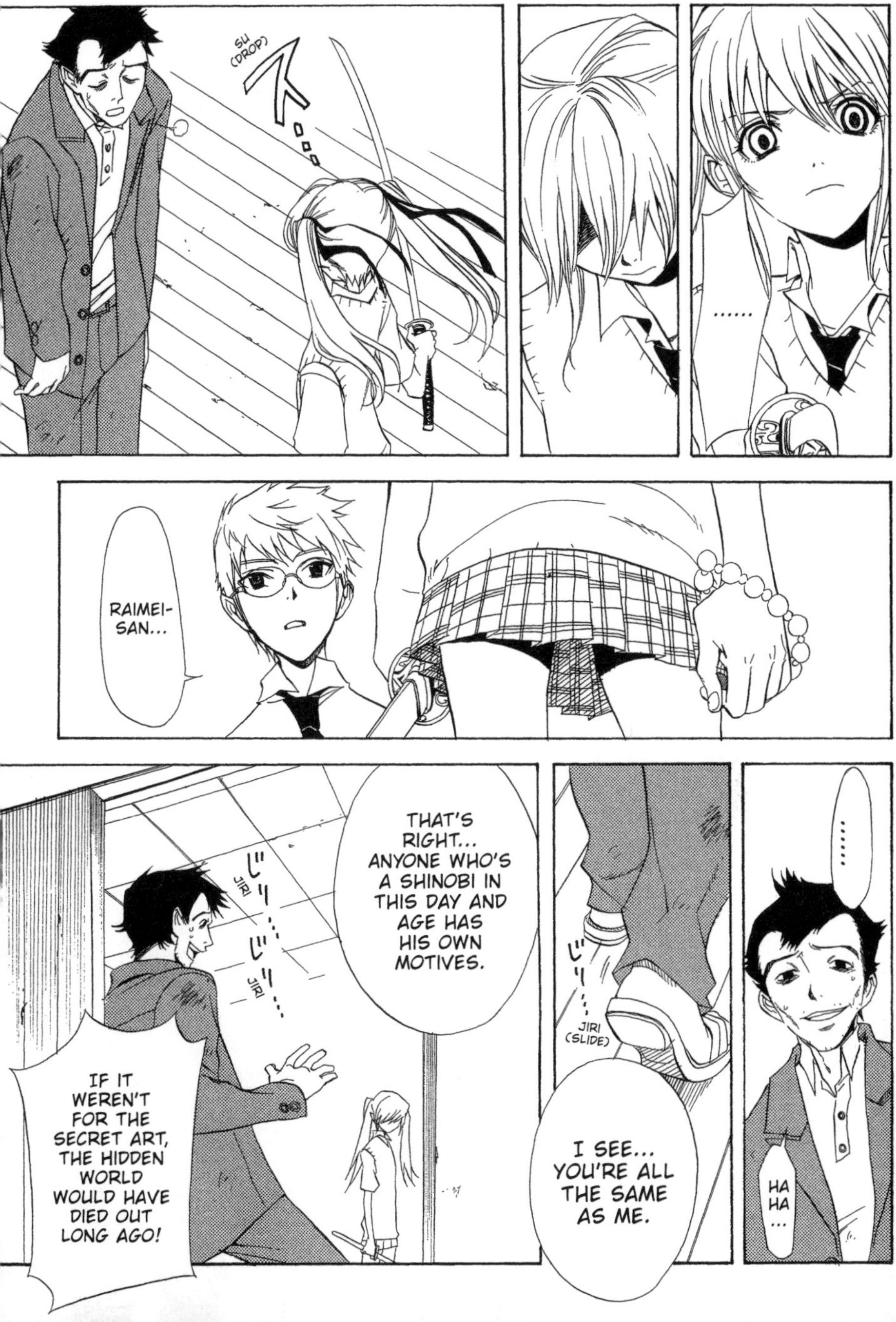
......
SU (DROP)
RAIMEI-SAN...
......
HA HA ...
JIRI (SLIDE)
I SEE... YOU'RE ALL THE SAME AS ME.
THAT'S RIGHT... ANYONE WHO'S A SHINOBI IN THIS DAY AND AGE HAS HIS OWN MOTIVES.
JIRI
JIRI
IF IT WEREN'T FOR THE SECRET ART, THE HIDDEN WORLD WOULD HAVE DIED OUT LONG AGO!

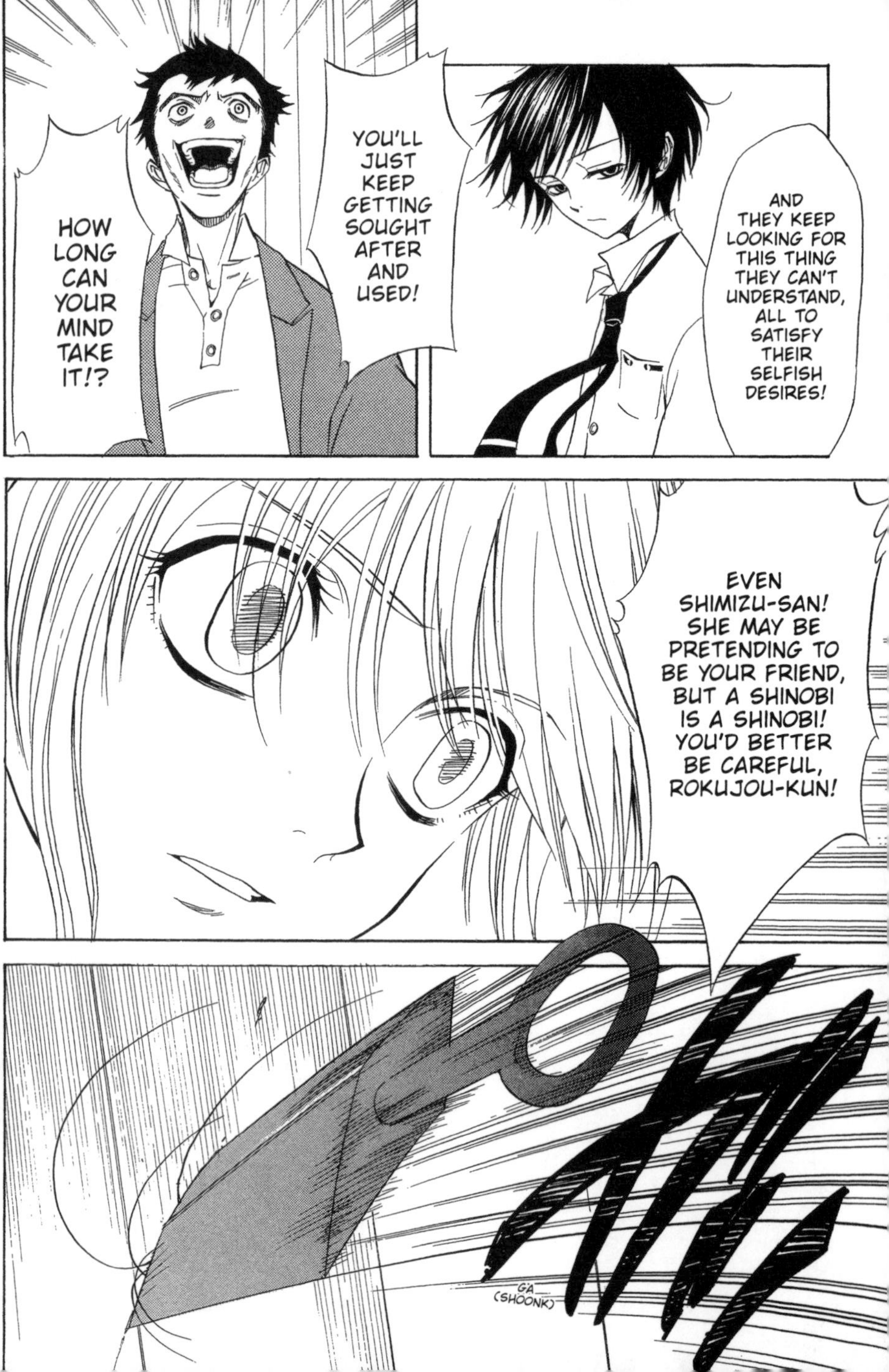
AND THEY KEEP LOOKING FOR THIS THING THEY CAN'T UNDERSTAND, ALL TO SATISFY THEIR SELFISH DESIRES!
YOU'LL JUST KEEP GETTING SOUGHT AFTER AND USED!
HOW LONG CAN YOUR MIND TAKE IT!?
EVEN SHIMIZU-SAN! SHE MAY BE PRETENDING TO BE YOUR FRIEND, BUT A SHINOBI IS A SHINOBI! YOU'D BETTER BE CAREFUL, ROKUJOU-KUN!
GA (SHOONK)

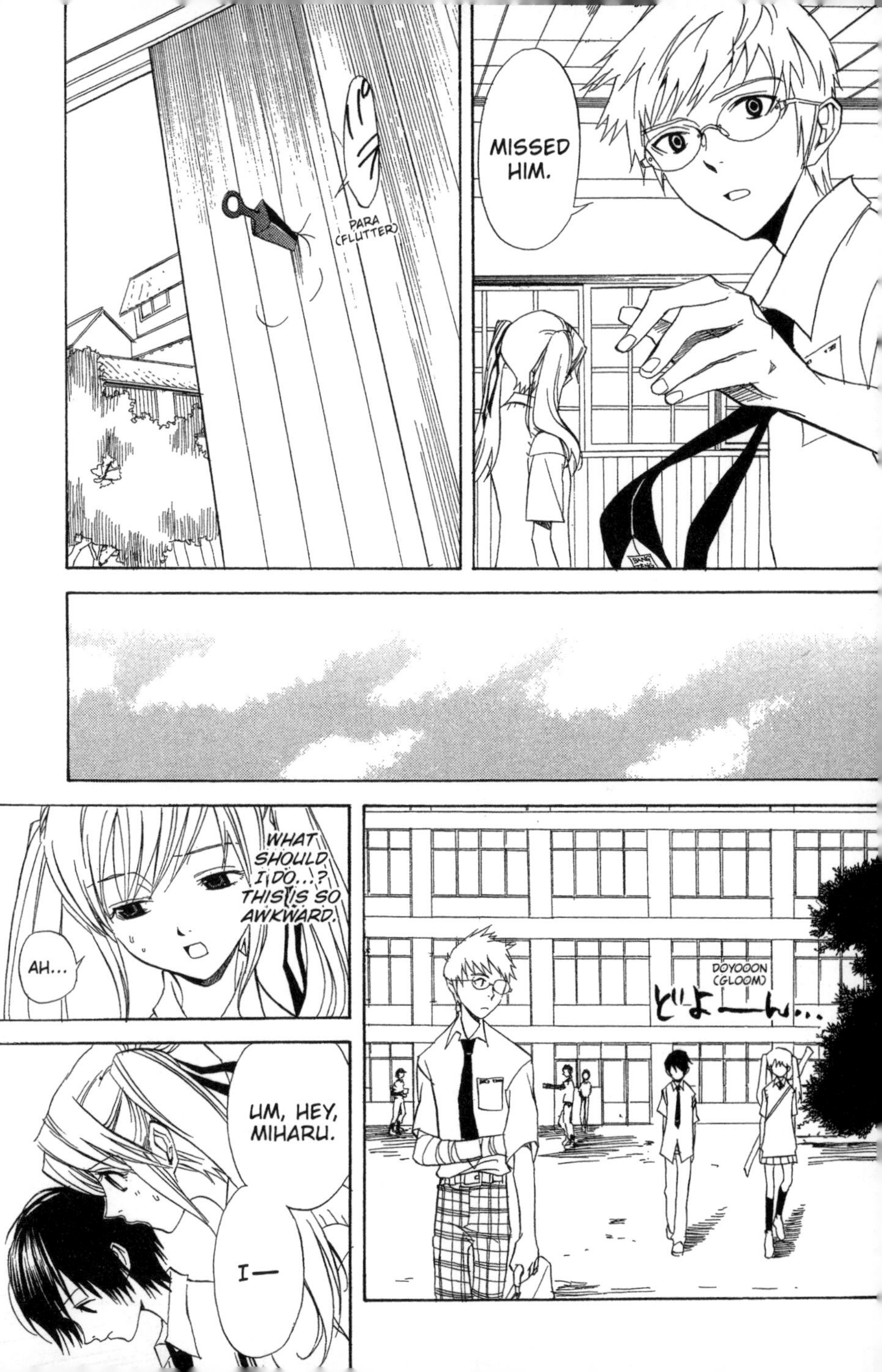
MISSED HIM.
PARA (FLUTTER)
DOYOOON (GLOOM)
どよーん..
WHAT SHOULD I DO...? THIS IS SO AWKWARD.
AH...
UM, HEY, MIHARU.
I—

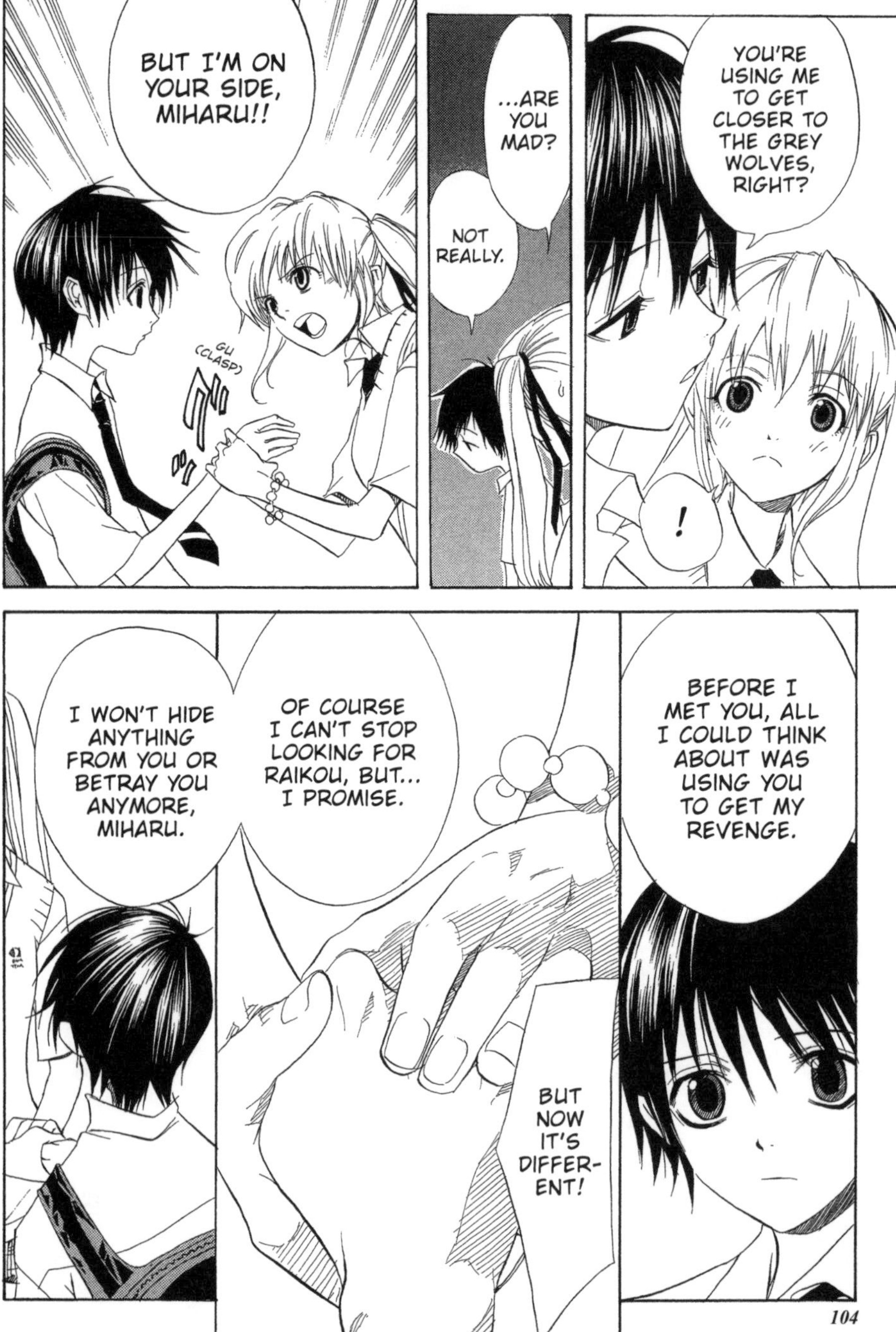
YOU'RE USING ME TO GET CLOSER TO THE GREY WOLVES, RIGHT?
!
...ARE YOU MAD?
NOT REALLY.
GU (CLASP)
BUT I'M ON YOUR SIDE, MIHARU!!
BEFORE I MET YOU, ALL I COULD THINK ABOUT WAS USING YOU TO GET MY REVENGE.
BUT NOW IT'S DIFFER-ENT!
OF COURSE I CAN'T STOP LOOKING FOR RAIKOU, BUT... I PROMISE.
I WON'T HIDE ANYTHING FROM YOU OR BETRAY YOU ANYMORE, MIHARU.

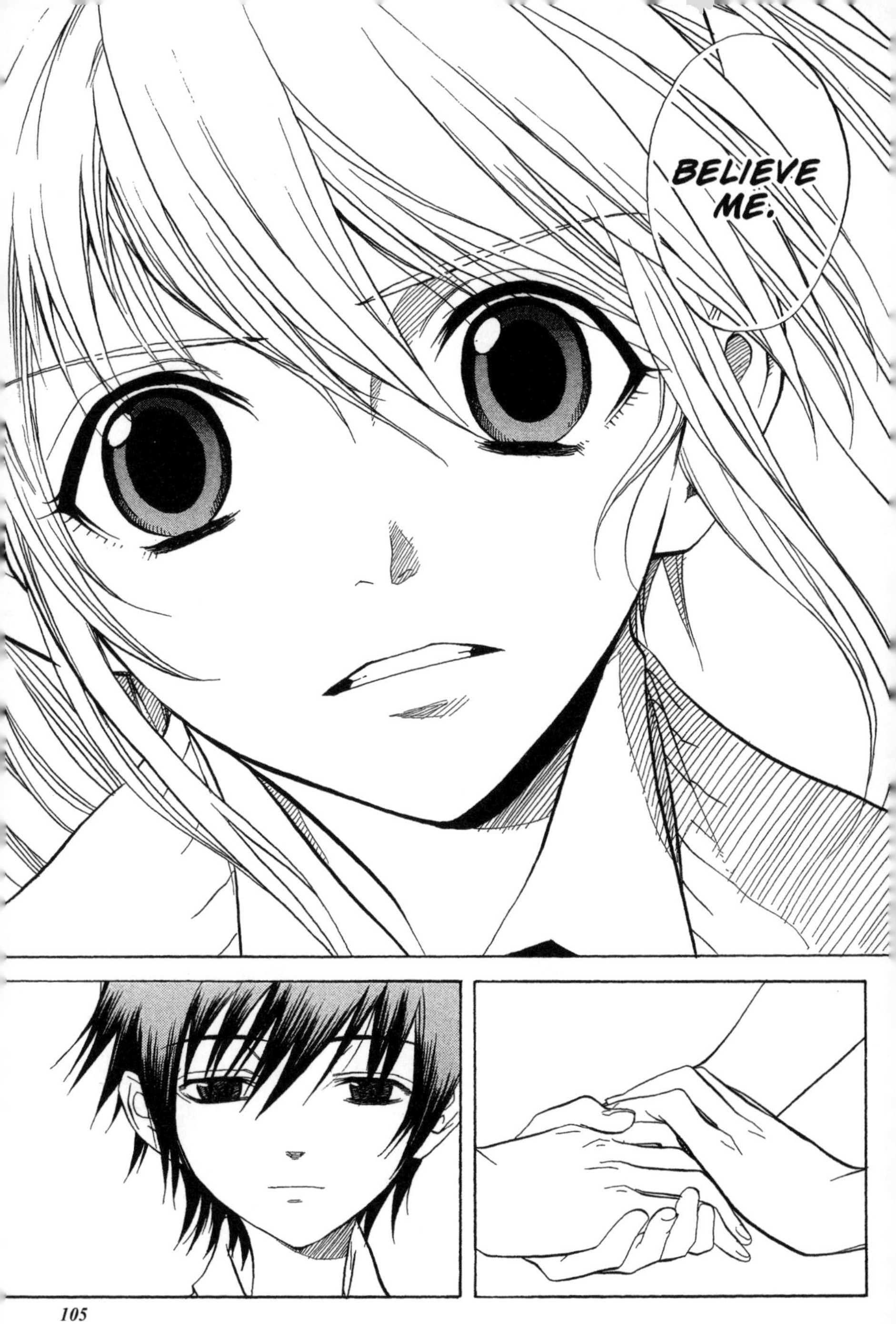
BELIEVE ME.

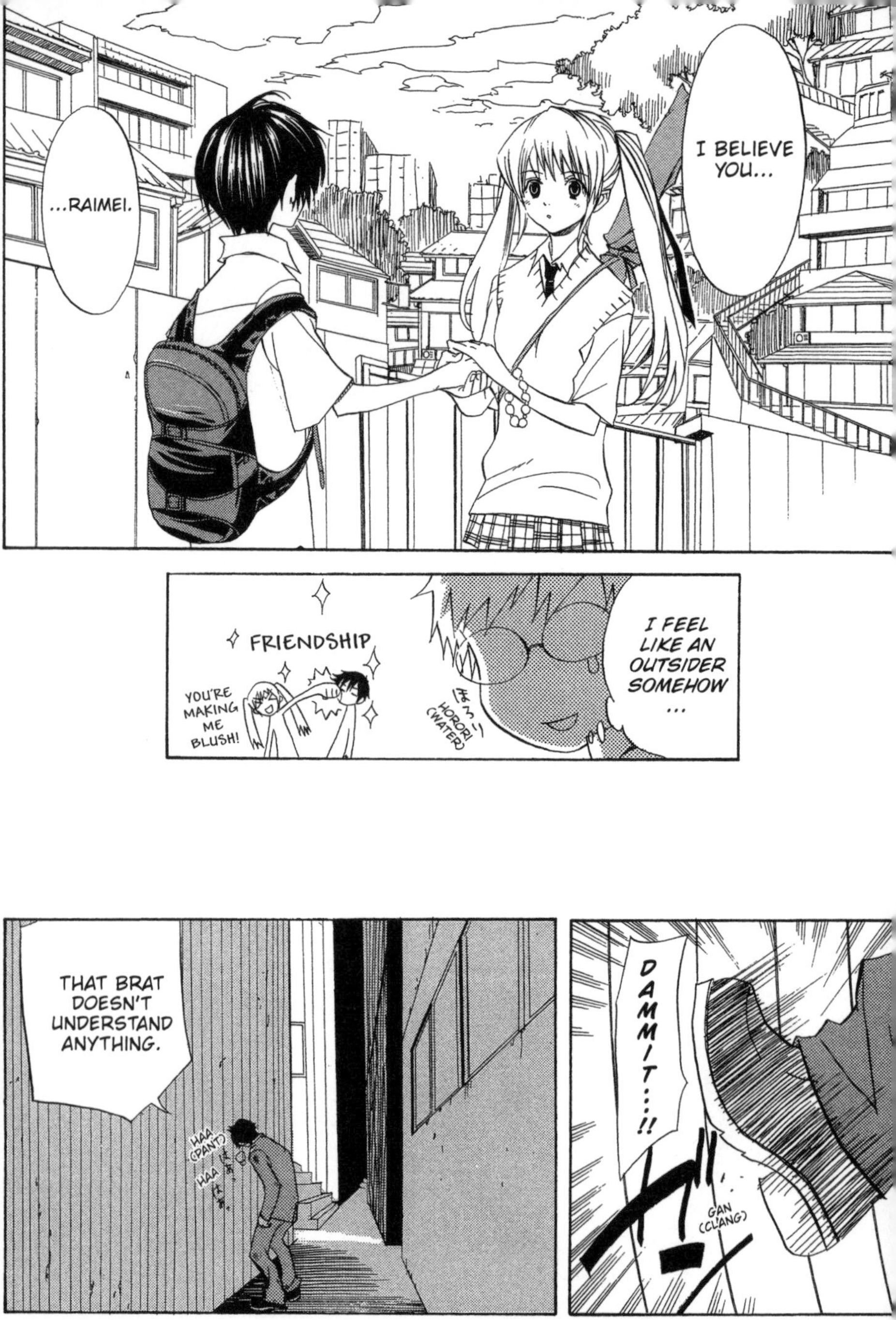
I BELIEVE YOU...
...RAIMEI.
I FEEL LIKE AN OUTSIDER SOMEHOW ...
HORORI (WATER)
FRIENDSHIP
YOU'RE MAKING ME BLUSH!
DAMMIT...!!
GAN (CLANG)
THAT BRAT DOESN'T UNDERSTAND ANYTHING.
HAA (PANT) HAA

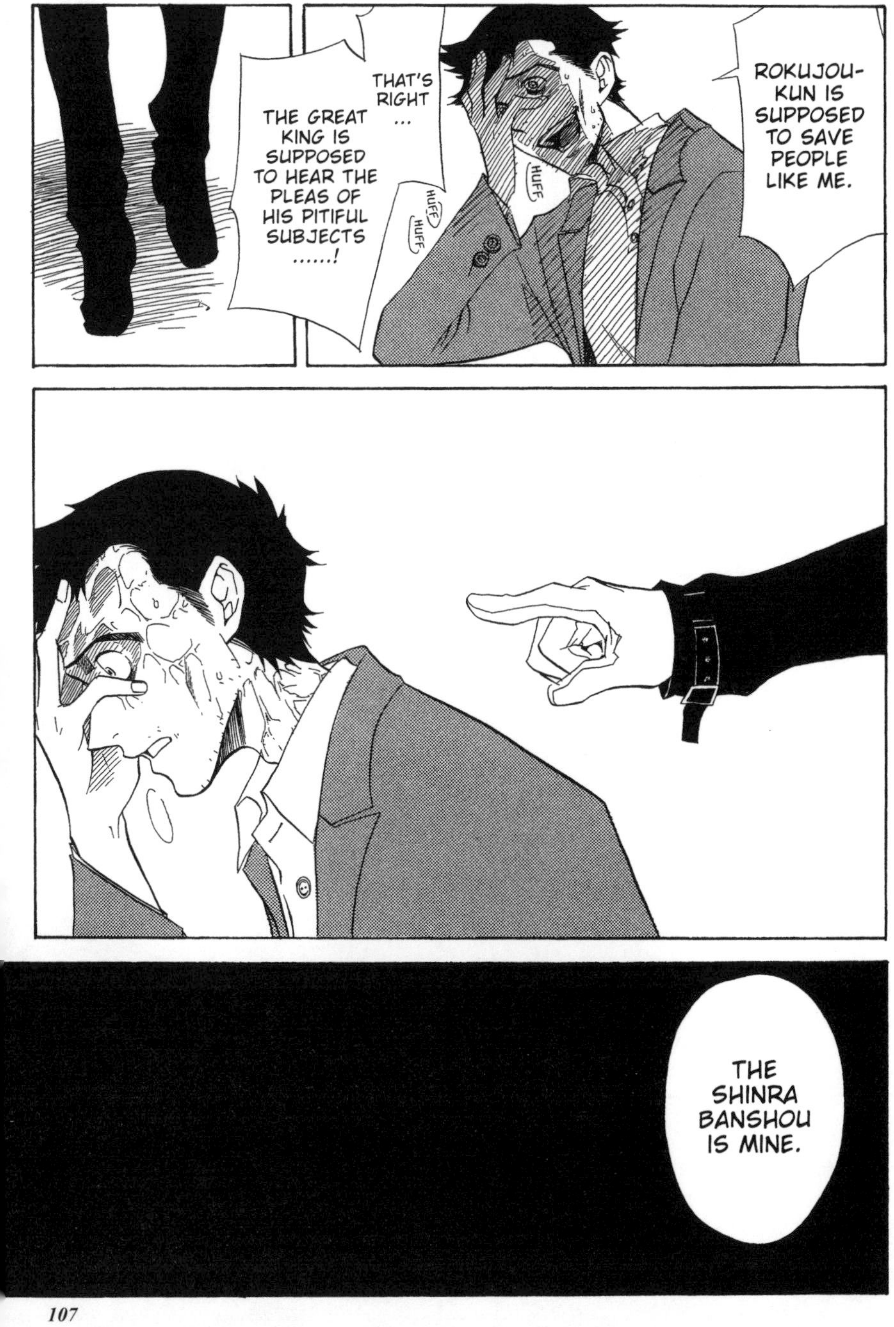
ROKUJOU-KUN IS SUPPOSED TO SAVE PEOPLE LIKE ME.
THAT'S RIGHT ...
HUFF HUFF HUFF
THE GREAT KING IS SUPPOSED TO HEAR THE PLEAS OF HIS PITIFUL SUBJECTS ......!
THE SHINRA BANSHOU IS MINE.

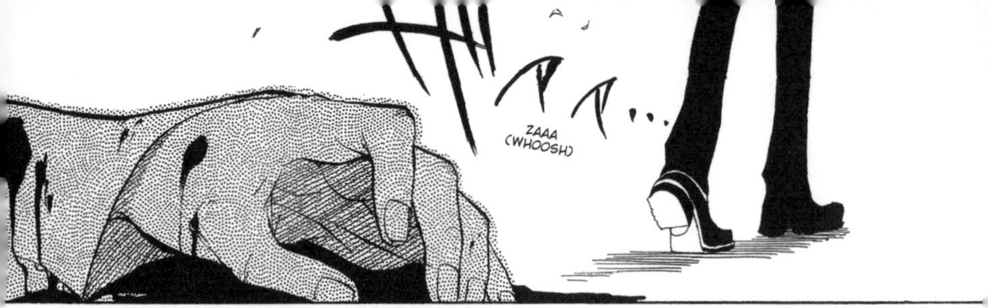
ザァァ...
ZAAA
(WHOOSH)

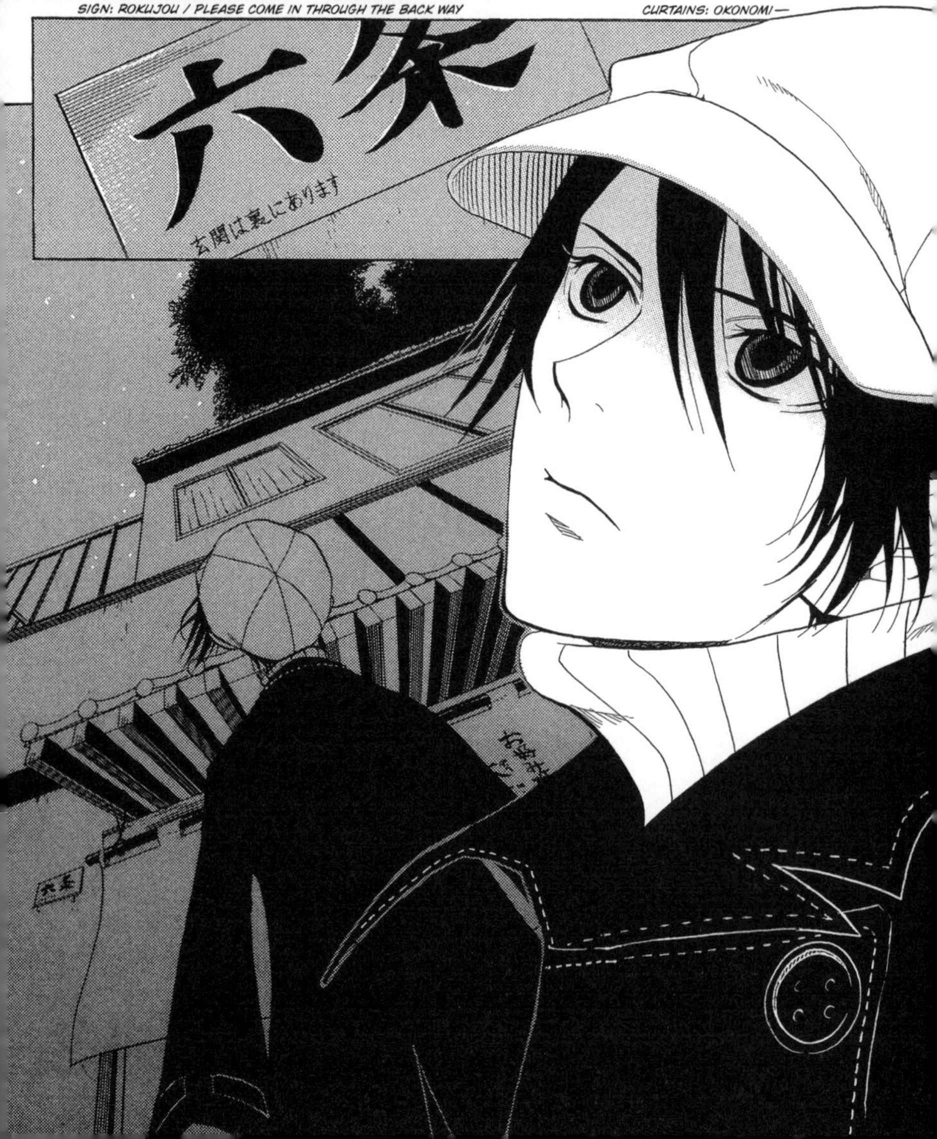
SIGN: ROKUJOU / PLEASE COME IN THROUGH THE BACK WAY
CURTAINS: OKONOMI—
六条
玄関は裏にあります

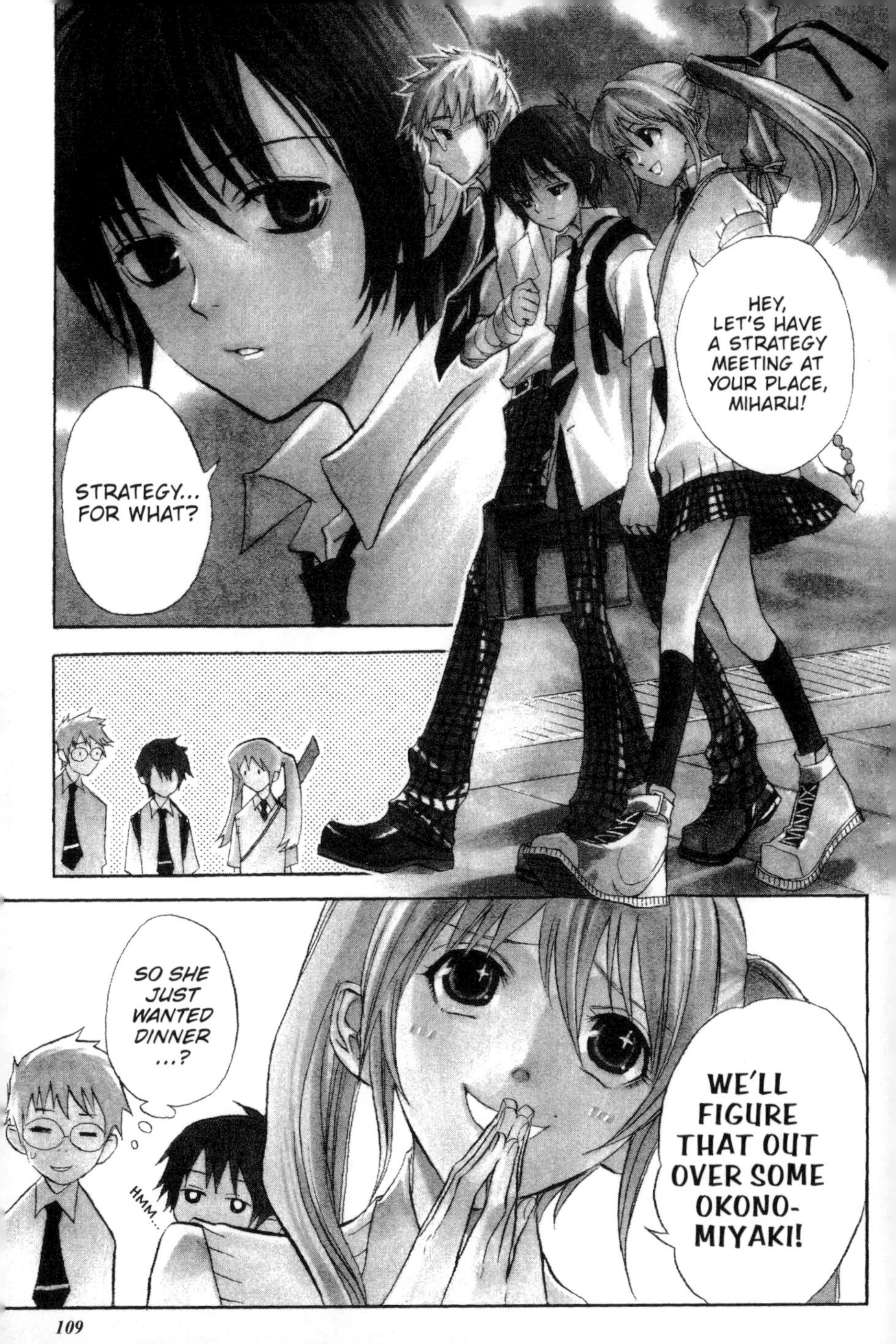
HEY, LET'S HAVE A STRATEGY MEETING AT YOUR PLACE, MIHARU!
STRATEGY... FOR WHAT?
WE'LL FIGURE THAT OUT OVER SOME OKONO-MIYAKI!
SO SHE JUST WANTED DINNER ...?
HMM...

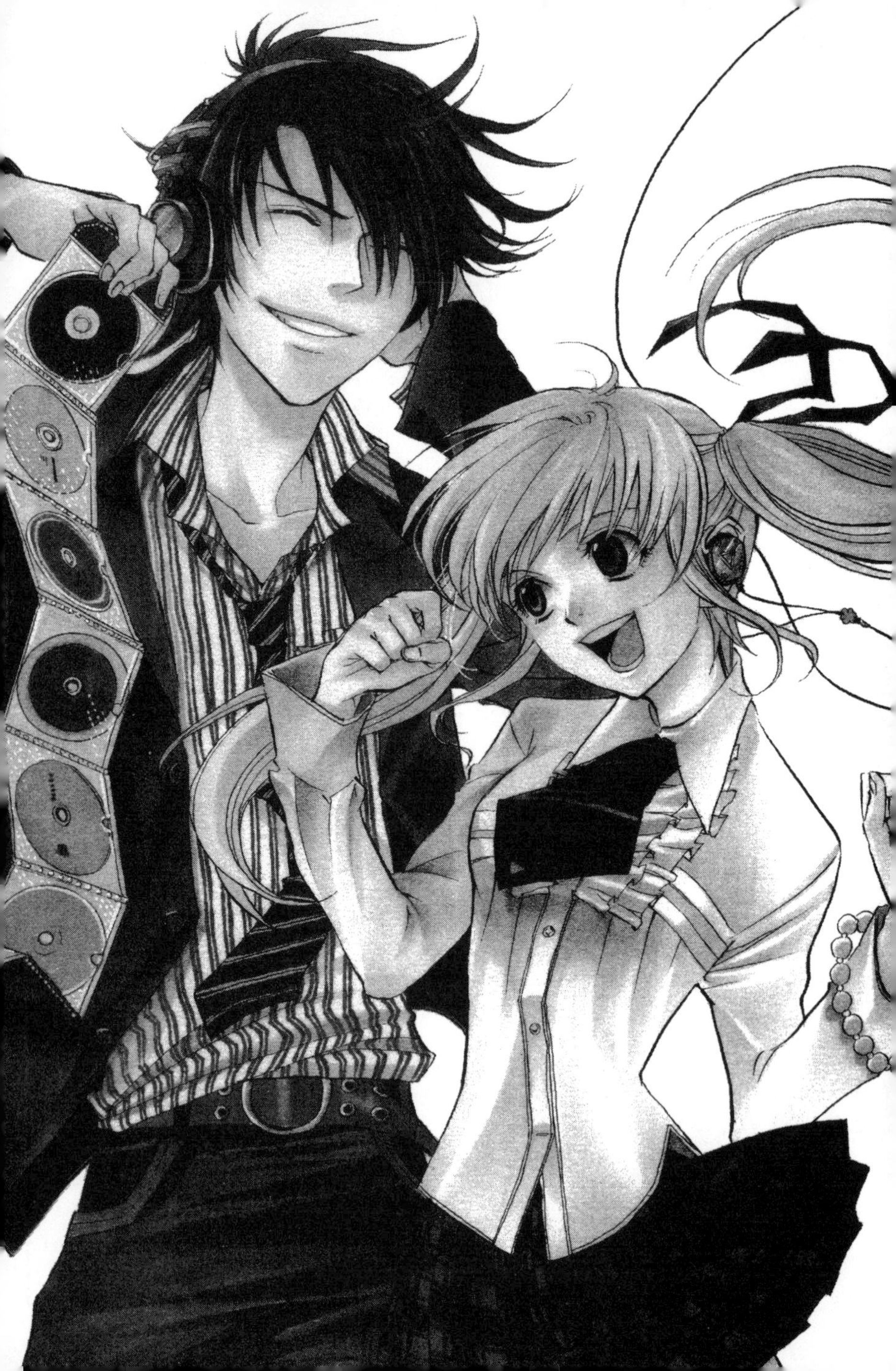

CHAPTER NINE: PALMS

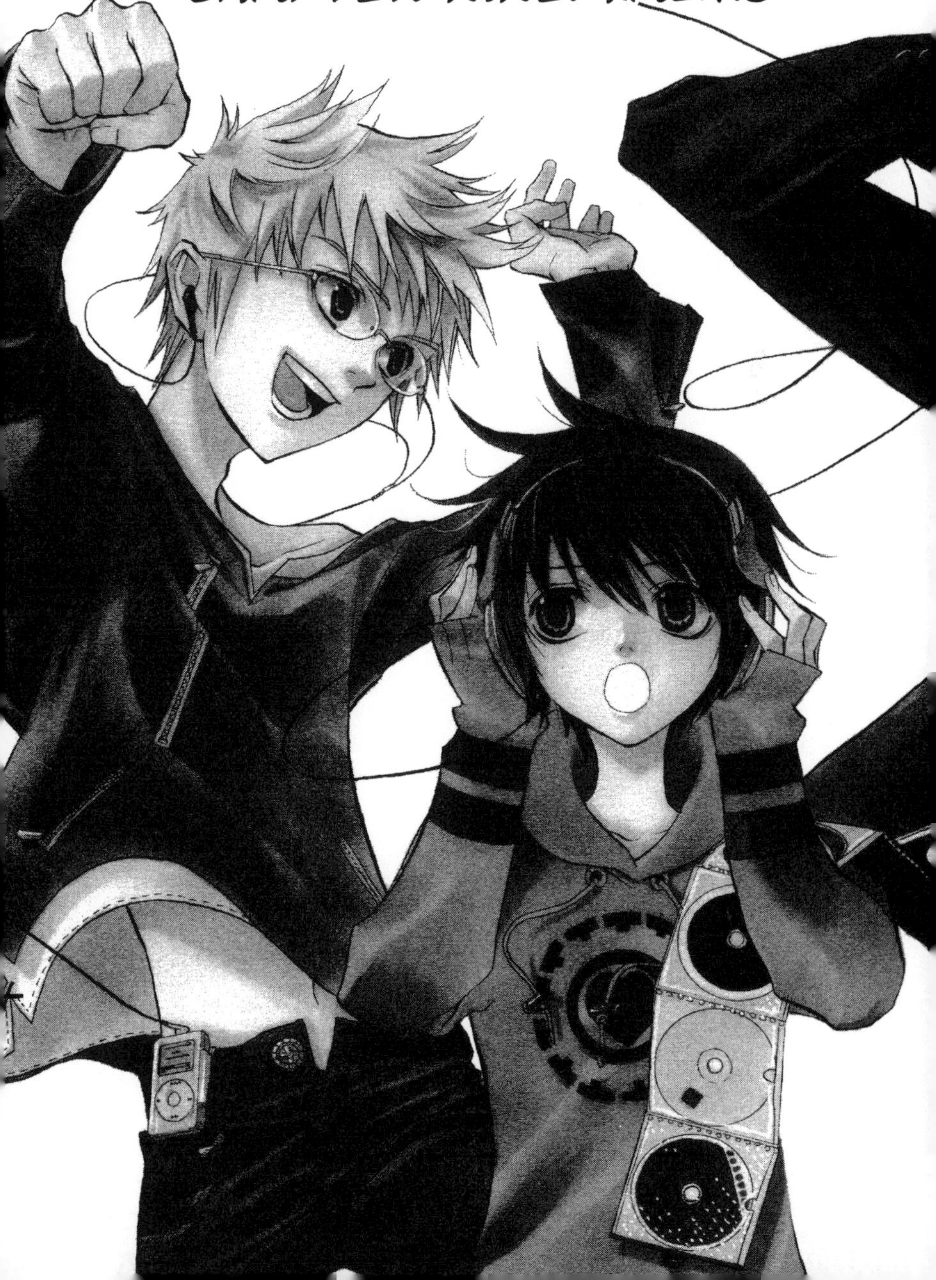

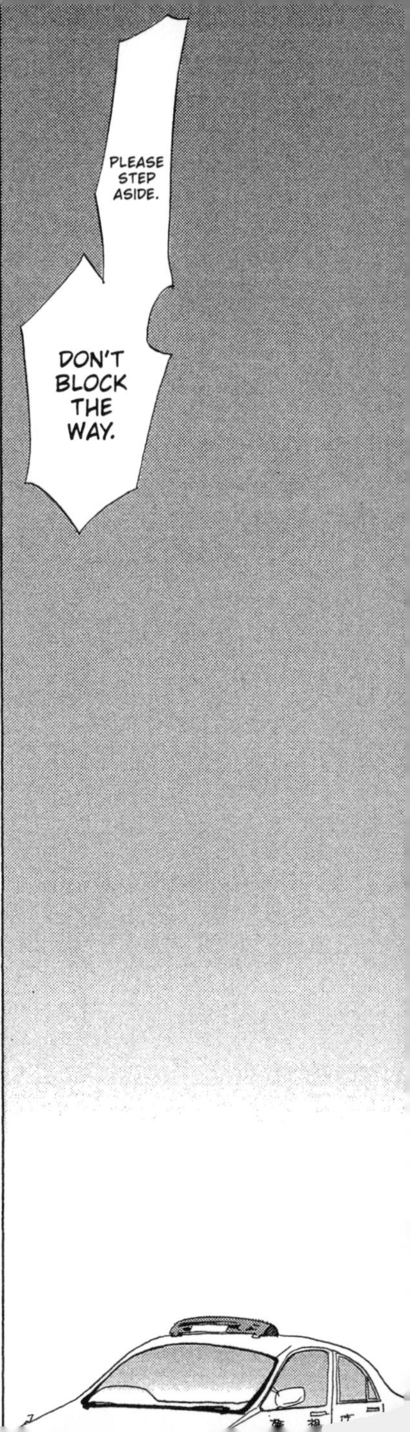
PLEASE STEP ASIDE.
DON'T BLOCK THE WAY.

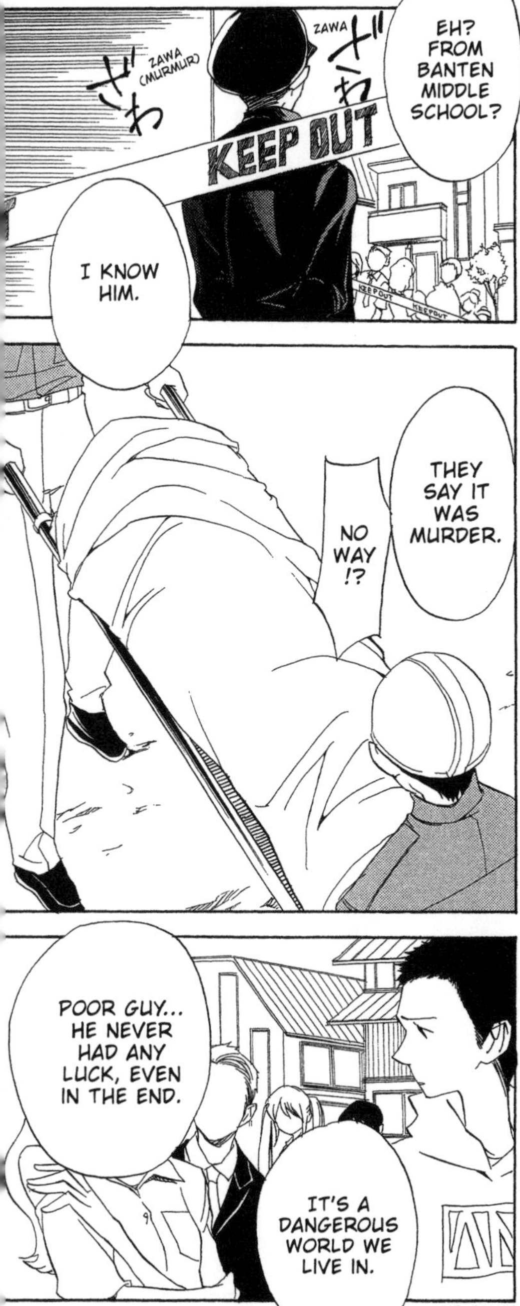
EH? FROM BANTEN MIDDLE SCHOOL?
ZAWA
ZAWA (MURMUR)
KEEP OUT
I KNOW HIM.
THEY SAY IT WAS MURDER.
NO WAY !?
POOR GUY... HE NEVER HAD ANY LUCK, EVEN IN THE END.
IT'S A DANGEROUS WORLD WE LIVE IN.

CAR: POLICE

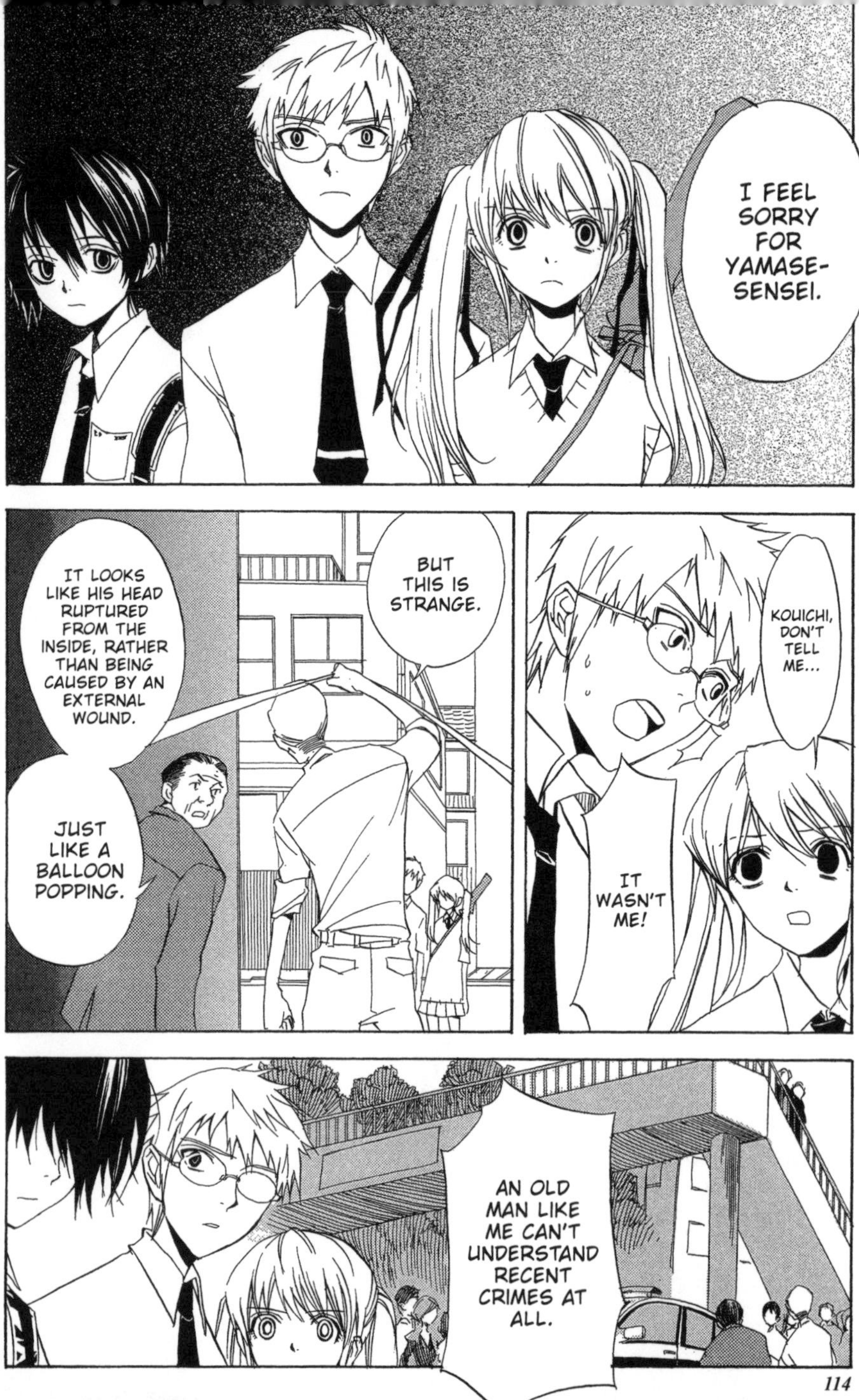
I FEEL SORRY FOR YAMASE-SENSEI.
KOUICHI, DON'T TELL ME...
IT WASN'T ME!
BUT THIS IS STRANGE.
IT LOOKS LIKE HIS HEAD RUPTURED FROM THE INSIDE, RATHER THAN BEING CAUSED BY AN EXTERNAL WOUND.
JUST LIKE A BALLOON POPPING.
AN OLD MAN LIKE ME CAN'T UNDERSTAND RECENT CRIMES AT ALL.

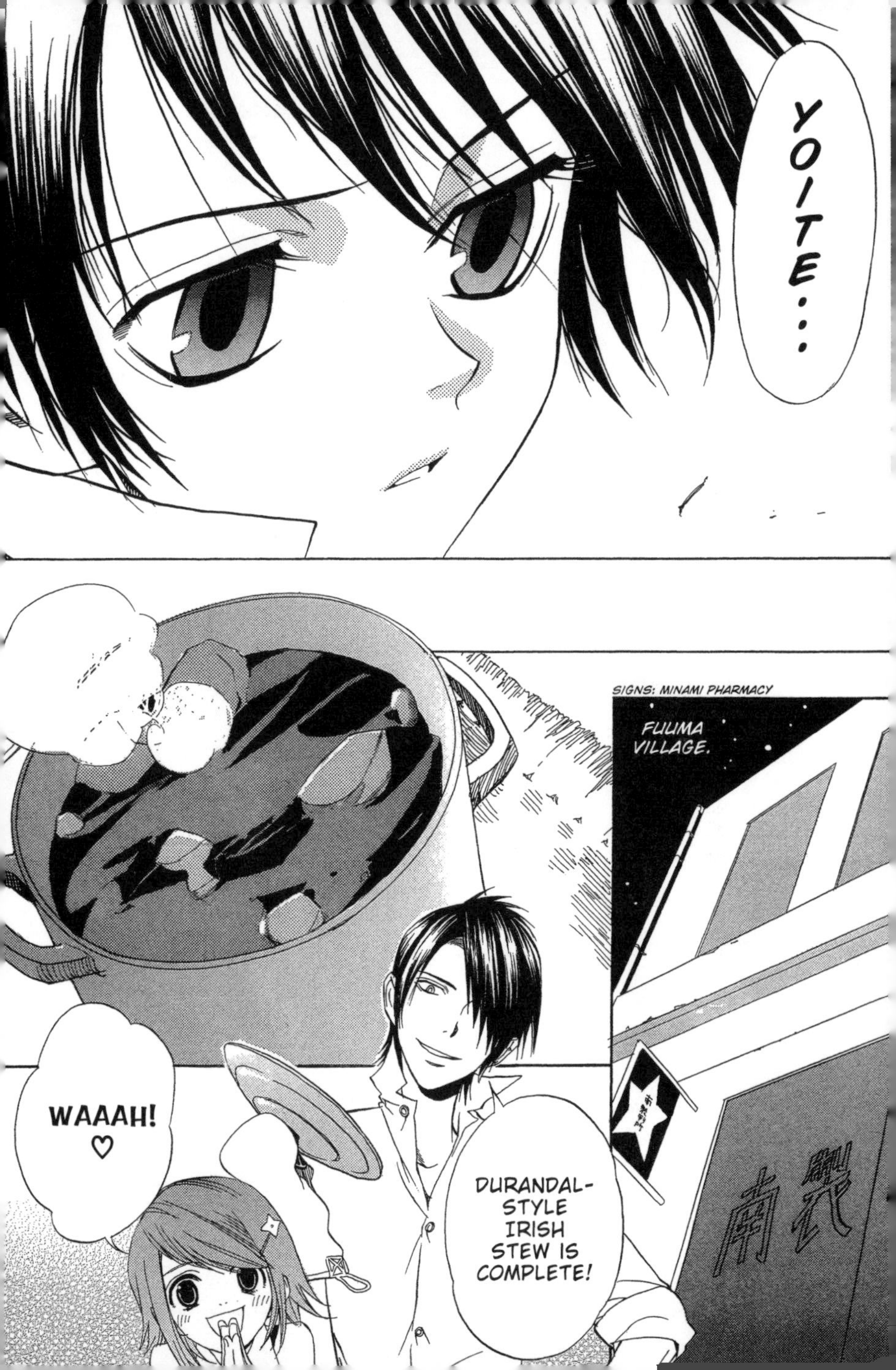
YOITE...
SIGNS: MINAMI PHARMACY
FUUMA VILLAGE.
DURANDAL-STYLE IRISH STEW IS COMPLETE!
WAAAH! ♡

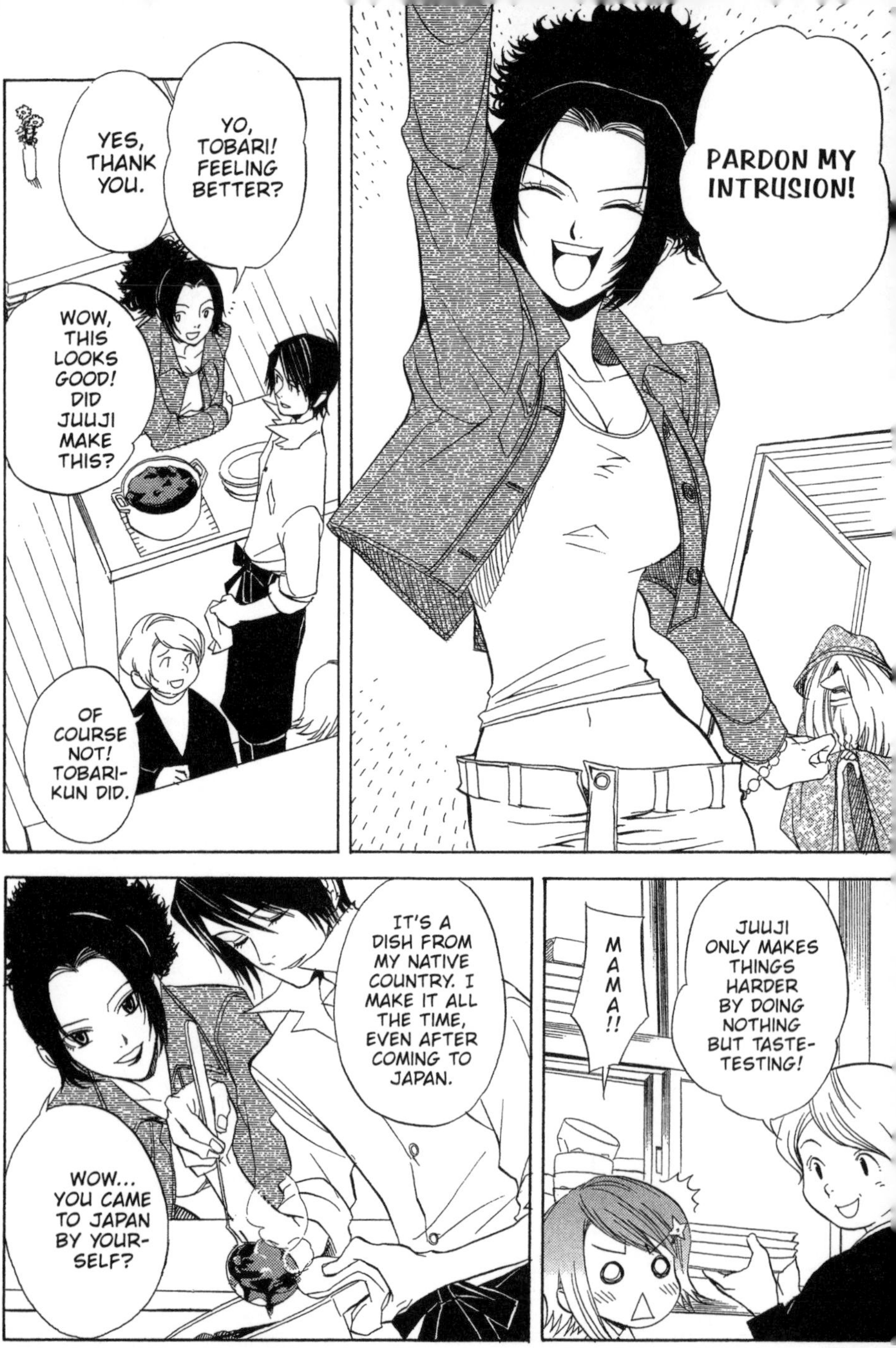
PARDON MY INTRUSION!
YO, TOBARI! FEELING BETTER?
YES, THANK YOU.
WOW, THIS LOOKS GOOD! DID JUUJI MAKE THIS?
OF COURSE NOT! TOBARI-KUN DID.
JUUJI ONLY MAKES THINGS HARDER BY DOING NOTHING BUT TASTE-TESTING!
MAMA!!
IT'S A DISH FROM MY NATIVE COUNTRY. I MAKE IT ALL THE TIME, EVEN AFTER COMING TO JAPAN.
WOW... YOU CAME TO JAPAN BY YOURSELF?

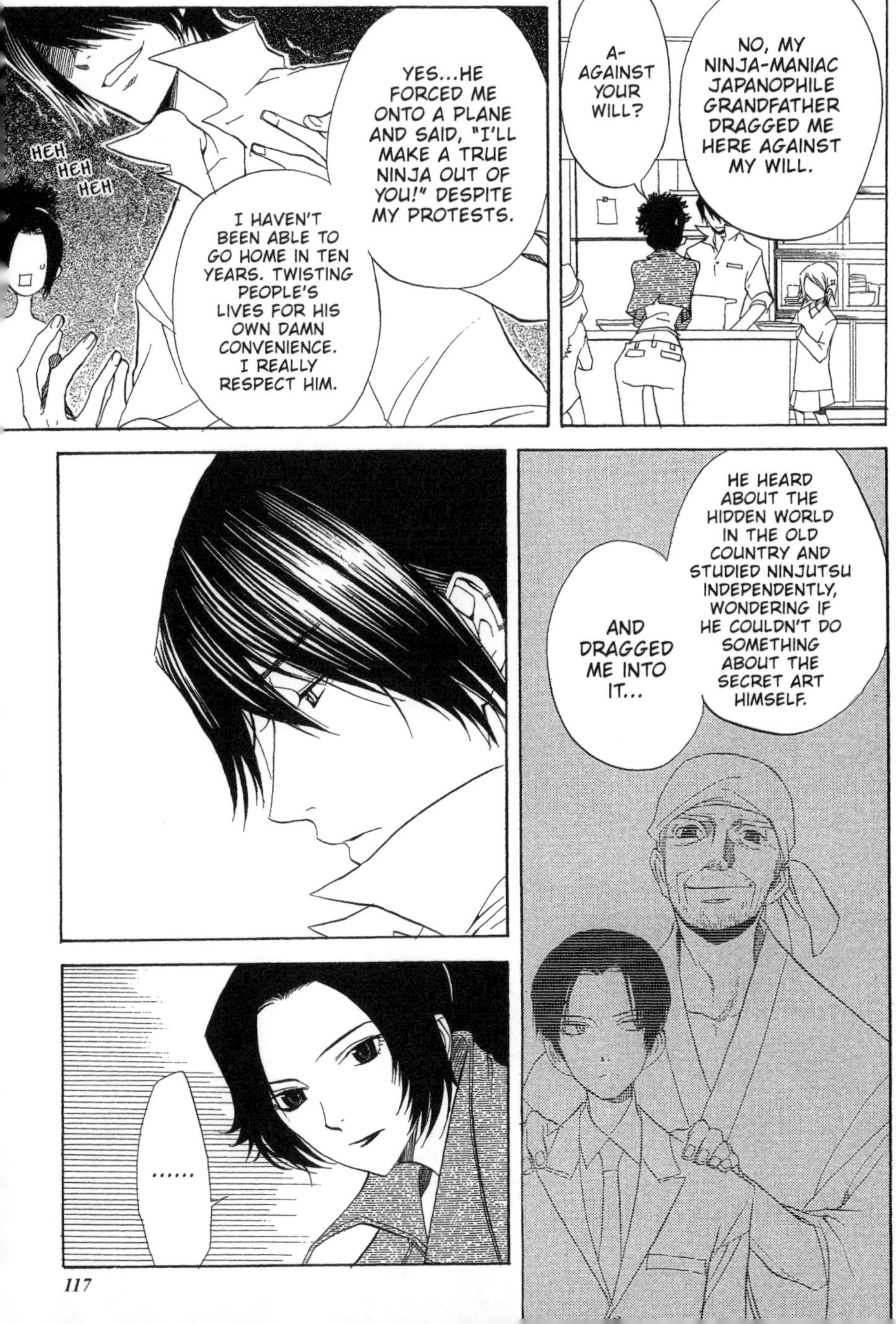
NO, MY NINJA-MANIAC JAPANOPHILE GRANDFATHER DRAGGED ME HERE AGAINST MY WILL.
A- AGAINST YOUR WILL?
YES...HE FORCED ME ONTO A PLANE AND SAID, "I'LL MAKE A TRUE NINJA OUT OF YOU!" DESPITE MY PROTESTS.
I HAVEN'T BEEN ABLE TO GO HOME IN TEN YEARS. TWISTING PEOPLE'S LIVES FOR HIS OWN DAMN CONVENIENCE. I REALLY RESPECT HIM.
HEH HEH HEH
HE HEARD ABOUT THE HIDDEN WORLD IN THE OLD COUNTRY AND STUDIED NINJUTSU INDEPENDENTLY, WONDERING IF HE COULDN'T DO SOMETHING ABOUT THE SECRET ART HIMSELF.
AND DRAGGED ME INTO IT...
......

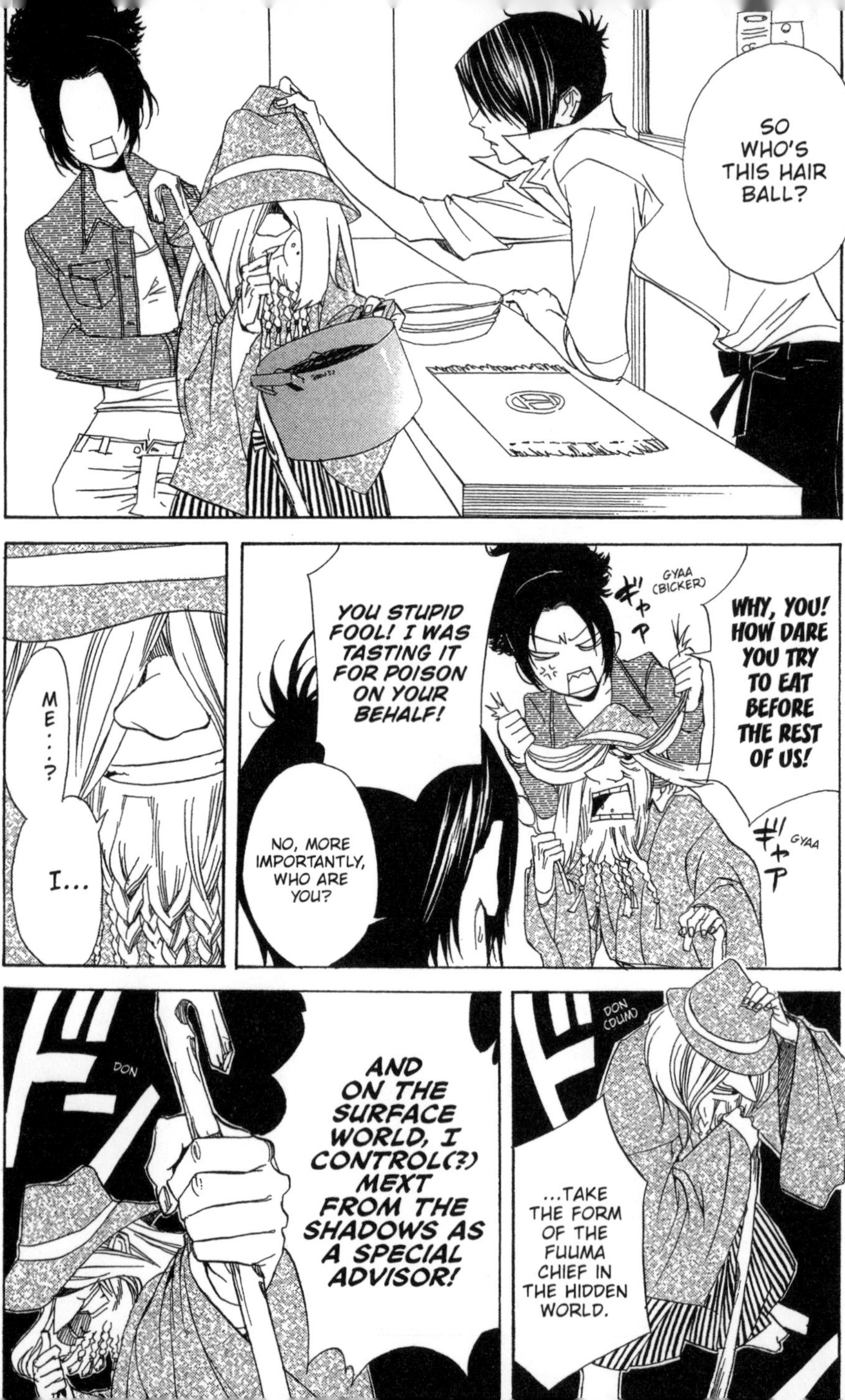

SO WHO'S THIS HAIR BALL?
GYAA (BICKER)
WHY, YOU! HOW DARE YOU TRY TO EAT BEFORE THE REST OF US!
GYAA
YOU STUPID FOOL! I WAS TASTING IT FOR POISON ON YOUR BEHALF!
NO, MORE IMPORTANTLY, WHO ARE YOU?
ME...?
I...
DON (DUM)
...TAKE THE FORM OF THE FUUMA CHIEF IN THE HIDDEN WORLD.
DON
AND ON THE SURFACE WORLD, I CONTROL(?) MEXT FROM THE SHADOWS AS A SPECIAL ADVISOR!

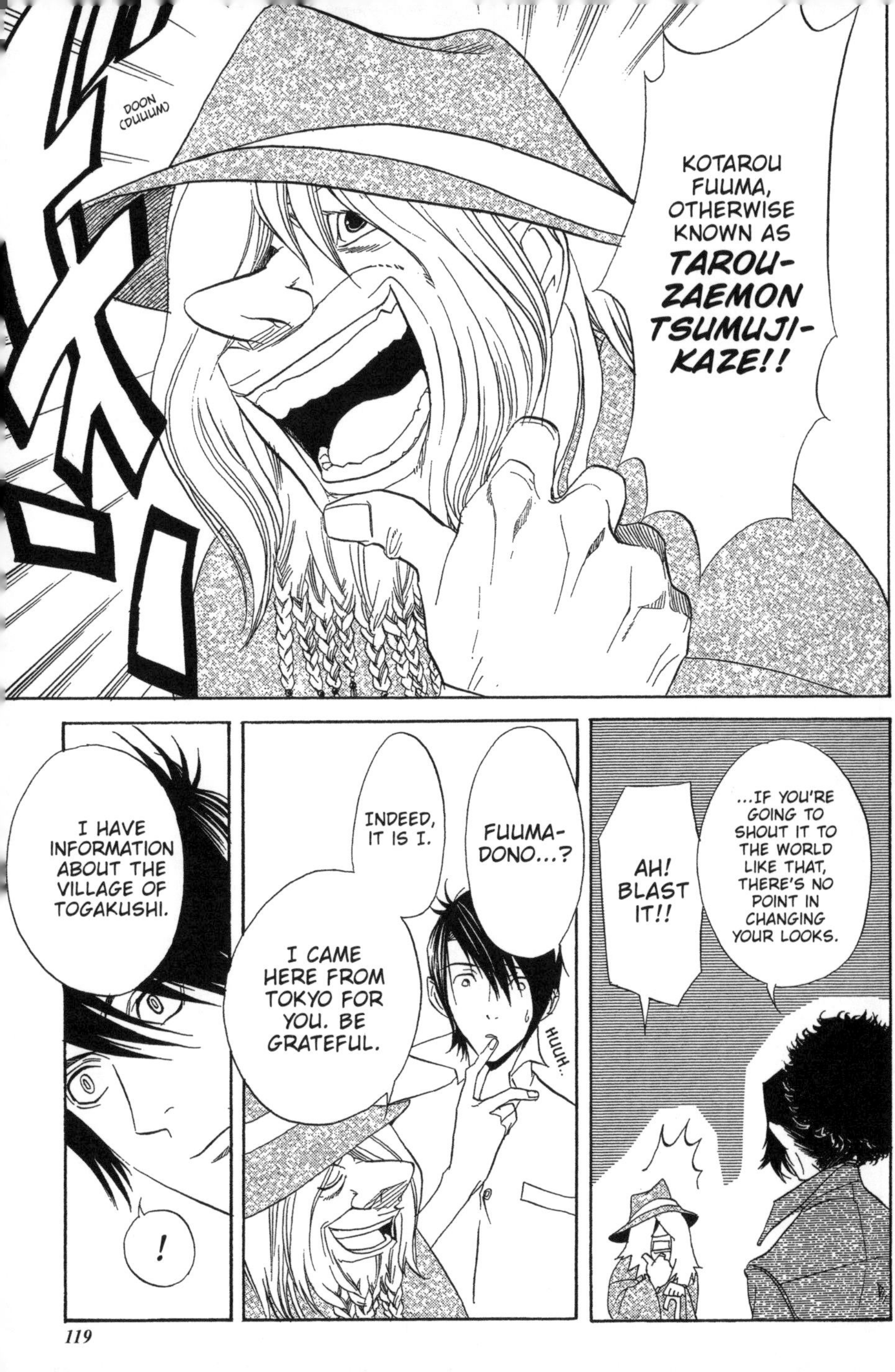
KOTAROU FUUMA, OTHERWISE KNOWN AS TAROU-ZAEMON TSUMUJI-KAZE!!
DOON (DUUUM)
...IF YOU'RE GOING TO SHOUT IT TO THE WORLD LIKE THAT, THERE'S NO POINT IN CHANGING YOUR LOOKS.
AH! BLAST IT!!
FUUMA-DONO...?
INDEED, IT IS I.
HUUH..
I CAME HERE FROM TOKYO FOR YOU. BE GRATEFUL.
I HAVE INFORMATION ABOUT THE VILLAGE OF TOGAKUSHI.
!

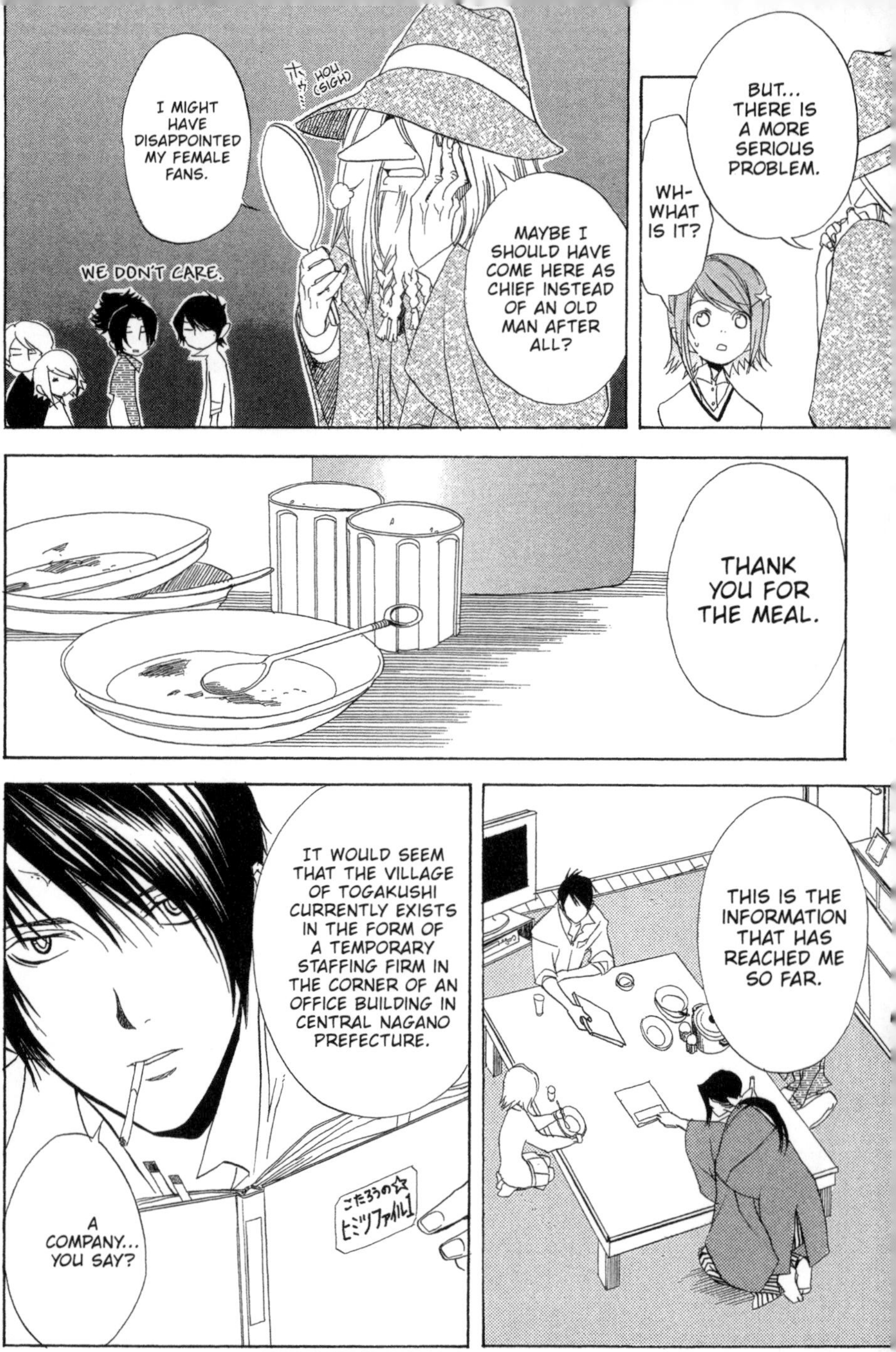
BUT... THERE IS A MORE SERIOUS PROBLEM.
WH- WHAT IS IT?
HOU (SIGH)
I MIGHT HAVE DISAPPOINTED MY FEMALE FANS.
MAYBE I SHOULD HAVE COME HERE AS CHIEF INSTEAD OF AN OLD MAN AFTER ALL?
WE DON'T CARE.
THANK YOU FOR THE MEAL.
THIS IS THE INFORMATION THAT HAS REACHED ME SO FAR.
IT WOULD SEEM THAT THE VILLAGE OF TOGAKUSHI CURRENTLY EXISTS IN THE FORM OF A TEMPORARY STAFFING FIRM IN THE CORNER OF AN OFFICE BUILDING IN CENTRAL NAGANO PREFECTURE.
こたろうの☆ ヒミツファイル1
A COMPANY... YOU SAY?

BOOK: KOTAROU'S SECRET FILE 1

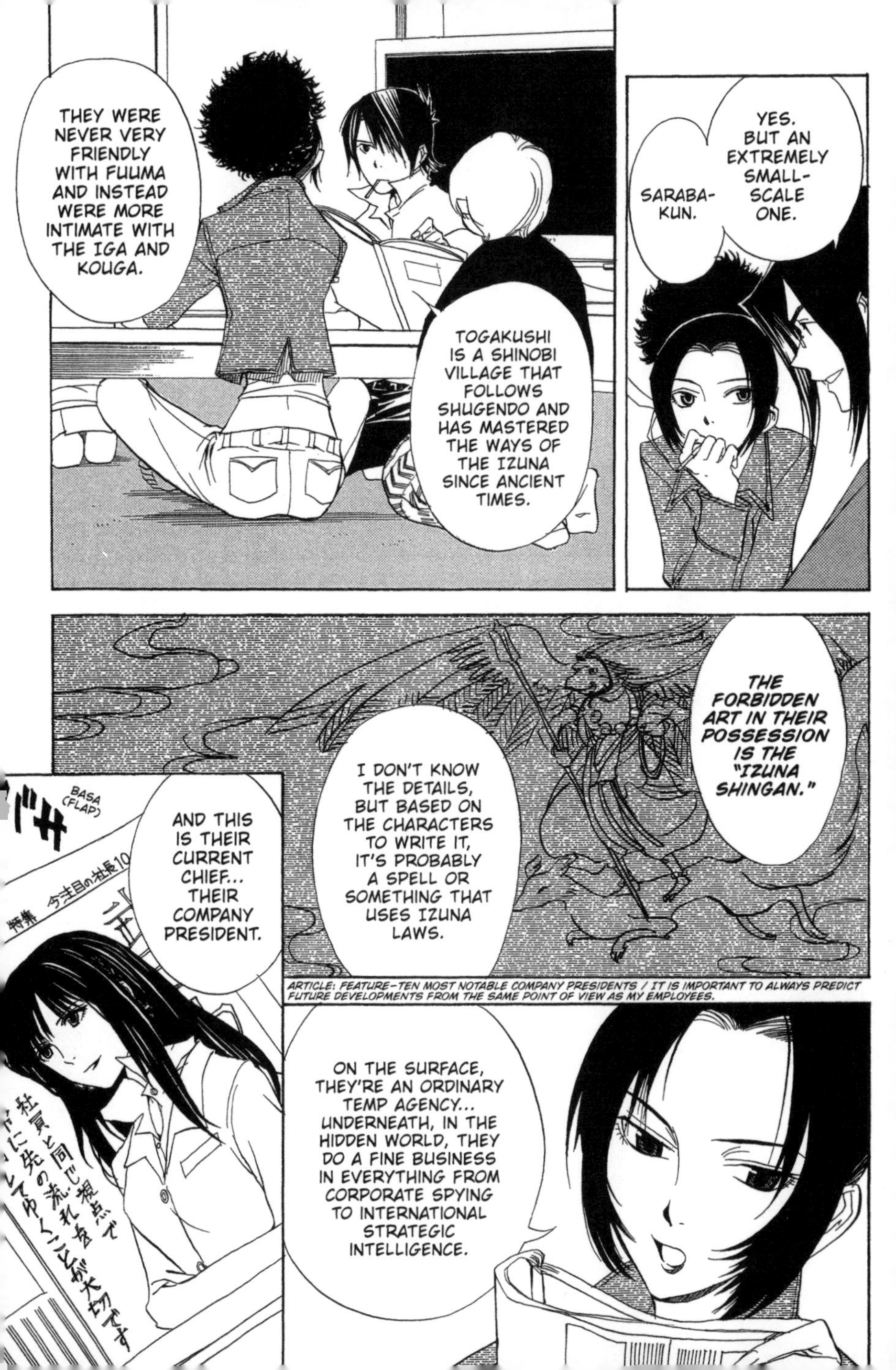
YES. BUT AN EXTREMELY SMALL-SCALE ONE.
SARABA-KUN.
THEY WERE NEVER VERY FRIENDLY WITH FUUMA AND INSTEAD WERE MORE INTIMATE WITH THE IGA AND KOUGA.
TOGAKUSHI IS A SHINOBI VILLAGE THAT FOLLOWS SHUGENDO AND HAS MASTERED THE WAYS OF THE IZUNA SINCE ANCIENT TIMES.
THE FORBIDDEN ART IN THEIR POSSESSION IS THE "IZUNA SHINGAN."
I DON'T KNOW THE DETAILS, BUT BASED ON THE CHARACTERS TO WRITE IT, IT'S PROBABLY A SPELL OR SOMETHING THAT USES IZUNA LAWS.
ON THE SURFACE, THEY'RE AN ORDINARY TEMP AGENCY... UNDERNEATH, IN THE HIDDEN WORLD, THEY DO A FINE BUSINESS IN EVERYTHING FROM CORPORATE SPYING TO INTERNATIONAL STRATEGIC INTELLIGENCE.
ARTICLE: FEATURE—TEN MOST NOTABLE COMPANY PRESIDENTS / IT IS IMPORTANT TO ALWAYS PREDICT FUTURE DEVELOPMENTS FROM THE SAME POINT OF VIEW AS MY EMPLOYEES.
BASA (FLAP)
特集 今注目の社長10
AND THIS IS THEIR CURRENT CHIEF... THEIR COMPANY PRESIDENT.
社員と同じ視点で

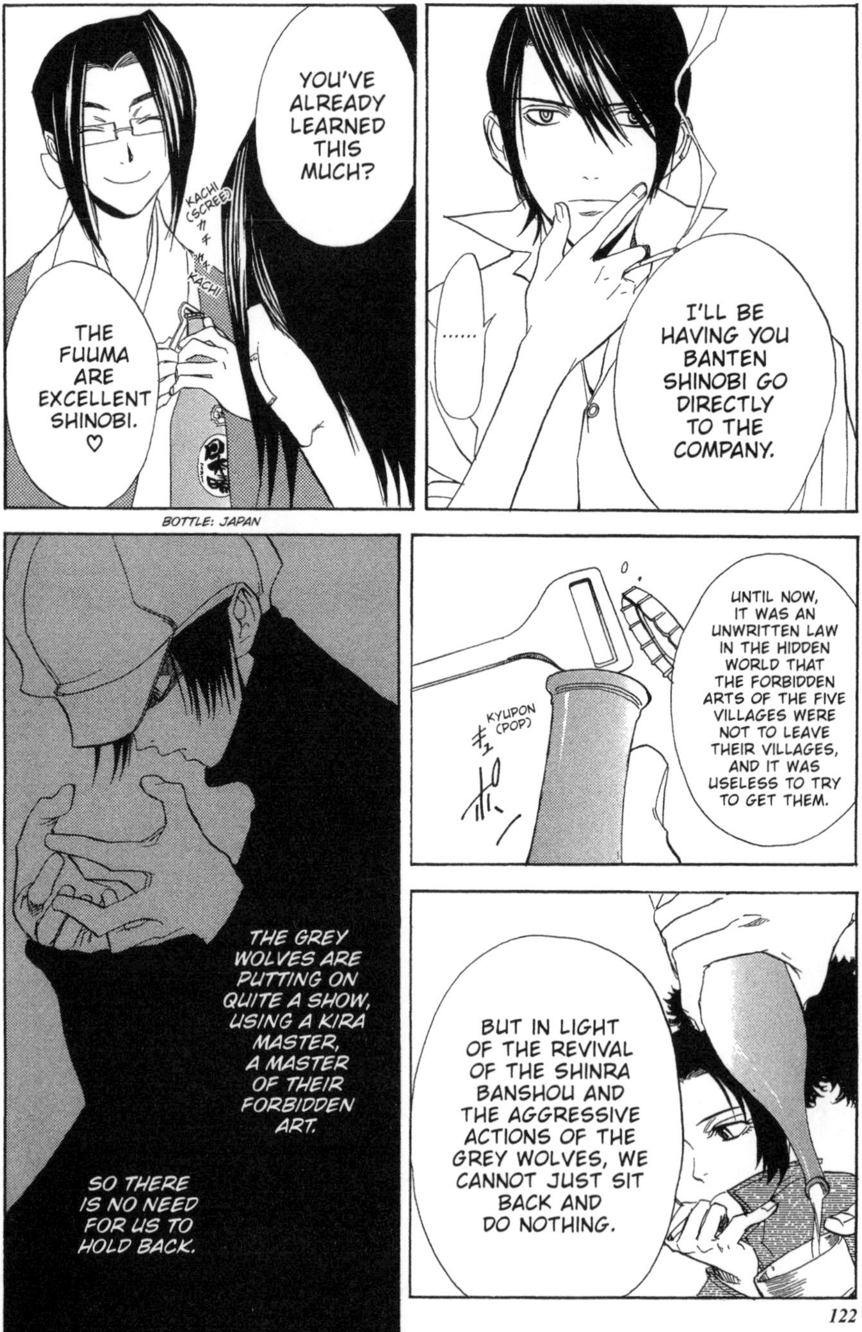
I'LL BE HAVING YOU BANTEN SHINOBI GO DIRECTLY TO THE COMPANY.
......
YOU'VE ALREADY LEARNED THIS MUCH?
KACHI (SCREE) KACHI
THE FUUMA ARE EXCELLENT SHINOBI. ♡
BOTTLE: JAPAN
UNTIL NOW, IT WAS AN UNWRITTEN LAW IN THE HIDDEN WORLD THAT THE FORBIDDEN ARTS OF THE FIVE VILLAGES WERE NOT TO LEAVE THEIR VILLAGES, AND IT WAS USELESS TO TRY TO GET THEM.
KYUPON (POP)
BUT IN LIGHT OF THE REVIVAL OF THE SHINRA BANSHOU AND THE AGGRESSIVE ACTIONS OF THE GREY WOLVES, WE CANNOT JUST SIT BACK AND DO NOTHING.
THE GREY WOLVES ARE PUTTING ON QUITE A SHOW, USING A KIRA MASTER, A MASTER OF THEIR FORBIDDEN ART.
SO THERE IS NO NEED FOR US TO HOLD BACK.

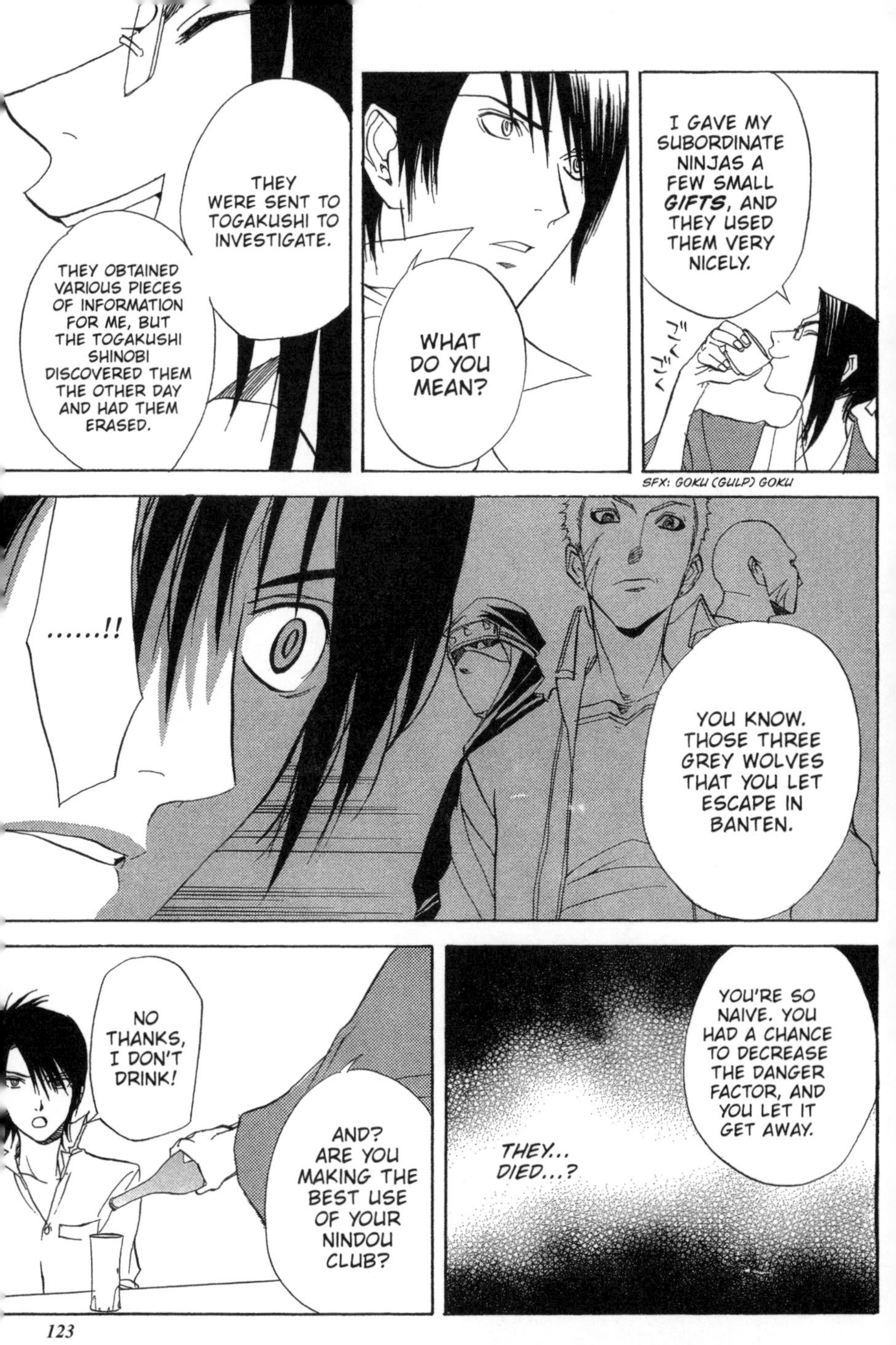
I GAVE MY SUBORDINATE NINJAS A FEW SMALL **GIFTS**, AND THEY USED THEM VERY NICELY.
SFX: GOKU (GULP) GOKU
WHAT DO YOU MEAN?
THEY WERE SENT TO TOGAKUSHI TO INVESTIGATE.
THEY OBTAINED VARIOUS PIECES OF INFORMATION FOR ME, BUT THE TOGAKUSHI SHINOBI DISCOVERED THEM THE OTHER DAY AND HAD THEM ERASED.
YOU KNOW. THOSE THREE GREY WOLVES THAT YOU LET ESCAPE IN BANTEN.
......!!
YOU'RE SO NAIVE. YOU HAD A CHANCE TO DECREASE THE DANGER FACTOR, AND YOU LET IT GET AWAY.
THEY... DIED...?
AND? ARE YOU MAKING THE BEST USE OF YOUR NINDOU CLUB?
NO THANKS, I DON'T DRINK!

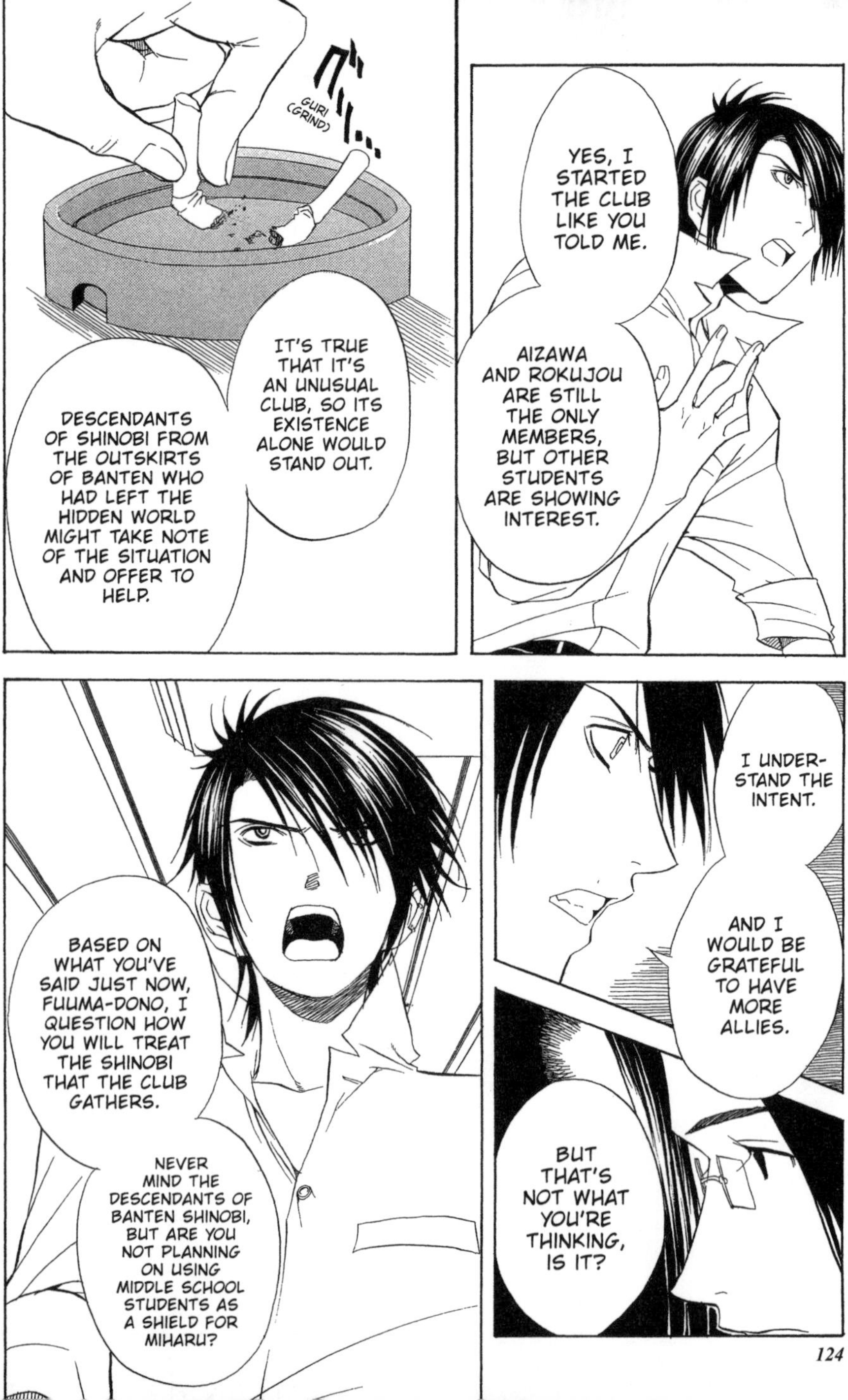
YES, I STARTED THE CLUB LIKE YOU TOLD ME.
AIZAWA AND ROKUJOU ARE STILL THE ONLY MEMBERS, BUT OTHER STUDENTS ARE SHOWING INTEREST.
GURI (GRIND)
IT'S TRUE THAT IT'S AN UNUSUAL CLUB, SO ITS EXISTENCE ALONE WOULD STAND OUT.
DESCENDANTS OF SHINOBI FROM THE OUTSKIRTS OF BANTEN WHO HAD LEFT THE HIDDEN WORLD MIGHT TAKE NOTE OF THE SITUATION AND OFFER TO HELP.
I UNDERSTAND THE INTENT.
AND I WOULD BE GRATEFUL TO HAVE MORE ALLIES.
BUT THAT'S NOT WHAT YOU'RE THINKING, IS IT?
BASED ON WHAT YOU'VE SAID JUST NOW, FUUMA-DONO, I QUESTION HOW YOU WILL TREAT THE SHINOBI THAT THE CLUB GATHERS.
NEVER MIND THE DESCENDANTS OF BANTEN SHINOBI, BUT ARE YOU NOT PLANNING ON USING MIDDLE SCHOOL STUDENTS AS A SHIELD FOR MIHARU?

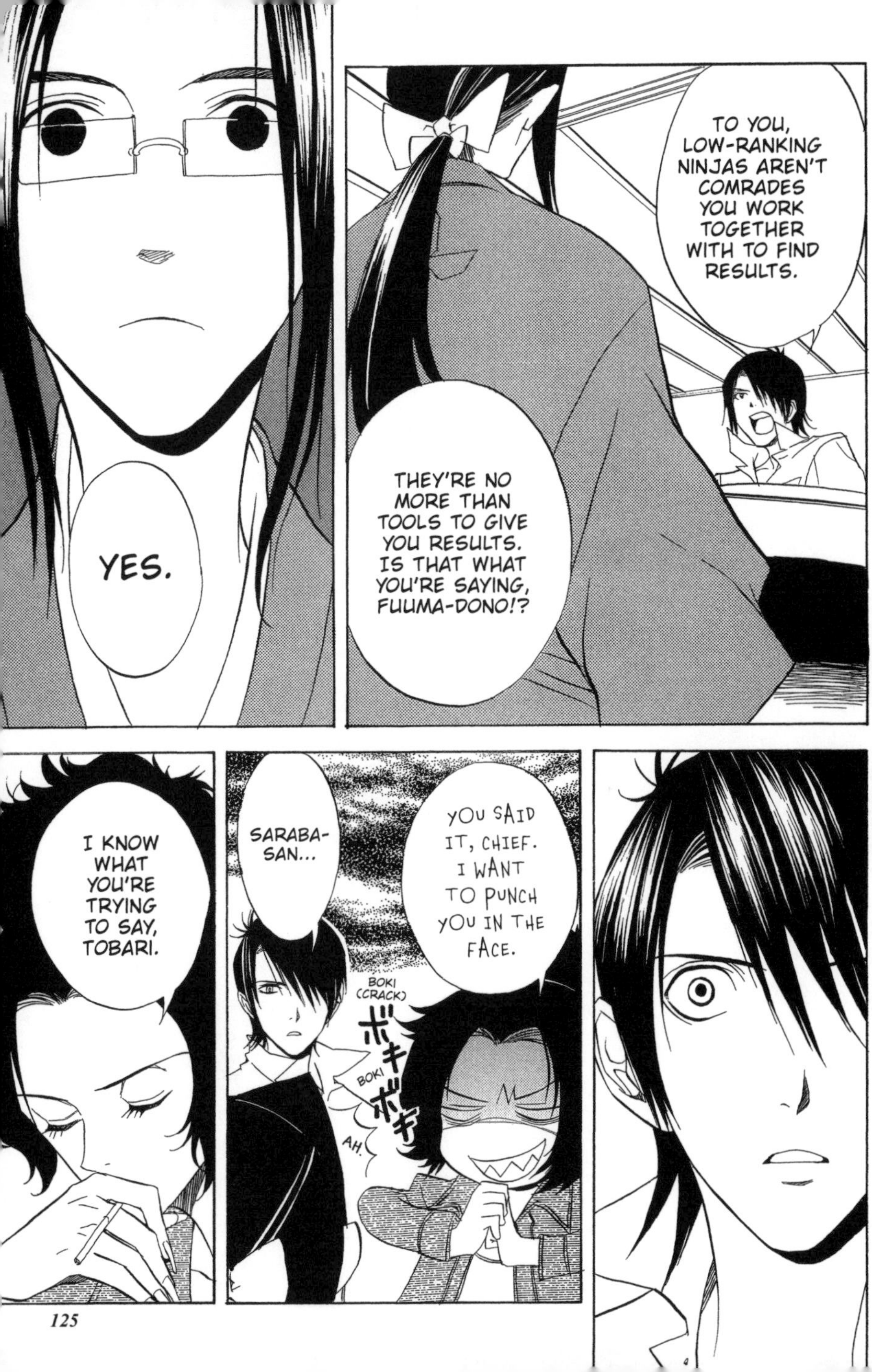

TO YOU, LOW-RANKING NINJAS AREN'T COMRADES YOU WORK TOGETHER WITH TO FIND RESULTS.
THEY'RE NO MORE THAN TOOLS TO GIVE YOU RESULTS. IS THAT WHAT YOU'RE SAYING, FUUMA-DONO!?
YES.
YOU SAID IT, CHIEF. I WANT TO PUNCH YOU IN THE FACE.
SARABA-SAN...
ボキ
BOKI (CRACK)
ボキ
BOKI
AH.
I KNOW WHAT YOU'RE TRYING TO SAY, TOBARI.

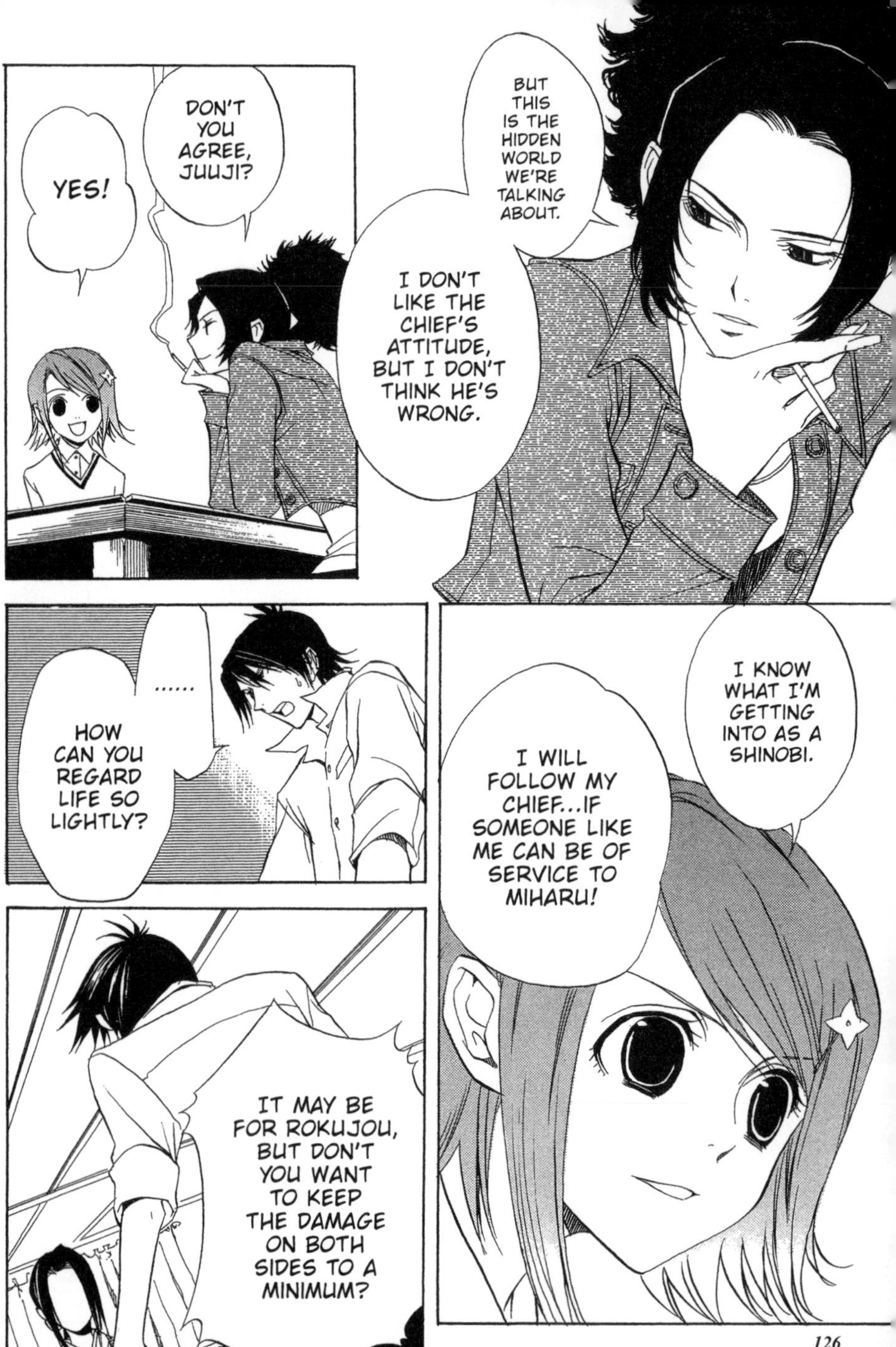
BUT THIS IS THE HIDDEN WORLD WE'RE TALKING ABOUT.
I DON'T LIKE THE CHIEF'S ATTITUDE, BUT I DON'T THINK HE'S WRONG.
DON'T YOU AGREE, JUUJI?
YES!
I KNOW WHAT I'M GETTING INTO AS A SHINOBI.
I WILL FOLLOW MY CHIEF...IF SOMEONE LIKE ME CAN BE OF SERVICE TO MIHARU!
......
HOW CAN YOU REGARD LIFE SO LIGHTLY?
IT MAY BE FOR ROKUJOU, BUT DON'T YOU WANT TO KEEP THE DAMAGE ON BOTH SIDES TO A MINIMUM?

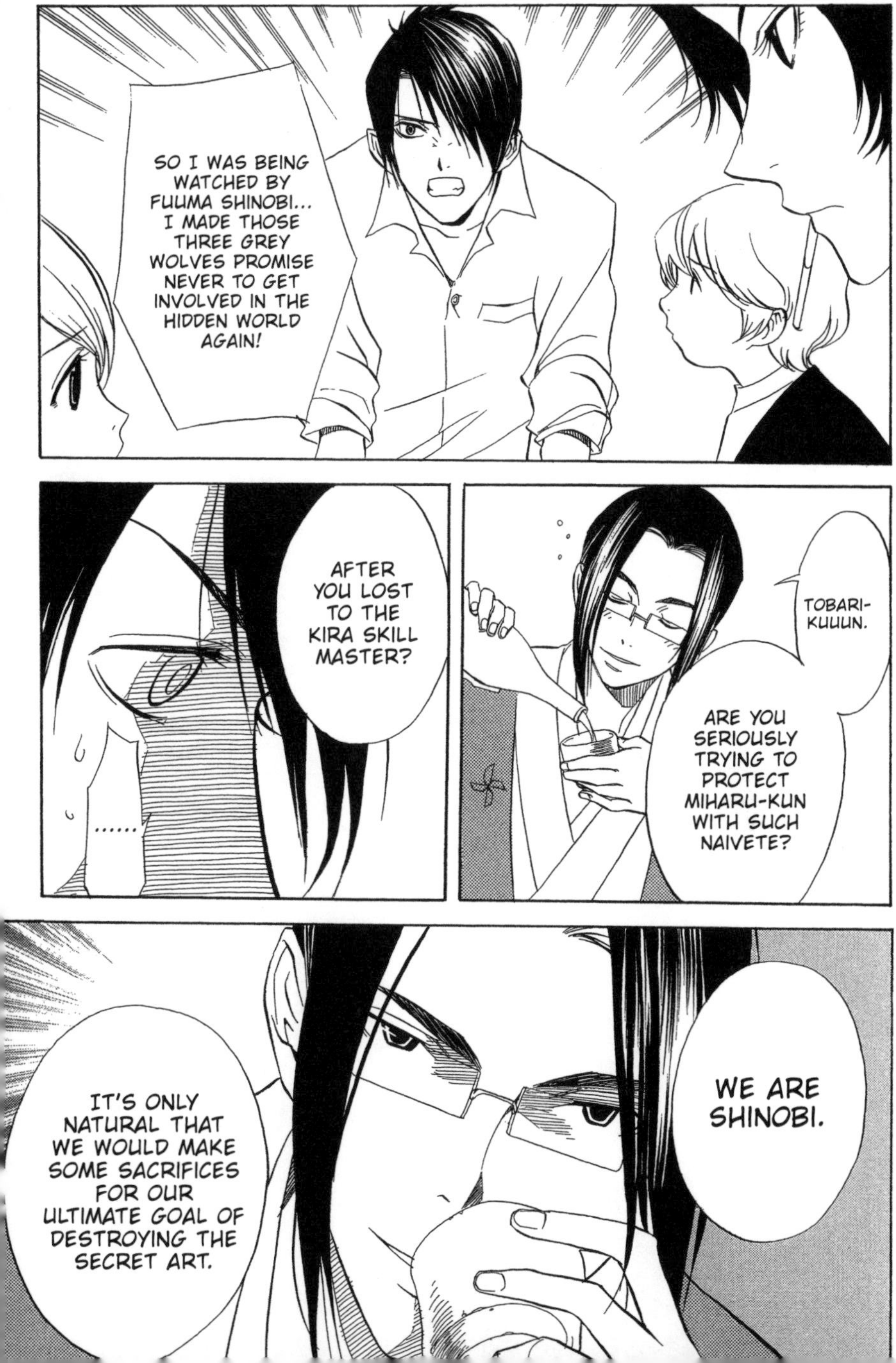
SO I WAS BEING WATCHED BY FUUMA SHINOBI... I MADE THOSE THREE GREY WOLVES PROMISE NEVER TO GET INVOLVED IN THE HIDDEN WORLD AGAIN!
TOBARI-KUUUN.
ARE YOU SERIOUSLY TRYING TO PROTECT MIHARU-KUN WITH SUCH NAIVETE?
AFTER YOU LOST TO THE KIRA SKILL MASTER?
......
WE ARE SHINOBI.
IT'S ONLY NATURAL THAT WE WOULD MAKE SOME SACRIFICES FOR OUR ULTIMATE GOAL OF DESTROYING THE SECRET ART.

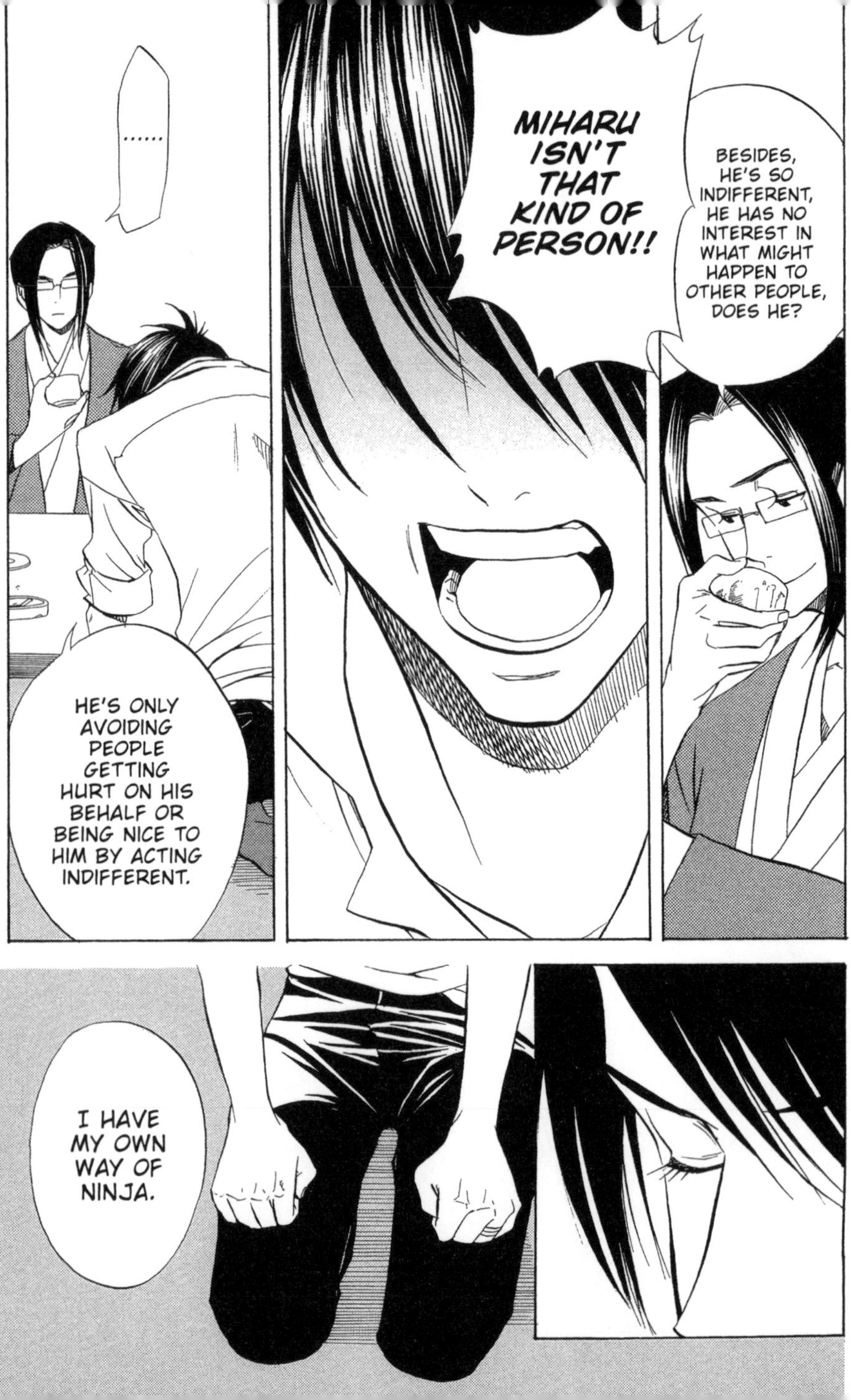
BESIDES, HE'S SO INDIFFERENT, HE HAS NO INTEREST IN WHAT MIGHT HAPPEN TO OTHER PEOPLE, DOES HE?
MIHARU ISN'T THAT KIND OF PERSON!!
......
HE'S ONLY AVOIDING PEOPLE GETTING HURT ON HIS BEHALF OR BEING NICE TO HIM BY ACTING INDIFFERENT.
I HAVE MY OWN WAY OF NINJA.

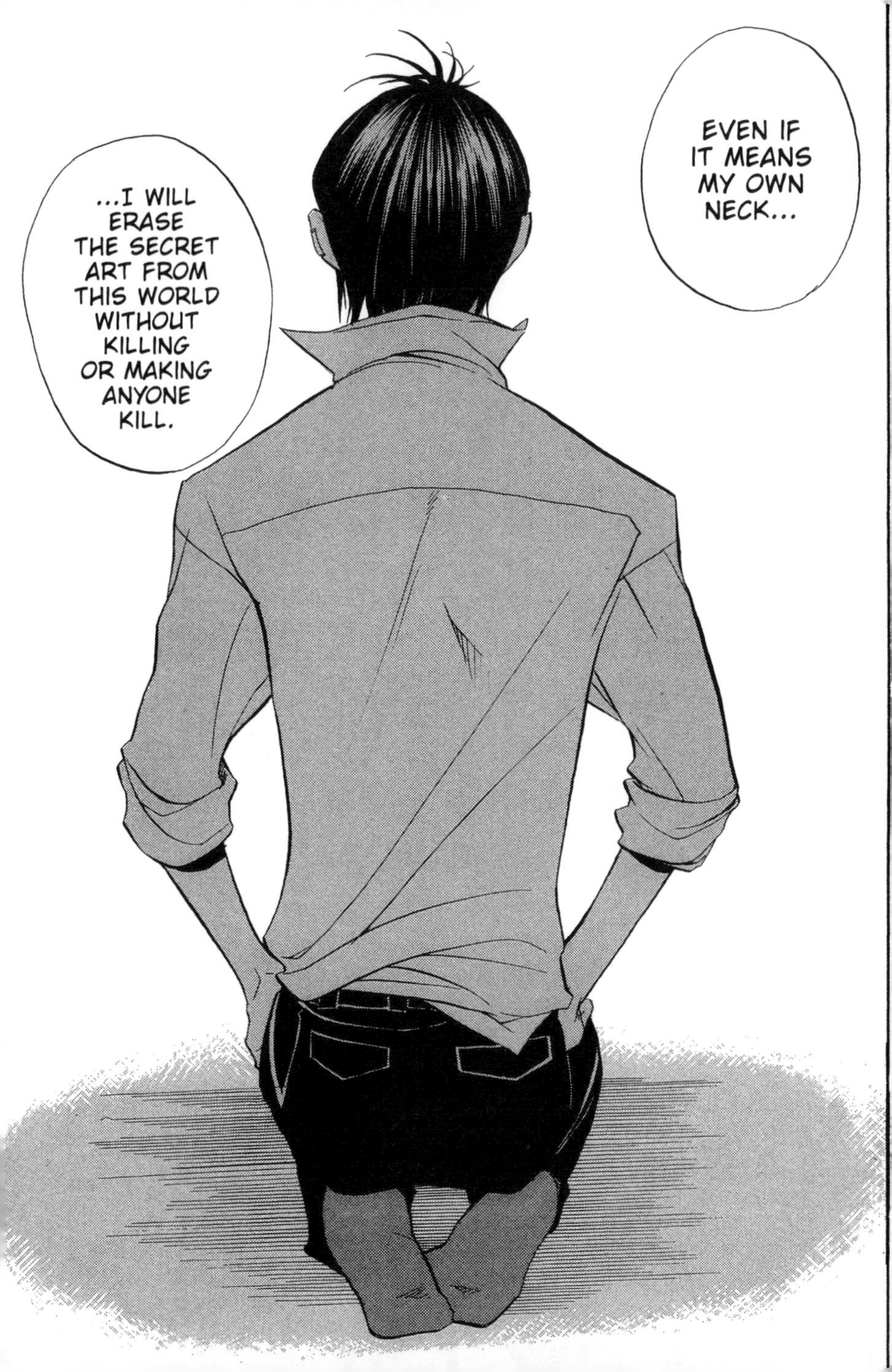
EVEN IF IT MEANS MY OWN NECK...
...I WILL ERASE THE SECRET ART FROM THIS WORLD WITHOUT KILLING OR MAKING ANYONE KILL.

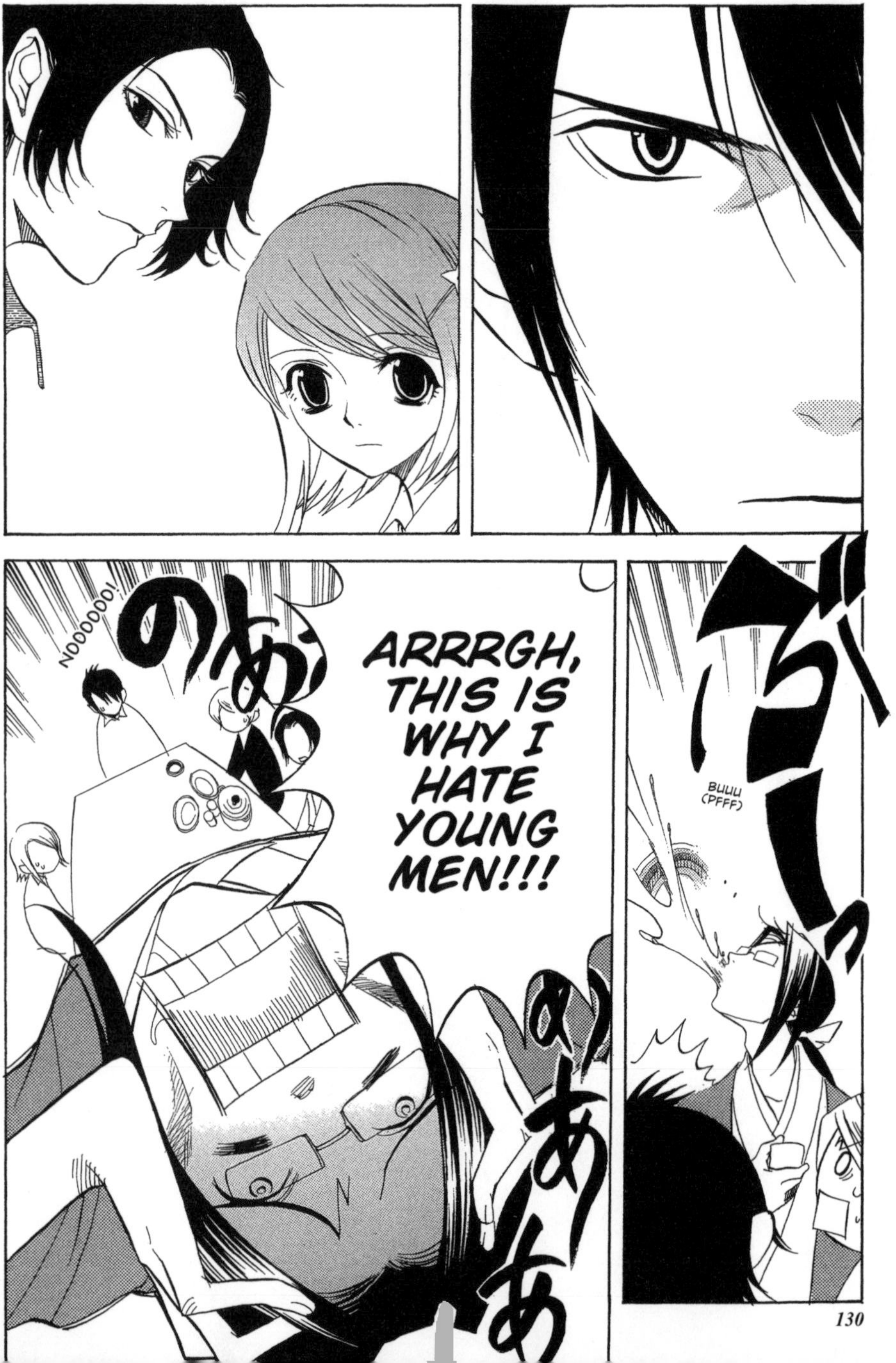
BUUU
(PFFF)
NOOOOOO!
ARRRGH, THIS IS WHY I HATE YOUNG MEN!!!

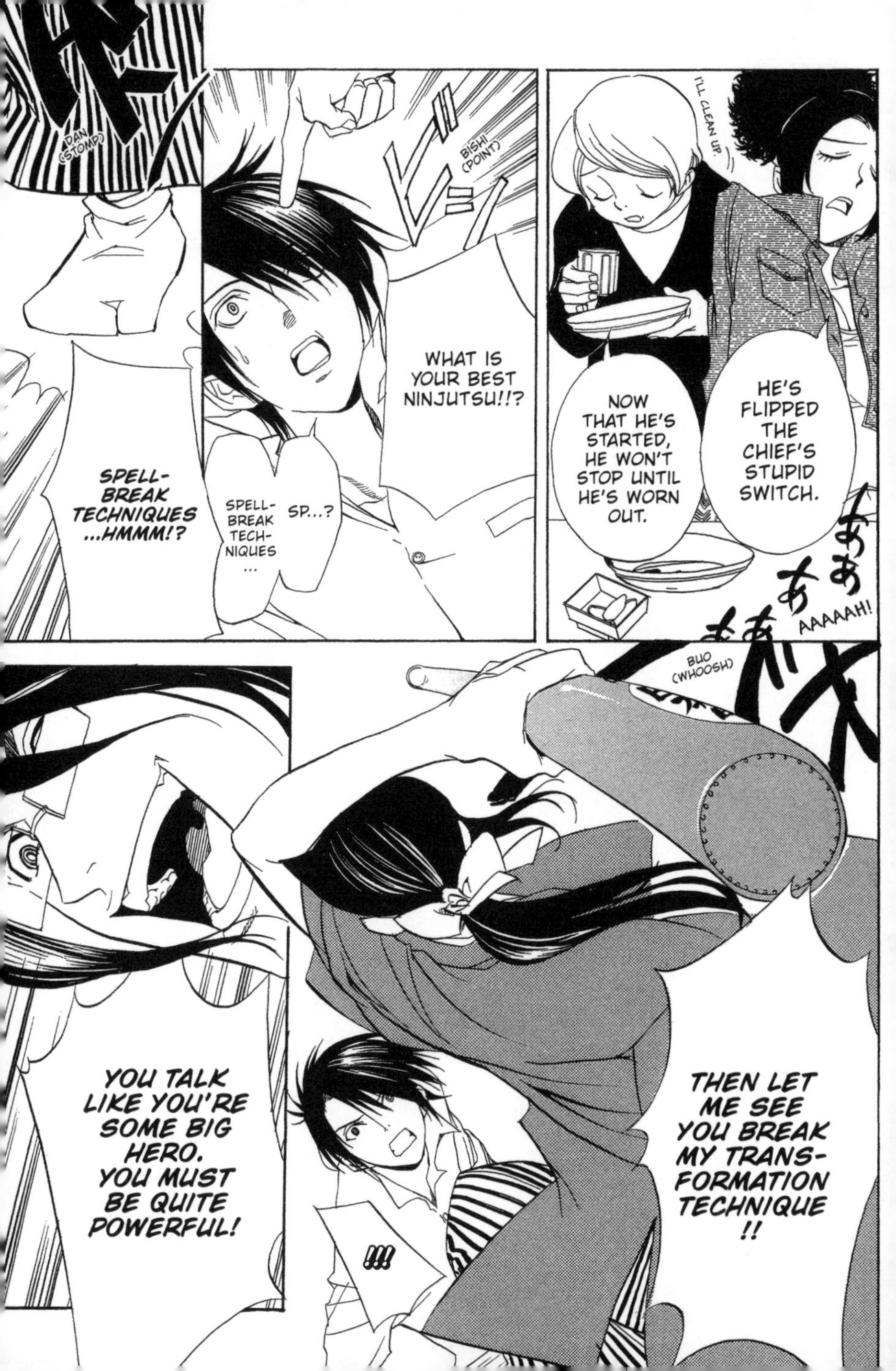
I'LL CLEAN UP.
HE'S FLIPPED THE CHIEF'S STUPID SWITCH.
NOW THAT HE'S STARTED, HE WON'T STOP UNTIL HE'S WORN OUT.
AAAAAH!
BISHI (POINT)
WHAT IS YOUR BEST NINJUTSU!!?
SP...?
SPELL-BREAK TECH-NIQUES ...
DAN (STOMP)
SPELL-BREAK TECHNIQUES ...HMMM!?
BUO (WHOOSH)
THEN LET ME SEE YOU BREAK MY TRANS-FORMATION TECHNIQUE !!
YOU TALK LIKE YOU'RE SOME BIG HERO. YOU MUST BE QUITE POWERFUL!
!!!

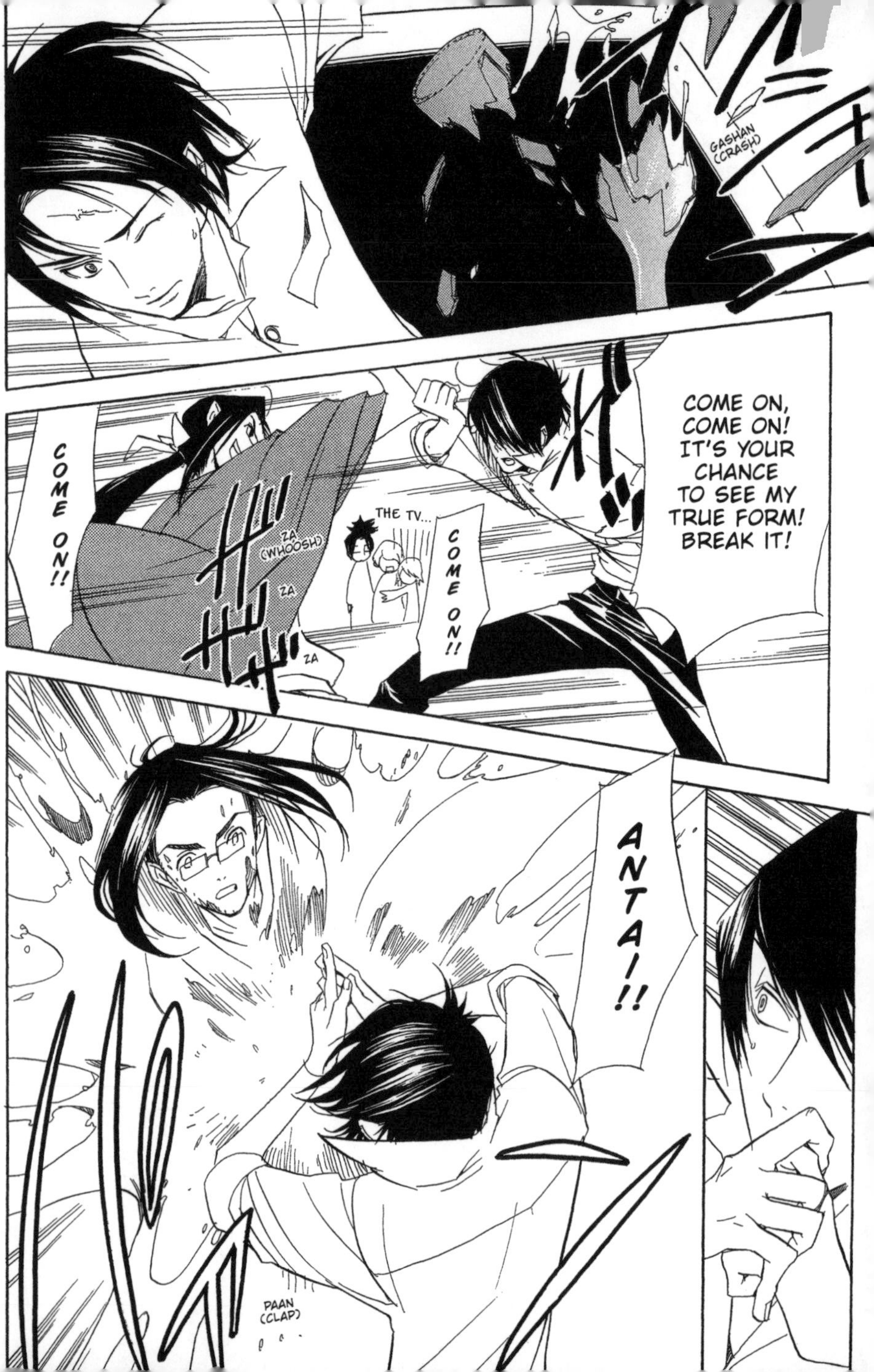
GASHAN (CRASH)
COME ON, COME ON! IT'S YOUR CHANCE TO SEE MY TRUE FORM! BREAK IT!
COME ON!!
THE TV...
ZA (WHOOSH)
ZA
ZA
COME ON!!
ANTA!!
PAAN (CLAP)

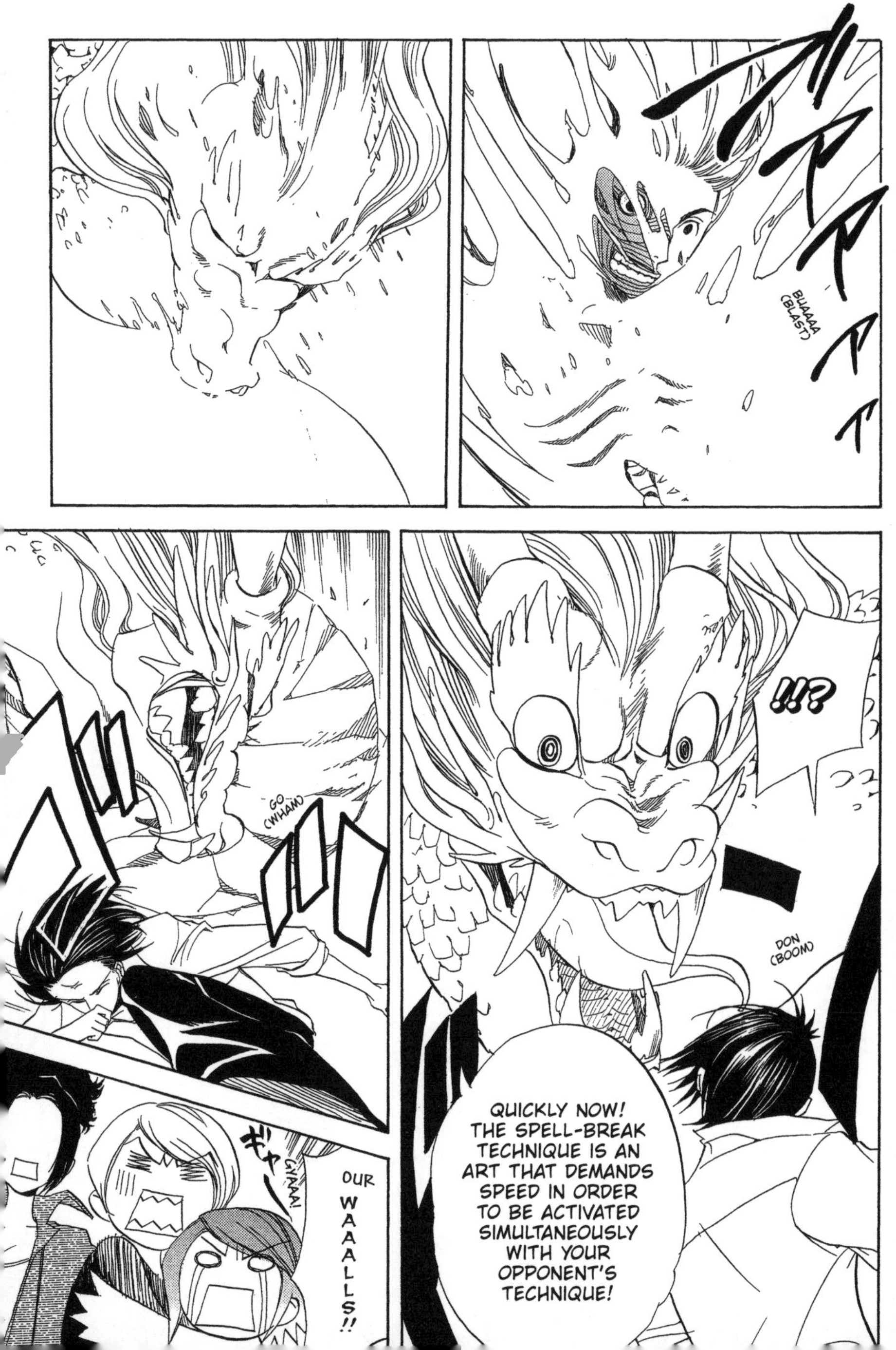
BUAAAA (BLAST)
!!?
DON (BOOM)
QUICKLY NOW! THE SPELL-BREAK TECHNIQUE IS AN ART THAT DEMANDS SPEED IN ORDER TO BE ACTIVATED SIMULTANEOUSLY WITH YOUR OPPONENT'S TECHNIQUE!
GO (WHAM)
ギャー
GYAAA!
OUR WAAAALLS!!

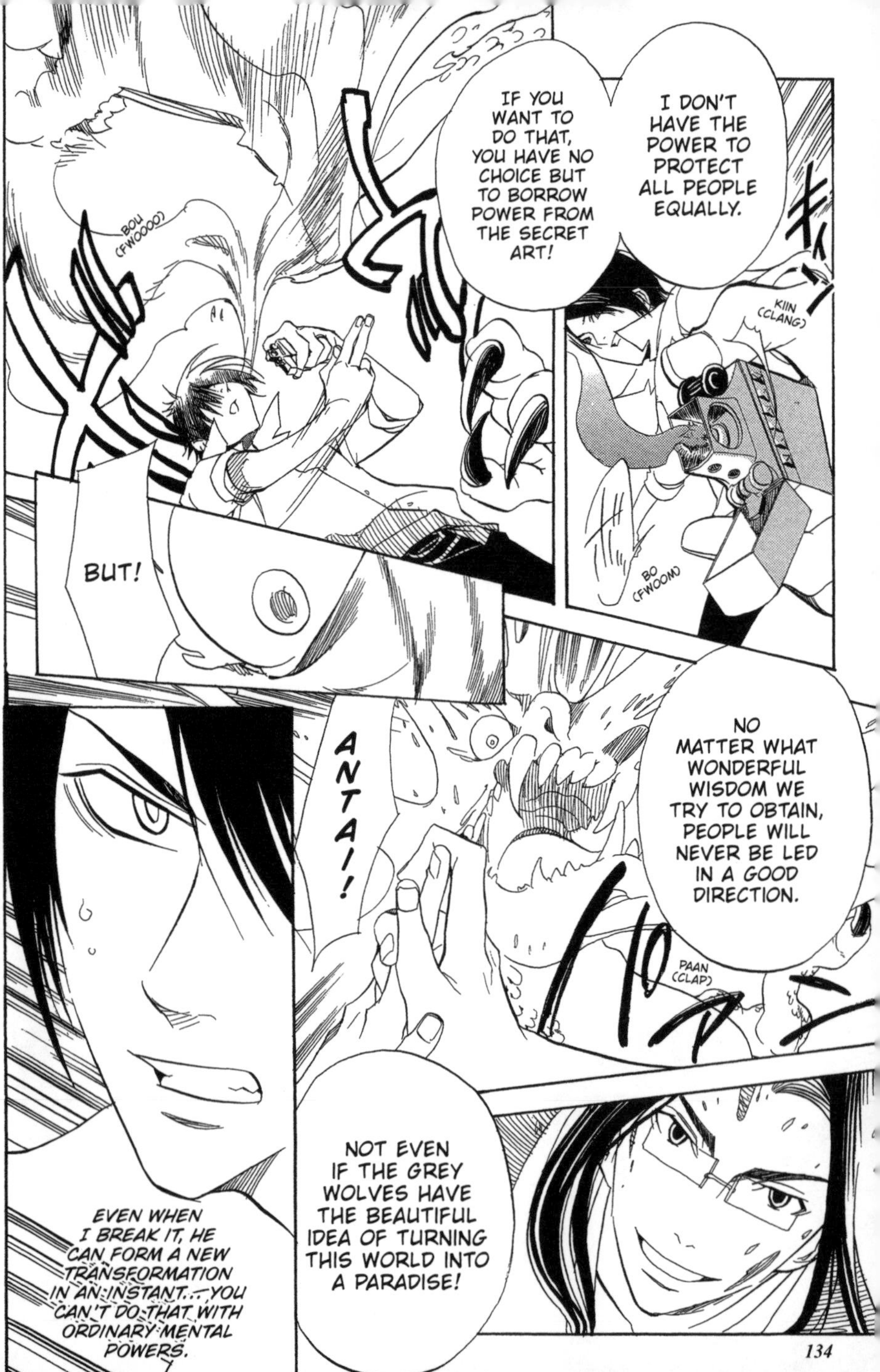
I DON'T HAVE THE POWER TO PROTECT ALL PEOPLE EQUALLY.
KIIN (CLANG)
BO (FWOOM)
IF YOU WANT TO DO THAT, YOU HAVE NO CHOICE BUT TO BORROW POWER FROM THE SECRET ART!
BOU (FWOOOO)
BUT!
NO MATTER WHAT WONDERFUL WISDOM WE TRY TO OBTAIN, PEOPLE WILL NEVER BE LED IN A GOOD DIRECTION.
PAAN (CLAP)
ANTA!!
NOT EVEN IF THE GREY WOLVES HAVE THE BEAUTIFUL IDEA OF TURNING THIS WORLD INTO A PARADISE!
EVEN WHEN I BREAK IT, HE CAN FORM A NEW TRANSFORMATION IN AN INSTANT... YOU CAN'T DO THAT WITH ORDINARY MENTAL POWERS.

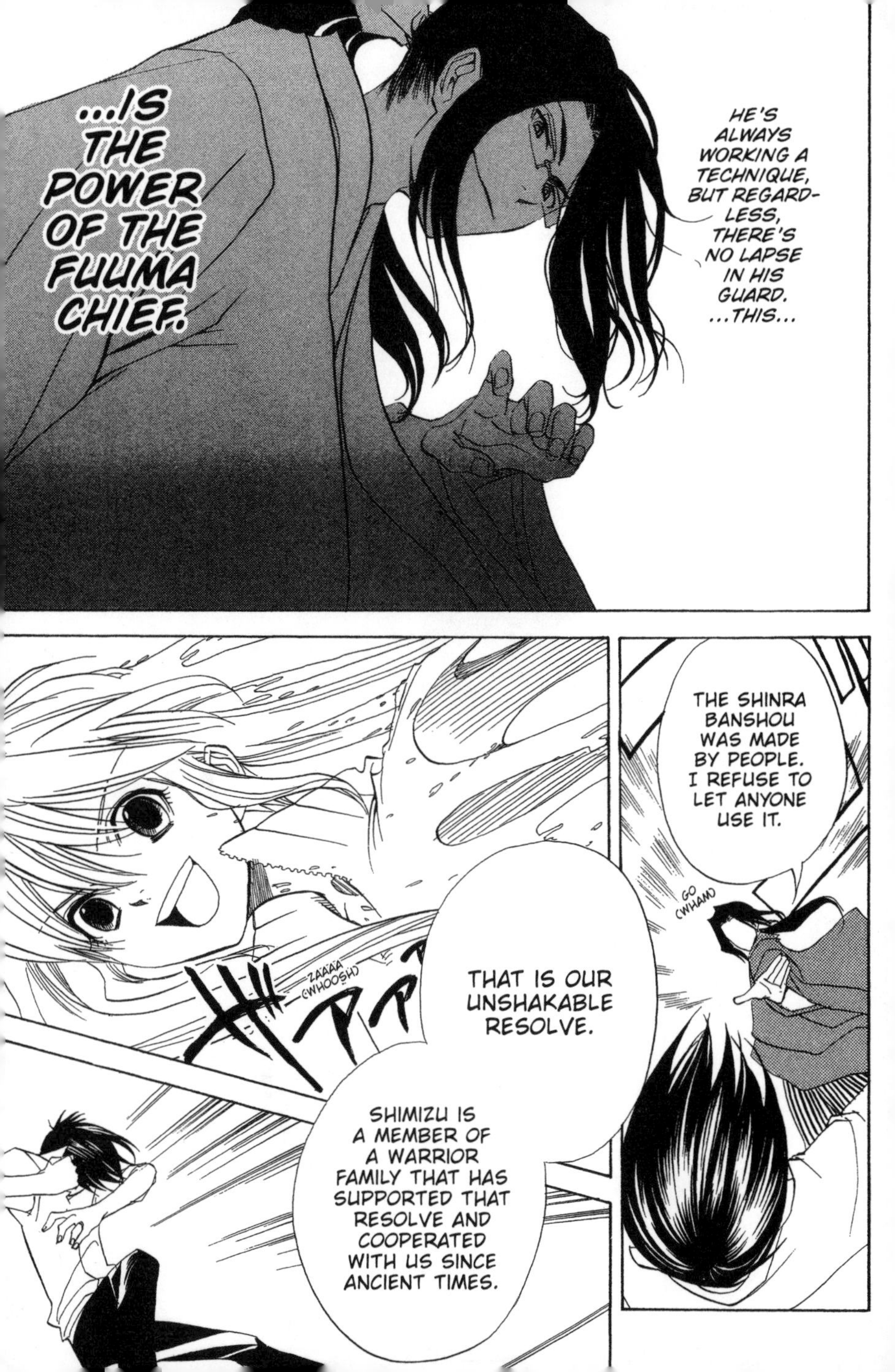
HE'S ALWAYS WORKING A TECHNIQUE, BUT REGARDLESS, THERE'S NO LAPSE IN HIS GUARD. ...THIS...
...IS THE POWER OF THE FUUMA CHIEF.
THE SHINRA BANSHOU WAS MADE BY PEOPLE. I REFUSE TO LET ANYONE USE IT.
GO (WHAM)
THAT IS OUR UNSHAKABLE RESOLVE.
ZAAAA (WHOOSH)
SHIMIZU IS A MEMBER OF A WARRIOR FAMILY THAT HAS SUPPORTED THAT RESOLVE AND COOPERATED WITH US SINCE ANCIENT TIMES.

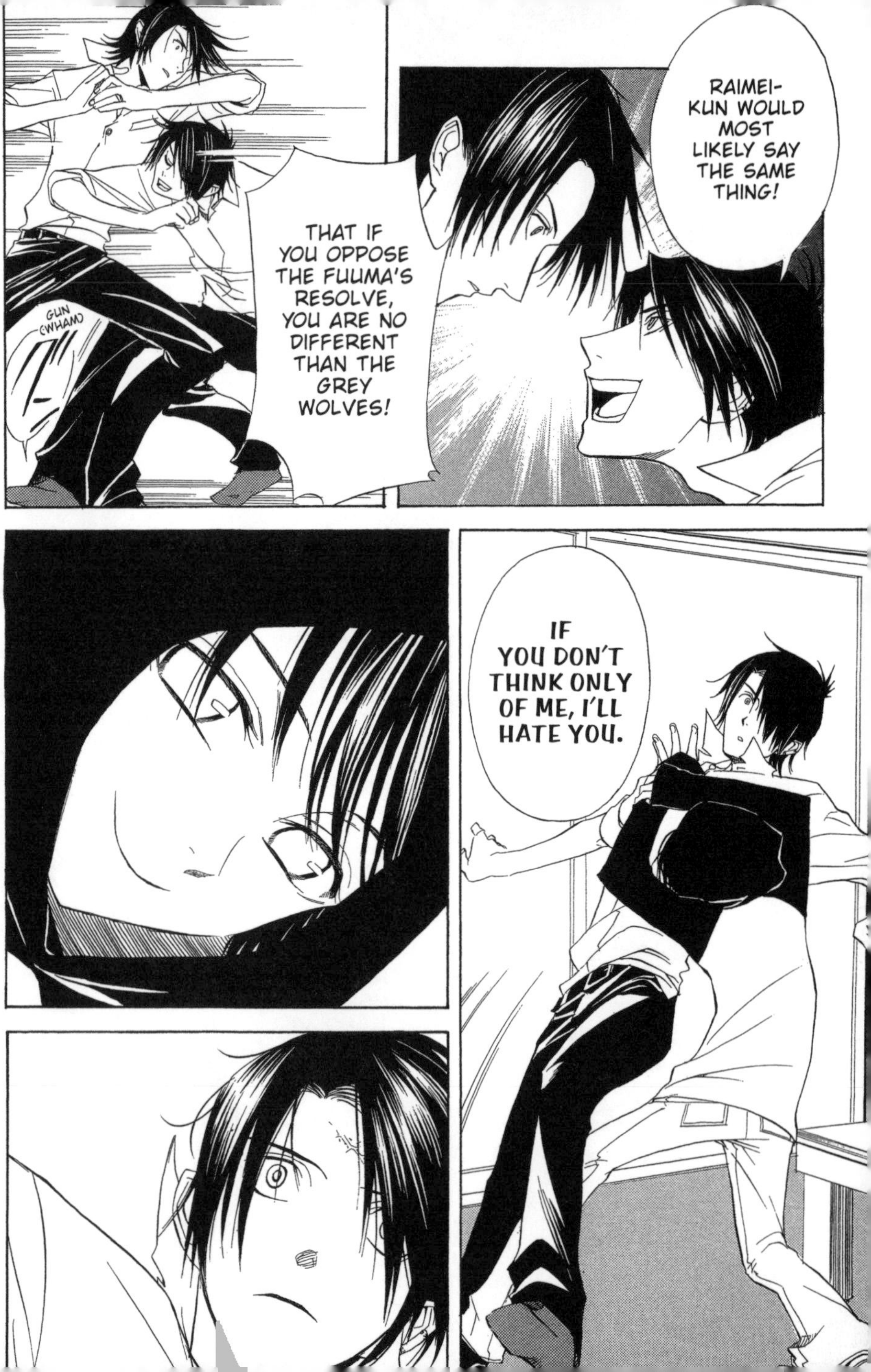
RAIMEI-KUN WOULD MOST LIKELY SAY THE SAME THING!
THAT IF YOU OPPOSE THE FUUMA'S RESOLVE, YOU ARE NO DIFFERENT THAN THE GREY WOLVES!
GUN (WHAM)
IF YOU DON'T THINK ONLY OF ME, I'LL HATE YOU.

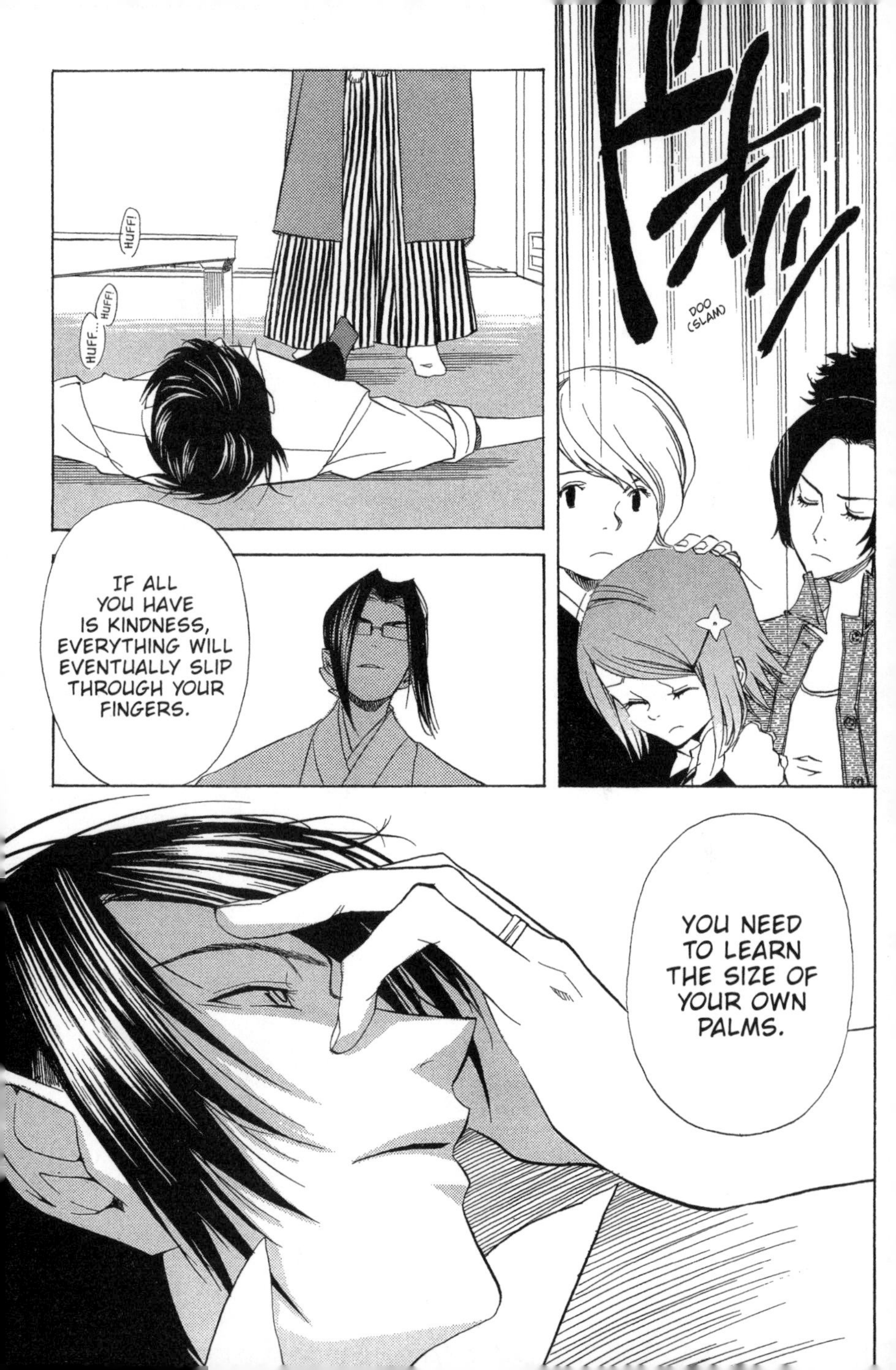
ドォッ
DOO (SLAM)
HUFF!
HUFF... HUFF!
IF ALL YOU HAVE IS KINDNESS, EVERYTHING WILL EVENTUALLY SLIP THROUGH YOUR FINGERS.
YOU NEED TO LEARN THE SIZE OF YOUR OWN PALMS.

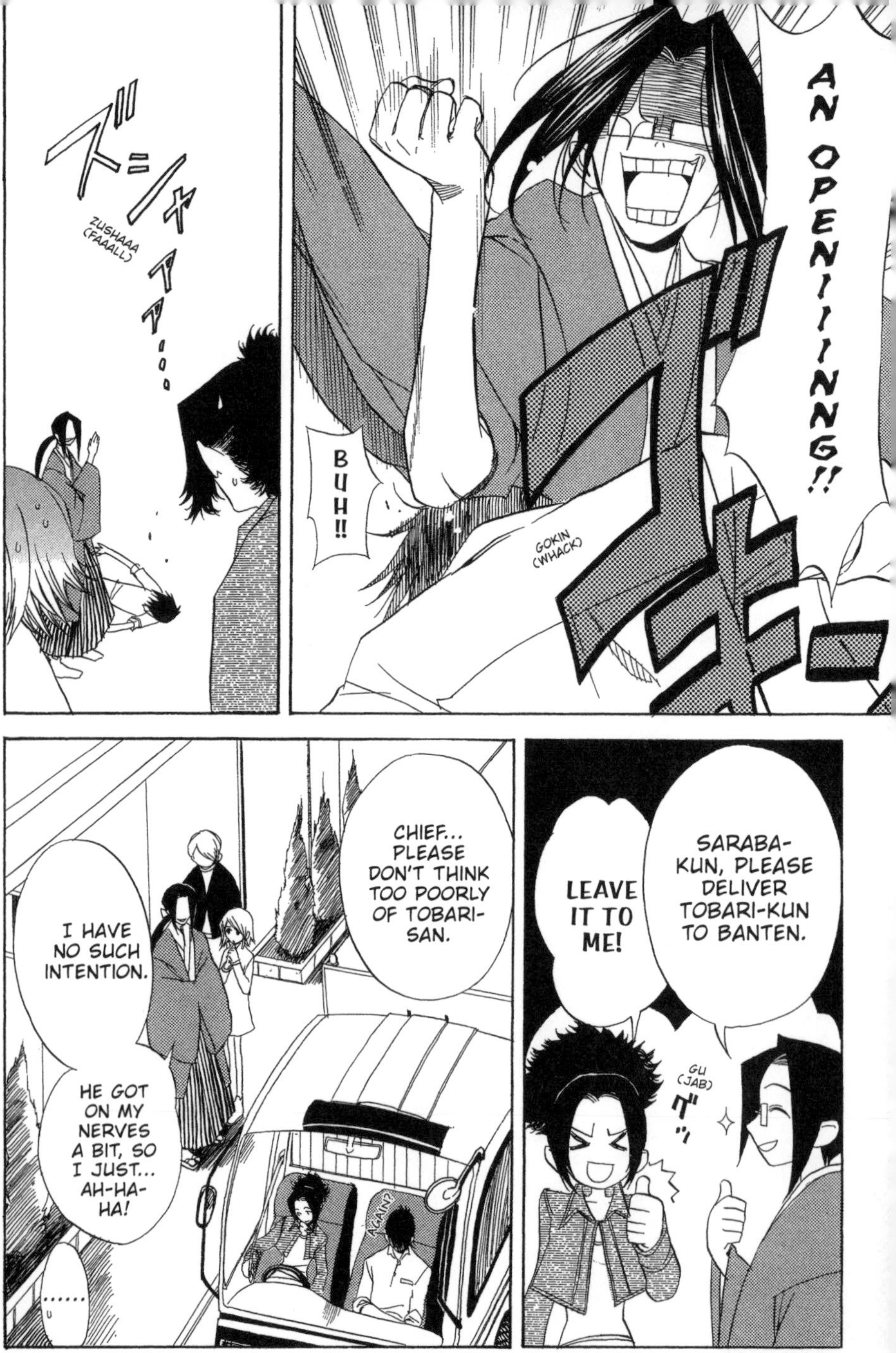
AN OPENIIINNG!!
BUH!!
GOKIN (WHACK)
ZUSHAAA (FAAALL)
SARABA-KUN, PLEASE DELIVER TOBARI-KUN TO BANTEN.
LEAVE IT TO ME!
GU (JAB)
CHIEF... PLEASE DON'T THINK TOO POORLY OF TOBARI-SAN.
I HAVE NO SUCH INTENTION.
HE GOT ON MY NERVES A BIT, SO I JUST... AH-HA-HA!
AGAIN?
......

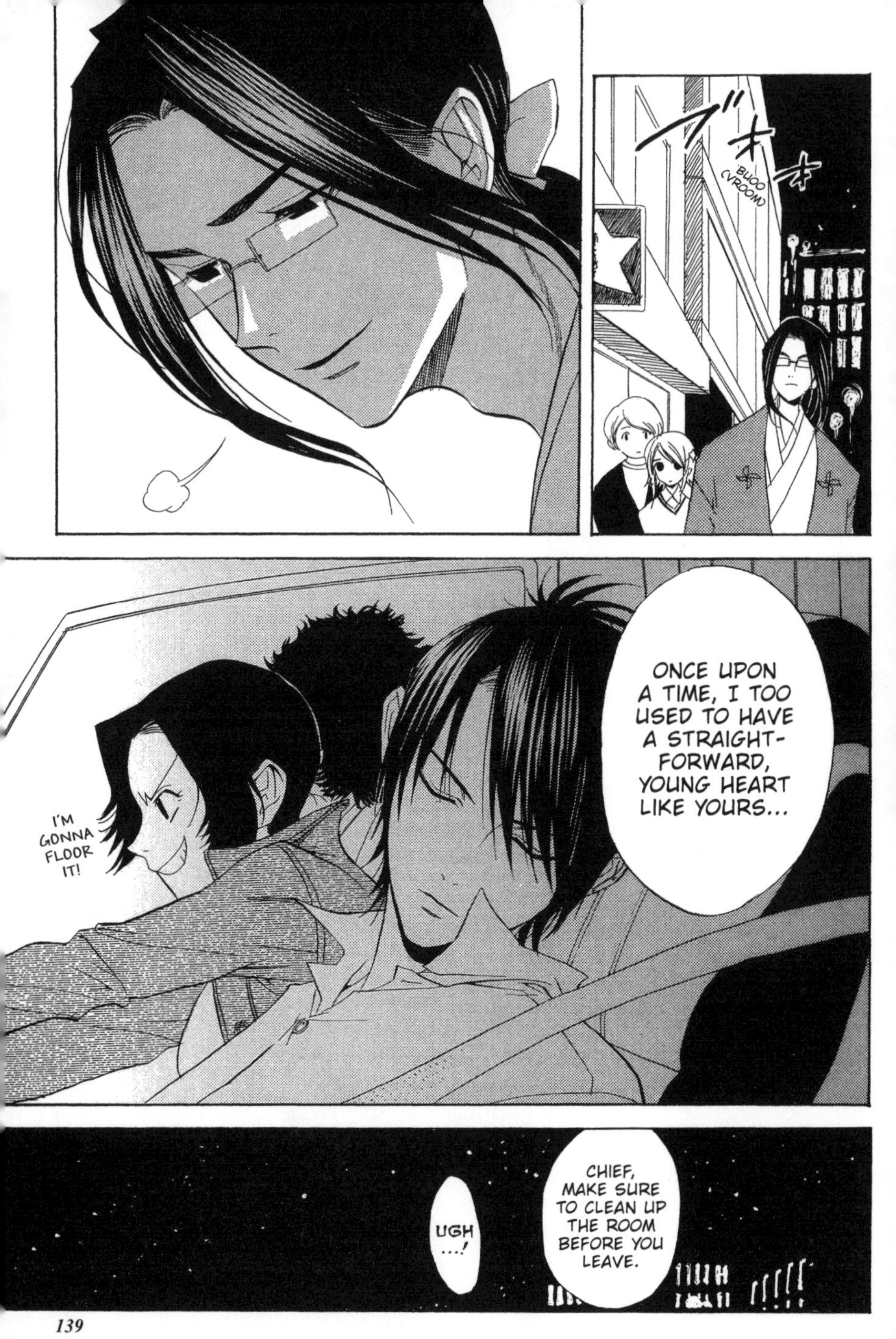
ブオオ
BUOO (VROOM)
ONCE UPON A TIME, I TOO USED TO HAVE A STRAIGHT-FORWARD, YOUNG HEART LIKE YOURS...
I'M GONNA FLOOR IT!
CHIEF, MAKE SURE TO CLEAN UP THE ROOM BEFORE YOU LEAVE.
UGH ...!

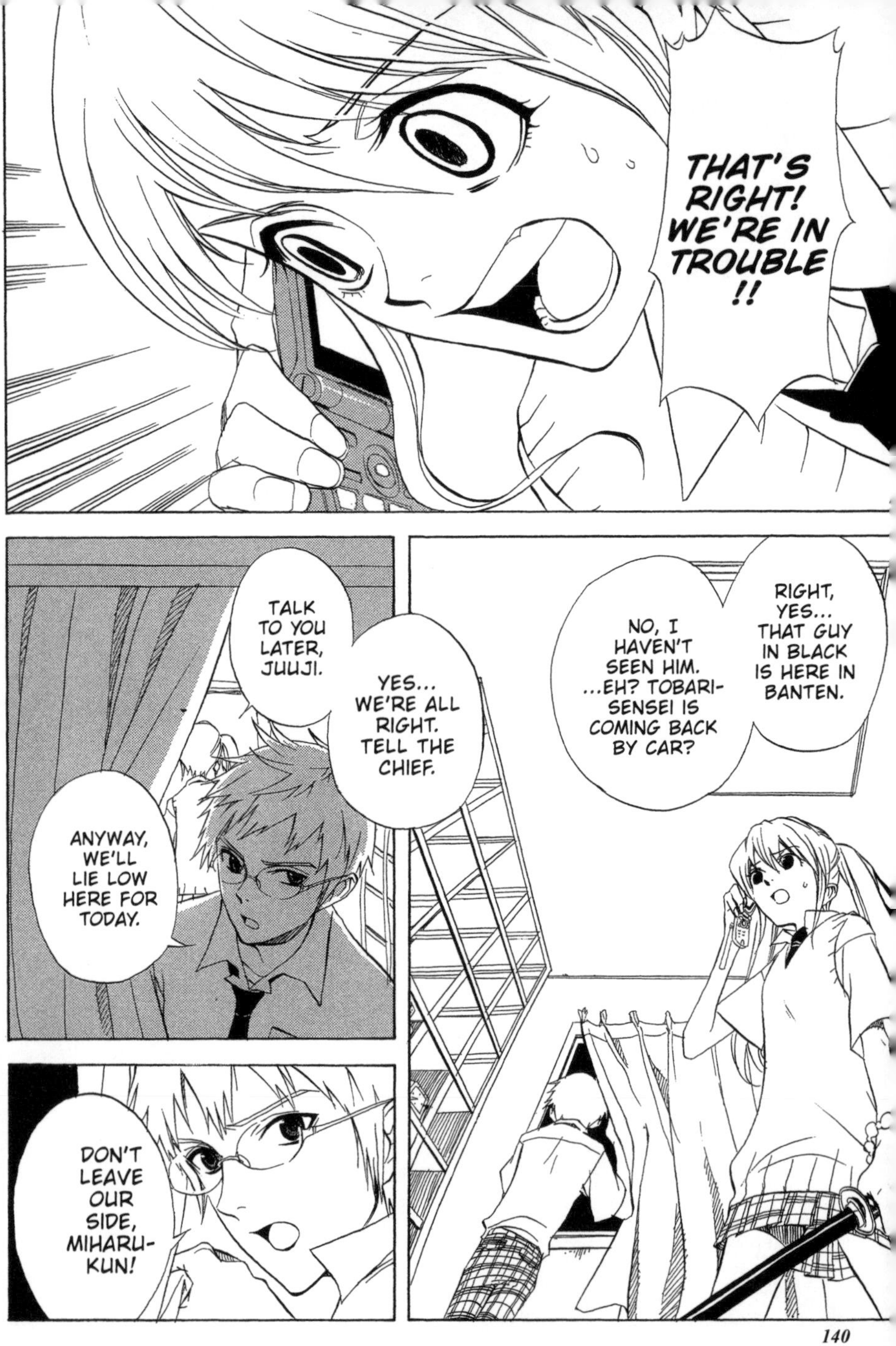
THAT'S RIGHT! WE'RE IN TROUBLE!!
RIGHT, YES... THAT GUY IN BLACK IS HERE IN BANTEN.
NO, I HAVEN'T SEEN HIM. ...EH? TOBARI-SENSEI IS COMING BACK BY CAR?
YES... WE'RE ALL RIGHT. TELL THE CHIEF.
TALK TO YOU LATER, JUUJI.
ANYWAY, WE'LL LIE LOW HERE FOR TODAY.
DON'T LEAVE OUR SIDE, MIHARU-KUN!

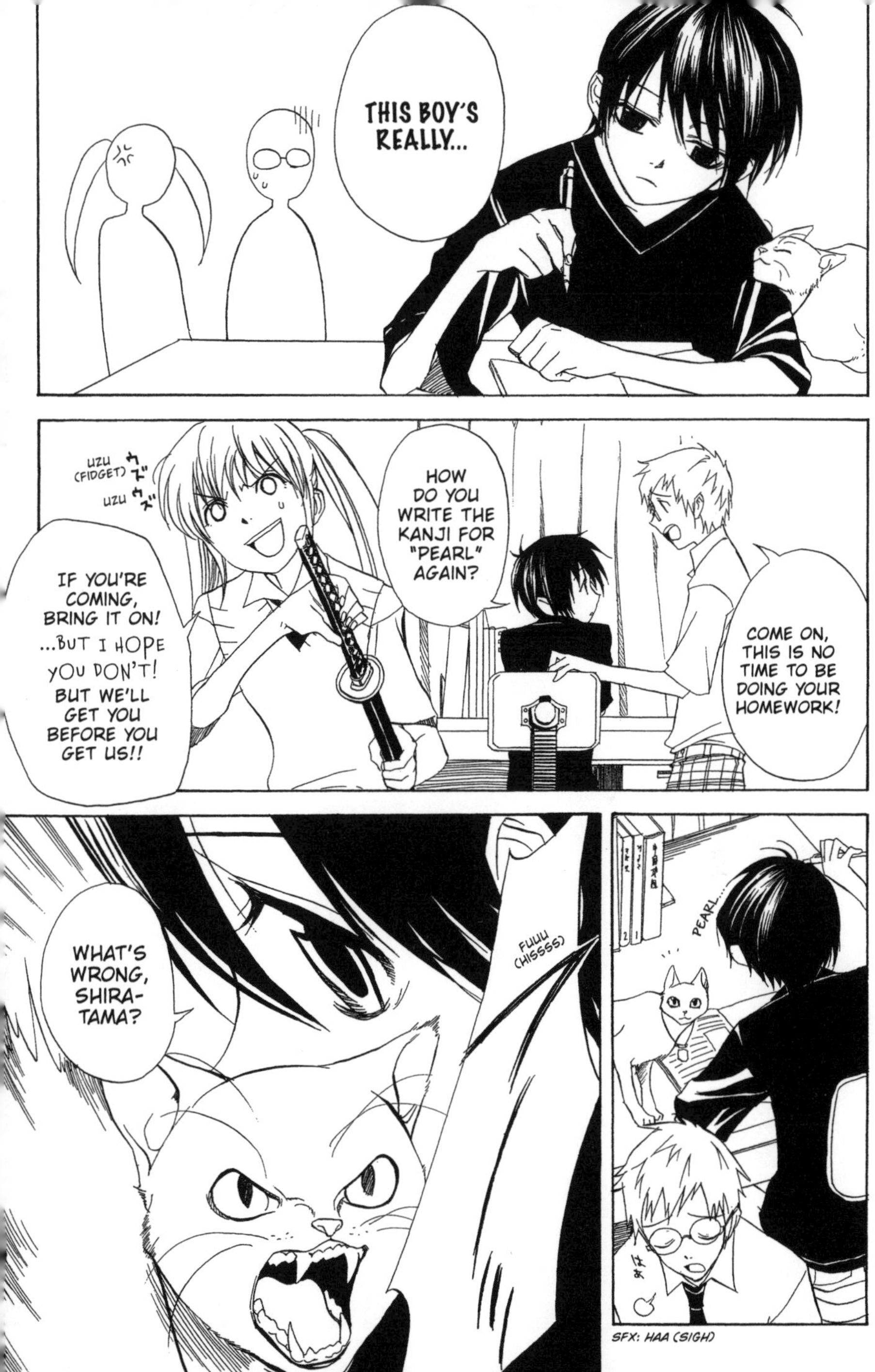
THIS BOY'S REALLY...
COME ON, THIS IS NO TIME TO BE DOING YOUR HOMEWORK!
HOW DO YOU WRITE THE KANJI FOR "PEARL" AGAIN?
UZU (FIDGET) ウズ
UZU ウズ
IF YOU'RE COMING, BRING IT ON! ...BUT I HOPE YOU DON'T! BUT WE'LL GET YOU BEFORE YOU GET US!!
PEARL....
FUUU (HISSSS)
WHAT'S WRONG, SHIRA-TAMA?
SFX: HAA (SIGH)

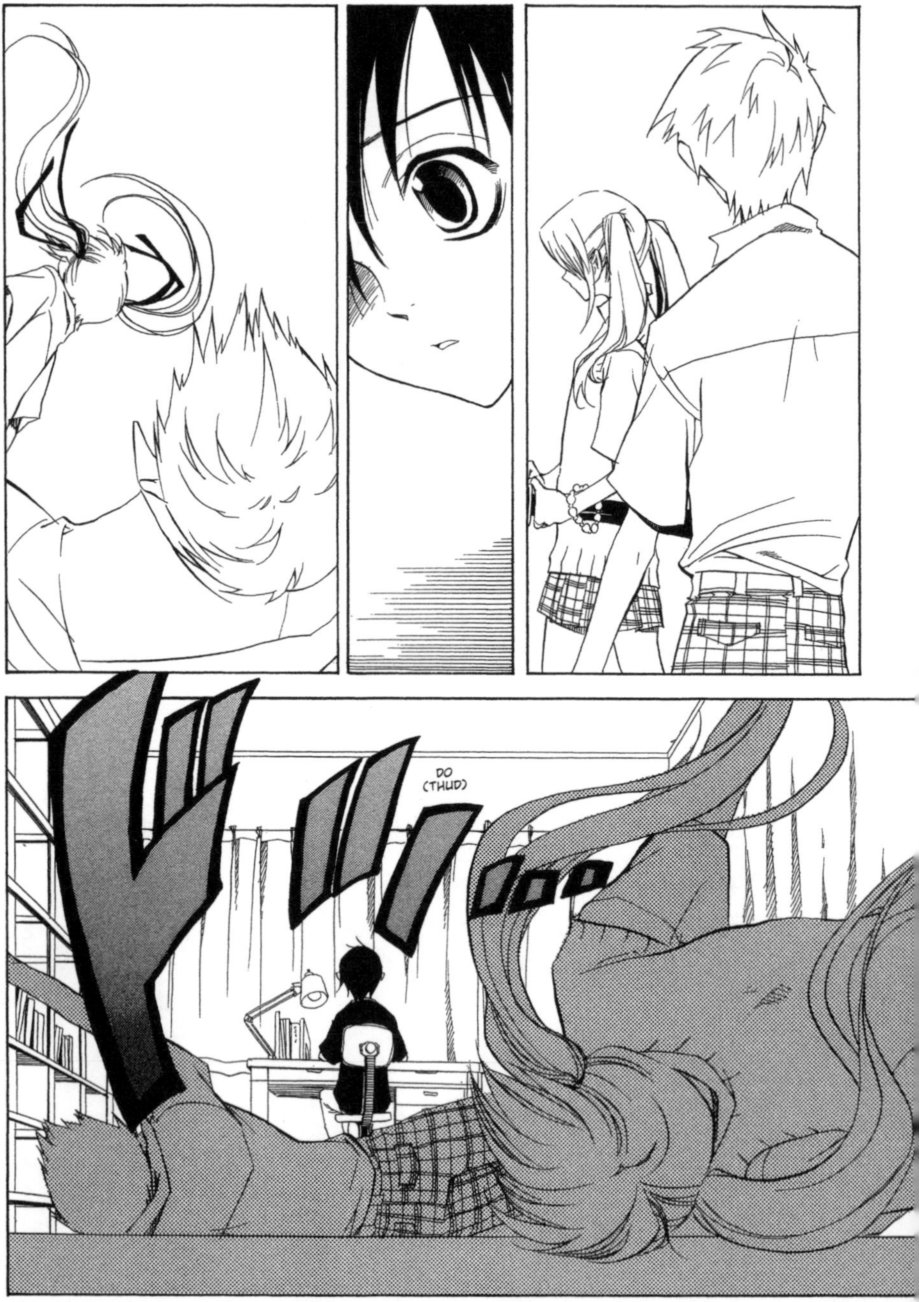
DO
(THUD)

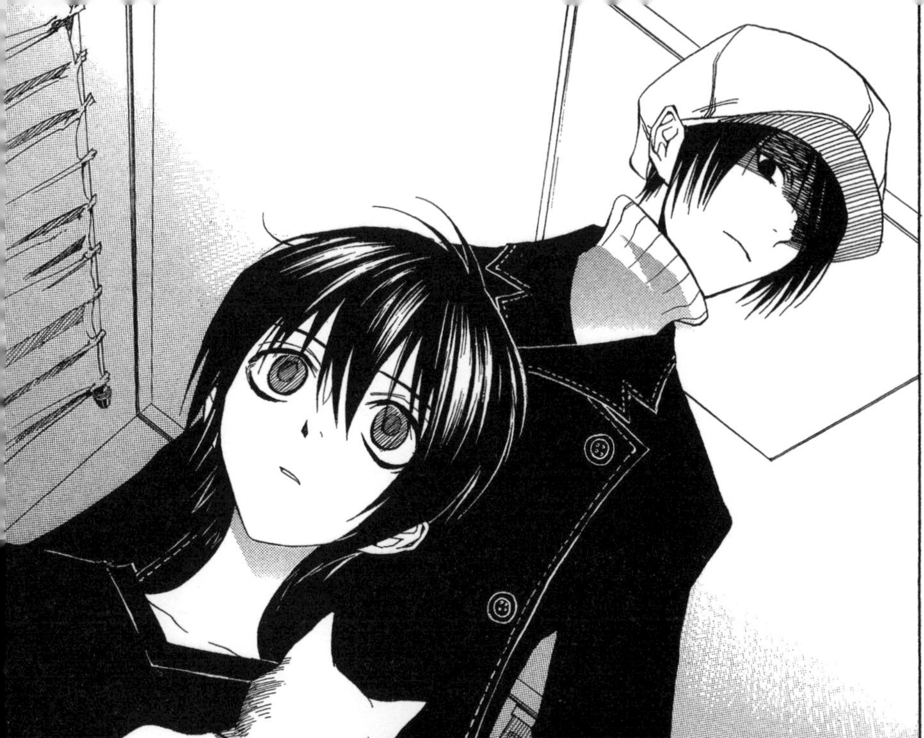

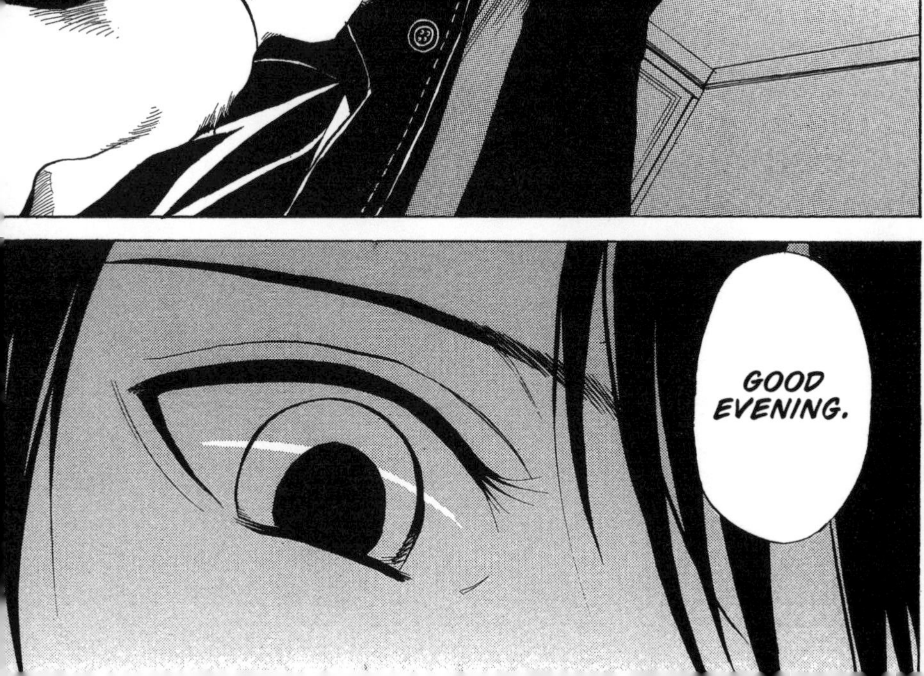
GOOD EVENING.

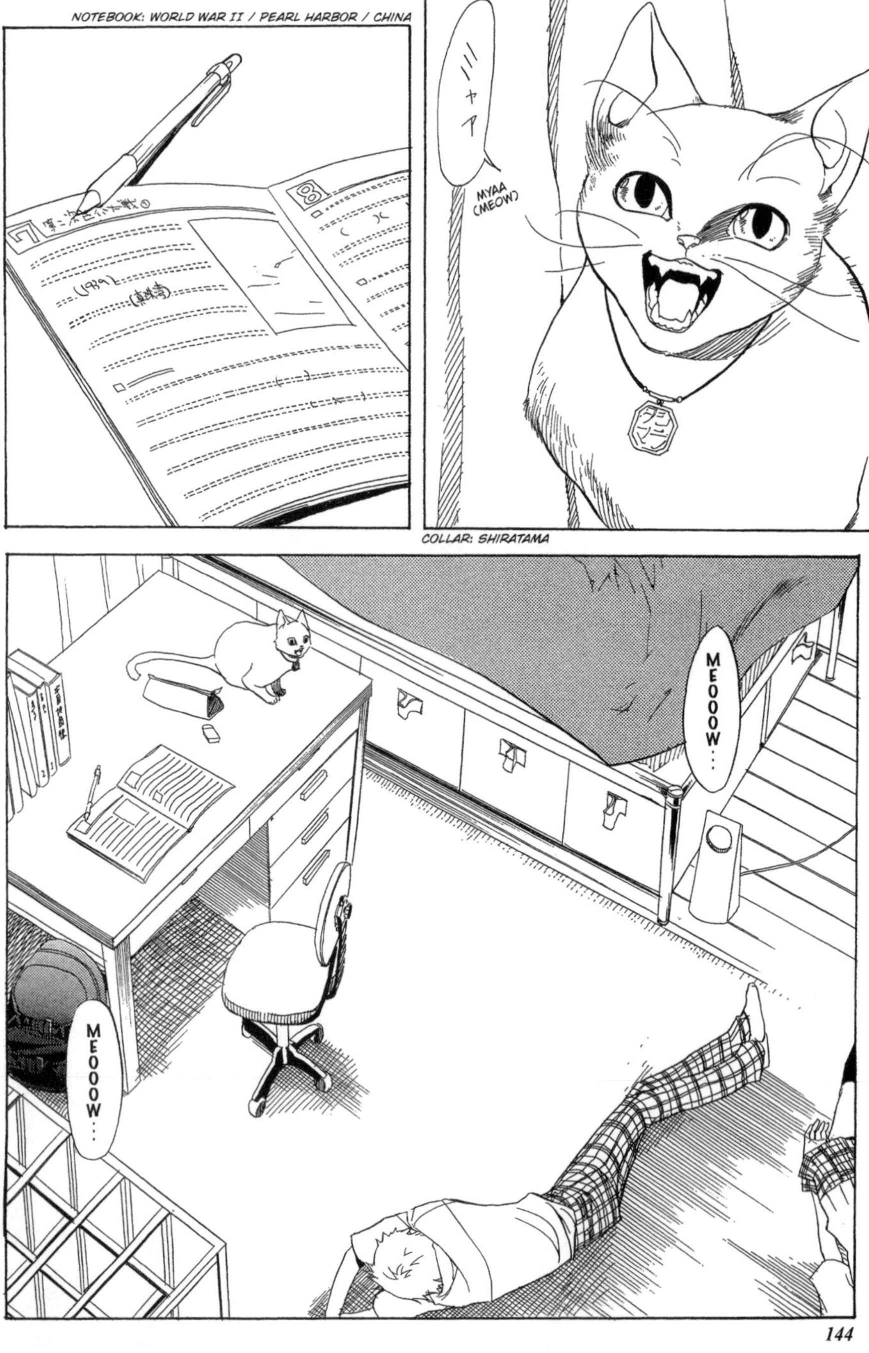
ミャア
MYAA (MEOW)
COLLAR: SHIRATAMA
NOTEBOOK: WORLD WAR II / PEARL HARBOR / CHINA
MEOOOW...
MEOOOW...

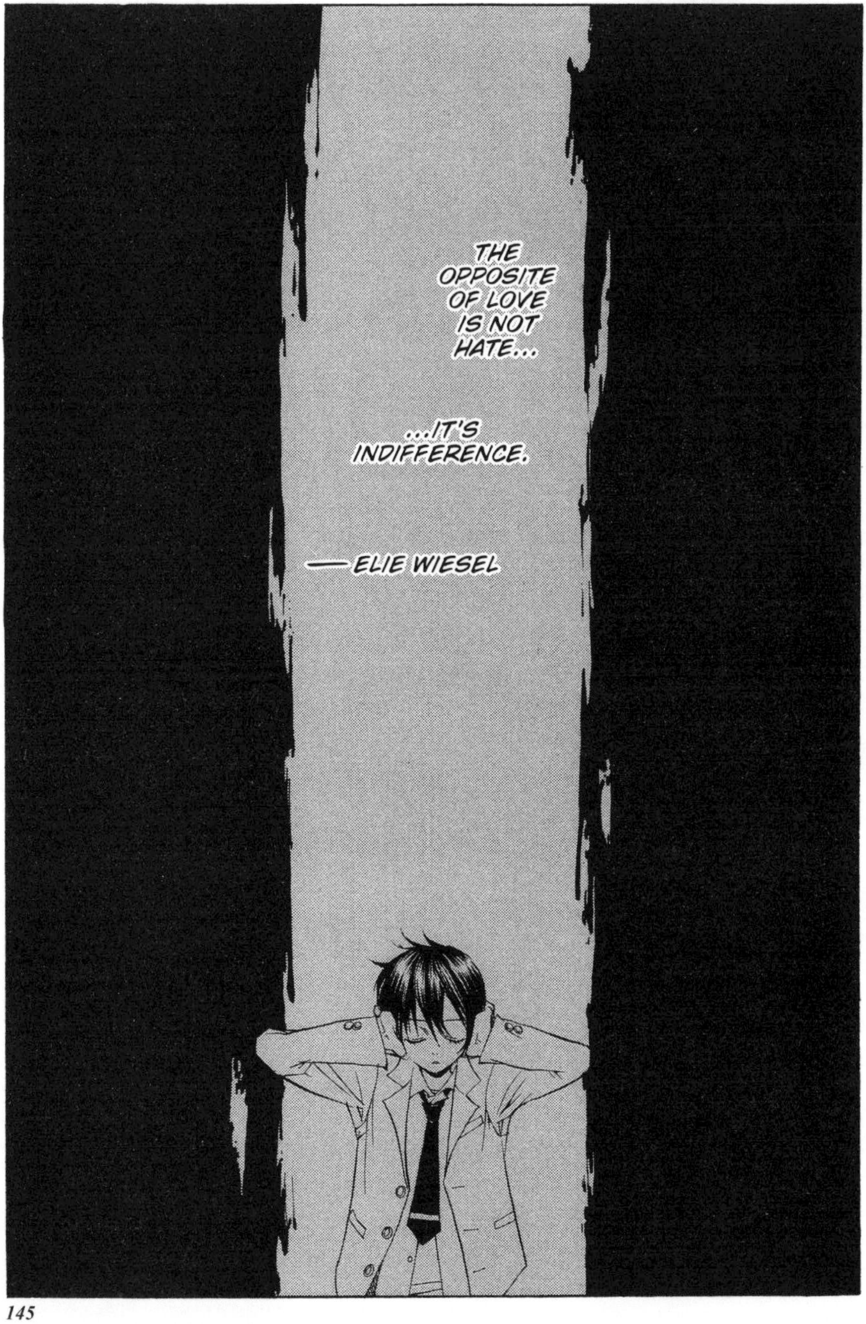
THE OPPOSITE OF LOVE IS NOT HATE...
...IT'S INDIFFERENCE.
—ELIE WIESEL

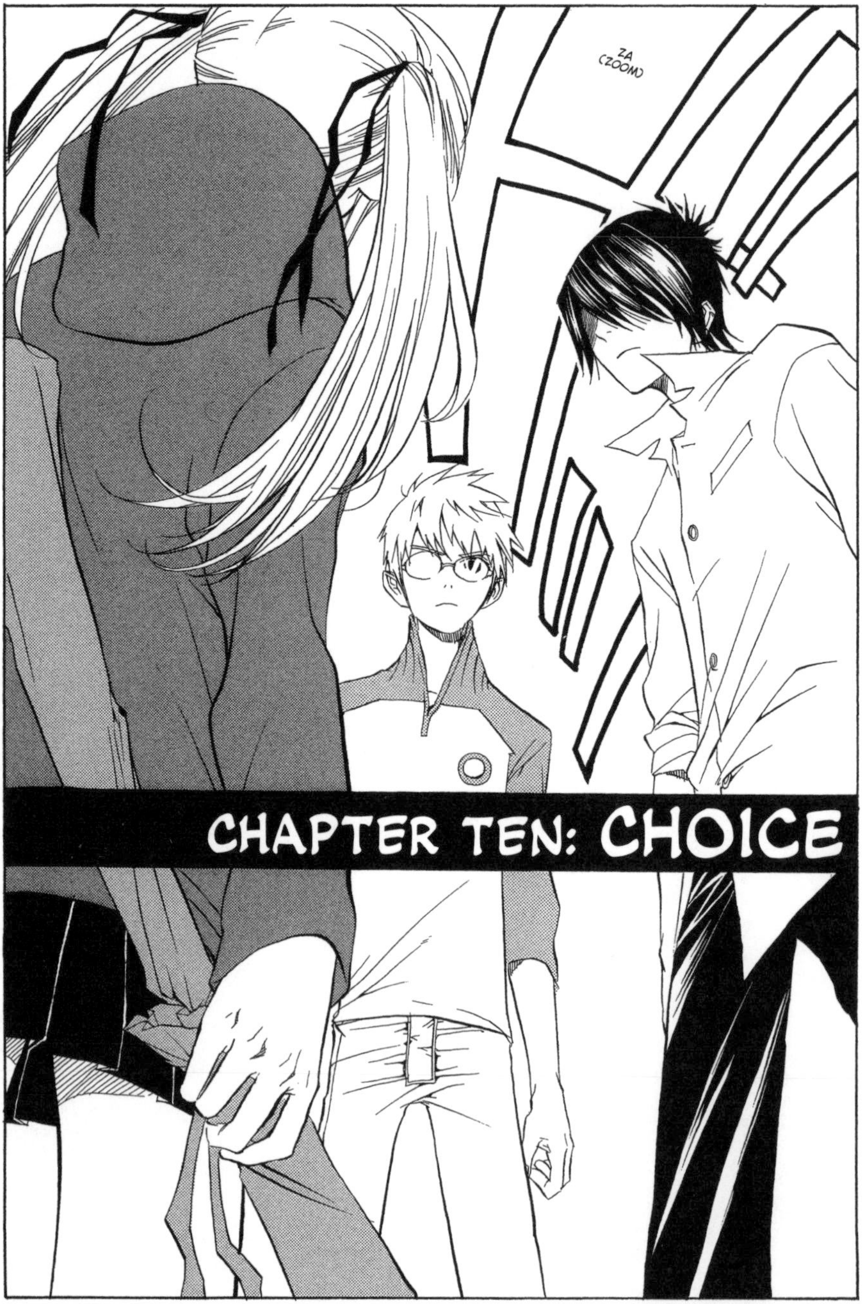
ZA
(ZOOM)
CHAPTER TEN: CHOICE

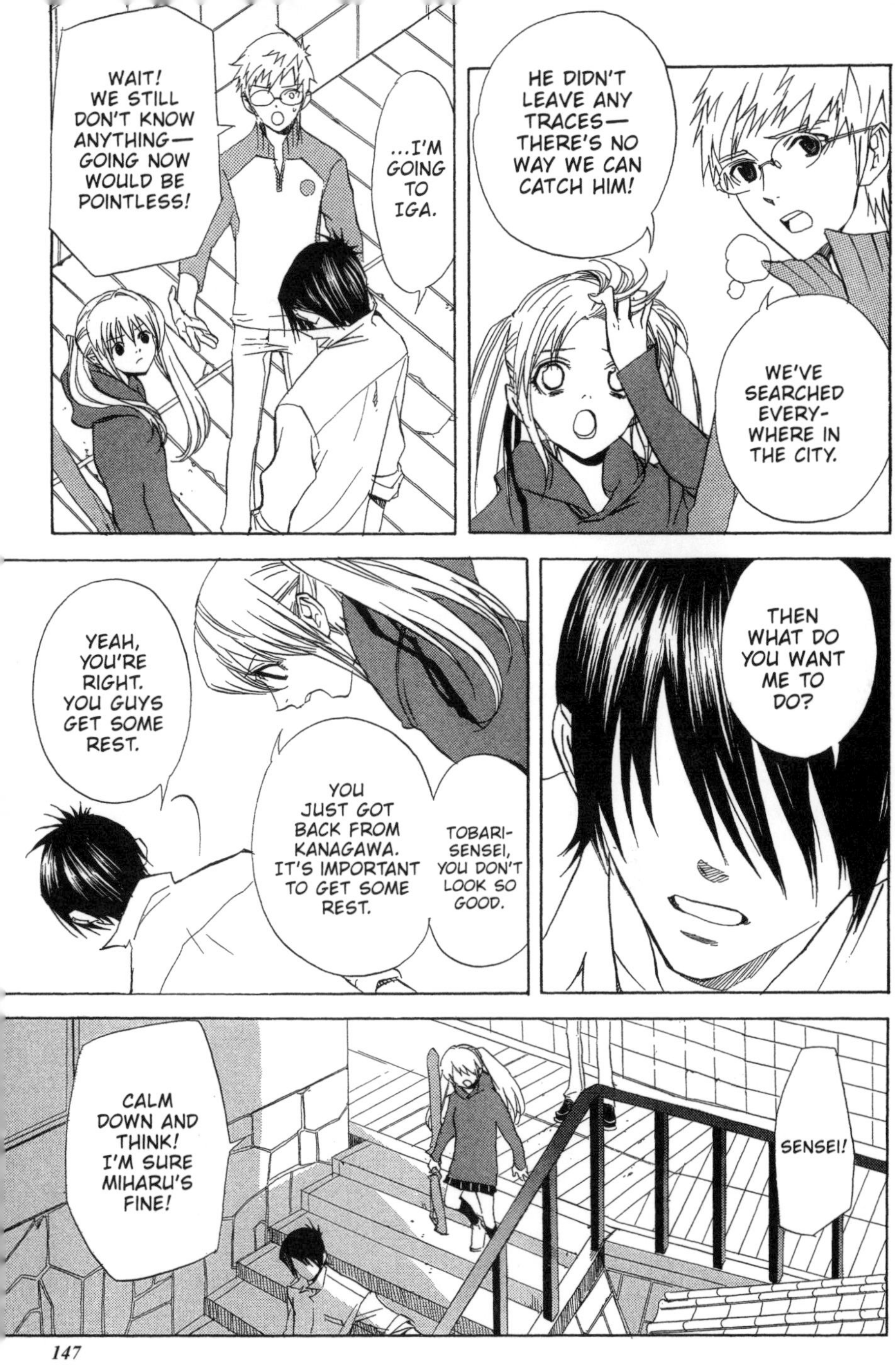
HE DIDN'T LEAVE ANY TRACES— THERE'S NO WAY WE CAN CATCH HIM!
WE'VE SEARCHED EVERY-WHERE IN THE CITY.
...I'M GOING TO IGA.
WAIT! WE STILL DON'T KNOW ANYTHING— GOING NOW WOULD BE POINTLESS!
THEN WHAT DO YOU WANT ME TO DO?
TOBARI-SENSEI, YOU DON'T LOOK SO GOOD.
YOU JUST GOT BACK FROM KANAGAWA. IT'S IMPORTANT TO GET SOME REST.
YEAH, YOU'RE RIGHT. YOU GUYS GET SOME REST.
SENSEI!
CALM DOWN AND THINK! I'M SURE MIHARU'S FINE!

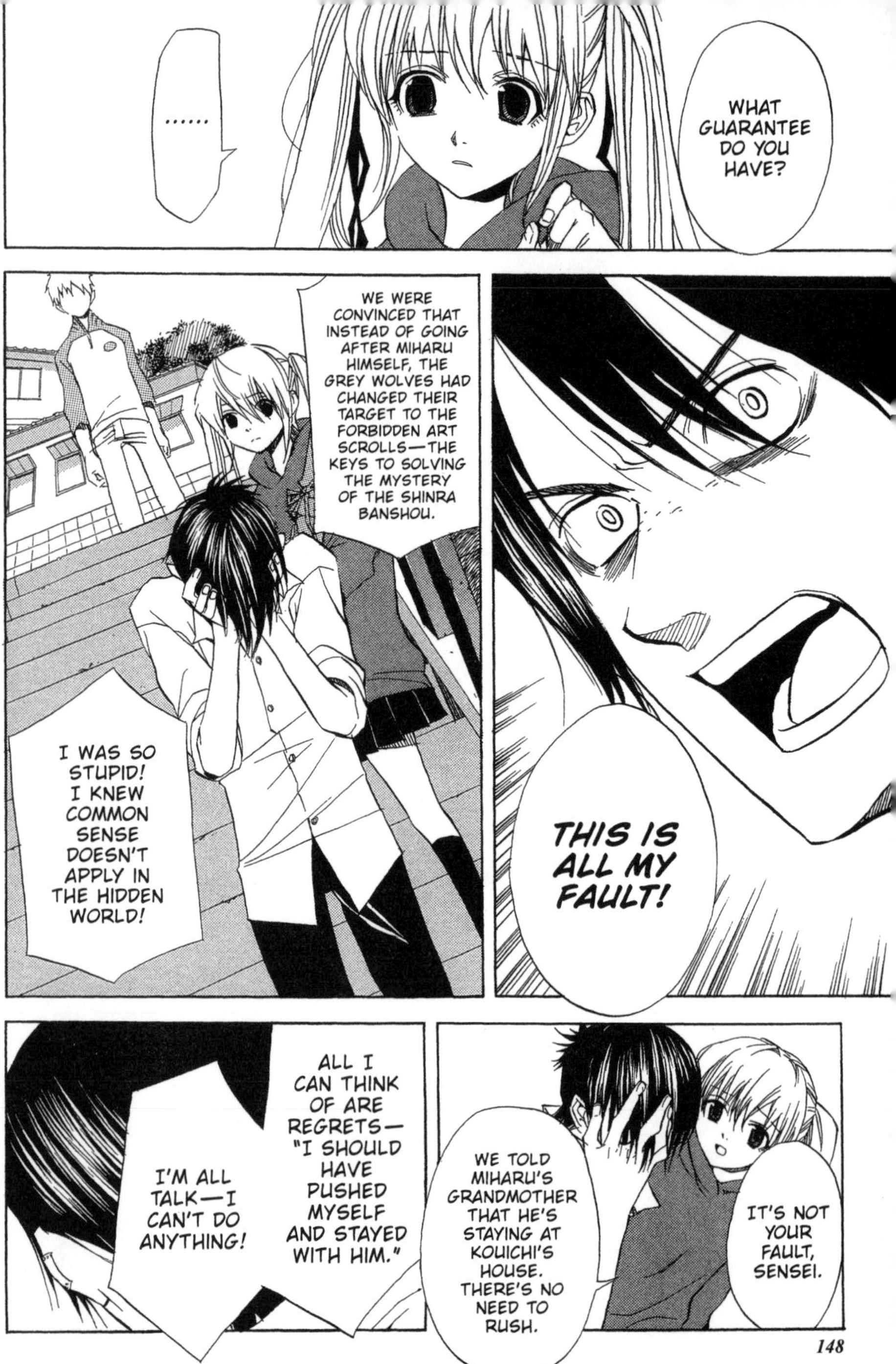
WHAT GUARANTEE DO YOU HAVE?
......
THIS IS ALL MY FAULT!
WE WERE CONVINCED THAT INSTEAD OF GOING AFTER MIHARU HIMSELF, THE GREY WOLVES HAD CHANGED THEIR TARGET TO THE FORBIDDEN ART SCROLLS—THE KEYS TO SOLVING THE MYSTERY OF THE SHINRA BANSHOU.
I WAS SO STUPID! I KNEW COMMON SENSE DOESN'T APPLY IN THE HIDDEN WORLD!
IT'S NOT YOUR FAULT, SENSEI.
WE TOLD MIHARU'S GRANDMOTHER THAT HE'S STAYING AT KOUICHI'S HOUSE. THERE'S NO NEED TO RUSH.
ALL I CAN THINK OF ARE REGRETS—"I SHOULD HAVE PUSHED MYSELF AND STAYED WITH HIM."
I'M ALL TALK—I CAN'T DO ANYTHING!

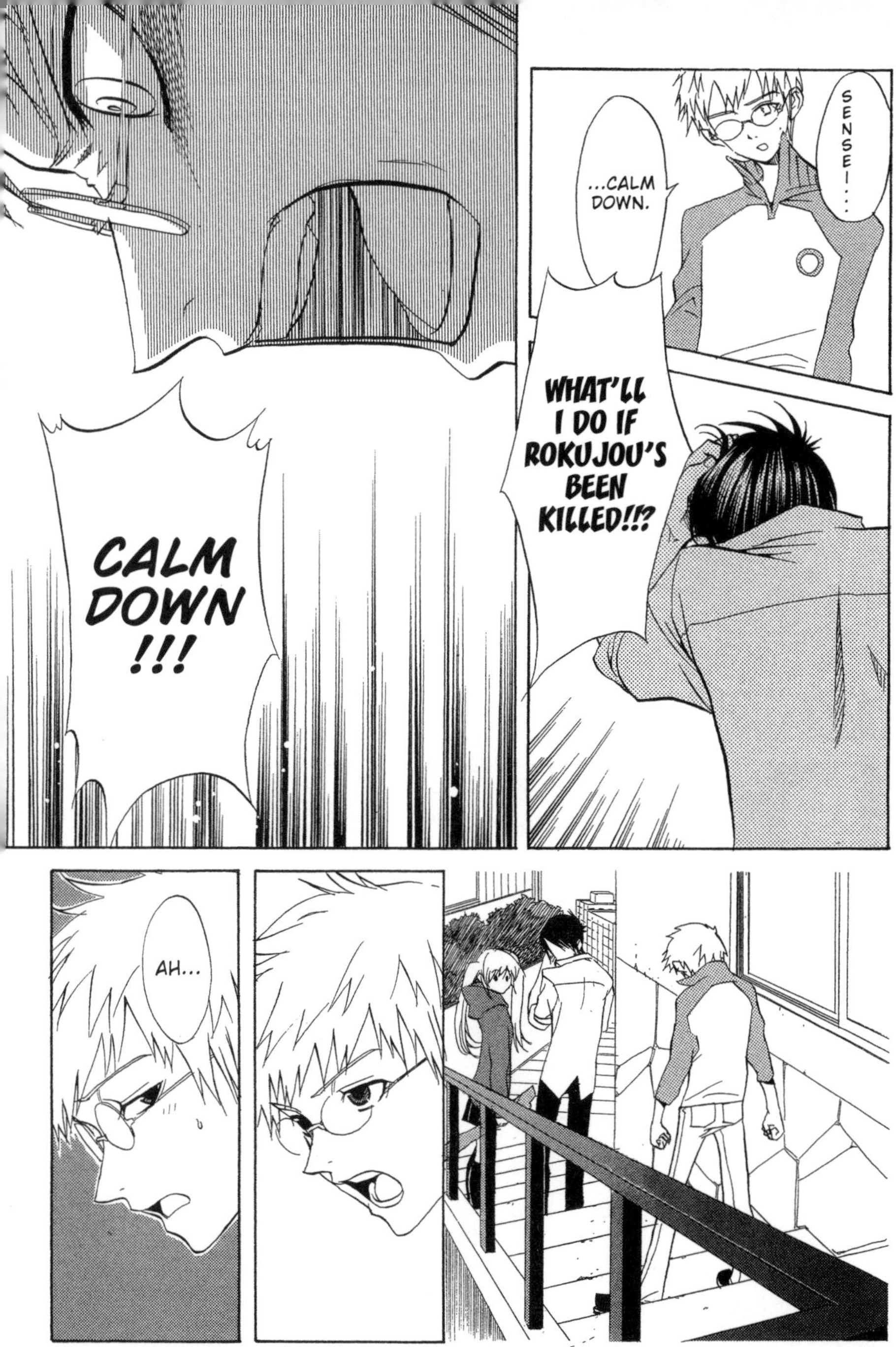
SENSEI...
...CALM DOWN.
WHAT'LL I DO IF ROKUJOU'S BEEN KILLED!!?
CALM DOWN!!!
AH...

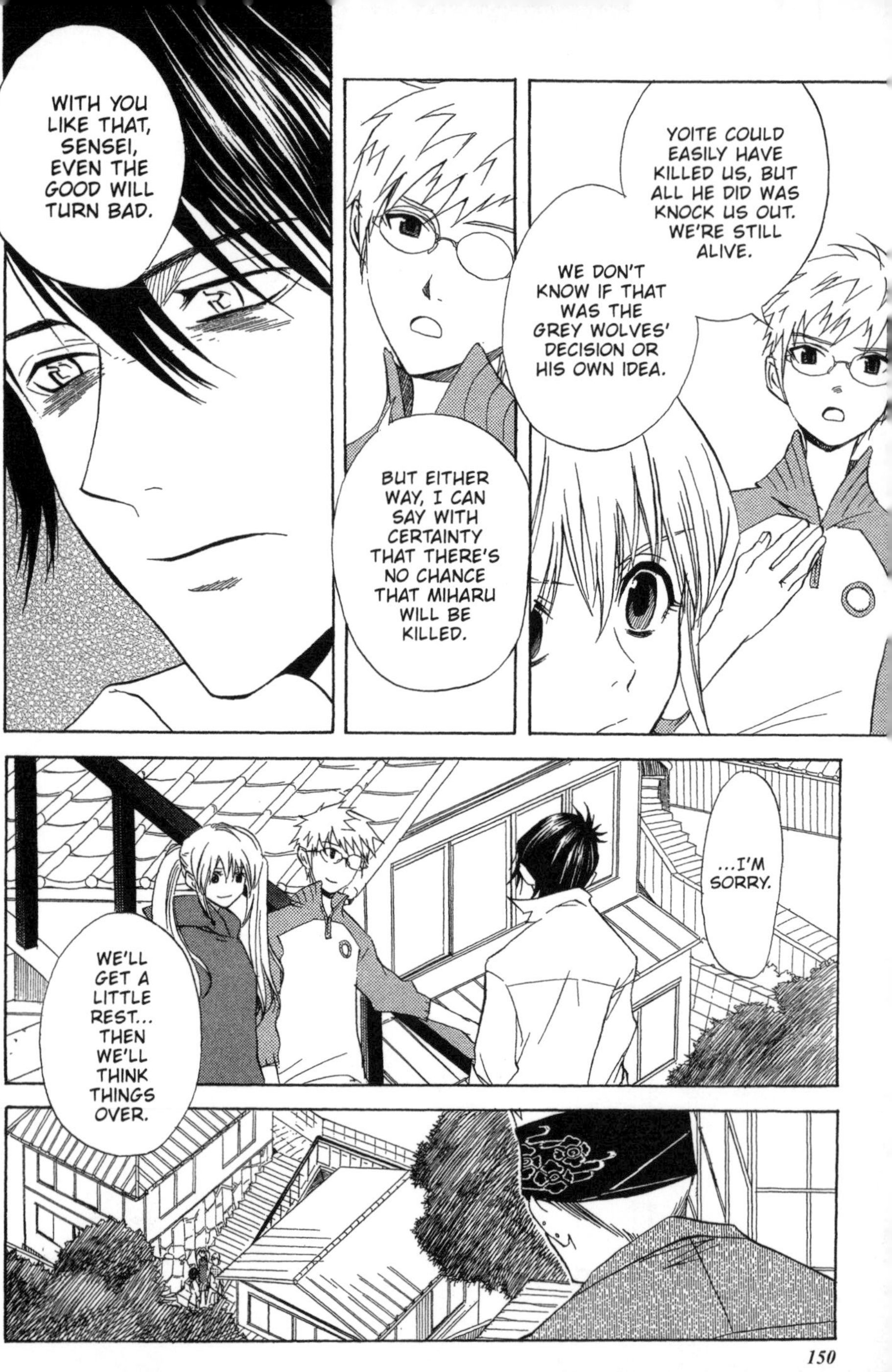
YOITE COULD EASILY HAVE KILLED US, BUT ALL HE DID WAS KNOCK US OUT. WE'RE STILL ALIVE.
WE DON'T KNOW IF THAT WAS THE GREY WOLVES' DECISION OR HIS OWN IDEA.
BUT EITHER WAY, I CAN SAY WITH CERTAINTY THAT THERE'S NO CHANCE THAT MIHARU WILL BE KILLED.
WITH YOU LIKE THAT, SENSEI, EVEN THE GOOD WILL TURN BAD.
...I'M SORRY.
WE'LL GET A LITTLE REST... THEN WE'LL THINK THINGS OVER.

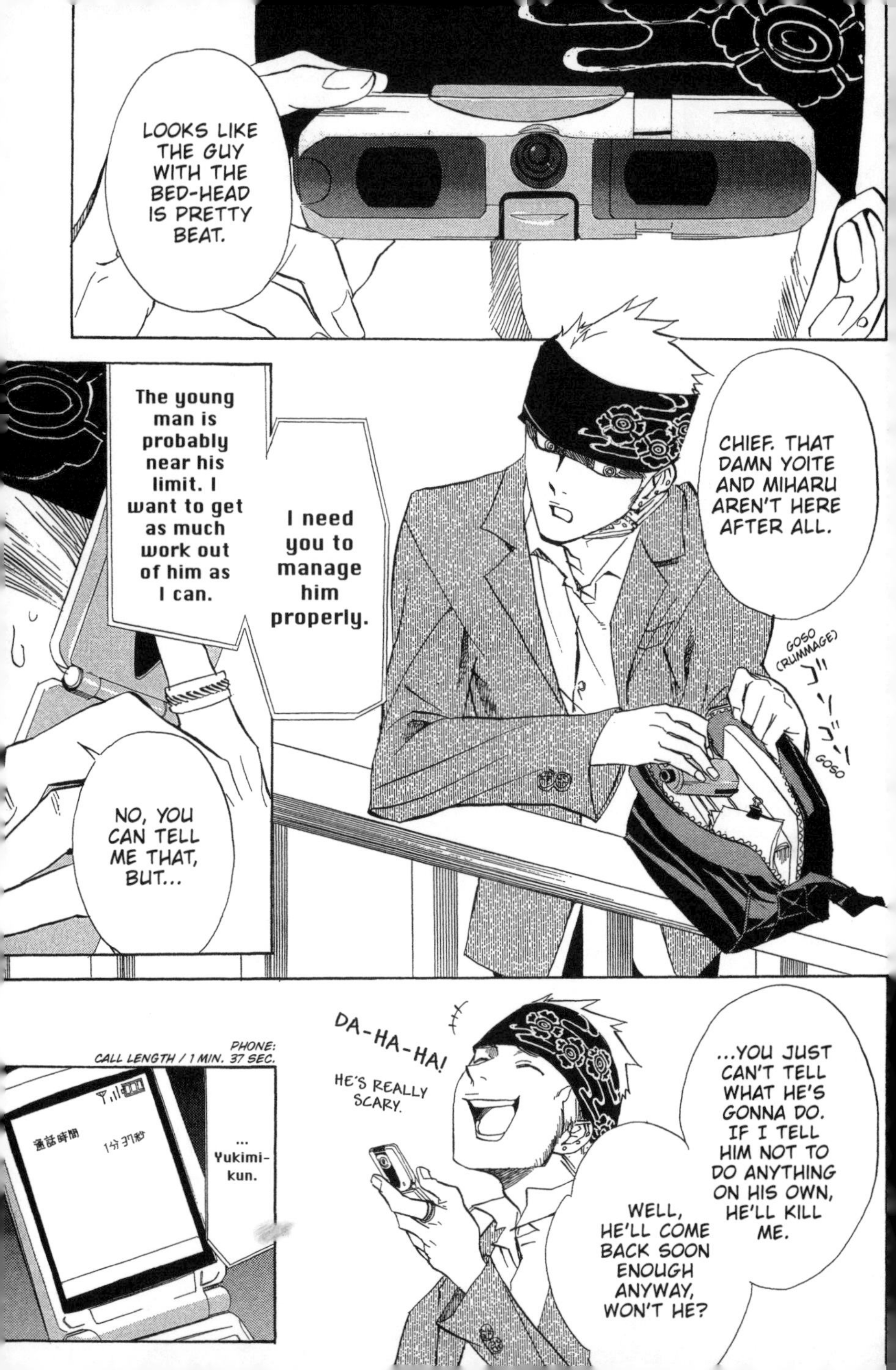
LOOKS LIKE THE GUY WITH THE BED-HEAD IS PRETTY BEAT.
CHIEF. THAT DAMN YOITE AND MIHARU AREN'T HERE AFTER ALL.
GOSO (RUMMAGE)
GOSO
The young man is probably near his limit. I want to get as much work out of him as I can.
I need you to manage him properly.
NO, YOU CAN TELL ME THAT, BUT...
...YOU JUST CAN'T TELL WHAT HE'S GONNA DO. IF I TELL HIM NOT TO DO ANYTHING ON HIS OWN, HE'LL KILL ME.
DA-HA-HA!
HE'S REALLY SCARY.
WELL, HE'LL COME BACK SOON ENOUGH ANYWAY, WON'T HE?
PHONE: CALL LENGTH / 1 MIN. 37 SEC.
通話時間
1分37秒
...Yukimi-kun.

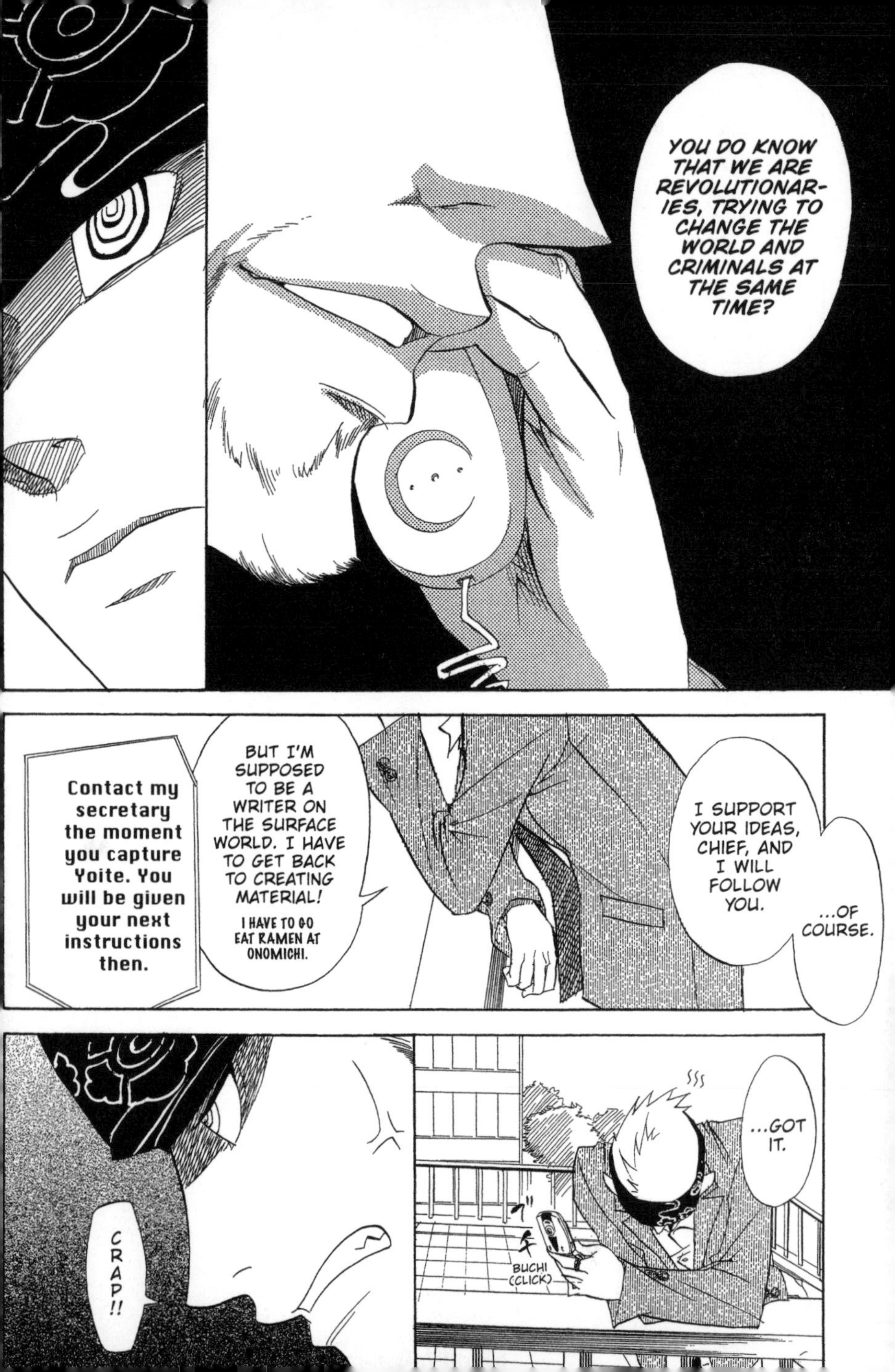
YOU DO KNOW THAT WE ARE REVOLUTIONARIES, TRYING TO CHANGE THE WORLD AND CRIMINALS AT THE SAME TIME?
I SUPPORT YOUR IDEAS, CHIEF, AND I WILL FOLLOW YOU.
...OF COURSE.
BUT I'M SUPPOSED TO BE A WRITER ON THE SURFACE WORLD. I HAVE TO GET BACK TO CREATING MATERIAL!
I HAVE TO GO EAT RAMEN AT ONOMICHI.
Contact my secretary the moment you capture Yoite. You will be given your next instructions then.
...GOT IT.
BUCHI (CLICK)
CRAP!!

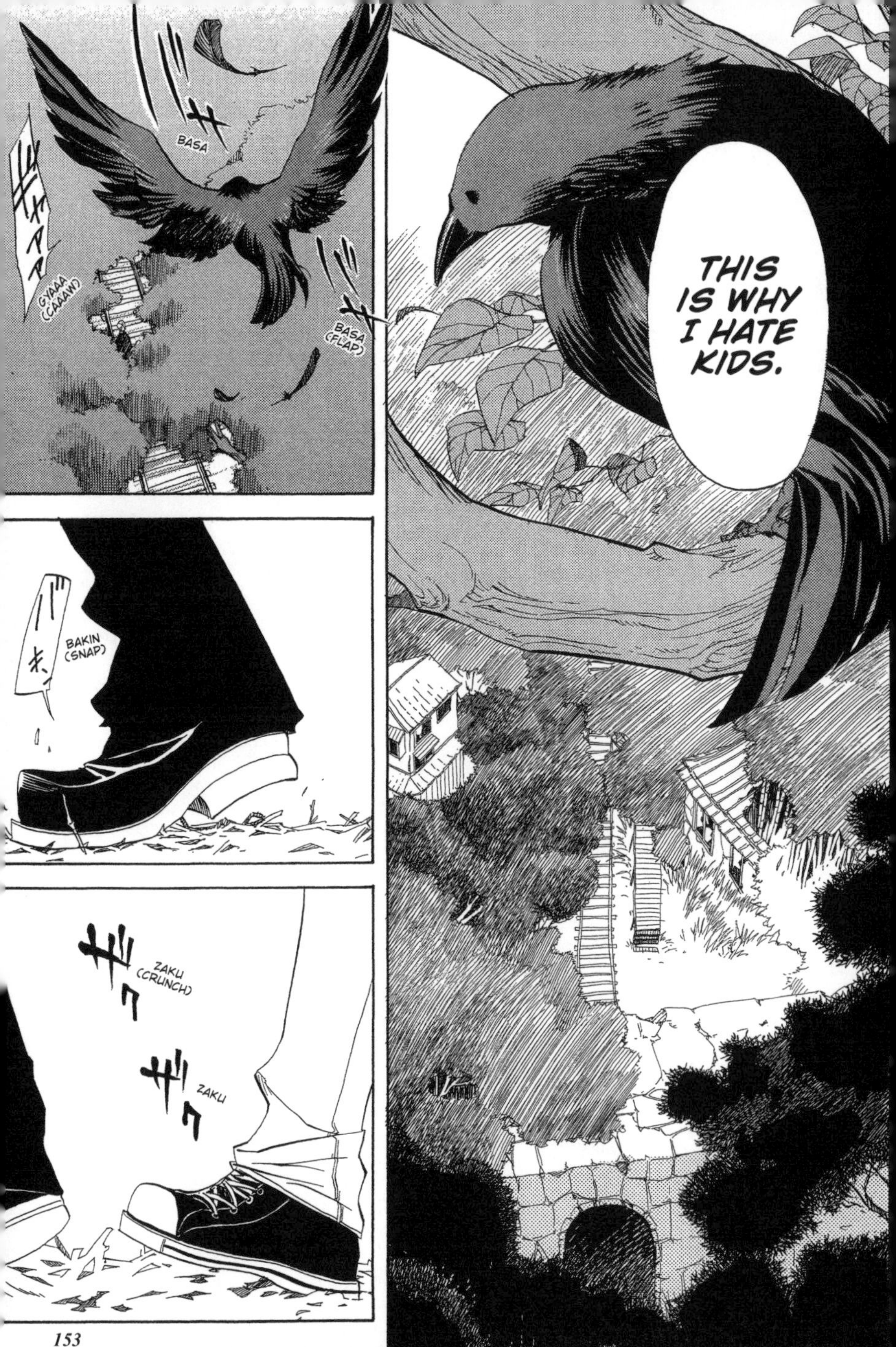
THIS IS WHY I HATE KIDS.
BASA
BASA (FLAP)
GYAAA (CAAAW)
BAKIN (SNAP)
ZAKU (CRUNCH)
ZAKU

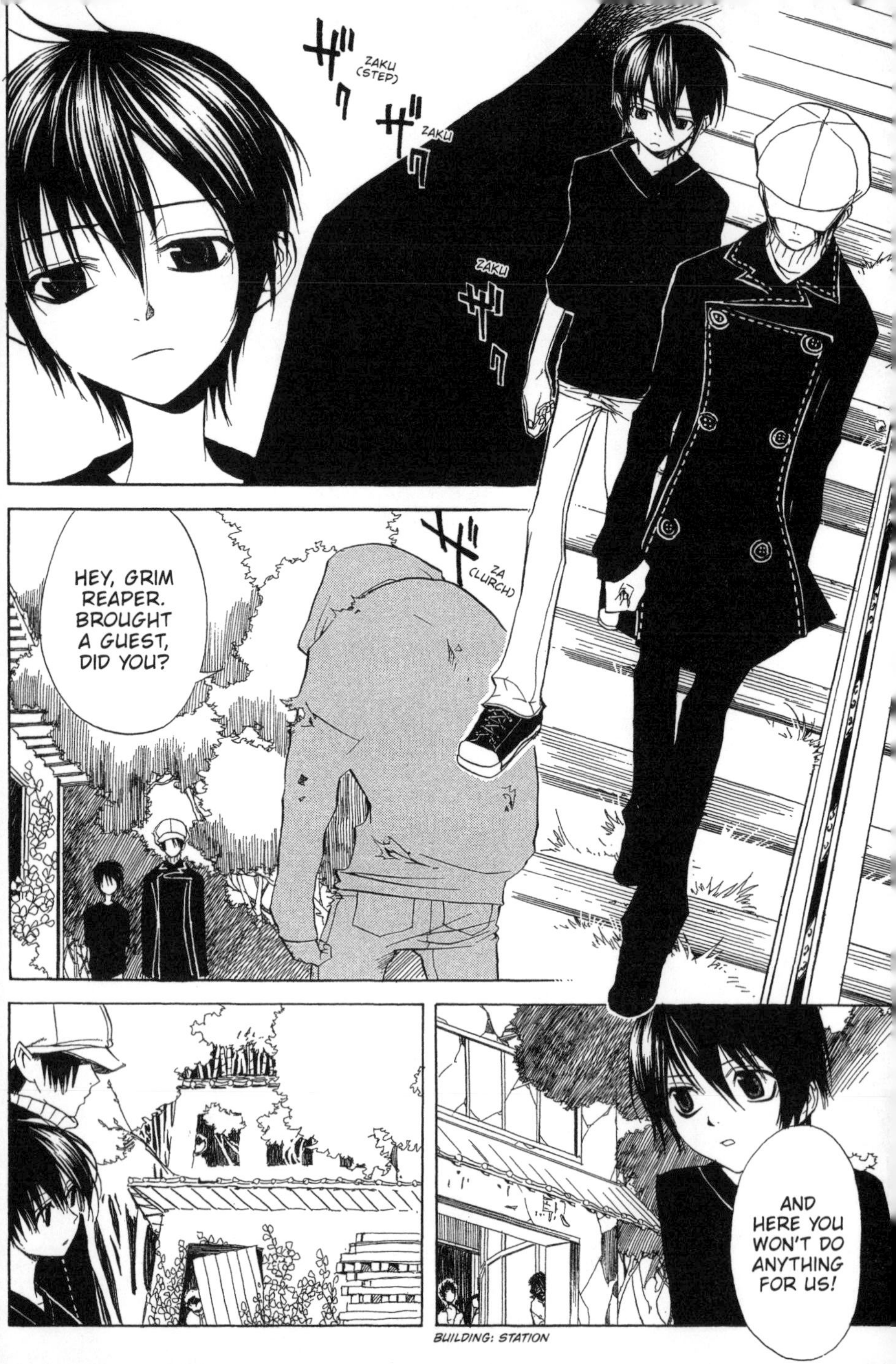
ZAKU (STEP)
ZAKU
ZAKU
ZA (LURCH)
HEY, GRIM REAPER. BROUGHT A GUEST, DID YOU?
AND HERE YOU WON'T DO ANYTHING FOR US!

BUILDING: STATION

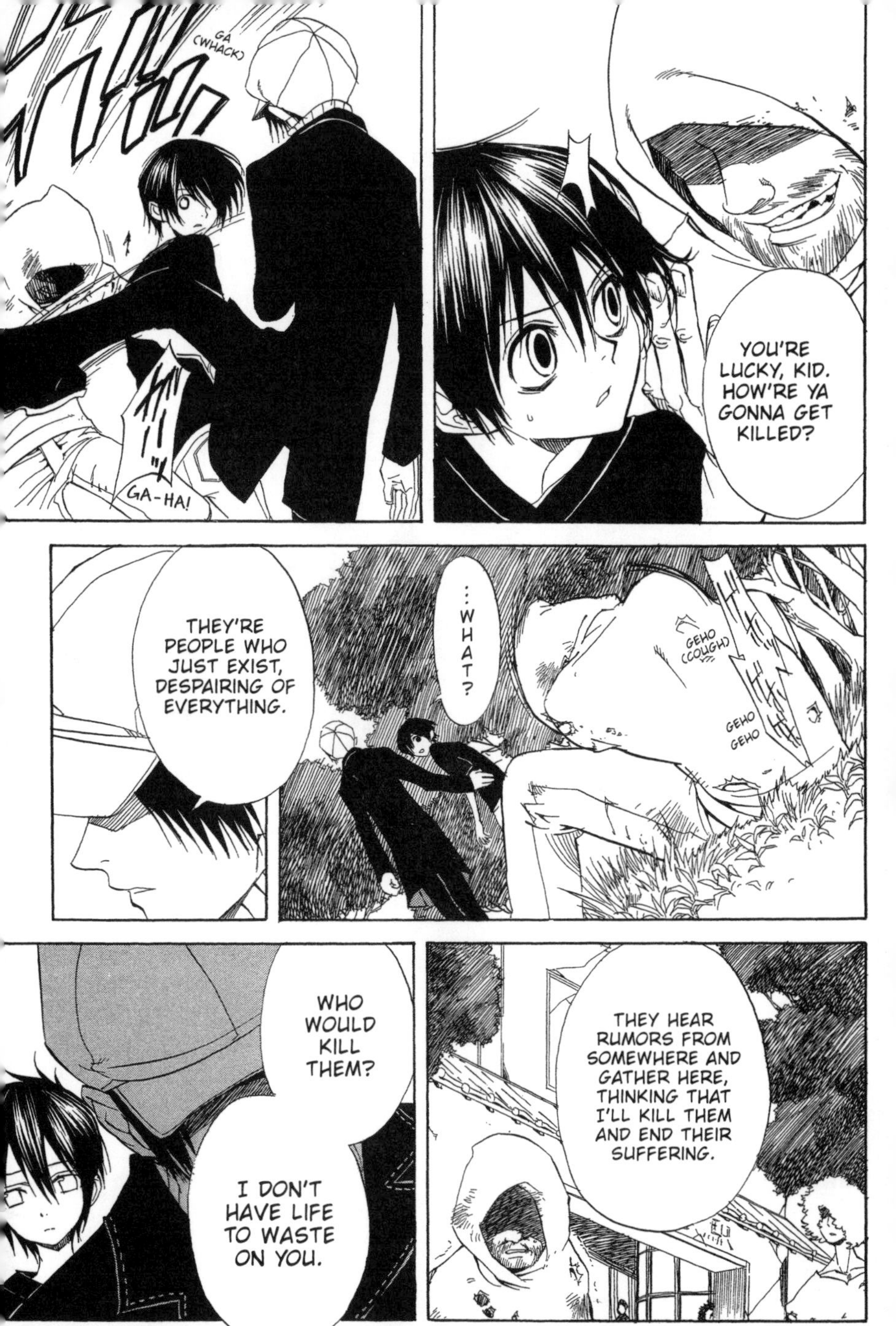

YOU'RE LUCKY, KID. HOW'RE YA GONNA GET KILLED?
GA (WHACK)
GA-HA!
GEHO (COUGH)
GEHO GEHO
...WHAT?
THEY'RE PEOPLE WHO JUST EXIST, DESPAIRING OF EVERYTHING.
THEY HEAR RUMORS FROM SOMEWHERE AND GATHER HERE, THINKING THAT I'LL KILL THEM AND END THEIR SUFFERING.
WHO WOULD KILL THEM?
I DON'T HAVE LIFE TO WASTE ON YOU.

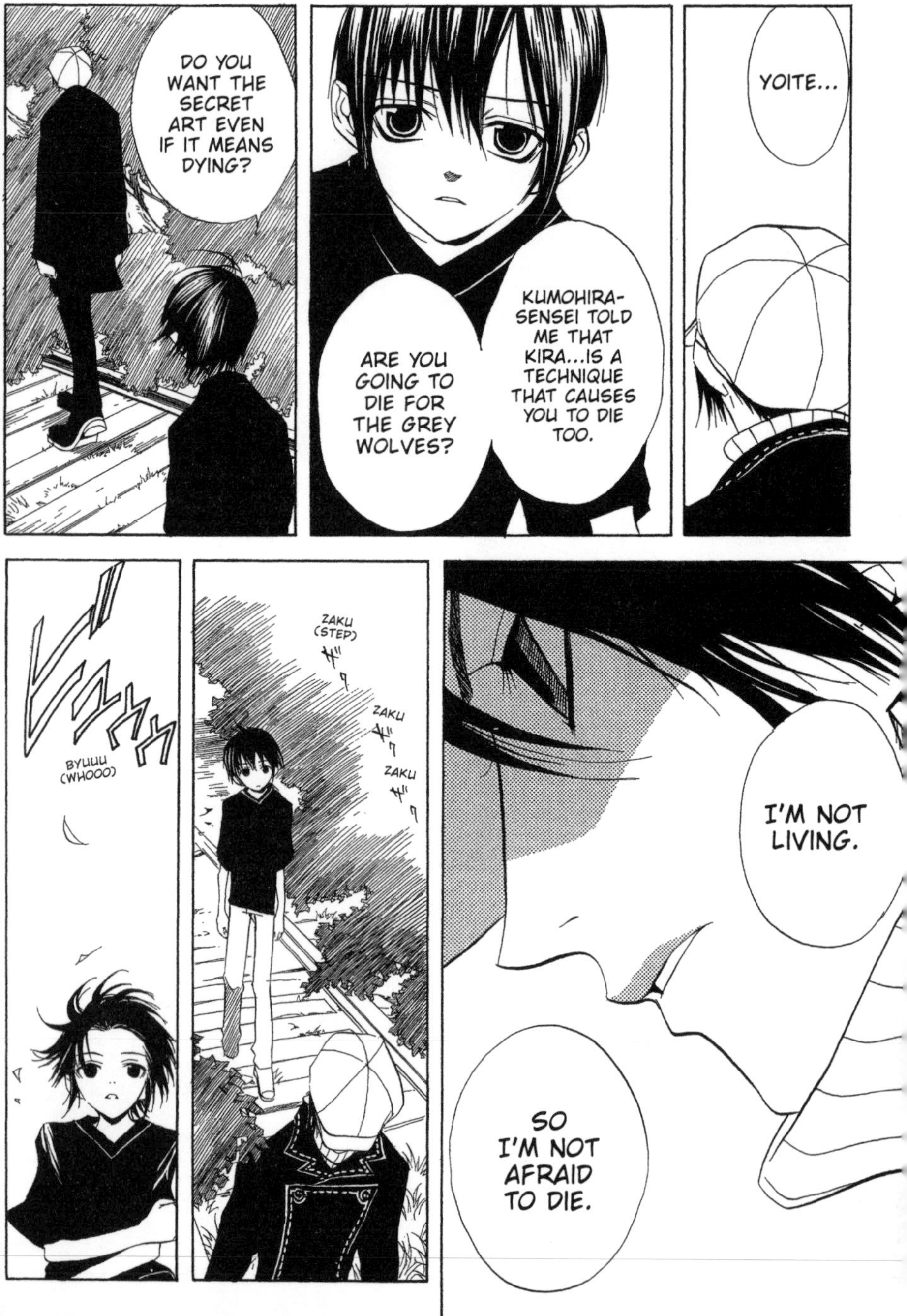
YOITE...
KUMOHIRA-SENSEI TOLD ME THAT KIRA...IS A TECHNIQUE THAT CAUSES YOU TO DIE TOO.
ARE YOU GOING TO DIE FOR THE GREY WOLVES?
DO YOU WANT THE SECRET ART EVEN IF IT MEANS DYING?
I'M NOT LIVING.
SO I'M NOT AFRAID TO DIE.
ZAKU (STEP)
ZAKU
ZAKU
BYUUU (WHOOO)

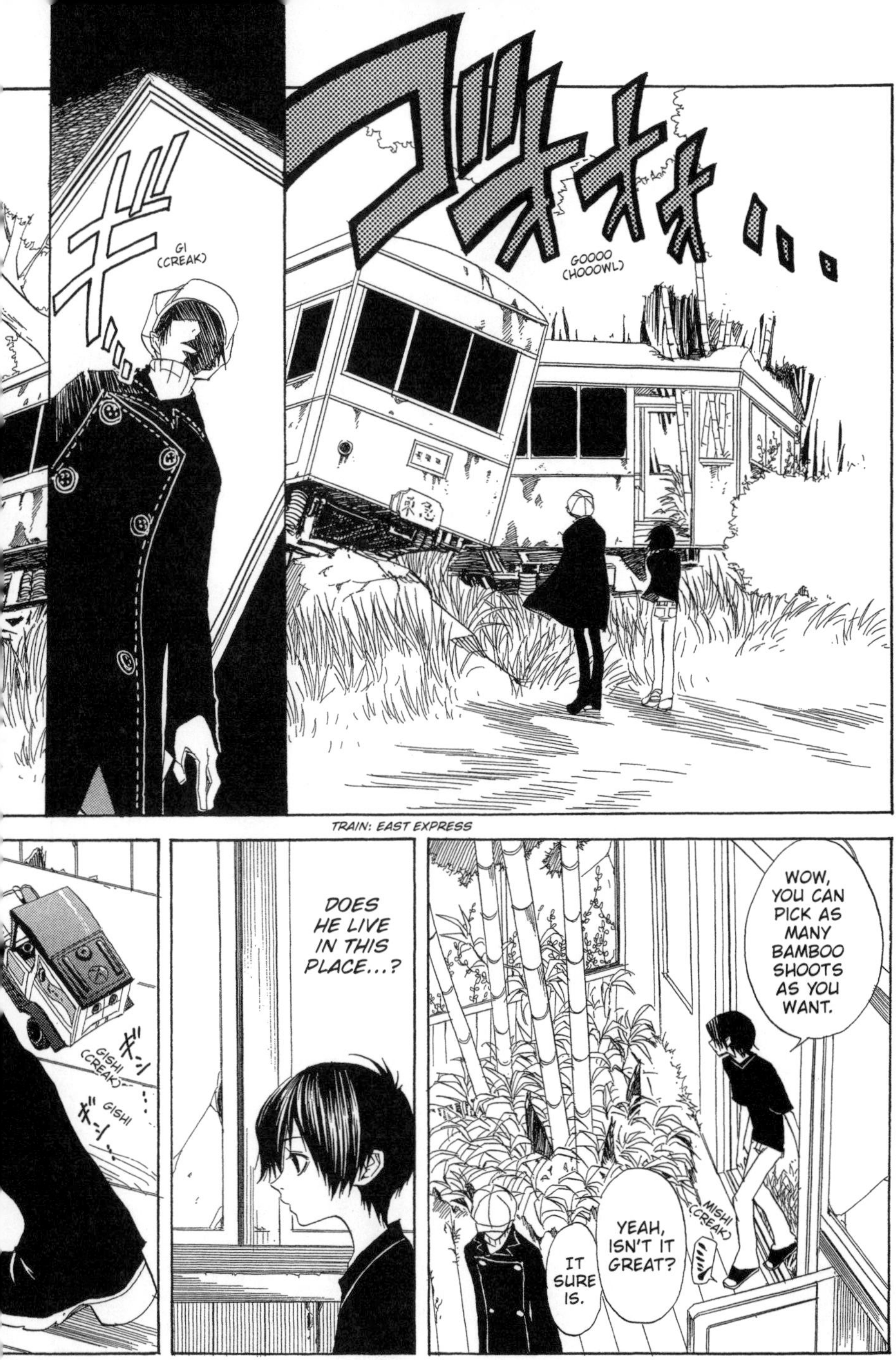
GOOOO (HOOOWL)
GI (CREAK)
TRAIN: EAST EXPRESS
WOW, YOU CAN PICK AS MANY BAMBOO SHOOTS AS YOU WANT.
MISHI (CREAK)
YEAH, ISN'T IT GREAT?
IT SURE IS.
DOES HE LIVE IN THIS PLACE...?
GISHI (CREAK)
GISHI

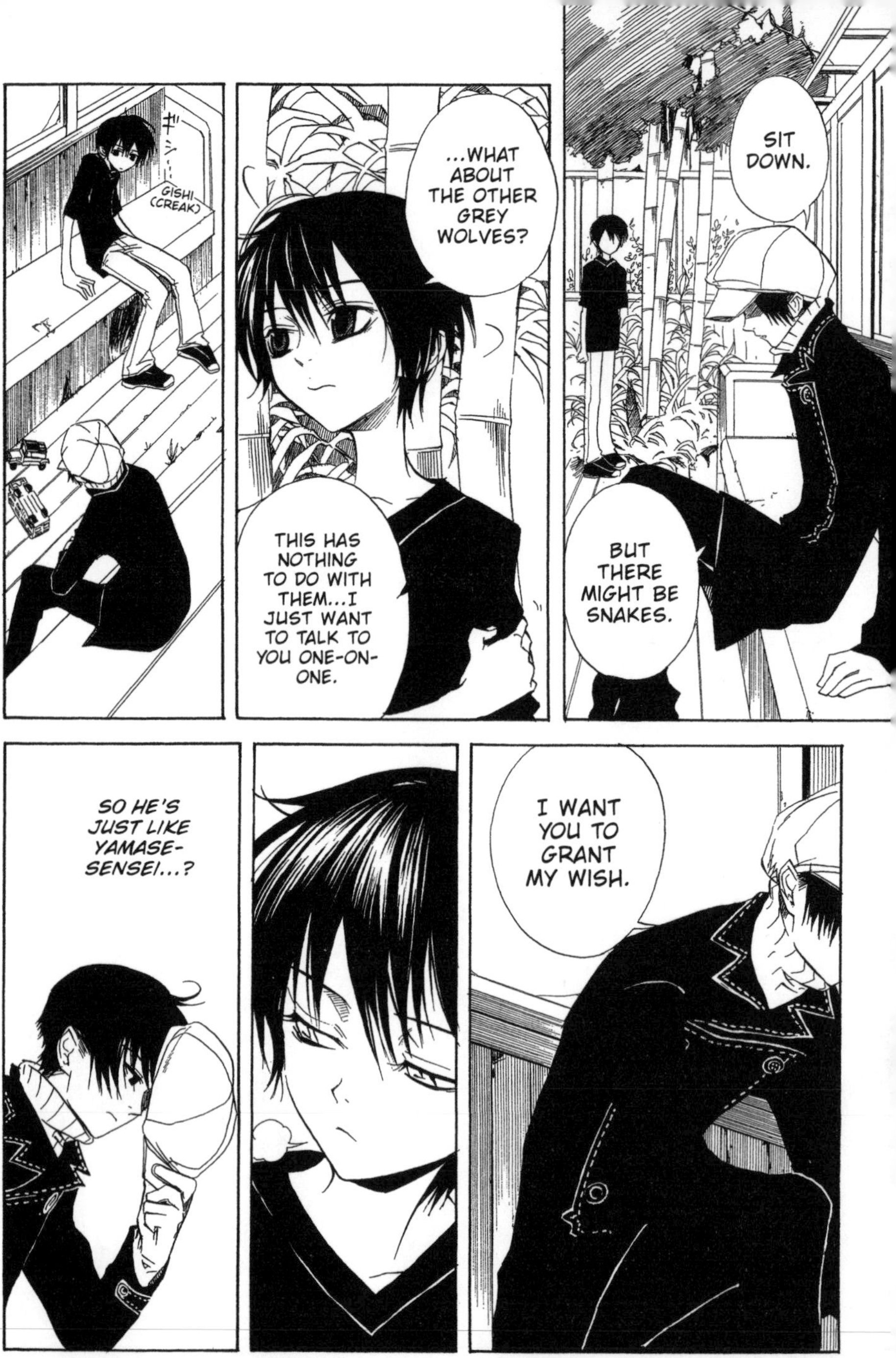
SIT DOWN.
BUT THERE MIGHT BE SNAKES.
...WHAT ABOUT THE OTHER GREY WOLVES?
THIS HAS NOTHING TO DO WITH THEM...I JUST WANT TO TALK TO YOU ONE-ON-ONE.
ギシ
GISHI (CREAK)
I WANT YOU TO GRANT MY WISH.
SO HE'S JUST LIKE YAMASE-SENSEI...?

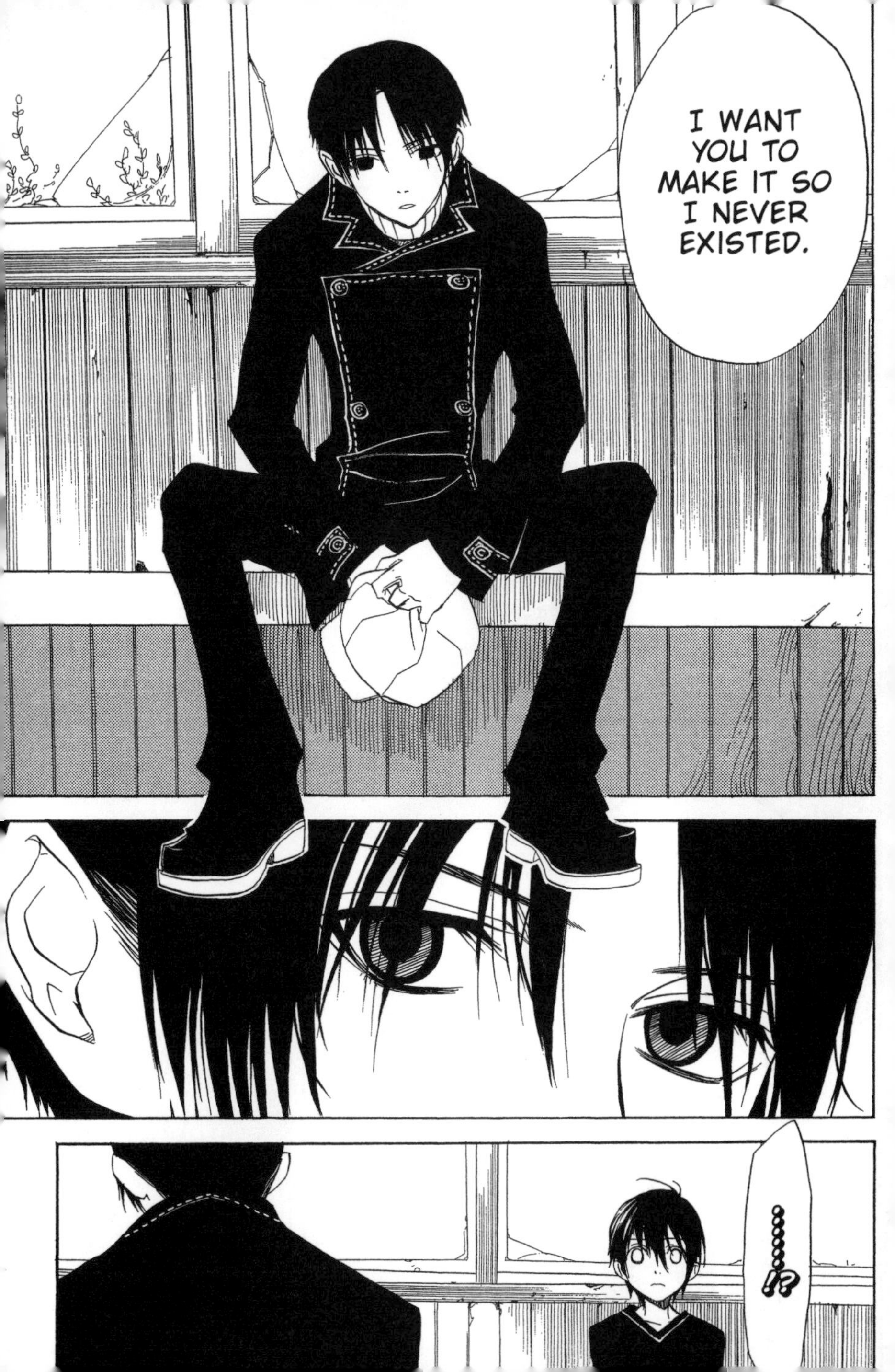
I WANT YOU TO MAKE IT SO I NEVER EXISTED.
.......!?

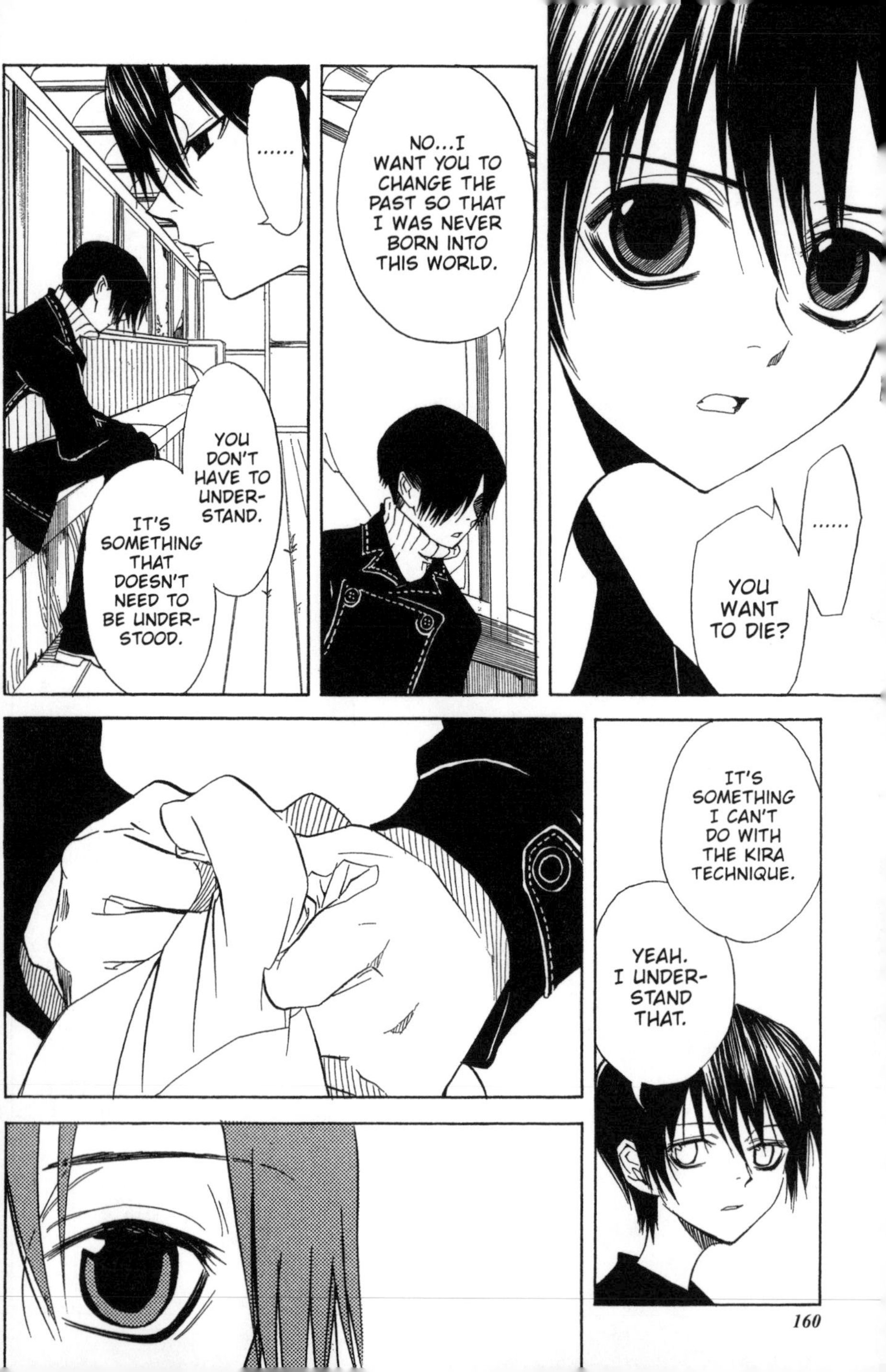
......
YOU WANT TO DIE?
NO...I WANT YOU TO CHANGE THE PAST SO THAT I WAS NEVER BORN INTO THIS WORLD.
......
YOU DON'T HAVE TO UNDERSTAND.
IT'S SOMETHING THAT DOESN'T NEED TO BE UNDERSTOOD.
IT'S SOMETHING I CAN'T DO WITH THE KIRA TECHNIQUE.
YEAH. I UNDERSTAND THAT.

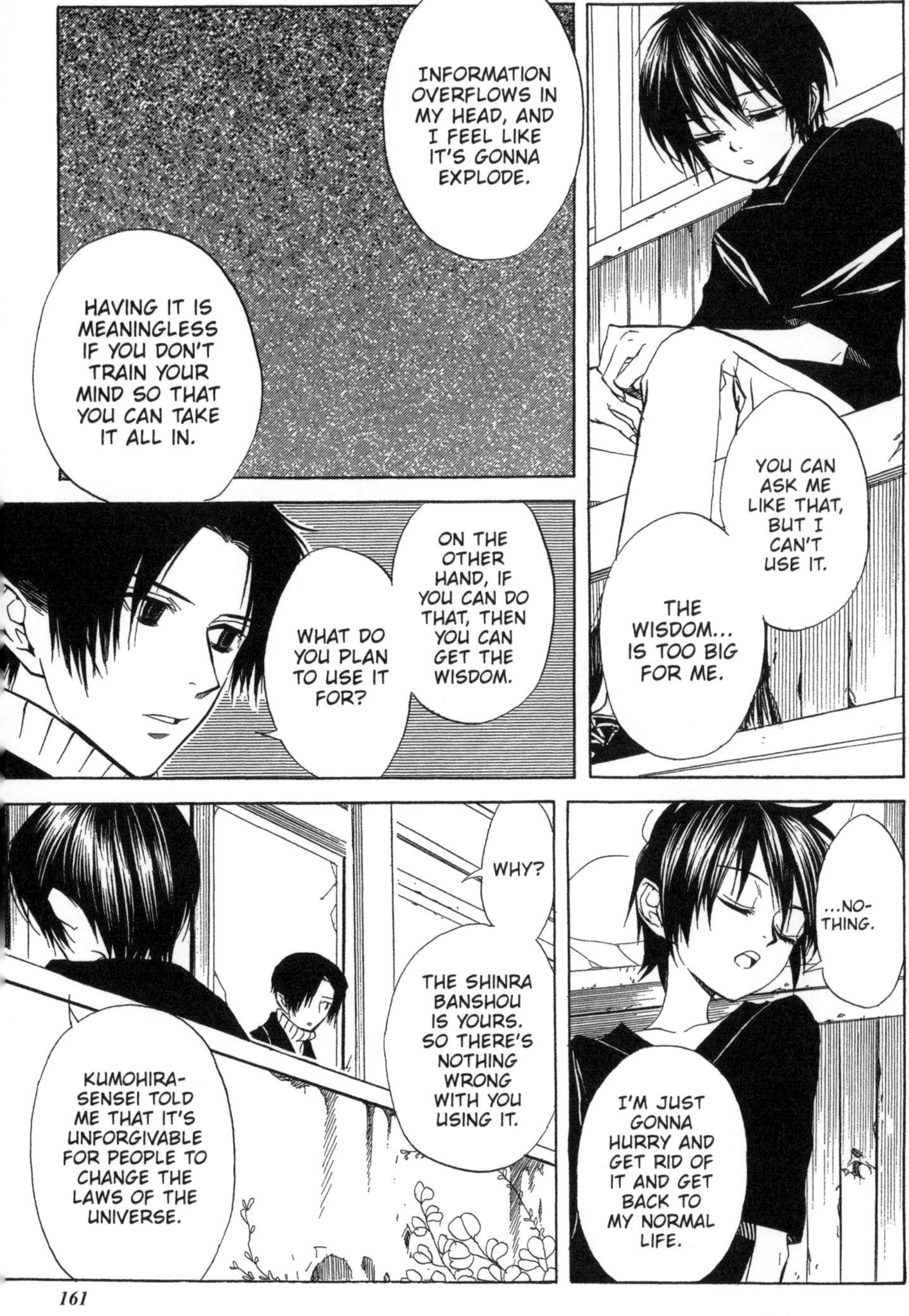
YOU CAN ASK ME LIKE THAT, BUT I CAN'T USE IT.
THE WISDOM... IS TOO BIG FOR ME.
INFORMATION OVERFLOWS IN MY HEAD, AND I FEEL LIKE IT'S GONNA EXPLODE.
HAVING IT IS MEANINGLESS IF YOU DON'T TRAIN YOUR MIND SO THAT YOU CAN TAKE IT ALL IN.
ON THE OTHER HAND, IF YOU CAN DO THAT, THEN YOU CAN GET THE WISDOM.
WHAT DO YOU PLAN TO USE IT FOR?
...NO-THING.
I'M JUST GONNA HURRY AND GET RID OF IT AND GET BACK TO MY NORMAL LIFE.
WHY?
THE SHINRA BANSHOU IS YOURS. SO THERE'S NOTHING WRONG WITH YOU USING IT.
KUMOHIRA-SENSEI TOLD ME THAT IT'S UNFORGIVABLE FOR PEOPLE TO CHANGE THE LAWS OF THE UNIVERSE.

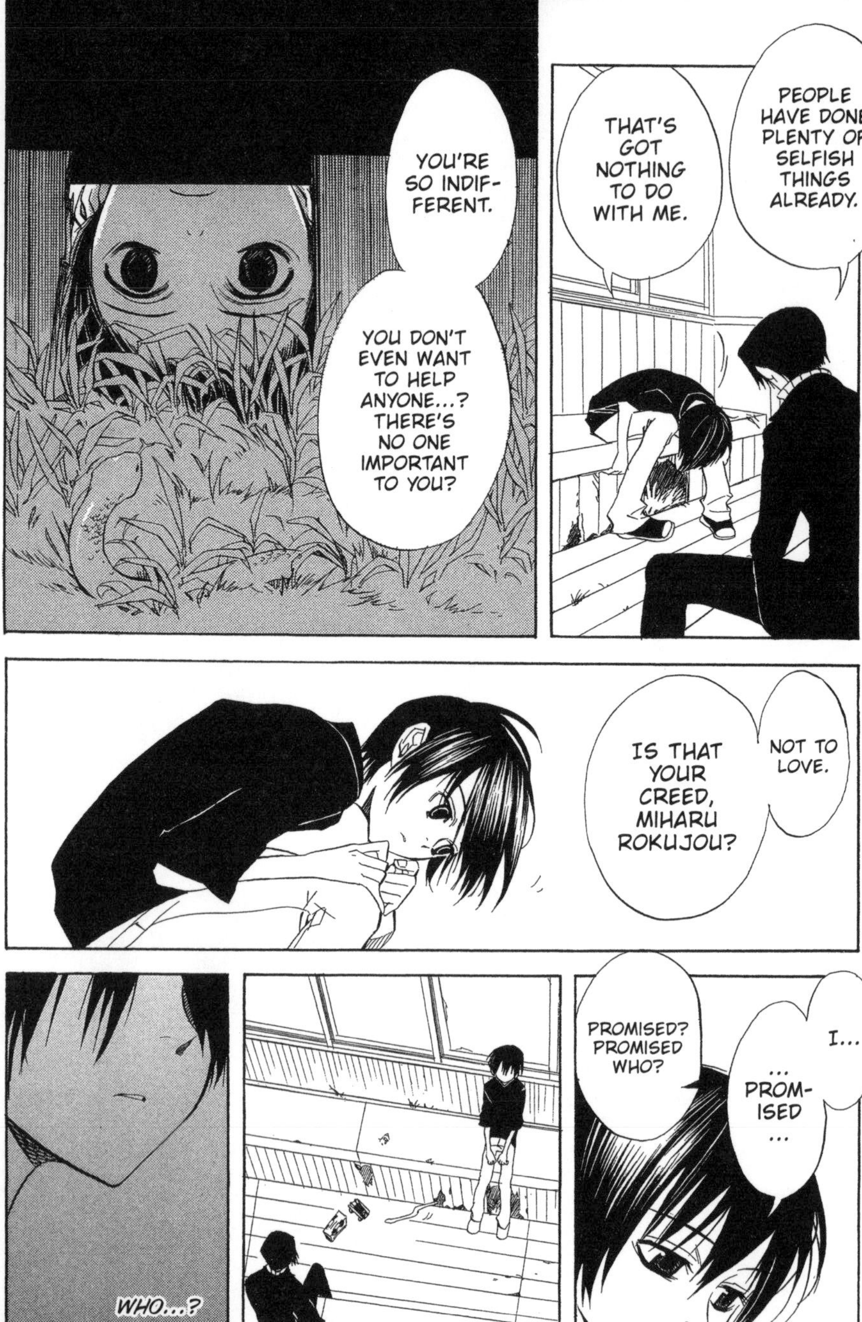
PEOPLE HAVE DONE PLENTY OF SELFISH THINGS ALREADY.
THAT'S GOT NOTHING TO DO WITH ME.
YOU'RE SO INDIF-FERENT.
YOU DON'T EVEN WANT TO HELP ANYONE...? THERE'S NO ONE IMPORTANT TO YOU?
NOT TO LOVE.
IS THAT YOUR CREED, MIHARU ROKUJOU?
I...
...PROM-ISED...
PROMISED? PROMISED WHO?
WHO...?

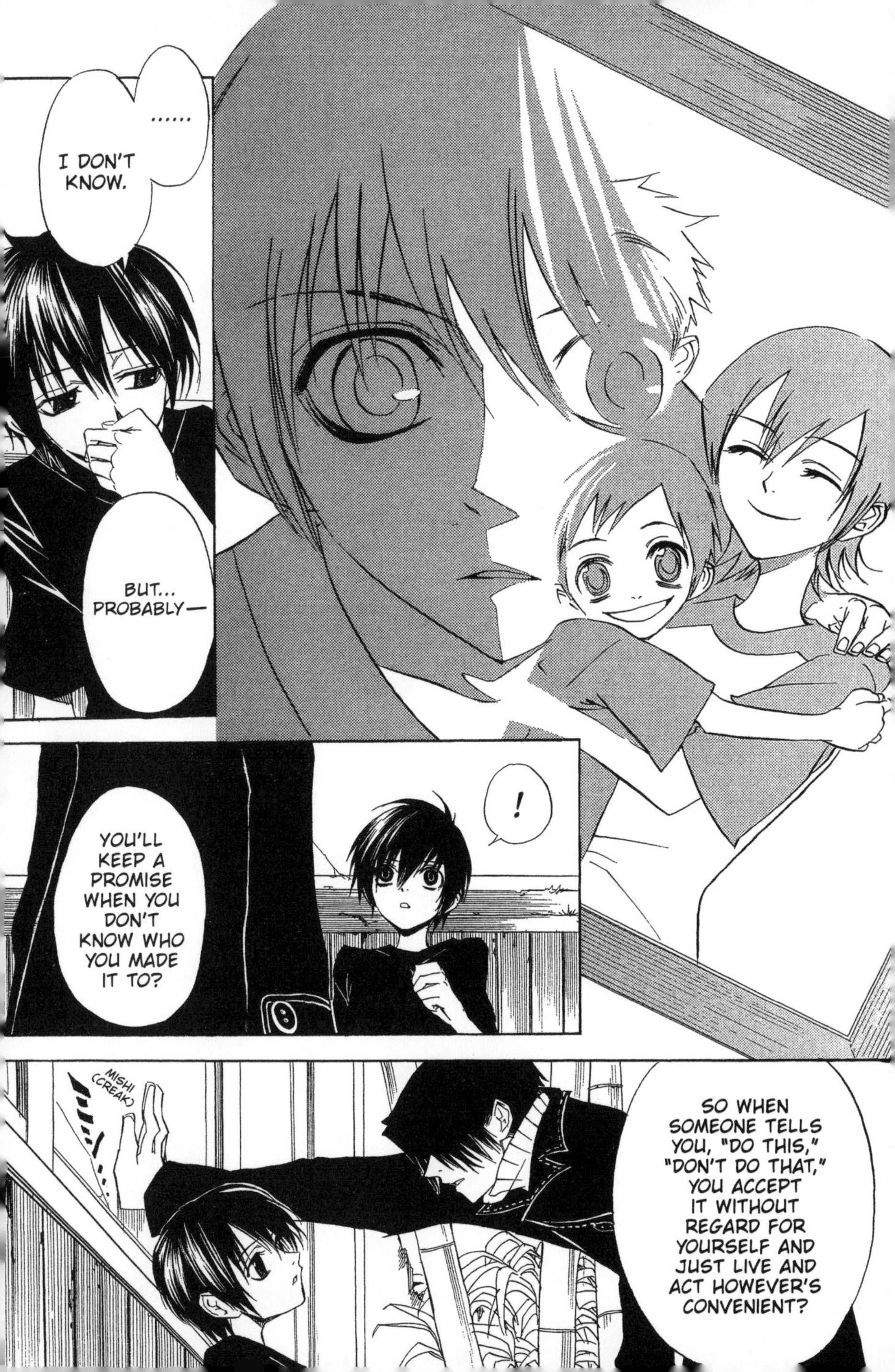
......
I DON'T KNOW.
BUT... PROBABLY—
!
YOU'LL KEEP A PROMISE WHEN YOU DON'T KNOW WHO YOU MADE IT TO?
SO WHEN SOMEONE TELLS YOU, "DO THIS," "DON'T DO THAT," YOU ACCEPT IT WITHOUT REGARD FOR YOURSELF AND JUST LIVE AND ACT HOWEVER'S CONVENIENT?
MISHI (CREAK)

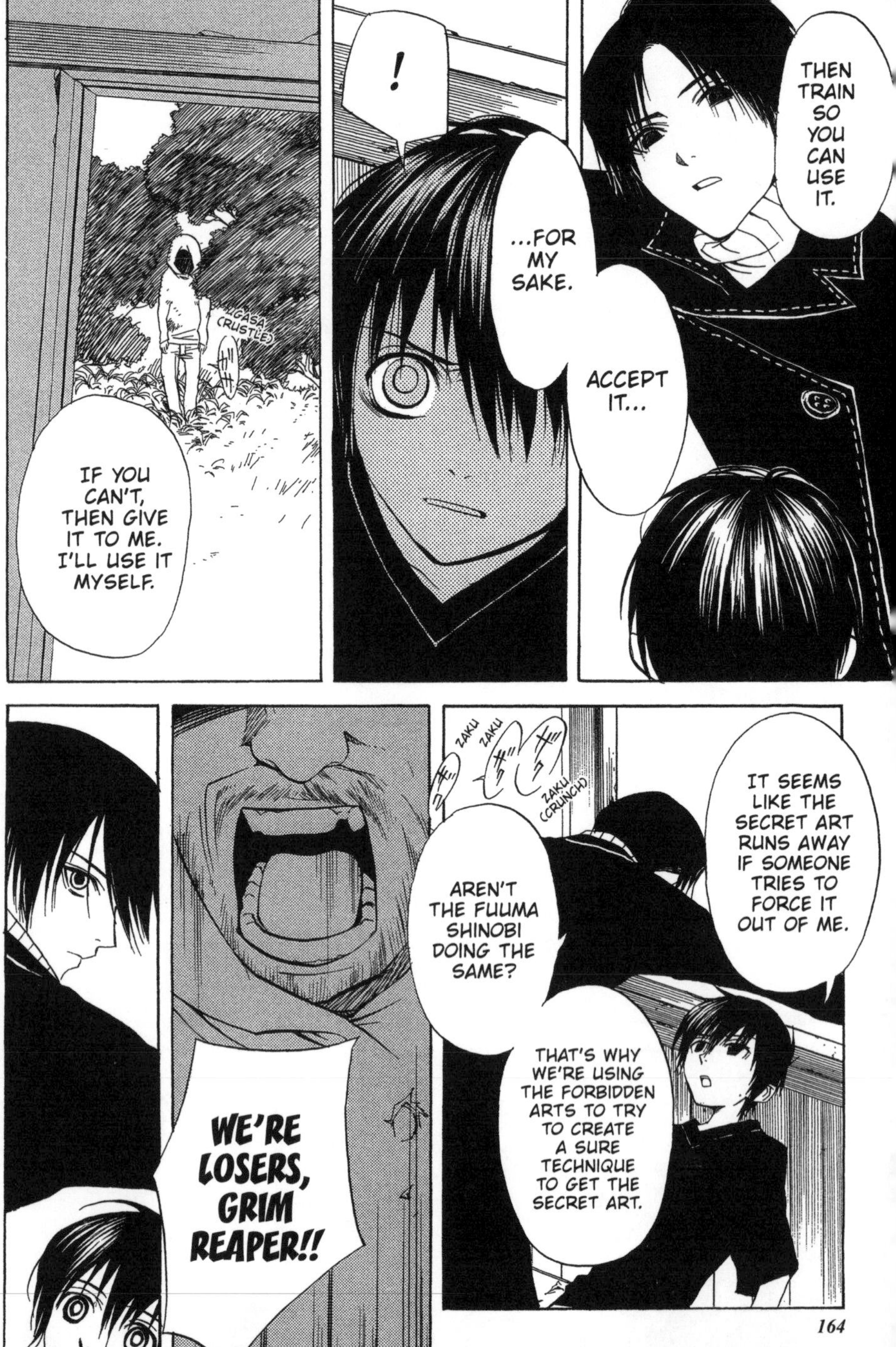
THEN TRAIN SO YOU CAN USE IT.
ACCEPT IT...
...FOR MY SAKE.
!
GASA (RUSTLE)
IF YOU CAN'T, THEN GIVE IT TO ME. I'LL USE IT MYSELF.
ZAKU
ZAKU
ZAKU (CRUNCH)
IT SEEMS LIKE THE SECRET ART RUNS AWAY IF SOMEONE TRIES TO FORCE IT OUT OF ME.
AREN'T THE FUUMA SHINOBI DOING THE SAME?
THAT'S WHY WE'RE USING THE FORBIDDEN ARTS TO TRY TO CREATE A SURE TECHNIQUE TO GET THE SECRET ART.
WE'RE LOSERS, GRIM REAPER!!

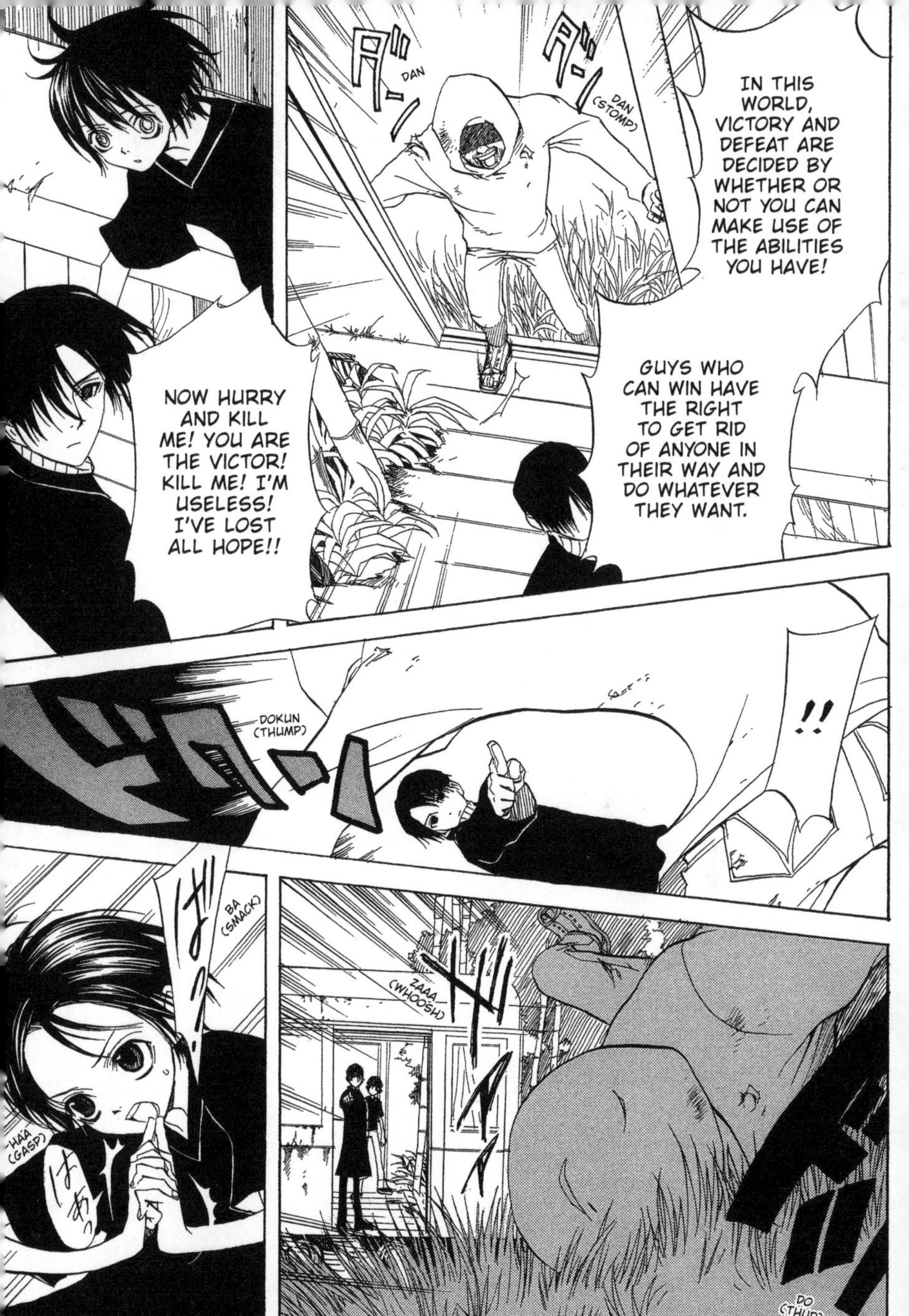
IN THIS WORLD, VICTORY AND DEFEAT ARE DECIDED BY WHETHER OR NOT YOU CAN MAKE USE OF THE ABILITIES YOU HAVE!
DAN (STOMP)
DAN
GUYS WHO CAN WIN HAVE THE RIGHT TO GET RID OF ANYONE IN THEIR WAY AND DO WHATEVER THEY WANT.
NOW HURRY AND KILL ME! YOU ARE THE VICTOR! KILL ME! I'M USELESS! I'VE LOST ALL HOPE!!
!!
DOKUN (THUMP)
ZAAA (WHOOSH)
DO (THUD)
BA (SMACK)
HAA (GASP)

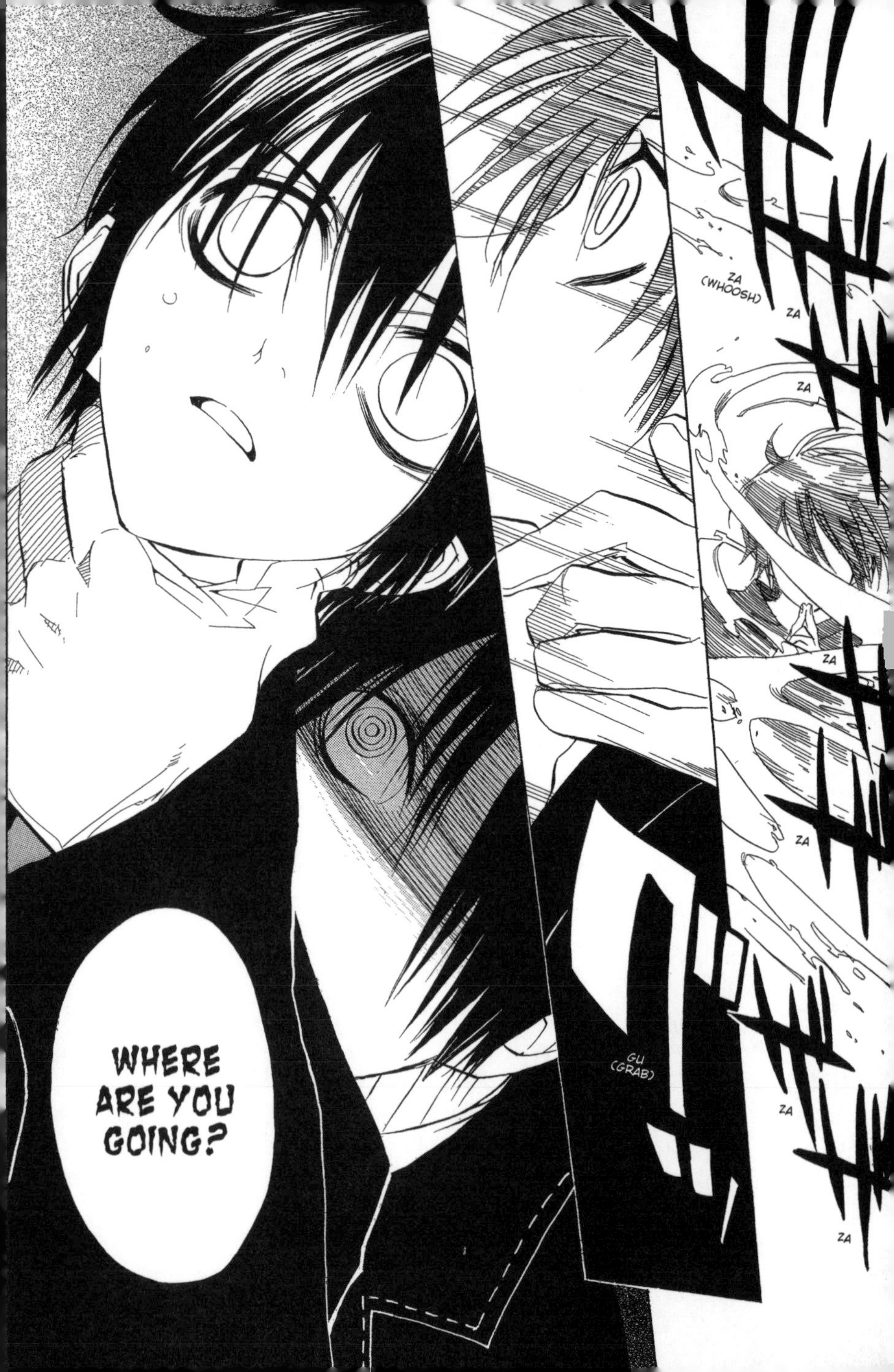
ZA (WHOOSH)
ZA
ZA
ZA
ZA
ZA
ZA
GU (GRAB)
WHERE ARE YOU GOING?

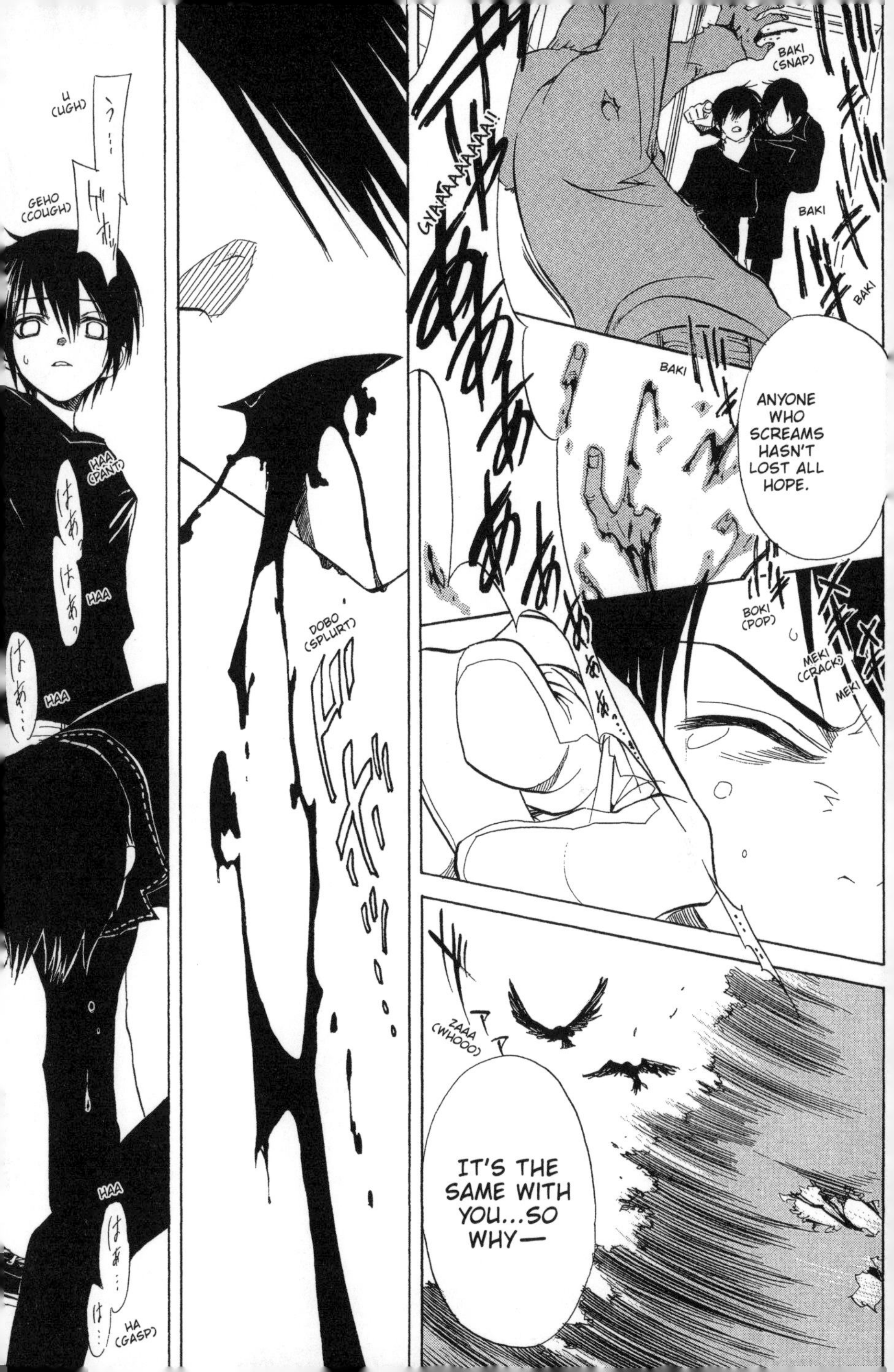

BAKI (SNAP)
BAKI
BAKI
GYAAAAAAAAAA!!
BAKI
ANYONE WHO SCREAMS HASN'T LOST ALL HOPE.
BOKI (POP)
MEKI (CRACK)
MEKI
ZAAA (WHOOO)
IT'S THE SAME WITH YOU...SO WHY—
DOBO (SPLURT)
U (UGH)
う…
GEHO (COUGH)
ゲホッ
HAA (PANT)
はあっ はあっ
HAA
HAA
はあ…
HAA
はあ… は…
HA (GASP)

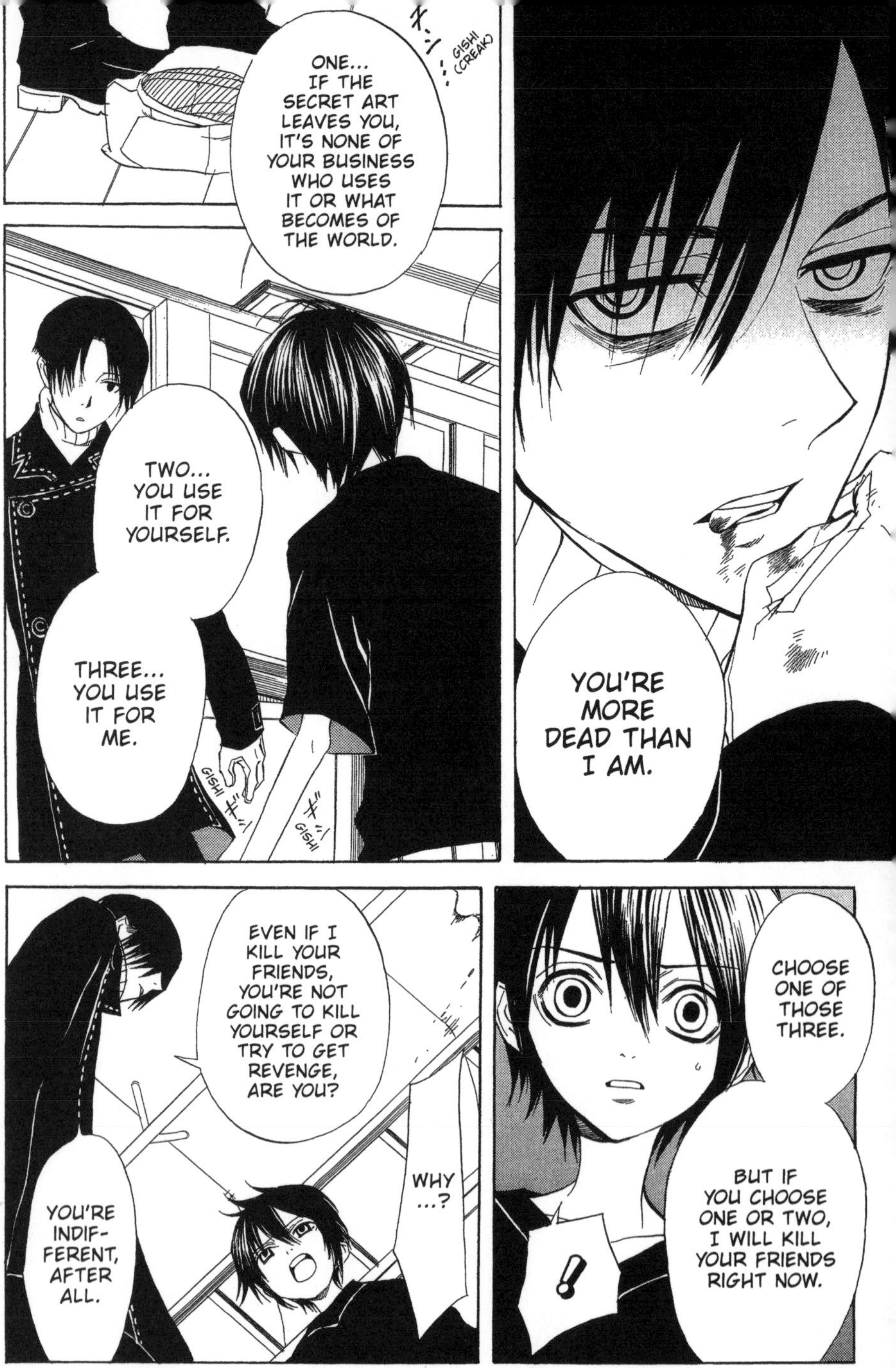
YOU'RE MORE DEAD THAN I AM.
GISHI (CREAK)
ONE... IF THE SECRET ART LEAVES YOU, IT'S NONE OF YOUR BUSINESS WHO USES IT OR WHAT BECOMES OF THE WORLD.
TWO... YOU USE IT FOR YOURSELF.
THREE... YOU USE IT FOR ME.
GISHI
GISHI
CHOOSE ONE OF THOSE THREE.
BUT IF YOU CHOOSE ONE OR TWO, I WILL KILL YOUR FRIENDS RIGHT NOW.
!
EVEN IF I KILL YOUR FRIENDS, YOU'RE NOT GOING TO KILL YOURSELF OR TRY TO GET REVENGE, ARE YOU?
WHY ...?
YOU'RE INDIF-FERENT, AFTER ALL.

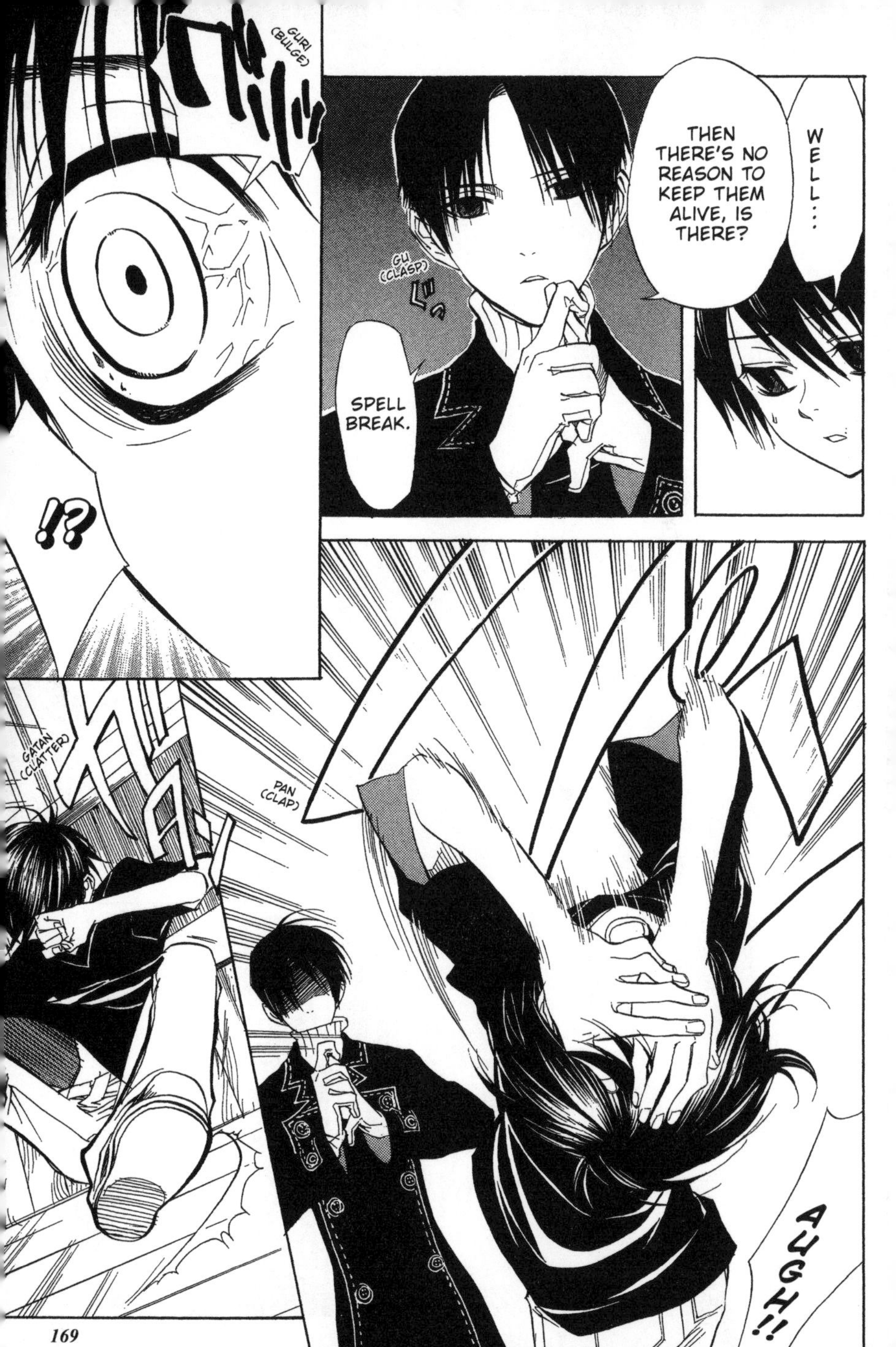
WELL...
THEN THERE'S NO REASON TO KEEP THEM ALIVE, IS THERE?
GU (CLASP)
SPELL BREAK.
GURI (BULGE)
!?
AUGH!!
PAN (CLAP)
GATAN (CLATTER)

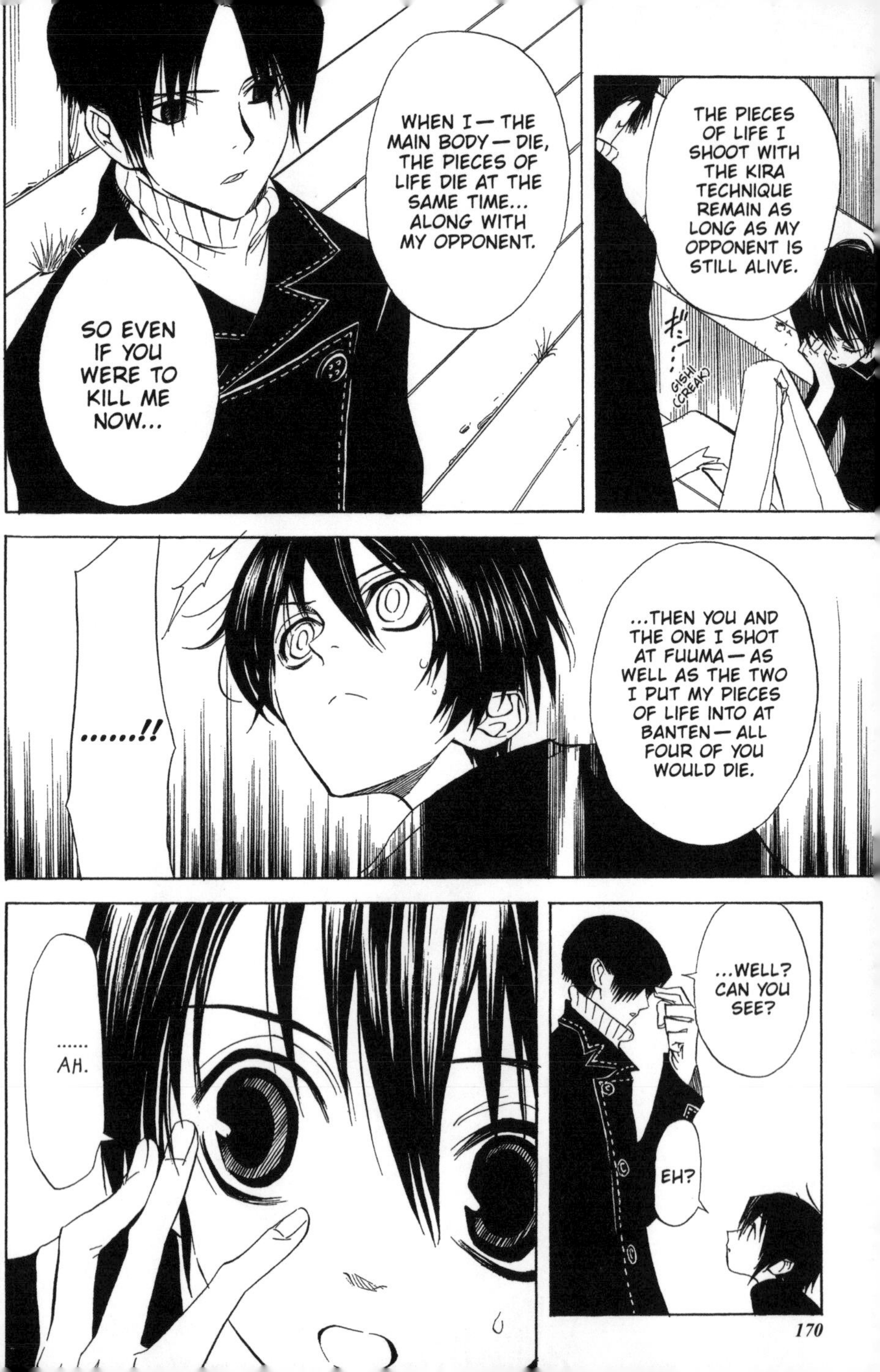
THE PIECES OF LIFE I SHOOT WITH THE KIRA TECHNIQUE REMAIN AS LONG AS MY OPPONENT IS STILL ALIVE.
GISHI (CREAK)
WHEN I— THE MAIN BODY— DIE, THE PIECES OF LIFE DIE AT THE SAME TIME... ALONG WITH MY OPPONENT.
SO EVEN IF YOU WERE TO KILL ME NOW...
...THEN YOU AND THE ONE I SHOT AT FUUMA— AS WELL AS THE TWO I PUT MY PIECES OF LIFE INTO AT BANTEN— ALL FOUR OF YOU WOULD DIE.
......!!
...WELL? CAN YOU SEE?
EH?
...... AH.

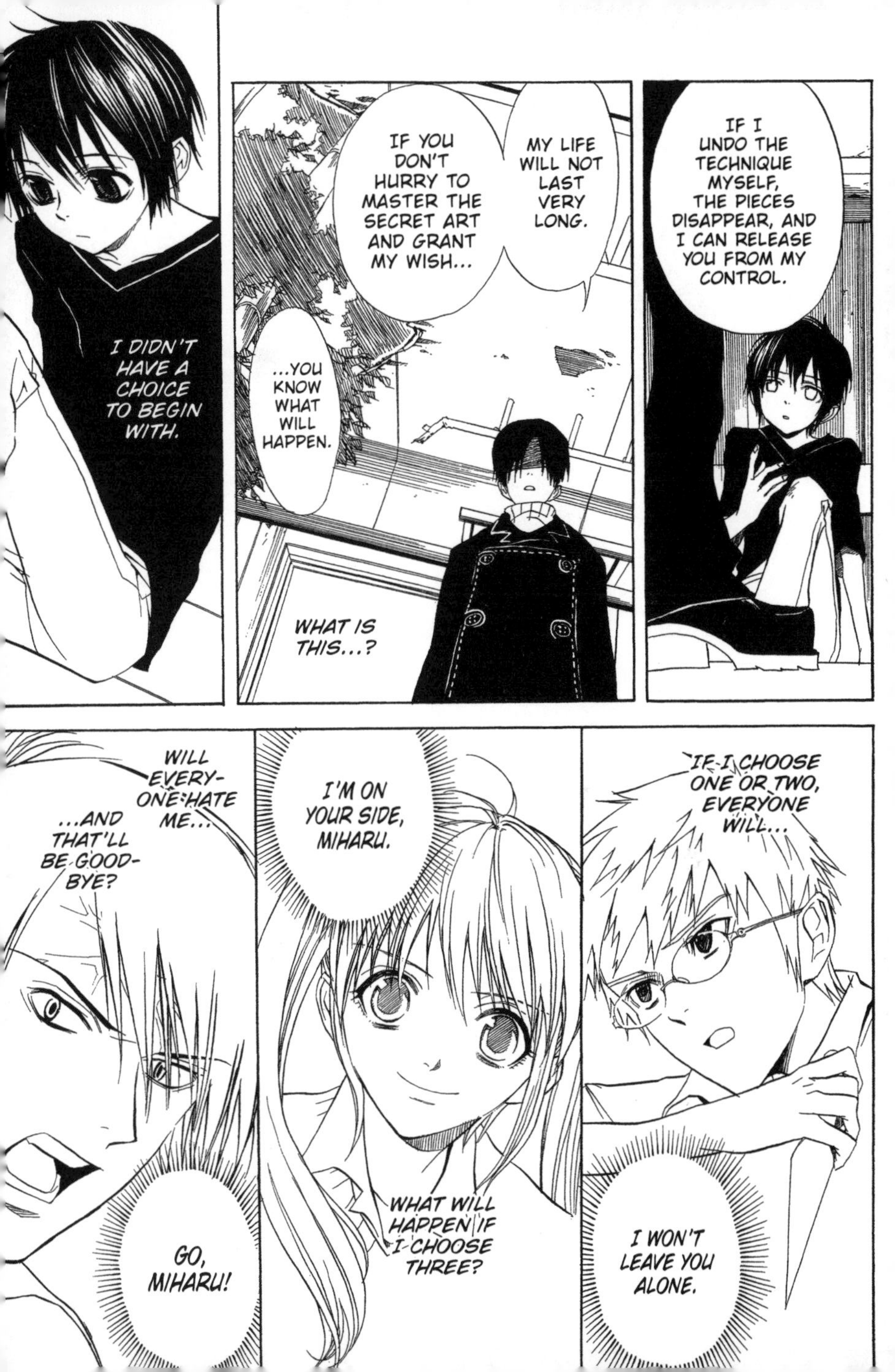
IF I UNDO THE TECHNIQUE MYSELF, THE PIECES DISAPPEAR, AND I CAN RELEASE YOU FROM MY CONTROL.
MY LIFE WILL NOT LAST VERY LONG.
IF YOU DON'T HURRY TO MASTER THE SECRET ART AND GRANT MY WISH...
...YOU KNOW WHAT WILL HAPPEN.
WHAT IS THIS...?
I DIDN'T HAVE A CHOICE TO BEGIN WITH.
IF I CHOOSE ONE OR TWO, EVERYONE WILL...
I WON'T LEAVE YOU ALONE.
I'M ON YOUR SIDE, MIHARU.
WHAT WILL HAPPEN IF I CHOOSE THREE?
WILL EVERYONE HATE ME...
...AND THAT'LL BE GOOD-BYE?
GO, MIHARU!

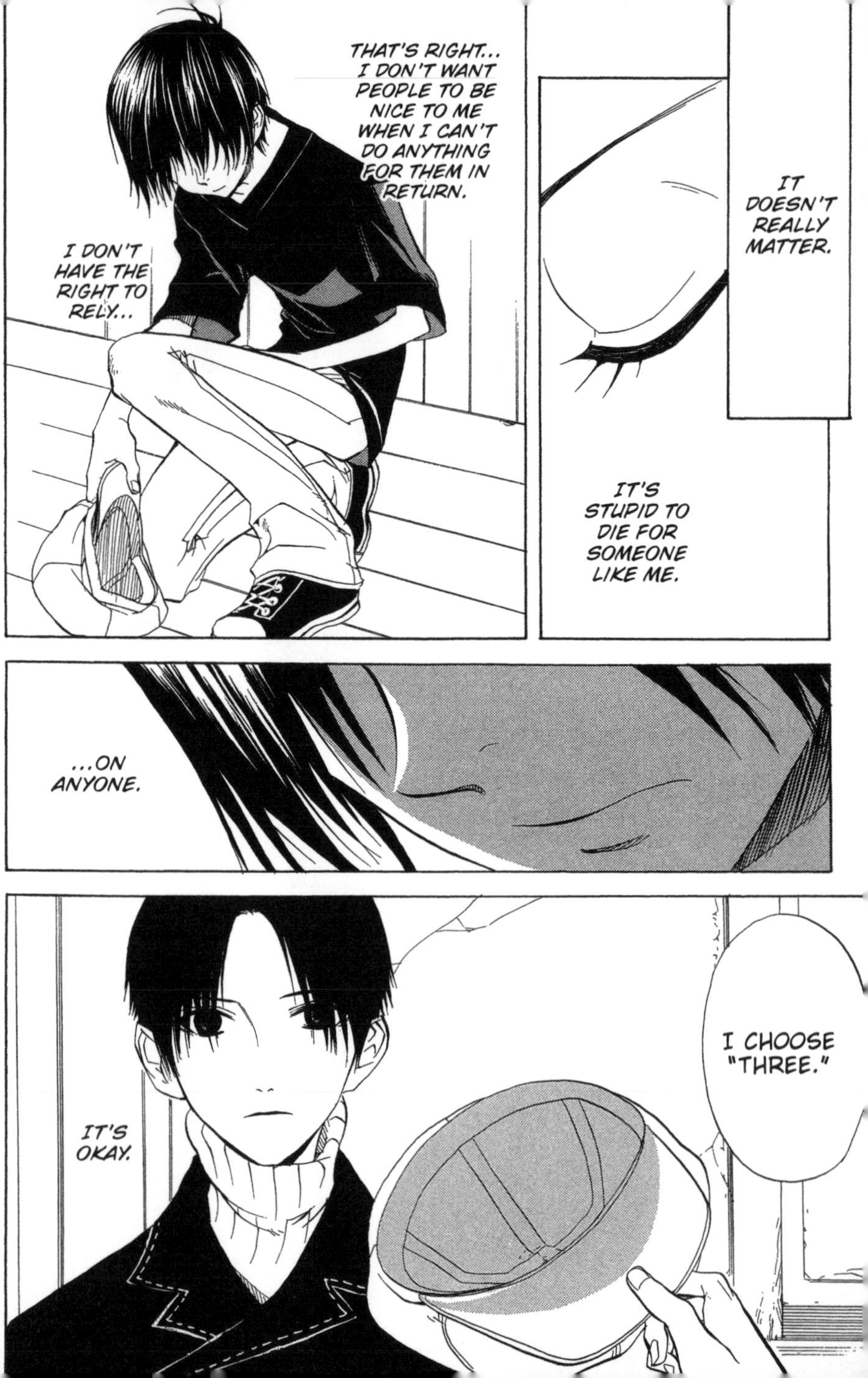
IT DOESN'T REALLY MATTER.
IT'S STUPID TO DIE FOR SOMEONE LIKE ME.
THAT'S RIGHT... I DON'T WANT PEOPLE TO BE NICE TO ME WHEN I CAN'T DO ANYTHING FOR THEM IN RETURN.
I DON'T HAVE THE RIGHT TO RELY...
...ON ANYONE.
I CHOOSE "THREE."
IT'S OKAY.

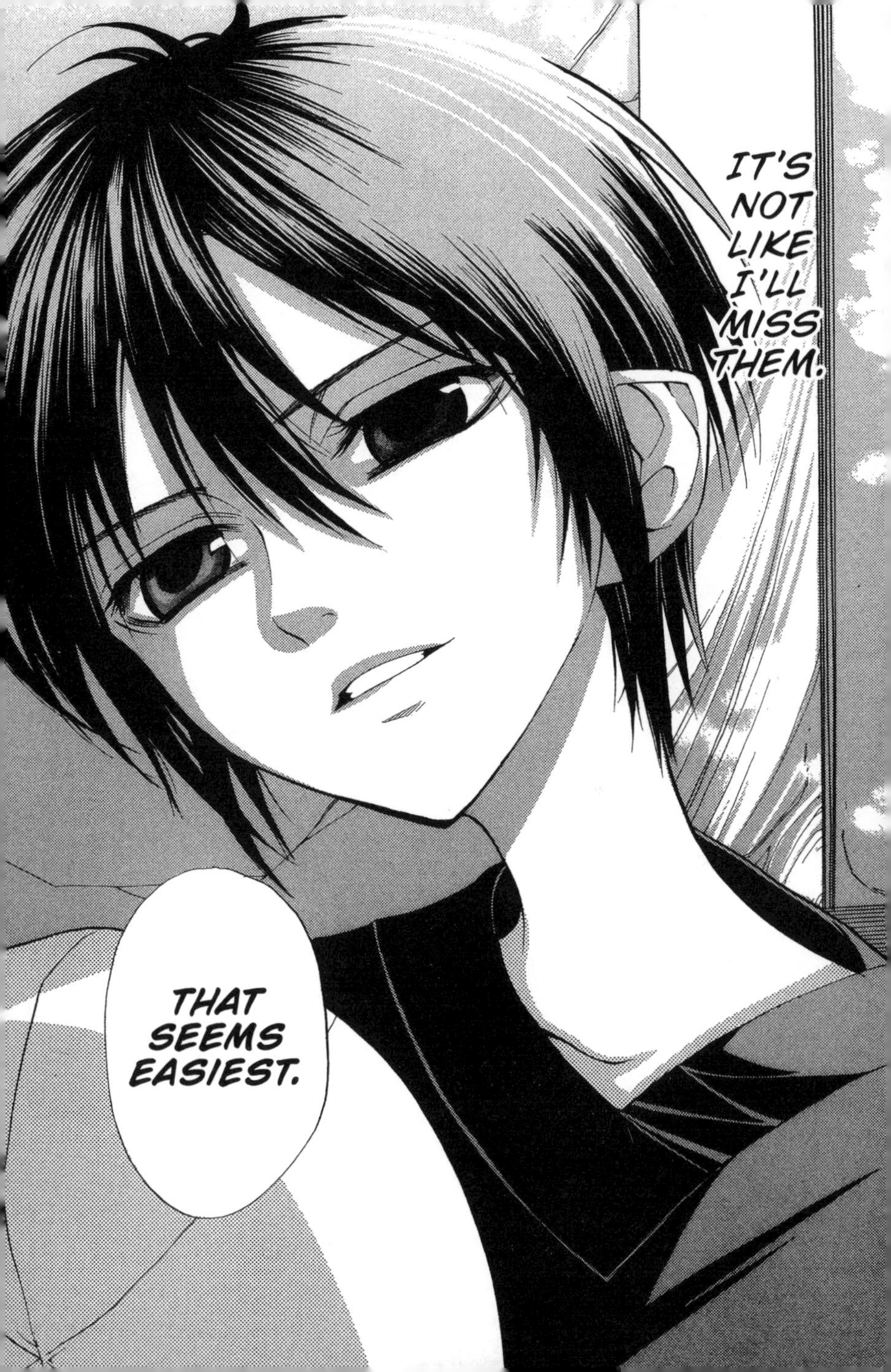
IT'S NOT LIKE I'LL MISS THEM.
THAT SEEMS EASIEST.

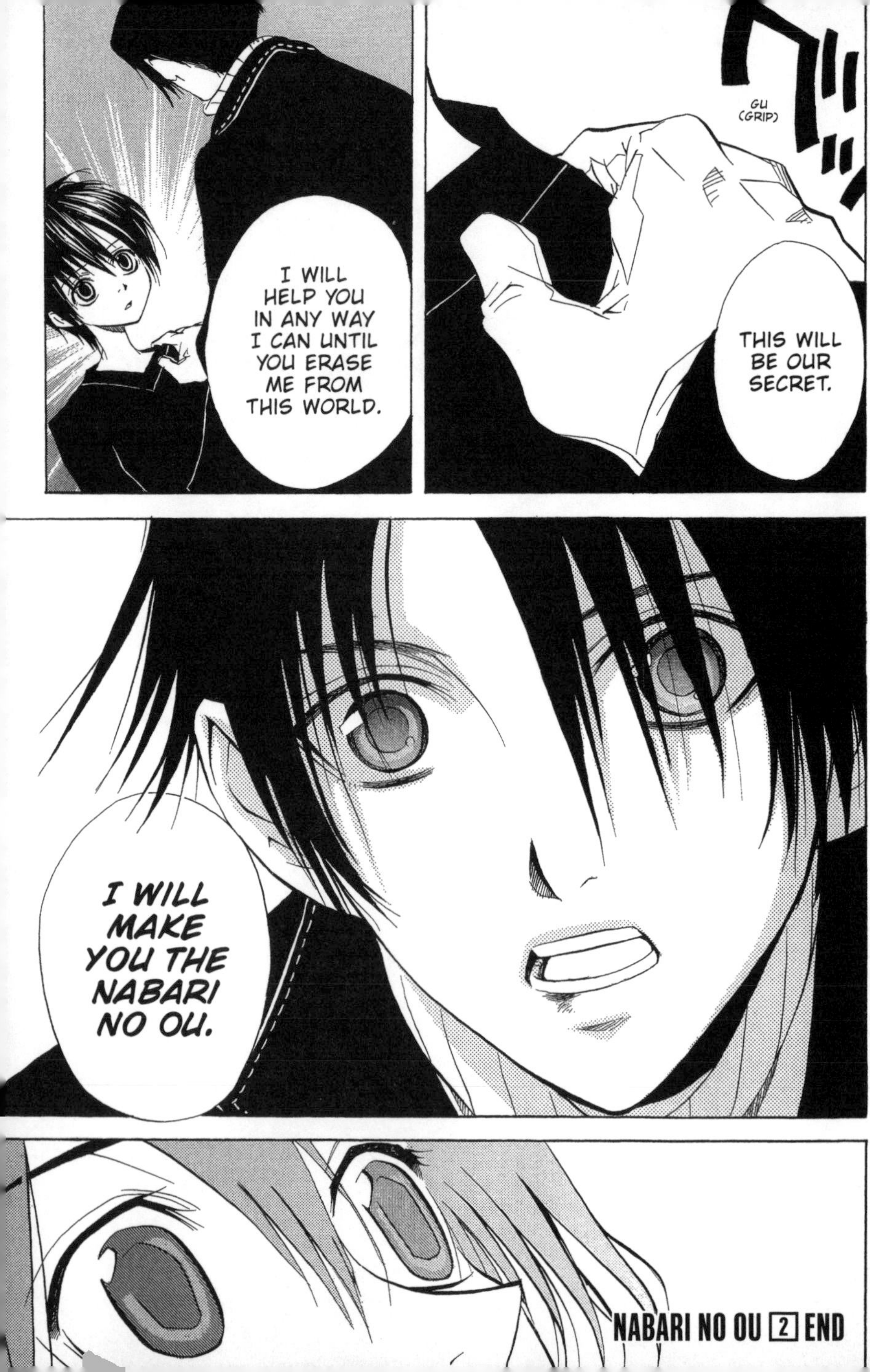
GU (GRIP)
THIS WILL BE OUR SECRET.
I WILL HELP YOU IN ANY WAY I CAN UNTIL YOU ERASE ME FROM THIS WORLD.
I WILL MAKE YOU THE NABARI NO OU.
NABARI NO OU 2 END

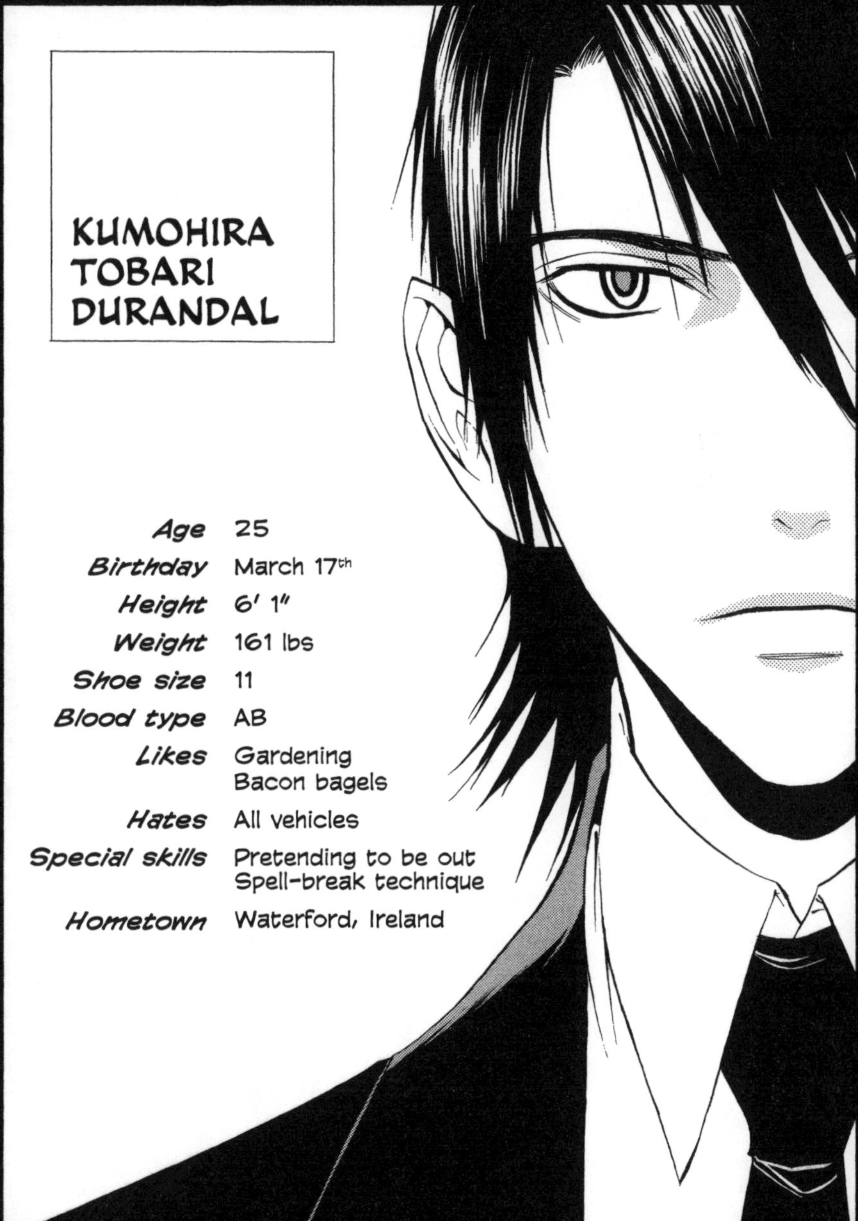

KUMOHIRA TOBARI DURANDAL

Age	25
Birthday	March 17th
Height	6′ 1″
Weight	161 lbs
Shoe size	11
Blood type	AB
Likes	Gardening Bacon bagels
Hates	All vehicles
Special skills	Pretending to be out Spell-break technique
Hometown	Waterford, Ireland

YOU'RE SO MEAN, SENSEI!

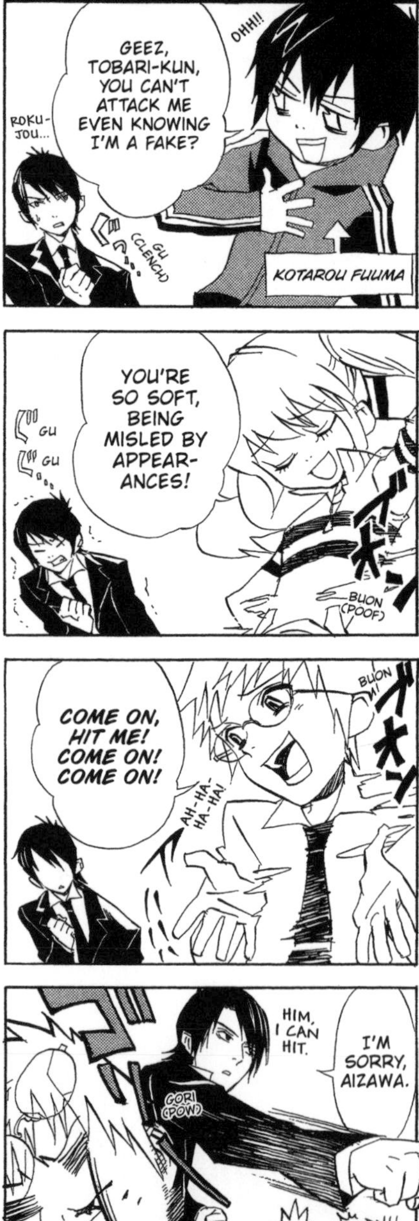
OHH!!
GEEZ, TOBARI-KUN, YOU CAN'T ATTACK ME EVEN KNOWING I'M A FAKE?
ROKU-JOU...
GU (CLENCH)
KOTAROU FUUMA
YOU'RE SO SOFT, BEING MISLED BY APPEARANCES!
GU
GU
BUON (POOF)
BUON!
COME ON, HIT ME! COME ON! COME ON!
AH-HA-HA-HA!
I'M SORRY, AIZAWA.
HIM, I CAN HIT.
GORI (POW)
EEH!?

LAID-BACK DUO

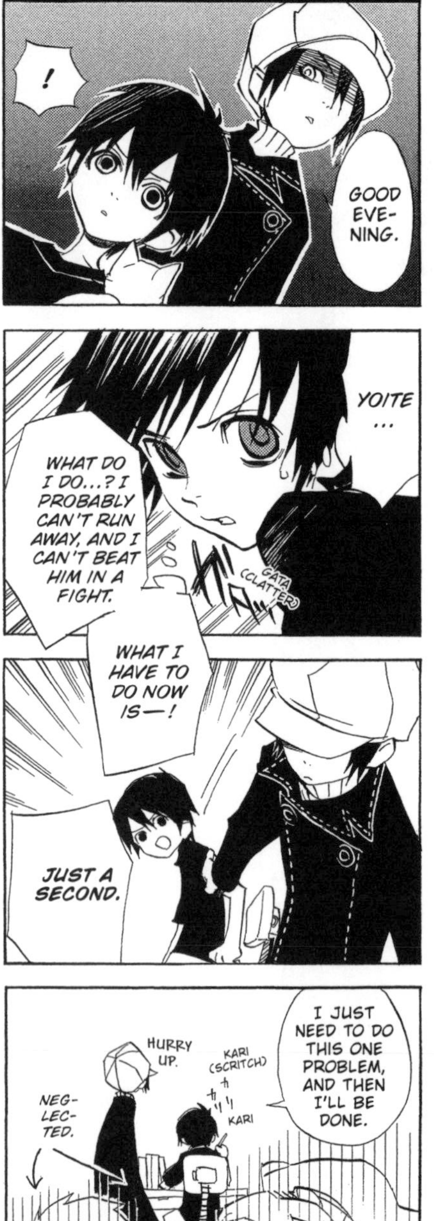
GOOD EVE-NING.
!
YOITE...
WHAT DO I DO...? I PROBABLY CAN'T RUN AWAY, AND I CAN'T BEAT HIM IN A FIGHT.
GATA (CLATTER)
WHAT I HAVE TO DO NOW IS—!
JUST A SECOND.
I JUST NEED TO DO THIS ONE PROBLEM, AND THEN I'LL BE DONE.
KARI (SCRITCH)
KARI
HURRY UP.
NEG-LEC-TED.

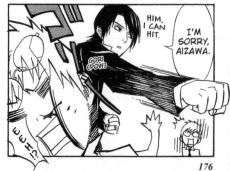

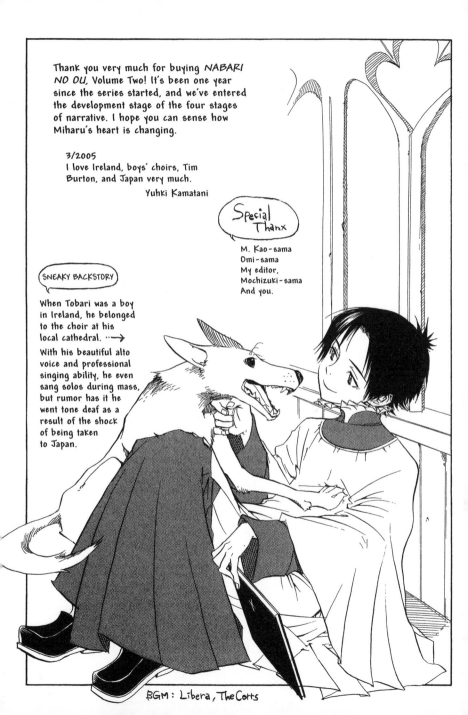

Thank you very much for buying *NABARI NO OU*, Volume Two! It's been one year since the series started, and we've entered the development stage of the four stages of narrative. I hope you can sense how Miharu's heart is changing.

3/2005
I love Ireland, boys' choirs, Tim Burton, and Japan very much.

Yuhki Kamatani

Special Thanx

M. Kao-sama
Omi-sama
My editor, Mochizuki-sama
And you.

SNEAKY BACKSTORY

When Tobari was a boy in Ireland, he belonged to the choir at his local cathedral. ··→ With his beautiful alto voice and professional singing ability, he even sang solos during mass, but rumor has it he went tone deaf as a result of the shock of being taken to Japan.

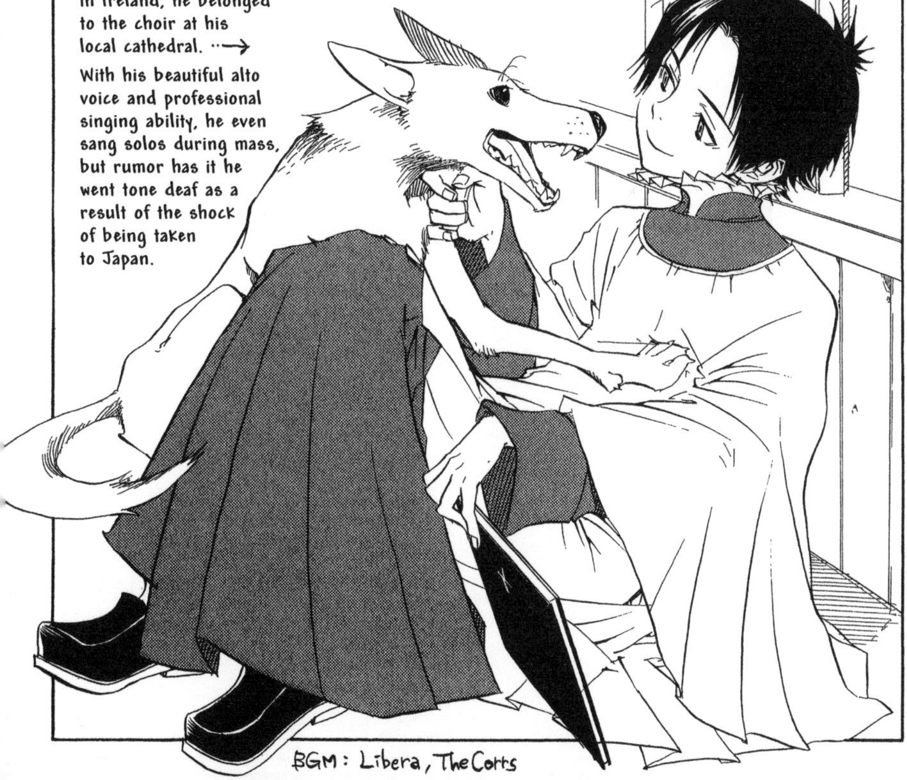

BGM: Libera, The Corrs

TRANSLATION NOTES

page 15, *Ichigo ichie*
Literally means "one lifetime, one encounter," and is a reminder that chances only come once and should be taken advantage of and cherished.

page 20, *Kunoichi*
Slang for "female." It is derived by taking each line of the kanji meaning "female" and reading them one by one. It is also a term for female ninja.

page 57, *Sengoku Era*
A period in Japan's history in which the country was at civil war. It was a time of war, natural disasters, and poverty that lasted for about a hundred years, from the late 1400s to the late 1500s, and it's no wonder that ninja of the time would want to create an art so powerful as the Shinra Banshou in an effort to end it.

page 58, *Heisei Era*
This refers to the reign of Emperor Heisei, from 1989 to the present.

page 59, *Izuna*
A type of fox spirit used by Izuna masters as familiars. They can do good, like telling the future, or evil, like possessing people and making them sick.

page 63, *Donburi*
A *donburi* is a porcelain bowl, usually filled with rice, that is then topped with food like a pork cutlet or fried shrimp.

page 121, *Shugendo*
Shugendo, the way of training and testing, is a religion that combines elements of Shintoism, Buddhism, and other eastern religions. Its purpose is to gain spiritual experiences by secluding oneself in the mountains and going through severe training.

page 157, *Bamboo shoots*
Commonly used in Asian food. Miharu is commenting that Yoite can eat as much as he wants, since he has bamboo growing right in his yard.

page 177, *Four stages of narrative*
The four stages of Japanese and Chinese narratives are "*ki shou ten ketsu.*" Introduction (*ki*, literally "awakening"), development (*shou*), turn (*ten*, the plot twist), and conclusion (*ketsu*).

Nabari No Ou

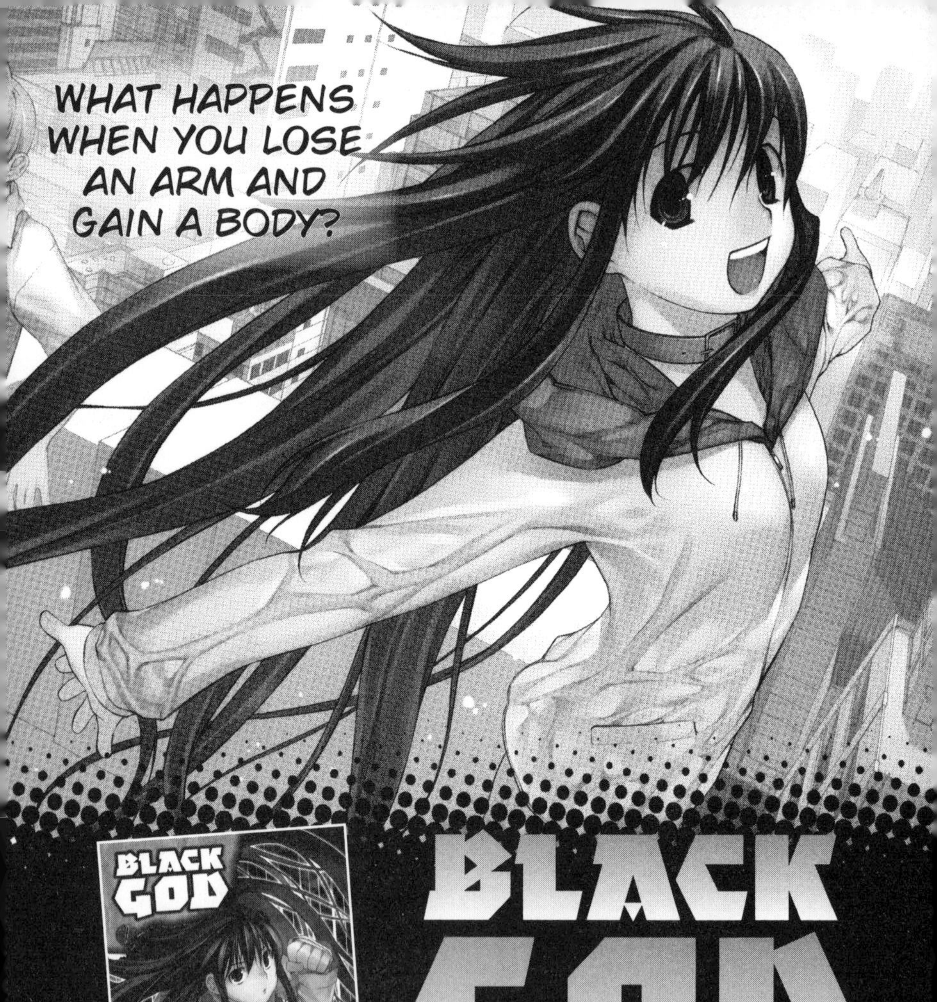
WHAT HAPPENS
WHEN YOU LOSE
AN ARM AND
GAIN A BODY?

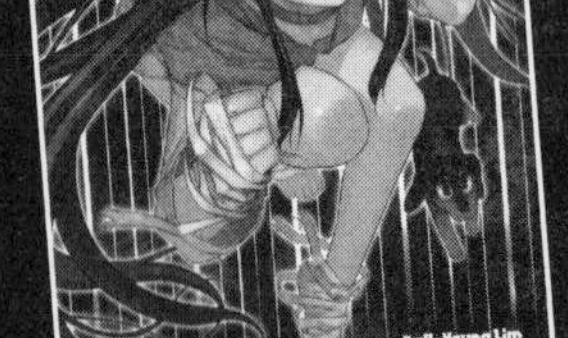
BLACK
GOD
Story by Dall-Young Lim
Art by Sung-Woo Park

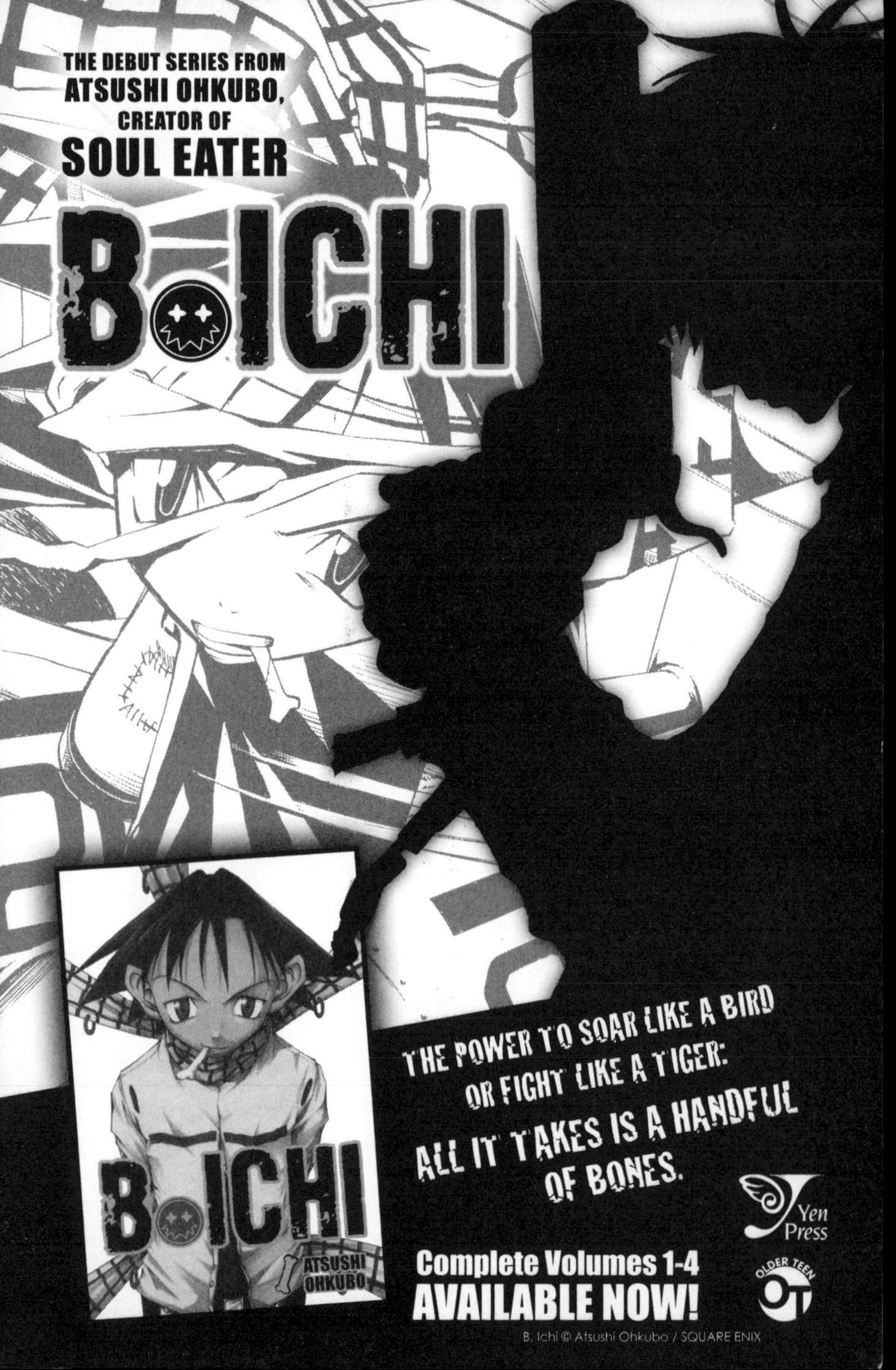
THE DEBUT SERIES FROM
ATSUSHI OHKUBO,
CREATOR OF
SOUL EATER
B. ICHI
THE POWER TO SOAR LIKE A BIRD
OR FIGHT LIKE A TIGER:
ALL IT TAKES IS A HANDFUL
OF BONES.
B. ICHI
ATSUSHI OHKUBO
Yen Press
Complete Volumes 1-4
AVAILABLE NOW!
OLDER TEEN OT
B. Ichi © Atsushi Ohkubo / SQUARE ENIX

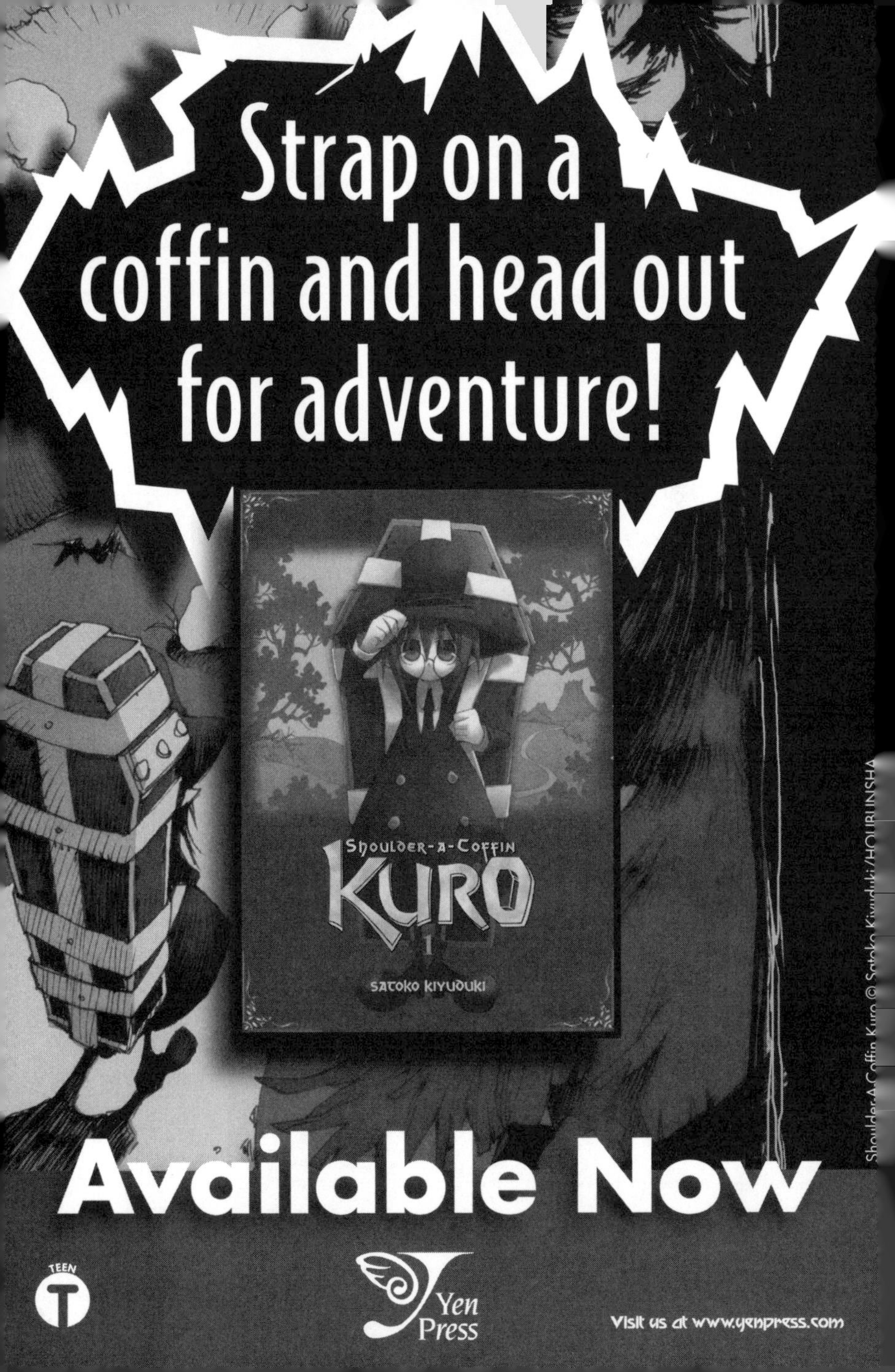
Strap on a coffin and head out for adventure!
Shoulder-a-Coffin
KURO
1
SATOKO KIYUDUKI
Available Now
TEEN
T
Yen Press
Visit us at www.yenpress.com
Shoulder-A-Coffin Kuro © Satoko Kiyuduki/HOUBUNSHA

Kieli sees ghosts.
Harvey cannot die.
He will throw
her world into
chaos...
...and become her
one true friend.

STORY BY **Yukako Kabei**
ART BY **Shiori Teshirogi**

KIELI

IT'S AN ALL-OUT CAT FIGHT ON CAMPUS...

Cat-lovers flock to Matabi Academy, where each student is allowed to bring their pet cat to the dorms.

Unfortunately, the grounds aren't just crawling with cats...

...an ancient evil lurks on campus, and only the combined efforts of student and feline can hold them at bay...

1

CAT
PARADISE

YUJI IWAHARA

IN STORES NOW!

OLDER TEEN
OT

Yen Press

Hello! This is YOTSUBA!

Guess what? Guess what?
Yotsuba and Daddy just moved here from waaaay over there!

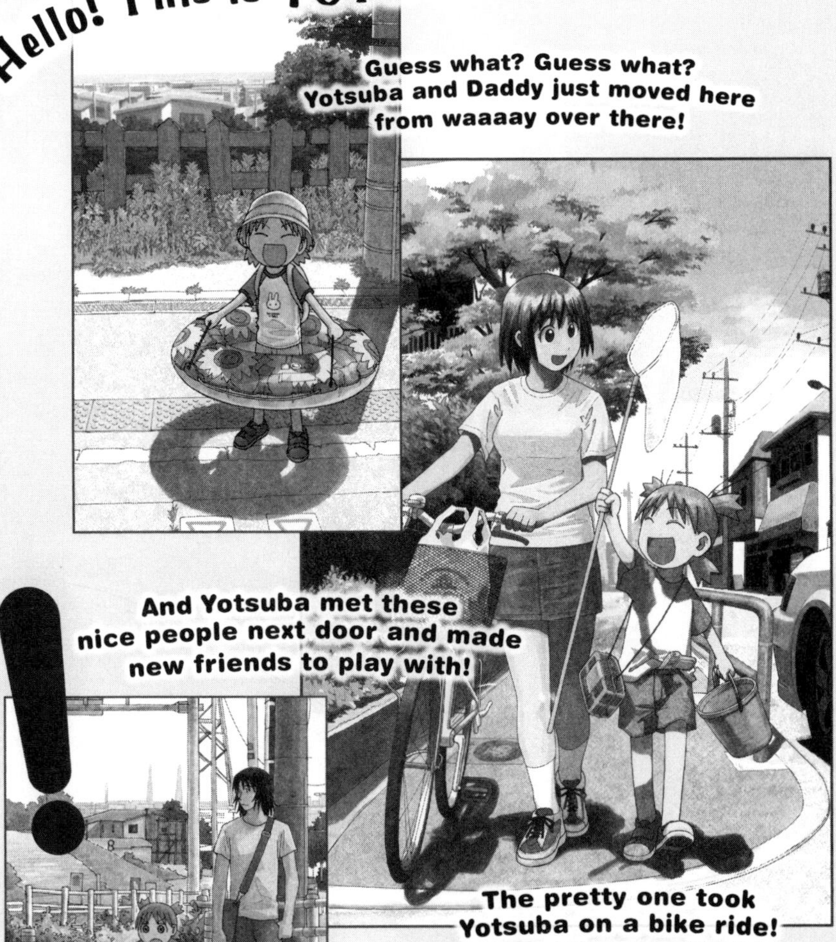

And Yotsuba met these nice people next door and made new friends to play with!

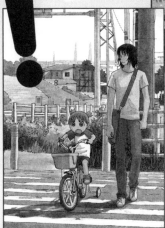

The pretty one took Yotsuba on a bike ride!
(Whoooa! There was a big hill!)

And Ena's a good drawer!
(Almost as good as Yotsuba!)

And their mom always gives Yotsuba ice cream!
(Yummy!)

And...
And...
OHHHH!

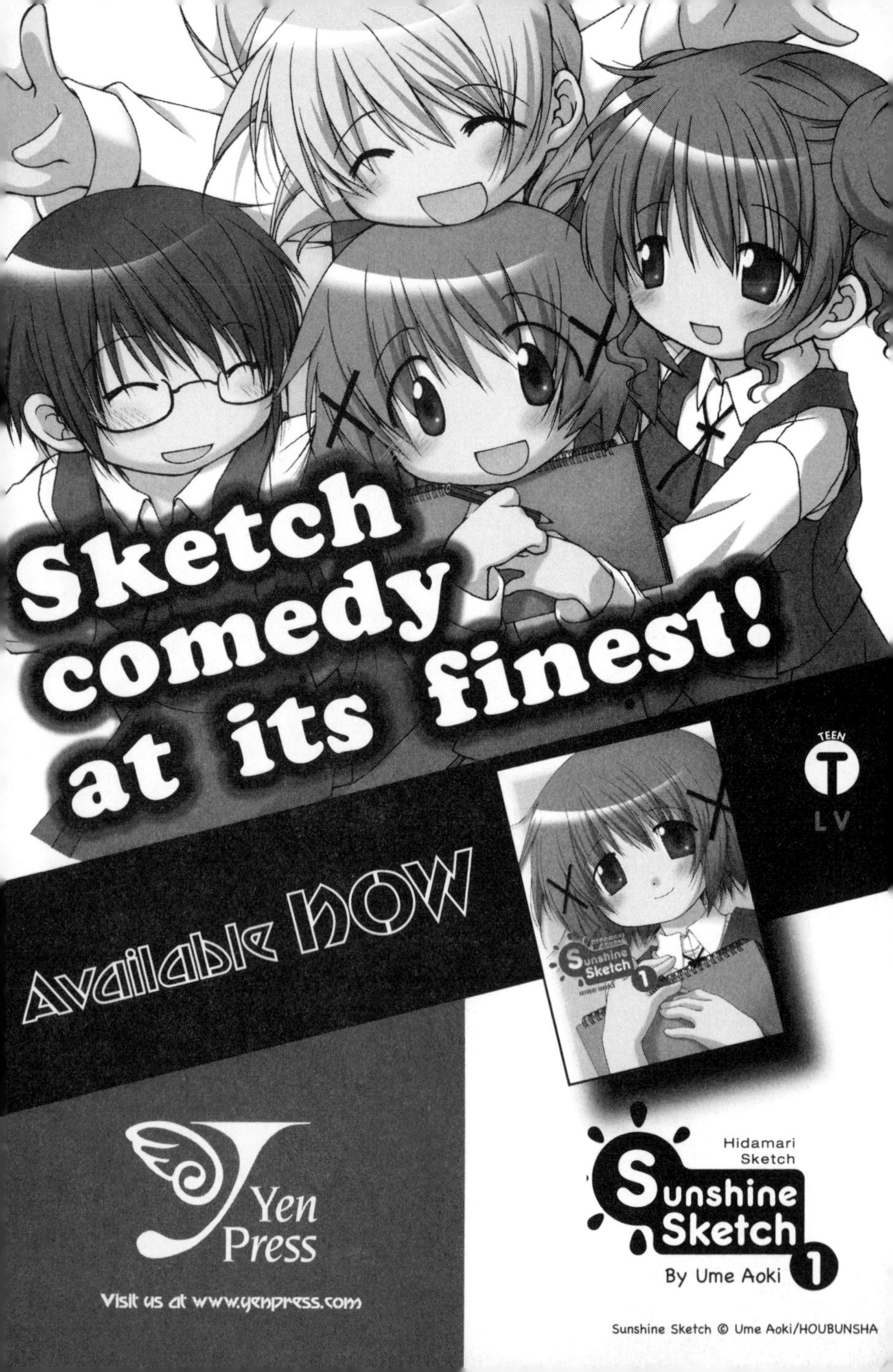
Sketch
comedy
at its finest!
TEEN
T
LV
Available NOW
Sunshine Sketch 1
ume aoki
Yen Press
Visit us at www.yenpress.com
Hidamari Sketch
Sunshine Sketch
1
By Ume Aoki
Sunshine Sketch © Ume Aoki/HOUBUNSHA

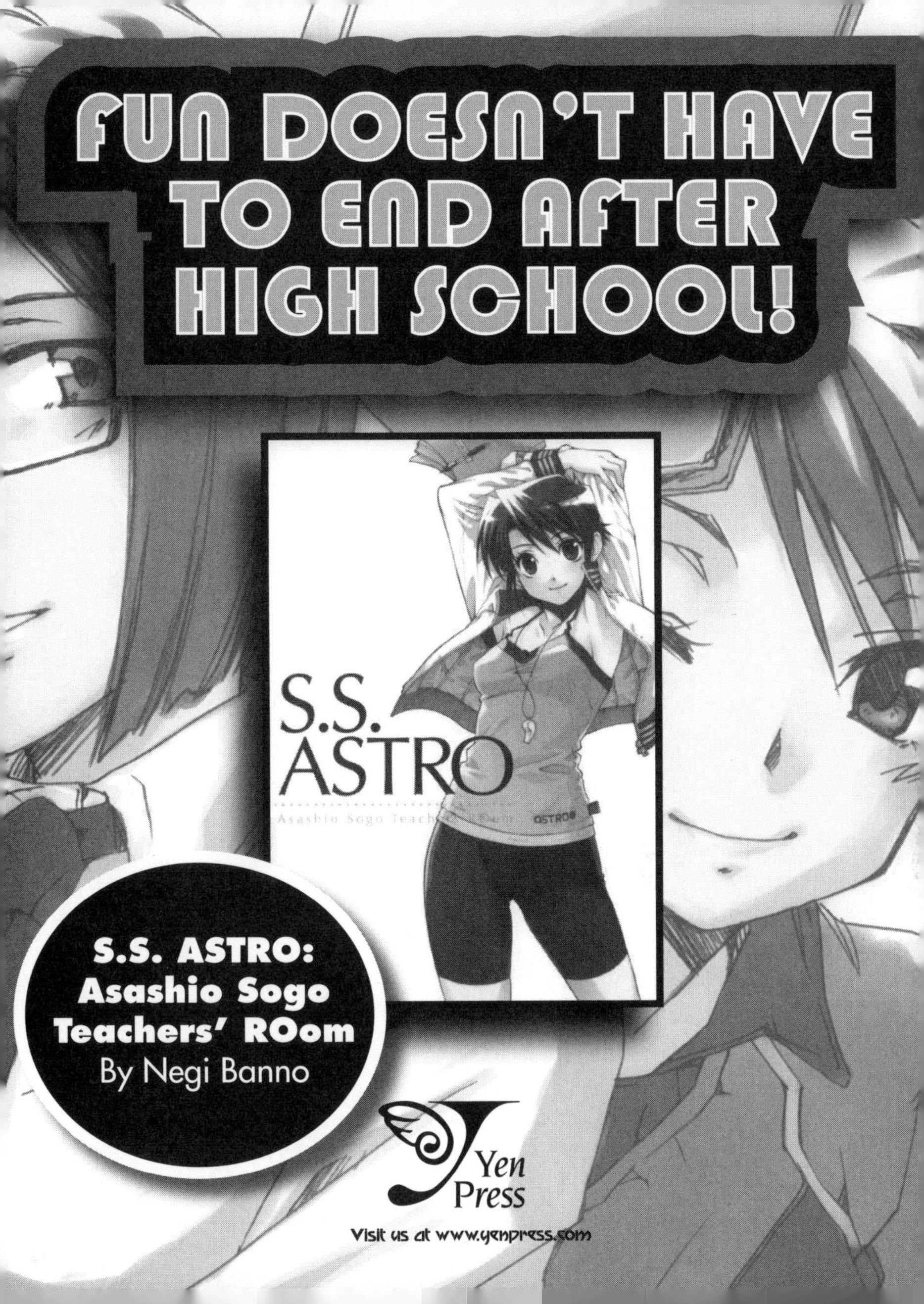
FUN DOESN'T HAVE TO END AFTER HIGH SCHOOL!
S.S. ASTRO
Asashio Sogo Teach
ASTRO
S.S. ASTRO: Asashio Sogo Teachers' ROom
By Negi Banno
Yen Press
Visit us at www.yenpress.com

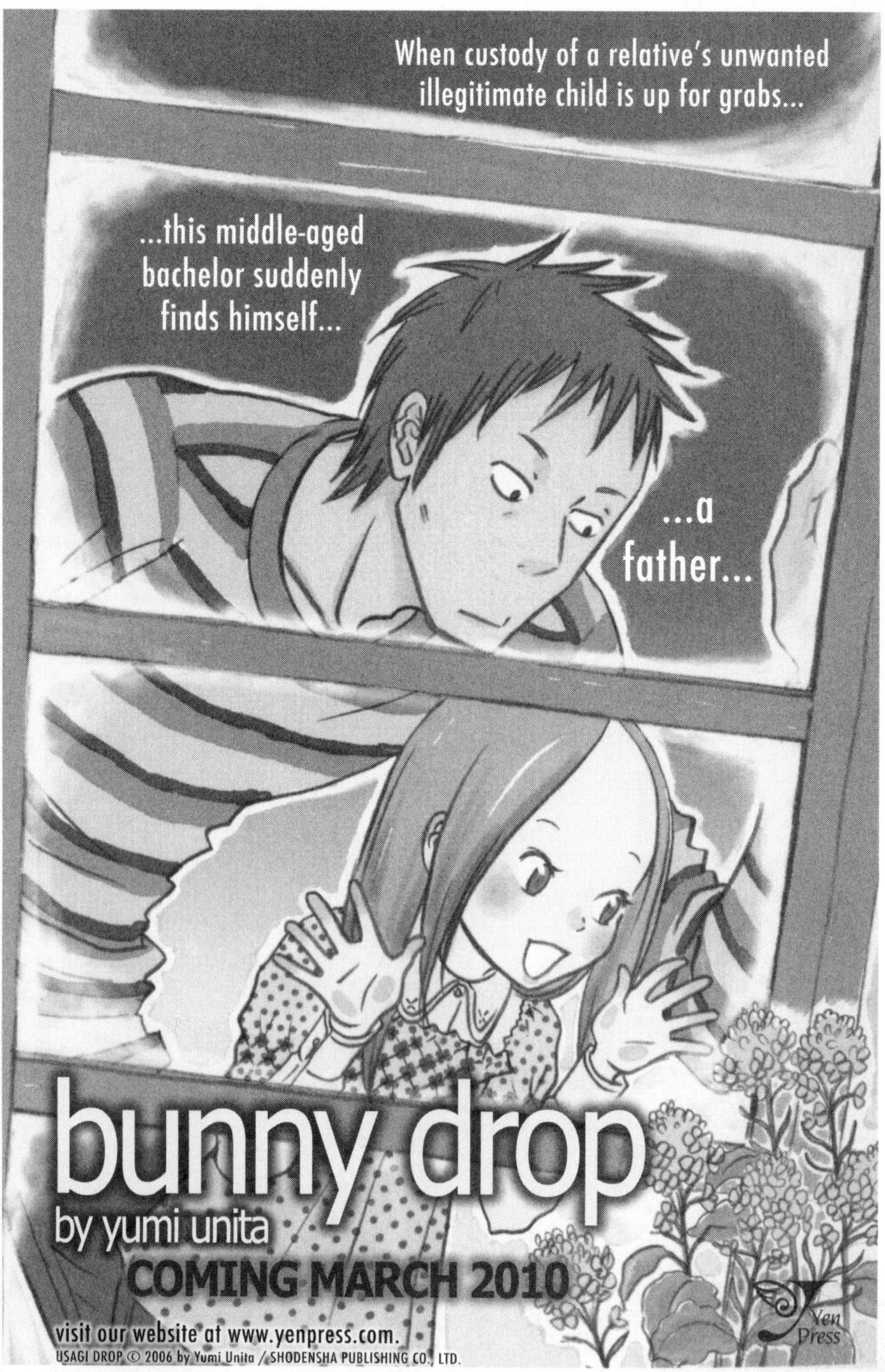
When custody of a relative's unwanted illegitimate child is up for grabs...
...this middle-aged bachelor suddenly finds himself...
...a father...
bunny drop
by yumi unita
COMING MARCH 2010
visit our website at www.yenpress.com.
Yen Press

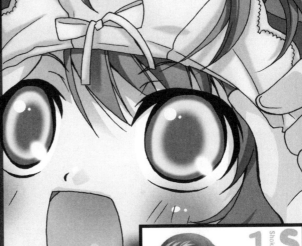

This one will make you PURR!

Suzunari!

By Shoko Iwami

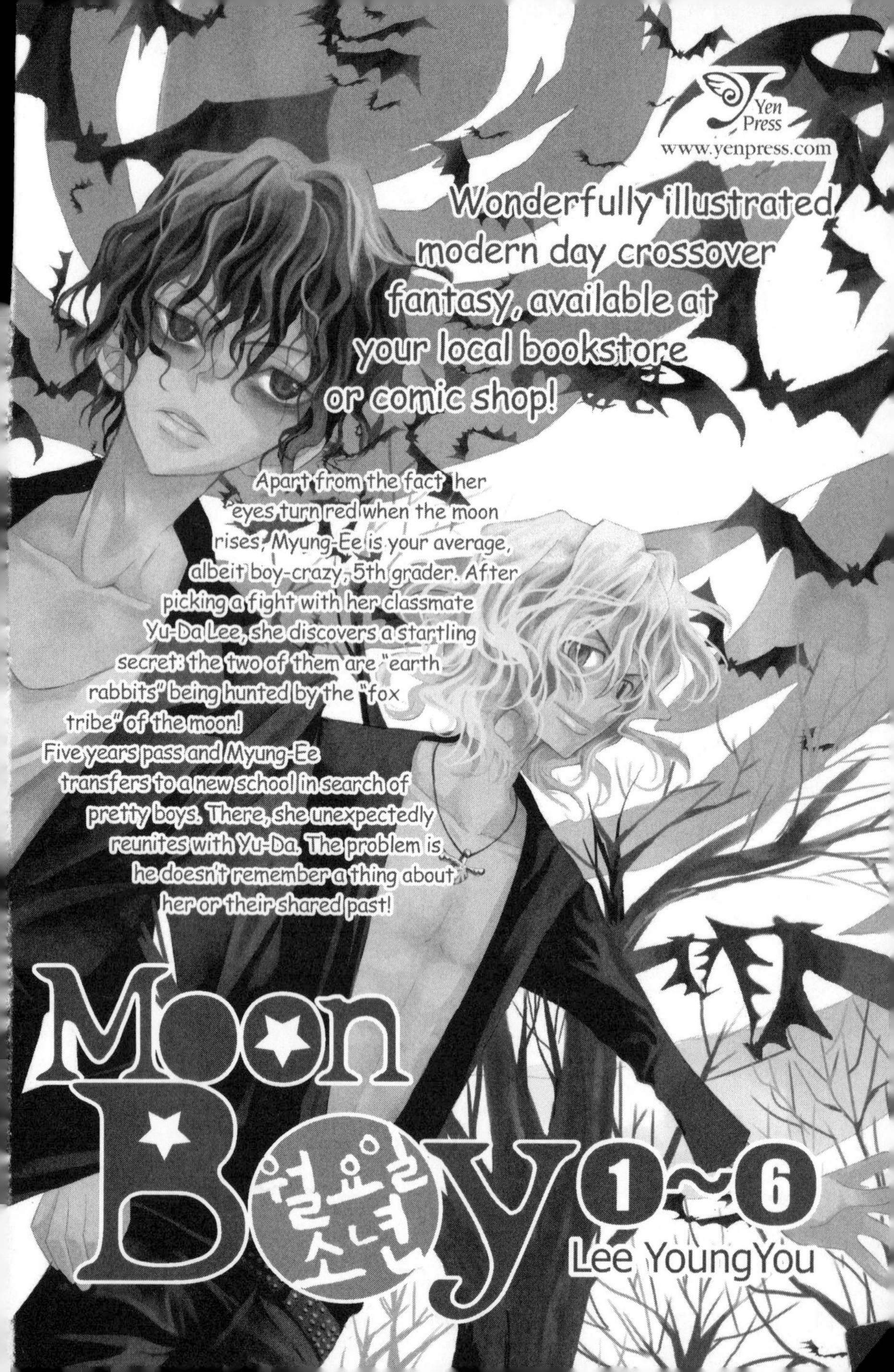
Yen Press
www.yenpress.com
Wonderfully illustrated modern day crossover fantasy, available at your local bookstore or comic shop!
Apart from the fact her eyes turn red when the moon rises, Myung-Ee is your average, albeit boy-crazy, 5th grader. After picking a fight with her classmate Yu-Da Lee, she discovers a startling secret: the two of them are "earth rabbits" being hunted by the "fox tribe" of the moon!
Five years pass and Myung-Ee transfers to a new school in search of pretty boys. There, she unexpectedly reunites with Yu-Da. The problem is he doesn't remember a thing about her or their shared past!
Moon Boy
월요일 소년
1~6
Lee YoungYou

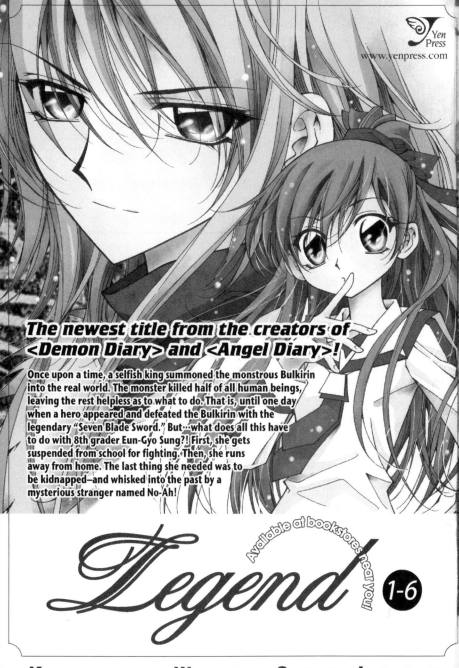

The newest title from the creators of <Demon Diary> and <Angel Diary>!

Once upon a time, a selfish king summoned the monstrous Bulkirin into the real world. The monster killed half of all human beings, leaving the rest helpless as to what to do. That is, until one day when a hero appeared and defeated the Bulkirin with the legendary "Seven Blade Sword." But...what does all this have to do with 8th grader Eun-Gyo Sung?! First, she gets suspended from school for fighting. Then, she runs away from home. The last thing she needed was to be kidnapped—and whisked into the past by a mysterious stranger named No-Ah!

Legend

Available at bookstores near you!

1-6

Kara · Woo SooJung

NABARI NO OU ❷

YUHKI KAMATANI

Translation: Alethea Nibley and Athena Nibley

Lettering: Alexis Eckerman

NABARI NO OU Vol. 2 © 2005 Yuhki Kamatani / SQUARE ENIX. All rights reserved. First published in Japan in 2005 by SQUARE ENIX CO., LTD. English translation rights arranged with SQUARE ENIX CO., LTD. and Hachette Book Group through Tuttle-Mori Agency, Inc.

Translation © 2009 by SQUARE ENIX CO., LTD.

Yen Press
Hachette Book Group
237 Park Avenue, New York, NY 10017

Visit our websites at www.HachetteBookGroup.com and www.YenPress.com.

Yen Press is an imprint of Hachette Book Group, Inc. The Yen Press name and logo are trademarks of Hachette Book Group, Inc.

First Yen Press Edition: October 2009

ISBN-13: 978-0-7595-3036-2

10 9 8 7 6 5 4 3 2 1

BVG

Printed in the United States of America